Scottish Culture
and Scottish Education
1800-1980

Scottish Culture and Scottish Education

1800-1980

Edited by
WALTER M. HUMES
and
HAMISH M. PATERSON

Department of Education,
University of Glasgow

JOHN DONALD PUBLISHERS LTD
EDINBURGH

ISBN 0 85976 086 3

Exclusive distribution in the United States of America and Canada by Humanities Press Inc., Atlantic Highlands, NJ 07716, U.S.A.

Phototypesetting by Burns & Harris Limited., Dundee
Printed in Great Britain by Bell & Bain Ltd., Glasgow

Contents

Introduction

> The historical evidence is there, in its primary form, not to disclose its own meaning, but to be interrogated . . .
>
> E. P. Thomson, *The Poverty of Theory and other essays*, 1978

THE history of education in Scotland has for long attracted the attention and efforts of writers and scholars of some distinction. James Craigie points out that, since the 1860s, no fewer than fifteen attempts have been made to construct a general and comprehensive history of Scottish education.[1] Some of these are small, impressionistic and relatively superficial but others are of considerable scholarly standing and scope, offering a more or less detailed account of educational events. This narrative tradition in the writing of Scottish educational history culminated in 1969 in James Scotland's massively researched two-volume work; the sheer amount of information it contains and the enormous time-span it covers would be almost enough to ensure that — as was the case with the work of Knox, Morgan, and Kerr in their time — the history is now accepted as a standard work. By 'standard' histories of Scottish education we mean, first, accounts which attempt to be comprehensive and authoritative in their coverage. However, since not all comprehensive, authoritative accounts are accepted as standard, a further criterion has to be applied: for us, this is to be found in the prescription of certain histories by members of the academic community, whose work and teaching serve to define the field.[2]

Taken in total, the standard histories of Scottish education indicate a continued fascination with the country's educational tradition, a wish to preserve what is valuable in that tradition and a desire to promulgate these virtues by reminding others (often English legislators but also Scots themselves) of the reflection in Scottish educational practices of a unique Scottish culture and identity which it would be unwise to ignore and fatal to forget. These motives help to explain the *kind* of history of Scottish education that has been written — narrative in form, broadly nationalistic in tone — but it is important to note the *consequences* of the favoured approach and the kind of understanding of cultural processes it allows.

In seeking to preserve 'a heritage worth remembering and building upon',[3] James Scotland and his predecessors are both defining the nature of that heritage and confirming its place in conventional accounts of Scottish cultural

1

identity. In the process, the standard histories become themselves part of the educational tradition they seek to describe and preserve: in effect, they seek to confirm a particular version of the cultural processes they claim to elucidate. There is a 'story' (some might say a 'myth') embedded in the history.

A realisation of this complex set of relationships — between the writing of narrative accounts of the history of Scottish education, the cultural functions they serve and the sort of understandings they permit — helps to explain why a sustained reading of the standard histories ultimately leaves the reader uneasy and dissatisfied. There would appear to be three main sources for this dissatisfaction. The first can be traced to the fact that many of the histories (despite their stated aims) do not even succeed in recounting an accurate or comprehensible narrative. Donald Withrington has described the factual inaccuracies and the restricted evidential base of many writings on Scottish education, including the standard works.[4] Even James Scotland's largely scrupulous history presents the reader, at times, with severe problems of formulating a clear narrative account: his treatment of the development of state-supported post-elementary and secondary education after 1872 — a complicated but important topic — is one example.

The second unsatisfactory aspect is more crucial — the story behind the history fails to convince. In the worst cases it fails to engage our understanding of events in any way (let alone convince) because of the working of two powerful assumptions — that the story of Scottish education is a story of uniform and steady progress and that, since this is the case, nothing is required of the historian other than an account of the steps (usually legislative) by which that progress was achieved. By far the worst offender here is Alexander Morgan, who describes his *Rise and Progress of Scottish Education* as an account which is '. . . purely historical, a record of facts based as far as possible on documentary evidence and official Reports, and free from speculation and personal opinion'.[5] The unwitting irony of 'purely historical' (indeed, a suspicion that freedom from 'speculation or personal opinion' may be largely illusory) is sharpened by the claim on the very first page of the text:

> Progress in education, experience everywhere has shown, is not by alternate destructions and reconstructions but by a continuous growth of old into new and better forms. Evolution, which rules organic life with irresistible sway, has in education its highest authorisation, and any attempt to violate it by short-cuts or arbitrary codes or regulations bring their own reward.[6]

The evolutionism is assumed, not argued for, and the relative lack of a sufficiently elaborated and plainly stated explanatory framework vitiates the intellectual standing of the history.

Morgan is not alone in failing to make clear the grounds on which his history is constructed, or in pre-judging the nature of the story which is embedded in it. H. M. Knox's *Two Hundred and Fifty Years of Scottish Education* illustrates well the lack of illumination and intellectual engagement characterised by an 'Acts and facts' approach. Knox sets out '. . . to supply a concise account of the development of the statutory system . . .'[7] and does so with some elegance and style. But the whole thrust of his history is of steady legislative progress; we glide through events and enactments with the minimum of fuss towards the pinnacle of the 1946 Act, the clauses of which represent '. . . two hundred and fifty years of steady progress in education . . .'[8] since they '. . . mark the limit of what is attainable under our present economic system'.[9] This also marks the limit of our attention and wakefulness; we lapse into a stupor, lulled by the constant and bland elision of problems, puzzles, debates and controversies but somewhat troubled by a severe inability to make much sense of this mass of factual and Act-ual data.

James Scotland's history probably marks the end of that era which started in the 1860s and in which educational historians tried to produce comprehensive factual accounts of the chronological development of Scottish schooling from the days of Columba. Scotland's interest in the detailed description of '. . . what went on in the classrooms of other centuries . . .'[10] is welcome; this emphasis humanises the basic factual structure of the book by injecting into the descriptive narrative an account of '. . . what people said and thought and felt, as well as what they did, especially in this case what children and their teachers felt and thought'.[11] In addition, there is less sign of the bland belief in 'progress' which undermines the work of Morgan and Knox: in fact, Scotland makes a point of deflating the rosy view ('The truth of the matter is, of course, that much of Scotland's pride in her educational tradition is unreasoning and unreasonable'[12]), and the frequent wit, the ironic remarks and the muscular style help to enliven the chronological forward march. Unlike Knox, Scotland does not evade entirely the problems, controversies and clashes of view which characterised much of the development of Scottish education; nor does he omit completely reference to a wider cultural context, both in Scotland and elsewhere. For these reasons, his history will doubtless remain for some time the standard modern work from which most studies of the subject will start and to which constant reference will be made.

But, if James Scotland's history represents the zenith of the narrative virtues, it also shows the basic weakness of this type of descriptive history, however thoroughly humanised. The basic framework is, after all, directly in the 'Acts and facts' tradition of assuming that events speak for themselves and do not require much in the way of an explicit interpretative context which aims to explain and understand these events as well as recount them. Of course, all historians write an interpretation of events by selecting, out of the available welter, some occurrences for discussion and ignoring or de-emphasising others. But, to the extent that interpretative assumptions remain implicit or hidden or disguised, the *reader's* attempt to decide if presented evidence is sufficient to confirm satisfactorily a hypothetical explanation for the events may be seriously undermined. By pre-empting the argument for the assumptive bases on which the history is constructed, narrative which claims to be 'purely historical' or which restricts itself to descriptions of the 'facts' tends to prejudge explanation and prevent understanding. A severe view of James

Scotland's effort to humanise his narrative, by the injection of real people's thoughts, feelings and deeds, would be that it is equivalent to the attempt to restore life to a semi-decayed corpse by a blood transfusion — the effort is wasted if the assumption of life cannot be sustained. Less metaphorically, it is not clear precisely what the *value* or *significance* of humanising detail might be, given that we do not have a frame, a context, of sufficient explicitness to indicate the import such detail may have in any explanation of what occurred; the accumulation of humanising detail will not *in itself* explain, or foster comprehension, or increase illumination for the reader. It is, then, the non-explicit or unwarranted explanatory frame of such histories which fails to convince; it is the suspected presence of covert assumptions which induces scepticism and, in some cases, disbelief; it is the seeming inability or unwillingness to generate hypotheses which are then *tested* in the face of evidence which leads to a failure to engage our attention. In short, most standard histories of Scottish education present no intellectual challenge, a deficiency which perhaps helps to explain the relative lack of interest in historical topics among students of education in recent years. It is our belief that the failure to challenge is mainly a consequence of the lack of a consciously articulated conceptual and explanatory frame or context. The presence of such a frame or context would immediately render problematic both the existence of, and the belief in, a tradition of uninterrupted 'progress' in Scottish education.

If the first source of dissatisfaction with the standard histories is disenchantment with the quality of the narrative and the second is disillusionment with the pre-emptive judgments embodied in a covert interpretative framework which succeeds only in evading the fundamental task of a search for explanations, then the third is their failure to locate the history of Scottish education within the context of Scottish culture as a whole. It is our firm belief that any real understanding of the development of Scottish education requires a much broader frame of reference than that provided by 'schooling', whether conceived in terms of 'what children and their teachers felt and thought' or in terms of legislative structures. The values embodied in any educational system are shaped by a wide range of cultural influences — deriving, for example, from new technologies, social and political changes, the growth and decline of particular forms of religious belief — which need to be taken into account if anything more than superficial understanding is to be achieved. More generally, broader movements in the history of ideas require to be teased out from the tangled skein of taken-for-granted grounds if we are even to begin the attempt to explain why certain educational practices found favour at any particular time and others did not.

The standard histories show a poor grasp of the way these wider forces operate but, ironically, this very deficiency is itself significant for a broader analysis of Scottish culture. Lying behind the sort of enterprise they represent, and the types of dissatisfaction they generate, is a vital historical question: what are the cultural reasons for, and consequences of, appeals to a Scottish educational 'tradition'?

One explanation could be that appeals to tradition tend to have the effect of forestalling critical discussion. The assumption of 'progress' in the works of Morgan and Knox is a clear example: they construct a representation of events which involves that abbreviation of debate we have previously described in an attempt to induce belief in the tradition. In effect, they are engaged in a proselytising exercise — an exercise which transforms history into ideology and story into myth. This transformation, and the cultural values embedded in it, invites several kinds of attention. The relation between evolutionist ways of thinking and assumptions of 'progress' is an obvious case. Again, the very idea of a Scottish educational tradition and the insistence on its distinctiveness implies a curious mixture of assertiveness and defensiveness which needs to be examined in depth. What precisely was the nature of the threat that Knox and Morgan imply (but do not discuss explicitly)? Can it all be explained in terms of the encroachments of English cultural imperialism or, as we suspect, is that too simplistic? Related to this, the *political* significance of the ideology and myth promoted by the standard histories is worthy of close inspection. It is notable that, characteristically, appeals to Scotland's educational tradition are often made by those who have power and influence in the construction of educational policy. Why do the authors of the standard histories appear to serve so well (however unwittingly) the interests of policy-makers? The importance of this kind of question shows the necessity of investigating political practices in any attempt to understand the place of Scottish education within the complex fabric of Scottish cultural life. All of these points reinforce our claim that the study of the history of Scottish education must be conducted with reference to many other aspects of national culture: we have suggested that, as part of this process, the cultural enlistments of the standard histories themselves need to be elucidated.

It could be argued that this poses a monumentally impossible set of tasks for the historian of Scottish education. To take our suggestions seriously would enlarge beyond reason the evidential base which would have to be drawn upon. Furthermore, the search for intellectually satisfying explanations would seem to be never-ending and the requirement that the location and status of such a search should be subjected to constant scrutiny would make history impossibly abstract and theoretical. We would not accept such arguments, although we would grant that the successful completion of such tasks is ultimately impossible: all history is provisional. But it is precisely because the remit of the historian of Scottish education has been too narrowly defined (and unjustifiably so) that we have standard histories which obscure and obfuscate rather than enlighten; it is precisely because the sources of Scottish history of education have been restricted to data on schools and schooling that these histories fail to give us sufficient grasp of the place and role of Scottish schools in the educational and cultural history of Scotland; it is precisely the apparent congruence between historians and policy-makers in their appeals to a tradition of progress which is in need of analysis.

In general, we seek to 'open up' and broaden the terms of the debate, in a number of ways. Our first priority, in compiling the present volume, was to encourage our contributors to write critical accounts of their respective topics. As an essential element of this critical stance, we encouraged them to adopt, whenever appropriate, an overt explanatory orientation and, in pursuit of this, not to eschew explicit interpretative stances (or even highly speculative ones) towards their material. It follows that the essays in this volume seek to broaden the evidential base from which historical accounts of Scottish education may, by interrogation, be constructed — by the detailed re-examination of known existing sources, by unearthing new sources (the files of the Scottish Record Office are an obvious treasure-house sorely in need of systematic pillage) and, most important of all, by extending the definition of 'educational evidence' so as to include sources more usually classed as economic, social, political, theological, literary or scientific, in an effort to begin the important task of analysing the interrelationships of educational and other cultural practices in Scotland.

Naturally the relative weighting of these recommended characteristics is not the same in all the contributions. The papers of David Hamilton and Tom Wilson are examples of re-examinations of existing accounts (of, respectively, Robert Owen's 'progressivism' and the reasons for the delay in implementing 'payment by results' in Scotland): in both cases, economic and political explanations are seen to underlie educational practices. Donald Withrington seeks to explain the origins and purposes of George Lewis's important pamphlet, *Scotland a Half-Educated Nation*, by locating it within the tensions in church and state during the 1830s: his account makes extensive use of previously neglected source material, which allows an appreciation of the differences between ostensible and underlying motives in public debates of the period. Jim Smith and Walter Humes draw on religious and scientific developments to explain the character of education (not just schooling) in nineteenth-century Scotland: their papers represent a conscious attempt to escape from the limitations of the 'Acts and facts' tradition by exploring broad movements in intellectual history. Three of the papers deal with Scottish teachers: Robert Bell, using new evidence, analyses the peculiar position of university departments of education in Scotland, describes the effects of this anomalous situation on members of staff within them, and examines the political-academic struggles which took place; Douglas Myers' concern is to discuss how, in spite of the considerable prestige and security of mid-nineteenth-century Scottish schoolmasters, their drive for professional autonomy and their attempts to influence policy were frustrated; Helen Corr's research indicates that the feminisation of the Scottish school-teaching profession was closely linked to broader socio-economic developments and had considerable effects on that profession. All three papers exemplify the notion that changes in the profession of teaching in Scotland cannot simply be explained in terms of narrowly defined 'educational' concerns but must be seen in a wider context of social interaction. Mary Finn and Hamish Paterson attempt to explain the development of state-financed secondary schools in Scotland in terms of the conceptual schemes held by influential bureaucratic policy-makers; in Finn's paper, the stress is on the ambivalent power of the notion of 'progress' in the construction of a 'modernised' school system; in Paterson's paper, the argument is that, under political pressures, an explicit rhetoric of class was abandoned in favour of the idea of 'ability'. Andrew McPherson draws on a wide range of evidence — oral, documentary and literary — in his extended discussion of the central position occupied by a selective vision of Scotland's educational tradition, the roots of that vision in a particular experience of the nature of civil society in Scotland and the effects of it on recent policy for Scotland's schools. Another influence on recent policy — that deriving from psychology — is examined by Frank McEnroe: by analysing a formative document in Scottish primary education, he demonstrates the potency of Freudian ideas in the thinking of policy-makers and their advisers, and speculates interestingly on the possible links between this and the governance of schools. These four papers (by Finn, Paterson, McPherson and McEnroe) are explicit attempts to understand events by reference to a much wider range of ideas and a much broader view of sources than is the norm — by reference to movements of ideas in society at large (progressivism), to prevalent political and psychological notions (class, ability, maturity, adjustment) and to versions of history held by educational elites.

The arrangement of the papers is broadly chronological. It will be seen that some of the contributors cover quite a wide time-span and so there is a measure of overlap in a few cases. In any event, it has been part of our plan to offer a balance between relatively intensive studies of specific topics and periods, and relatively extensive studies of themes and ideas. We have tried to ensure that coverage of the period as a whole (from 1800 to 1980) is also fairly well-balanced.

Finally, we can only hope that this collection of essays in the history of Scottish culture and education will have the effect of beginning a dialogue. It is not our intention to claim that final answers have been provided and we feel sure that our essayists would not wish to argue that their interpretations are the only possible ones. In addition, some of the topics are relatively un-explored in any depth and their inclusion here represents work in progress rather than work completed. If the volume does engender debate and dialogue, we would also hope that the effect on *students* of Scottish history of education (in universities, colleges and elsewhere) will be invigorating in that it will demonstrate that the field is rich in sources, in problems and in conflicting views.

Our thanks to our contributors for their patience in the face of editorial demands, and to Moira Duffy, David Hamilton, Leslie Hunter and John Tuck-well of John Donald Publishers for varieties of essential aid in the compilation of this volume.

W. M. Humes   University of Glasgow
H. M. Paterson

NOTES

1. James Craigie, review of James Scotland, *The History of Scottish Education* in *Scottish Educational Studies*, 2, 2, 1970, pp. 130-134.

2. We have canvassed the experience of academic colleagues and have perused some of the reading lists of universities and colleges in an attempt to settle on those histories which (since about 1900) appear to qualify as standard — these are, in chronological order of publication: John Kerr, *Scottish Education: School and University from Early Times to 1908* (Cambridge, 1910) and the second edition published in 1913; Alexander Morgan, *Rise and Progress of Scottish Education* (Edinburgh and London, 1927); H. M. Knox, *Two Hundred and Fifty Years of Scottish Education, 1696-1946* (Edinburgh and London, 1953); James Scotland, *The History of Scottish Education*, 2 volumes (London, 1969). Certain other volumes may be seen as standard works in their particular area — the leading examples would probably be James Grant, *History of the Burgh and Parish Schools of Scotland* (Glasgow and London, 1876) and John Strong, *A History of Secondary Education in Scotland* (Oxford, 1909), but their particularity exempts them from consideration here. In addition, a few historical works on Scottish education, which are *not* accepted as 'standard' but which nevertheless have been profoundly influential, come into a special category. These are histories which have pioneered the investigation of relatively new areas, or have made sustained attempts at explaining their evidence by placing it in a wider interpretative framework. We can think of only three such histories, which stand out in spite of their faults: L. J. Saunders, *Scottish Democracy, 1815-1840* (Edinburgh, 1950), in which the discussion of parish schools in their social, cultural and political context broke new ground, although the argument is finally less than completely convincing; G. E. Davie, *The Democratic Intellect* (Edinburgh, 1961), whose wilful analysis of the anglicisation of the Scottish universities in the nineteenth century nonetheless served to generate new interest and debate; and T. C. Smout, *A History of the Scottish People, 1560-1830* (Glasgow, 1969), which provides a badly needed social history in which education plays an important role. In addition, the collection of essays edited by T. R. Bone in *Studies in the History of Scottish Education, 1872-1939* (London, 1967) represents an attempt to look at specialised topics in some depth.

3. James Scotland, *op. cit.*, volume 2, p. 274.

4. Donald J. Withrington, 'What is and what might be: some reflections on the writing of Scottish educational history', *Scottish Educational Studies*, 2, 2, 1970, pp. 110-118.

5. Alexander Morgan, *op. cit.*, Preface. Morgan also provides us, in his *Makers of Scottish Education* (London, 1929), with a leading example of another debilitating tradition in the writing of Scottish history of education: mock-hagiography.

6. *Ibid.*, p. 1.

7. H. M. Knox, *op. cit.*, p. xi.

8. *Ibid.*, p. 242.

9. *Ibid.*, p. xiii.

10. James Scotland, *op. cit.*, volume 1, Preface.

11. *Ibid.*

12. *Ibid.*, volume 2, p. 257.

1

Robert Owen and Education: A Reassessment

David Hamilton

Let us, then take every means in our power to interest all those who have weight and influence in the city, to enter heartily into the support and extension of the Lancastrian system of education for the poor, until every child of that class shall find a place in one of the schools. There, in a manner peculiar to the system, they must learn the habits of obedience, order, regularity, industry and constant attention which are to them of more importance than merely learning to read, write and account.

(Robert Owen, Speech to the Lancastrian Society of Glasgow, 1812)[1]

Among the most widely discussed characteristics of the early factory system is the moral character of the masters. Usually the factories are divided into two types — those run by brutal, heartless capitalists who flogged their employees, especially the apprentices, and those run as 'model' communities by humanitarian masters. Empirically, the distinction is valid, if we view the outward behaviour of the capitalists and possibly their psychological make-up. From the standpoint of control of labour, however, both types of factory management display a concern with the enforcement of discipline, which was one of the most salient points of dissatisfaction with the earlier modes of production.

(Neil Smelser, *Social Change in the Industrial Revolution*, 1959)[2]

TWENTIETH-CENTURY accounts of Robert Owen's activities at New Lanark between 1800 and 1824 tend to focus preferentially on their radical, progressive and socialist elements.[3] But there is also a recent counter-current in the historiography of Owen — one that regards his philanthropic/benevolent stance merely as a shrewd but profitable 'human relations' approach to capitalist production. Educationists writing about Owen usually hold the first position, while economic historians usually adopt the latter.

The net result is that Owen has become a two-sided figure. To some commentators he is typical of the period, but to others he is remembered for his uniqueness. This essay suggests that a more adequate appraisal of Owen's endeavours at New Lanark requires a better integration of data from economic history and the history of ideas. Overall, it will have served its purpose if it gives credence to the view that Owen's contribution to education is still in need of further investigation.

The historical discovery of Owen dates back to the late nineteenth century when George Holyoake (in a series of writings starting with the *Life and Last Days of Robert Owen*, 1859) annexed Owen's work to his own propaganda in favour of consumers' co-operatives. The Fabians were next to rediscover Owen at the turn of the nineteenth century. Among other things the Fabian re-working produced Frank Podmore's *Robert Owen: A Biography* (1906) and, later, G. D. H. Cole's *Robert Owen* (1925). Podmore's volume remained 'the most useful standard source'[4] until at least 1971; and Cole's work was seminal in that it drew attention to the pivotal importance of Owen's educational ideas.

In the 1960s educationists like Silver, Stewart & McCann, and Simon, added new information to earlier studies but, like the Fabians, continued to locate Owen within a 'history of ideas'[5] framework (Silver) and continued to present him as a 'progressive'[6] innovator (Stewart & McCann) who worked 'single-handed'[7] (Simon) to translate novel ideas into educational practice. Significantly, none of these educationists attempted to set Owen's work against the peculiar conditions of the early nineteenth-century cotton industry.

Nevertheless, 'discordant elements'[8] in Owen's work had already been noted by Miliband in 1954. They are apparent, too, in the early biographies. Podmore, for instance, noted that while Owen effected a 'marvelous improve-ment', New Lanark continued to be run as a 'strictly limited monarchy' under the 'most benevolent of despots'.[9] Similarly, Cullen (in *Adventures in Socialism*, 1910) traced 'the inception of modern Socialism' to New Lanark but, at the same time, recorded that Owen's 'first aim' was to secure 'ample dividends to the commercial gentlemen who had invested their capital in the (New Lanark) Company'.[10] And finally, despite repeating Podmore's charac-terisation of Owen as a 'benevolent despot', G. D. H. Cole still felt able to draw attention to Owen's 'concern' for 'educational freedom'.[11]

In resolving these paradoxes economic historians have tended to be more cautious in their appraisal of Owen. They locate his philanthropy and mana-gerial style (and those of his mill-owning contemporaries) not so much within a democratic progressive tradition as within the monopolistic character and cyclical fortunes of the early nineteenth-century cotton trade. In 1965, for instance, Pollard (Professor of Economic History, University of Sheffield), made a direct connection between philanthropy and profitability:

> The few individuals among the cotton masters who stand out as having a social consciousness regarding their communities were favoured by cheap power, by cheap labour, or by being in the fine spinning trade, in which profits were much higher and conditions of survival much easier.[12]

More recently, Butt (now Professor of Economic History, University of

Strathclyde) extended the argument to include the claim that Owen's reforms were, in fact, perfectly consonant with the profit motive. From this standpoint Owen's benevolence was guided as much by economic rationality as by purblind emotion. For instance, in providing schooling for young children, not only could Owen draw upon female labour as required, but also raise family incomes without elevating wage-rates (and thereby lowering profitability).[13]

Indeed, Butt went so far as to suggest that Owen's heightened interest in education after 1810 (following almost a decade of apparent inaction) might validly be regarded as a direct response to the industrial unrest that swept Scotland at that time. That is, if other mill owners sought to stamp out disaffection by operating lockouts and blacklists (see below), Owen sought industrial control and re-direction through more effective management.

Whatever the status of these claims by economic and political historians, they have rarely received the critical attention of educationists. The accounts of the latter, therefore, suffer not so much from inaccuracy as from myopia. Two systematic defects can be discerned. First, an over-emphasis upon aspects of Owen's work that are thought to prefigure the present; and secondly, an excusable over-reliance (in the absence of other data) upon the chronology and *post hoc* explanations provided in Owen's autobiography.

The remainder of this essay, then, offers an enlarged view of Owen. Parts 1 and 2 focus on the systematic weaknesses described above. Parts 3 to 5 investigate Owen's latency period; scrutinise his originality as an innovator; and re-examine the dispute that led to Owen's departure from New Lanark. Part 6 provides an overview of the main conclusions.

1. The Present in the Past

A good example of 'presentism' in the historiography of Owen occurs in Margaret Cole's *Robert Owen of New Lanark* (1954). In the introduction to that work Owen was credited with pioneering all kinds of welfare-state ideas. With respect to education Cole claimed the following:

> Owen was the first to demand, and to set up nursery schools, the first to recognise the important function of play in education, and the first to suggest that school teachers should be trained for their work, if necessary by the state.[14]

In elaborating her argument Cole played down the apparently conservative aspects of Owen's work. They are de-coupled from the rest of his life. The net result is an account of Owen that bears only a tenuous relationship to the epoch in which he lived. Indeed, Cole underlined Owen's other-worldliness when she ascribed his originality to 'prescience'.[15] Like Pollard's claim that Owen was ' a man far ahead of his time',[16] Cole's appeal to 'prescience' is as unsatisfactory as it is ahistorical.

Another instance where Owen's twentieth-century reputation overrides other considerations occurs in Stewart & McCann's *The Educational Innovators* (1967). The authors' concern to locate Owen within the 'progressive tradition' tended to presume what it set out to demonstrate. Insofar as they regarded 'progressive', 'experimental' and 'radical' as educational synonyms,[17] Stewart & McCann were able to draw a theoretical mask over some of Owen's less progressive characteristics (for example, his autocratic managerial style). Owen may have been an innovator, but not all innovations are educationally radical.

Stewart & McCann's enthusiasm for Owen's work — 'an astonishing innovation in the education of the working class'[18] — created a further discrepancy in their analysis. For their summary of the New Lanark 'innovations' they relied upon Owen's autobiography and included, therefore, the 'introduction'[19] of music into the curriculum. Seven pages earlier, however, they had already noted that David Dale (Owen's predecessor) had (sporadically) employed a music master in the 1790s.[20]

2. *Owen's autobiography*

As the foregoing example indicates, Owen's autobiography — published in 1858 — is a suspect historical source. But its weakness relates not so much to its factual content as to the fact that Owen, like his biographers, re-interpreted events in the light of experience. Thus, historical accounts of Owen and New Lanark which rely on the autobiography have been doubly refracted — once by the circumstances of Owen's later life and once by the circumstances of his biographers (for example, nineteenth-century Owenites, twentieth-century Fabians, late twentieth-century progressives). In his autobiography, Owen offers a humanistic, communitarian, progressive account of his days at New Lanark; and it is the same traits that have appealed to educationists. But it does not necessarily follow that Owen's popular appeal between 1800 and 1825 derived from the same factors. Nor, indeed, that Owen had acted during those years for the same reasons that he adduced in 1858.

Nevertheless, it is important to reaffirm that there is no evidence in Owen's autobiography of conscious fabrication or intentional distortion. Rather, the account is misleading in a more subtle way. It is reasonable to assume that, during his managership at New Lanark, Owen's activities were shaped by all kinds of factors. These would include the state of the cotton industry, the availability of labour and the general political climate. In each instance, then, Owen weighed up a wide range of pros and cons before deciding on a course of action. Thus, the reasons given in his autobiography may, in truth, have been influential. But other, unreported factors may also have played a part. Here are two such instances: both relate to labour shortages.

In common with many other water-powered mills, New Lanark was in a relatively remote part of Scotland. When David Dale opened it in 1786, he faced a chronic labour shortage which, in part, was solved by importing orphan/pauper 'apprentices' from places like Glasgow and Edinburgh. Owen became manager in 1800 and, thereafter, gradually dispensed with the services of the unattached apprentices and replaced them with women and children from the factory community that grew up alongside the mill.

According to Cullen, Owen found the apprenticeship system 'distasteful'.[21] This may have been the case but it was also recognised to be more expensive than a system of 'free' child labour. Pauper children were taken on for a fixed period of years and, during that time, were supposed to be housed, fed, clothed, and instructed by the factory owners. The problem with pauper labour was that in times of slump it had to be maintained, whereas surplus 'free' labour could be dismissed.[22]

Labour shortages also provide an alternative explanation of Owen's behaviour during the four-month shutdown of the New Lanark mill in 1806. Owen kept on the workers and paid out over £7000 in wages. Cullen ascribed Owen's decision to 'generosity',[23] which Podmore had more cautiously described as 'wise generosity'.[24] Arguably, Owen's action was simply a calculated economic risk. The shutdown arose from an American embargo on cotton exports which, in turn, distorted the market. Rather than pay inflated prices, the British owners (who held a virtual monopoly on factory production) decided to run down their existing stocks and wait for normal supplies to resume. Indeed, it is not unreasonable to suggest that £7000 may have been a small price to pay — especially when set against future profits. Certainly, it was a small price to pay for the retention of a well-trained, well-disciplined and, henceforth, well-contented labour force.[25]

In these terms it is difficult to assess Owen's generosity — especially since there is (as yet) little evidence of the stance adopted by other mill owners. On the other hand, there is good evidence that mills in outlying areas (like New Lanark) suffered chronic labour problems at this time. In *An Economic History of Scotland* (1975) Lythe and Butt note that 'despite elaborate social provision' labour turnover in the early years of the nineteenth century reached 'staggering proportions'. In support of their argument they cite evidence from the Newton Stewart (Kirkcudbright) mill. By August 1801 the mill had lost nearly 35 per cent of the workforce that had been present twelve months earlier and a further 10 per cent who had joined and left during the course of the year.[26] Given these circumstances and the general problem of labour discipline in the industrial revolution, Owen's activities in the first decade of the nineteenth century could be regarded as much those of a profit-conscious businessman as those of a benevolent philanthropist.

3. Owen's Latency Period

Owen's autobiography has also been more generally misleading about his early years at New Lanark. The received view — supported by the autobiography — is that Owen came to Scotland with his educational ideas fully formed and that, therefore, his relative inactivity between 1800 and 1813 (his entry into partnership with a group of well-known philanthropists) derives, in G. D. H. Cole's terms, from the 'interference'[27] of his early partners. The latter part of this argument has substance — the terms of the 1813 partnership (and

Owen's improved financial position) provided considerable managerial freedom. But the early part merits reconsideration. The received view gained further support from Podmore who wrote:

> It is to be remarked that his first years at New Lanark shut him off to a great extent from such intercourse with educated men as he had enjoyed in Manchester.[28]

And, fifty years later, Margaret Cole repeated the same argument:

> During the fourteen years after (Owen) had left Manchester his mind had been working almost entirely in intellectual isolation . . . it is exceedingly doubtful whether during that period he talked with anyone who could as it were rub his intellectual nose.[29]

The implication of these arguments is that Owen's social ideas remained in a state of suspended animation for over a decade. This is highly unlikely. Just as Owen was an active member of the Manchester Literary and Philosophical Society in the 1790s, so he was probably a member of the Glasgow Literary and Commercial Society in the 1800s (and certainly presented papers in 1815 and 1818[30]). Moreover, as part-proprietor and manager of one of the largest cotton mills in Britain, and as a producer whose goods were sold all over the world, it is not unreasonable to assume that Owen was more worldly-wise than some of his biographers have imagined.

To understand more fully Owen's actions (and inactions) between 1800 and 1813 it is necessary to take a closer look at the economic, intellectual and political context of New Lanark. Specifically, it is important to examine the influence of the Scottish Enlightenment, the changing fortunes of the cotton trade and, not least, the industrial relations of the epoch.

It is well-known and widely accepted by educationists that Owen broke with the monitorial system after 1812. Although he accepted its cheapness and relative efficiency, he came to recognise that it was an insufficient mechanism for disciplining the minds of the learners. The monitorial system claimed to inculcate piety; Owen wanted to instill character. The causes of Owen's reconsideration are, as implied, likely to have been various, but the form and content of his educational innovations indicate the influence of Scottish philosophical and educational thought. As Harrison has suggested, therefore, the starting point of Owen's social theories was 'not Manchester but Scotland'.[31]

The task of pinning down the connection is difficult, since Owen made few explicit references to his sources, and claimed to have read very little during that time. But to a man who moved easily in commercial and intellectual circles there was no need, then or now, to do much reading.

Owen's general achievement, as Harrison has pointed out in *Robert Owen and the Owenites* (1969), was to harness a cluster of eighteenth-century ideas about reason, nature, and the potency of human action to the substance and consequences of the industrial revolution. The particular contribution of the Scottish Enlightenment to Owen's educational ideas seems to have taken two forms: a pedagogical theory of the schoolroom and a psychological theory of group processes. The immediate source of these notions, as shown below, was probably the new teaching methods adopted in certain departments of the Scottish universities.

Medieval pedagogic influences lasted well into eighteenth-century Scotland. Students were taught via formalised Latin lectures (or 'dictates') and their learning, accordingly, was a predominantly passive affair. During the middle of the century students increasingly began to receive instruction couched in the vernacular and delivered by more extempore methods. The overall intention (if not the result) of the reforms was to create a more active pedagogic discipline — one that took shape as an 'easy dialogue', between the lecturer and 'not more than thirty or forty' students.[32]

A further important feature of this new pedagogy was that teaching and assessment were brought much closer together. The formalised disputation was abandoned and teachers began to question students during the course of the lectures (as well as on separate occasions). These procedures — a precursor of simultaneous instruction — were explicitly designed to maintain the constant attention of all the members of the class.

Thus, there is a marked similarity between the methods adopted in the universities and the 'familiar' lectures given to 'classes of about forty to fifty'[33] at New Lanark after 1812. It is not yet clear whether Owen transposed these ideas directly from the universities, or whether he drew them from the general educational melting-pot of the day.[34] Certainly, he claimed to have been on 'most friendly terms' with the Glasgow professors, mentioning the major publicist for the new methods, George Jardine, by name.[35] On the other hand, Jardine does not appear to have made any reciprocal acknowledgement of Owen. But, even if Owen did not learn of the new methods from Jardine's immediate circle, it is just as plausible that he learned of them in the wider intellectual networks of the day (for example, the Glasgow Literary and Commercial Society).

The group psychology that Owen took on board with his pedagogy derived not only from continental materialists like Helvetius but also from Scottish moral philosophers like Francis Hutcheson, David Hume and Adam Smith. If Helvetius gave Owen the notion — expressed in 1814 — that the 'character of man is . . . always formed for him',[36] the latter group provided the important rider that the 'ideas and habits' which 'govern and direct [man's] conduct' are created and transmitted not in nature but in society.[37]

During the early years of the nineteenth century, then, it is quite possible that Owen moved beyond the individualistic notions of the continental philosophers (who still took Rousseau's *Emile* as the paradigmatic educational relationship[38]) and, under the direct influence of the Scottish Enlightenment, began to claim the importance of group dynamics to the conduct of society in general and schooling in particular.

The kind of group teaching described above was, therefore, as much an ideological response to the Scottish Enlightenment as it was a practical response to the immediate context of New Lanark. Owen believed that group teaching was superior to the conventional method of individualised instruction. In a phrase used by Owen's son, grouping would foster an atmosphere of 'friendly emulation'[39] that, in turn, would carry forward the weaker members of the group. Further, such group teaching was also a practical demonstration of the fact that, as in society, there was (in Owen's words) a 'clear and inseparable connection between the interest and happiness of each individual and the interest and happiness of every other individual'.[40]

These two rationalisations of class teaching point to the source of Owen's ideas. The 'happiness' quotation demonstrates the general influence of utilitarian thought; the rhetoric of 'friendly emulation', as shown below, links Owen to a peculiarly Scottish strain of utilitarianism.

A general feature of utilitarian thought is the 'identity of interests' thesis — that all humans operate with the same scale of values. In *The Growth of Philosophic Radicalism* (1928) Halevy has argued that, on the basis of their different social origins, three variants of the 'identity of interests' thesis can be distinguished: (1) the thesis of the 'natural' identity of interests presumes that the interests of individuals are harmonised via the operation of 'natural' (i.e. market) forces; (2) the thesis of the 'artificial' identity of interests assumes that harmonisation occurs through the intervention of legislators; and (3) the thesis of the 'fusion' of interests assumes that the identification of personal and general interest can obtain spontaneously through the psychological phenomena of 'sympathy' and 'fellow feeling'.

In fact, Halevy places Owen among those, like Godwin, who believed in the 'artificial' identification of interests (and the power of education to bring about such harmonisation). But it is also the case that the 'friendly emulation' statement is consonant with the 'fusion of interests' thesis which, as Halevy notes, owes much to thinkers of the Scottish Enlightenment (such as Hutcheson, Hume and Smith).[41]

From the foregoing evidence it is a reasonable hypothesis that Owen's thinking between 1800 and 1812 did not so much stagnate as undergo a subtle but pedagogically important realignment — one that left Owen more readily disposed to the kinds of practices adopted in the Scottish universities. But shifts in thinking are not enough to explain changes in pedagogic practice: the will to change is one thing, the capacity to change is something else. In Owen's case, the general economic buoyancy of the cotton trade during the Napoleonic Wars was a second factor that influenced his educational behaviour before and after 1810.

Butt has estimated that, between 1810 and 1814, the average return on Owen's capital was 46 per cent, whereas before and after that time it was only 15 per cent.[42] This profit not only enabled Owen to renegotiate various debts; it also gave him sufficient social credit to move easily in London society and sufficient commercial credit to attract, as trading partners, Bentham and other wealthy financier-philanthropists. Further, deployment of the residual profits of the New Lanark mill (that is, the portion remaining after the partnership obligations had been met) was, after 1813, left to the initiative of Owen. The 'fat' years after 1810 helped, no doubt, towards overcoming the resistance of Owen's partners and, in turn, towards the completion of the New Institute for the Formation of Character (begun by 1809 and opened in 1816).

Finally, the view that Owen's innovations were simply delayed after 1800 also fails to take account of the changing climate of industrial relations. In 1810-11, for instance, the Glasgow mill owners were troubled by an upsurge of unrest among their operatives. The operatives had (legally) established a (Friendly) Society of Operative Cotton Spinners in 1810 but, in the eyes of the owners, were illegally using its funds to support members who, the owners claimed, had been sacked for 'drunkenness, irregularity of attendance and other misdemeanors'.[43] The full details of these events have, it seems, not been researched or published but the tone of the employers' arguments suggests that the sackings (and the violence they provoked) took place at a time of surplus labour and were part of a widespread (if shortlived) decline in the living standards of the mill workers.

The issue of living standards also erupted the following year in the shape of the 'great weavers strike' which, supported from Aberdeen to Carlisle, lasted for twelve weeks. The handloom weavers had earlier petitioned parliament for the establishment of a minimum wage. But, according to Smout's *A History of the Scottish People* (1969), their efforts had fallen on 'stony ground'.[44] The formation of a union was the weavers' response; and the 1812 strike followed an unsuccessful attempt to establish the regulation of wages in Glasgow. The strike was finally broken when the leaders of the Glasgow Committee were sentenced to prison terms ranging from four to eighteen months.

The events of 1810 and 1812 mark an important change in the social climate. The over-supply of labour — particularly in the urban-located steam-powered mills — and the attendant increased exploitation of the textile workers created a volatile political situation. Owen's response to these developments was to blame them on the manufacturing system which, he claimed in 1815, had fostered a 'gross ferocity of character' among the labouring classes that 'sooner or later' would 'plunge the country into a formidable and perhaps inextricable state of danger'.[45]

As the Napoleonic wars came to a close, these problems were further exacerbated: a small localised surplus of 'hands' turned into a national reserve army of discontented able-bodied labour. These historically unprecedented developments gave a new edge to discussions about social control and reform. It is reasonable to assume, therefore, that Owen's nineteenth-century audience (unlike his twentieth-century biographers) paid rather less attention to his philosophical musings and rather more attention to his diagnoses and remedies. They, like Owen, believed that the 'direct object' was 'to effect the amelioration and avert the danger'.[46]

In 1815, Owen advanced the following proposals: (1) that the hours and conditions of factory employment should be regulated; and (2) that children should demonstrate competence in the three R's before being admitted to factory labour. Owen believed these policies would be beneficial to all parties — 'to the child, to the parent, to the employer and to the country'.[47] But insofar as Owen's audience was drawn from the economic and political elites of British society — copies were sent to all members of both houses of parliament — it is the arguments directed towards the investing and employing classes that presumably carried the most weight.

Owen used a language that the elites understood; he appealed to their pockets as well as to their hearts. To the employers, for instance, he claimed that children who had been 'best taught' not only made the 'best servants', but were also 'the most easily directed to do everything that was right and proper'. And to the tax-payers he reported that any increase in prices caused by improvements in working conditions would be more than offset by a diminution in the 'poors-rates'.[48]

In 1817, Owen turned from the problem of factory exploitation to the problem of post-war unemployment. As noted earlier, the impact of this problem was more widely recognised. It directly affected not just employers but everyone responsible for poor relief. Owen's solution was that the able-bodied poor should be placed in self-supporting residential establishments accommodating around 1,000 persons. He claimed that every part of society would be 'essentially benefited' by such means: the 'deep distress' of the manufacturing and labouring poor would be 'relieved'; and the need for charity and poor-rates would be overcome 'in one generation'.[49]

The philosophic, economic and political circumstances described above pass virtually unmentioned in Owen's autobiography. Their absence, of course, adds invisible support to Owen's claim that, 'unfettered by partners and ignorant prejudices', he would have transformed New Lanark in 'two years' (rather than sixteen).[50] A closer look at the historical record, however, suggests otherwise. In short, when Owen went to New Lanark he was under-capitalised — both financially and intellectually — for the kind of future that the industrial revolution was to force upon him.

4. Owen as Innovator

Owen's self-presentation as someone who worked unremittingly against the ignorance, opposition and incompetence of others is, as widely noted, a marked characteristic of his autobiography. It is a view that Owen projected beyond his partners to such important collaborators as Peter Drinkwater (who gave Owen his first job as manager of a large cotton mill in Manchester), David Dale (original owner of New Lanark) and James Buchanan (the superintendent of the New Lanark school from 1815-1818). Closer examination, however, suggests that Owen's success was rather more directly tied to the sponsorship and assistance of these men than he was prepared to admit. In a more general sense, a study of Owen's collaborators also provides further clues as to the source of his ideas and, more important, to the ways in which they resonated with contemporary conditions.

Owen described Drinkwater as 'totally ignorant of everything connected with cotton spinning'.[51] This was true to an extent: Drinkwater (like Dale) made his initial fortune as a middleman rather than a cotton yarn manufacturer. Nevertheless, in 1879 Drinkwater erected the first cotton mill in Manchester powered by a rotary steam engine. Further, Chaloner's twentieth-century judgment is that Drinkwater was a 'quick learner',[52] a man who readily appreciated, for instance, that the production of fine (i.e. more profitable) yarn presumed the existence of machinery that could work at an even tempo. Indeed, Chaloner even goes so far as to suggest that some of Owen's later success in yarn production derives from the knowledge he inherited from Drinkwater's own innovations.

Owen's judgment on Dale was that he paid insufficient attention to the welfare of the work-force. Again, recent research (by McLaren) suggests otherwise — that Dale was amongst the most innovative owners of his time, particularly with regard to the provision of schooling at New Lanark.[53] Dale, it should be recognised, was not alone in providing (evening) schooling for his pauper apprentices. But the unusually extensive, well-established, and closely regulated curriculum at New Lanark presumably owed something to Dale's wealth as a banker, his experience as Director of the Town's Hospital (that is, charity workhouse) of Glasgow and his calvinist convictions as a leader of the Old Scots Independents. Such schooling — with its division of the children into classes, its fortnightly examinations and its specification in writing of how far the teachers were to 'carry forward their scholars' — drew the same kind of attention as Owen's later experiments.[54] In 1792, the *Annual Register* described Dale as 'this extraordinary man';[55] in 1796, the Manchester Board of Health included New Lanark in its survey of factory schooling; and between 1796 and 1798 visitors to New Lanark included Henry Brougham, Robert Owen, Andrew Bell and Professor (Dugald?) Stewart, all of whom, then or later, showed a special interest in education and schooling.[56]

Owen described James Buchanan as a 'simple-minded kind-hearted' man who, upon his appointment as teacher at New Lanark could 'scarcely read, write, or spell'.[57] An alternative biography, prepared by Buchanan's granddaughter, suggests a more worldly-wise man who, besides being a weaver, had also served in the Militia (Home Guard) during the Napoleonic wars.[58] The family evidence, together with Rusk's claim that Buchanan was/had been a lay preacher in the Primitive Methodists[59] would, if true, cast doubt on Owen's appraisal of Buchanan's literacy. In the early nineteenth century, both weaving and lay preaching were associated with relatively high levels of self-education, certainly to the level of being able to read.

Owen also indicated that he spent a considerable amount of time inducting Buchanan into the work of the school. The Buchanan family records claim otherwise — that Buchanan was merely left to his own devices. Again, the Buchanan evidence, if true, would imply that the early methods followed at New Lanark owe as much to Buchanan as they do to Owen. But what was the source of Buchanan's ideas? One possibility is that Buchanan had already come into contact with new modes of teaching in the sabbath schools of the dissenting sects. Indeed, it may have been this experience, coupled with Buchanan's 'tractable and willing' disposition, that drew Owen's attention to him in the first place.[60]

5. Owen's departure from New Lanark

Explanations for Owen's departure from New Lanark generally point to the work of one of Owen's partners, the Quaker William Allen. Owen's criticism of established religion and the 'liberal modes of natural instruction'[61] followed at New Lanark are usually cited as the main bones of contention. The first of these is certainly plausible — even before signing the original partnership agreement, Allen had been concerned to establish that only the Holy Scriptures (that is, no sectarian texts) would be used at New Lanark.[62] And even after the agreement was signed Allen worried repeatedly about Owen's 'infidel principles' and their impact upon the school.[63]

The matter of 'liberal modes of instruction', however, does not figure in Allen's memoirs. He merely notes that, in 1823 (when matters were coming to a head), a visit by himself and two other partners led to the conclusion that New Lanark should be put under the 'control of the London parties'.[64] Owen claims that Allen's objections to the inclusion of music, dancing and military discipline in the New Lanark curriculum[65] stemmed from Allen's convictions as a Quaker. But even if this was the case (which is doubtful), it still does not explain why Allen finally chose to act against Owen in 1823.

A more reasonable precipitating factor stems not so much from Allen's religious views as from his standpoint as a businessman: Allen's first formal action against Owen — the calling of an extraordinary meeting of the partners — dates from 21st August 1822. Allen's purpose, as described in a letter to Bentham, was that the meeting should consider the 'propriety' of purchasing some of Owen's shares and of 'making regulations for the future conduct'[66] of New Lanark.

One reason for Allen's actions could be that, in the summer of 1822, he had first learned that the New Lanark mill had made a trading loss in 1821. 1822 was also the year that the expenses of the New Institution reached a maximum of £1394, having risen from £506 in 1817. The cash book for the New Institution also reveals that the amount recorded for 'sundries' in 1822 (£472) was more than four times the amount for any previous year. Further, the years after 1820 also show a substantial variation in the amount spent on 'clothing': five pounds was spent in 1820 and an average of £182 per annum between 1821 and 1823 (inclusive).[67]

All these facts suggest that Allen's disquiet may also have been prompted by economic factors. From this viewpoint Allen objected not so much to Owen's methods as to the financial burden they placed upon the company.

Such an interpretation accords with the terms renegotiated by Allen in 1824. Among other things, dancing was no longer to be taught at the expense of the company.[68] Normal dress (instead of uniforms) was to be resumed, and Catherine Vale Whitwell, who was paid nearly twice as much as the next highest paid teachers, was to be dismissed from her artist-in-residence position.[69] It seems likely, then, that changes in the economic climate rather than changes in Allen's educational viewpoint, were the immediate cause of the crisis among the partners. When profits were high, Owen had been able to deflect any ideological objections to his innovations. But the combination of an ideological and an economic crisis finally made the gulf between Owen and his partners unbridgeable.

6. Robert Owen: A Man of his Time

The opening paragraphs of this essay raised doubts about the conventional view of Robert Owen's educational work at New Lanark. With the aid of information not accessible to many of the earlier commentators, the remainder of the essay offers a revised interpretation. Two thrusts of the argument merit restatement. First, that Owen's innovations at New Lanark were perfectly compatible with the economic and political logic of capitalist production. And secondly, that the New Lanark innovations were not so much triggered by Owen's 'prescience' or 'humanity'[70] as by the particular set of ideological and material circumstances that came together in that place.

Owen's work at New Lanark was, therefore, the expression of an inheritance. He took the political belief, derived from Calvin and Knox, that investment in schooling was an essential element in the creation of piety and social virtue. He added the social-psychological notion, derived from the Scottish Enlightenment, that durable forms of schooling would follow from pedagogies that stressed group methods and pupil understanding. And he built upon David Dale's experiments in factory-, school- and pauper-management. Thereafter, Owen invested his intellectual legacy in the cotton trade which, in its uneven development between 1810 and 1816, yielded both new problems to tackle and new resources (that is, super-profits) to apply.

It was these factors, intersecting with Owen's biography, that created the peculiar character of New Lanark. It is not so much, therefore, his ideas that should be remembered as his capacity to put them into practice. Owen's tenure (and efforts) as manager of New Lanark coincided with the accumulation of great surplus wealth. A significant proportion of that wealth was not returned directly to the partners but, rather, reinvested in the general workings of the New Lanark Community. Such reinvestment had an important qualitative consequence. It enabled Owen to reshape the educational practices of working-class schooling. The net result was a pedagogic amalgam which, under the pressure of new constraints and new opportunities, underwent constant redefinition. It is not surprising, therefore, that twentieth-century commentators have produced contrasting representations of Robert Owen. In a very real sense most, if not all, are correct. In the course of his twenty-five years at New Lanark, Owen prefigured all kinds of educational futures. But even as we celebrate these futures, it is perhaps worth remembering the context that fostered them. To credit Owen with visionary powers or innate propensities is not only to misconstrue his work, it is also to devalue his undoubted achievements.

NOTES

1. R. Owen, Speech to the Lancastrian Society of Glasgow; reported in *The Glasgow Herald*, May 4th, 1812.

2. N. J. Smelser, *Social Change in the Industrial Revolution* (London, 1959), p. 105.

3. See, for instance, B. Simon (ed.), *The Radical Tradition in Education in Britain* (London, 1972); W. A. C. Stewart & P. McCann, *The Educational Innovators, 1750-1880* (London, 1967) and S. Castles & W. Wustenberg, *The Education of the Future: an Introduction to the Theory and Practice of Socialist Education* (London, 1979).

4. J. F. C. Harrison, 'A new view of Mr. Owen', in S. Pollard & J. Salt (eds.), *Robert Owen: Prophet of the Poor* (London, 1977), p. 2.

5. H. Silver, *The Concept of Popular Education* (London, 1965), p. 13 ff.

6. W. A. C. Stewart & P. McCann, *op. cit.*, p. 53.

7. B. Simon, *Studies in the History of Education 1780-1870* (London, 1960), p. 193.

8. R. Miliband, 'The politics of Robert Owen', *Journal of the History of Ideas*, 1954, *15*, p. 233. Miliband further comments that Owen's undoubted contribution to the development of Socialist doctrine in Britain should be set against his cautious and conservative approach to the politics of his own day, and to politics in general. For this reason, if no other, it is important to distinguish between Owen's ideas and Owenite ideas.

9. F. Podmore, *Robert Owen: a Biography* (London, 1906), pp. 82, 169.

10. A. Cullen, *Adventures in Socialism* (Glasgow, 1910), pp. 86, 29. It should be noted that Cullen, like many of his contemporaries, used 'socialism' more as an antonym of 'individualism' than of 'capitalism'.

11. G. D. H. Cole, *Robert Owen* (London, 1925), pp. 13, 155. Cole also reports that Owen's fame at New Lanark rested upon a claim, if not a demonstration, that 'philanthropy could be made to pay' (p. 14). For a general consideration of 'benevolence as investment' see O. Checkland, *Philanthropy in Victorian Scotland* (Edinburgh, 1980), pp. 1-7.

12. S. Pollard, *The Genesis of Modern Management* (London, 1965), p. 91.

13. J. Butt, 'Robert Owen of New Lanark: his critique of British Society', in J. Butt & I. F. Clarke (eds.), *The Victorians and Social Protest* (Newton Abbot, 1973), p. 22.

14. M. Cole, *Robert Owen of New Lanark* (London, 1953), p. 1.

15. *Ibid.*, p. 1.

16. S. Pollard, 'Introduction' to S. Pollard & J. Salt, *Robert Owen: Prophet of the Poor*, p. VIII. The fact that British educational historians have little experience of handling ideas from economic history can be matched by the uneven handling of ideological influences by economic historians.

17. W. A. C. Stewart & P. McCann, *op. cit.*, p. vix. See also the criticism in H. Silver, 'Aspects of neglect: the strange case of Victorian popular education', *Oxford Review of Education*, 1977, *3*, p. 58.

18. W. A. C. Stewart & P. McCann, *op. cit.*, p. 72.

19. *Ibid.*, p. 72.

20. *Ibid.*, p. 65. For a general discussion of the long-standing place of music in Scottish schools see J. Bulloch, The significance and contribution of the song schools in Scottish educational history, unpublished M.Ed. thesis, University of Glasgow, 1981.

21. A. Cullen, *op. cit.*, p. 34.

22. For comments on the poor cost-effectiveness of pauper apprentices, see N. Smelser, *op. cit.*, pp. 104-5; and S. Pollard, *op. cit.*, pp. 164-5. Smelser reports that 'in a classic statement in 1816,

Robert Peel claimed that apprenticeship was no longer a basic concern in the cotton manufacture because of . . . steam factories with their free child labour' (p. 187).

23. A. Cullen, *op. cit.*, p. 36.

24. F. Podmore, *op. cit.*, p. 84.

25. For a general discussion of recruitment and retention of skilled labour in the industrial revolution, see S. Pollard, *op. cit.*, pp. 166-172. Owen's actions in 1806 might be compared with Henry Ford's unprecedented increase in auto-workers' wages to five dollars a day in 1914. In his autobiography Ford wrote: 'the payment of five dollars a day for an eight-hour day was one of the finest cost-cutting moves we ever made' (quoted in H. Braverman, *Labour and Monopoly Capital,* New York, 1974, p. 150).

26. S. Lythe & J. Butt, *An Economic History of Scotland, 1100-1939* (Glasgow, 1975), p. 186.

27. G. D. H. Cole, *op. cit.*, p. 159; cf. 'the difficulties Owen encountered as a result of his partnerships are important only in that . . they delayed the application of his plans for education.' H. Silver, *op. cit.*, pp. 115-116.

28. F. Podmore, *op. cit.*, p. 111.

29. M. Cole, *op. cit.*, p. 74.

30. See T. Atkinson, *Sketch of the Origins and Progress of the Literary and Commercial Society of Glasgow,* Glasgow: Printed for private circulation, 1831. No indication is given of the date of Owen's admission to the society but he is recorded as giving papers in 1815 ('education and the formation of character') and 1818 ('observations on the effects of the manufacturing system, with hints for the improvement of those parts of it which are injurious to health and morals'). There is no reason to assume that the economic/intellectual climate of Glasgow around 1800 was any less important to the fermentation of Owen's ideas than it had been, forty years previously, to the formulation of Adam Smith's social theories.

31. J. F. C. Harrison, 'The steam engine of the New Moral World: Owenism and education 1817-1829', *Journal of British Studies,* 1967, 6, p. 81. See also J. F. C. Harrison, *Robert Owen and the Owenites in Britain and America* (London, 1969), pp. 83-87.

32. G. Jardine, *Outlines of Philosophical Education Illustrated by the Method of Teaching the Logic Class in the University of Glasgow* (Glasgow, 1825), pp. 464 and 426.

33. R. D. Owen, *An Outline of the System of Education at New Lanark* (1824), reprinted in B. Simon (ed.), *op. cit.*, p. 160. See also D. Hamilton, 'Adam Smith and the moral economy of the classroom system', *Journal of Curriculum Studies,* 1980, 12, pp. 281-298.

34. The intellectual/educational networks that existed in Scotland at the beginning of the nineteenth century will be reported more fully in the forthcoming M.Ed. theses (Glasgow University) of Eileen Brown and Rosalind Russell. Already, their work on Dugald Stewart and Elizabeth Hamilton suggests, for instance, that Pestalozzian ideas entered Scotland at a much earlier date than hitherto reported.

35. When Owen addressed the Lancastrian Society of Glasgow in 1812 he was 'supported on the right and left by Professors Jardine and Mylne', *Life of Robert Owen* (London, 1971), p. 107 (originally published in 1857).

36. R. Owen, *A New View of Society* (3rd. Essay, 1814), reprinted in B. Simon (ed.), *op. cit.*, p. 71.

37. *Ibid.*, p. 71.

38. For a valuable discussion of the educational views of continental thinkers like Helvetius, see H. Silver, *op. cit.*, pp. 60-65.

39. R. D. Owen, *A Outline of the System of Education at New Lanark* in B. Simon (ed.), *op. cit.*, p. 175. For the importance of 'emulation' to the organisation of early nineteenth-century schooling, see D. Hamilton, 'Adam Smith and the moral economy of the classroom system', *op. cit.*

40. R. Owen, *A New View of Society,* in B. Simon (ed.), *op. cit.*, p. 75.

41. E. Halevy, *The Growth of Philosophic Radicalism* (Boston, 1955, originally published in 1928), pp. 13-17. Halevy's analysis of the identity of interests thesis may help to explain Owen's care for humanity and social justice which 'many of the Utilitarians lacked' (see P. Gordon & D. Lawton, *Curriculum Change in the Nineteenth and Twentieth Centuries,* London, 1978, p. 54).

42. J. Butt, 'Robert Owen as businessman', in J. Butt (ed.), *Robert Owen: Prince of Cotton Spinners* (Newton Abbot, 1971), pp. 199-200.

43. (Minute Book of) Association of Master Cotton Spinners (Strathclyde Regional Archives, T-MJ 99).

44. T. C. Smout, *A History of the Scottish People 1560-1830* (Glasgow, 1975), pp. 397-8.

45. R. Owen, 'On the effect of the manufacturing system etc.' (1815), Appendix H of Volume 1A of *The Life of Robert Owen* (London, 1856), p. 41.

46. *Ibid.*, p. 41.

47. *Ibid.*, p. 41.

48. *Ibid.*, pp. 42-43.

49. R. Owen, 'Report to the committee of the association for the relief of the manufacturing and labouring poor' (1817), Appendix I of Volume 1A of *The Life of Robert Owen*, p. 64. The fact that Owen's proposals in 1815 and 1817 consciously sought to reassure the upper and middle classes had led at least one commentator to describe them as 'essentially conservative' (J. H. Treble, 'The social and economic thought of Robert Owen', in S. Butt (ed.), *op. cit.*, p. 42).

50. *Life of Robert Owen*, p. 79.

51. *Life of Robert Owen*, p. 26.

52. W. H. Chaloner, 'Robert Owen, Peter Drinkwater and the early factory system in Manchester, 1788-1800', *Bulletin of the John Rylands Library*, 1954, *37*, p. 91.

53. D. J. McLaren, 'A Bright Luminary to Scotland': a Life of Glasgow Entrepreneur David Dale, 1739-1806, M.Ed. thesis, University of Glasgow, 1981; cf. M. Sanderson, 'Education and the factory in industrial Lancashire, 1780-1840', *Economic History Review*, 1967, *20*, pp. 266-279; and R. Pallister, 'Schools for working class children in County Durham in the early nineteenth century', *Bulletin of the North East Group for the Study of Labour History*, 1971, *5*, pp. 9-12.

54. See 'Queries submitted to Mr. Dale of Glasgow by Mr Bayley of Manchester, in connection with the working conditions in the Mills at New Lanark', reprinted in T. Ferguson, *The Dawn of Scottish Welfare: a Survey from Medieval Times to 1863* (London, 1948), pp. 93-96.

55. Quoted in H. Silver, *op. cit.*, p. 110.

56. The surviving New Lanark Visitors' Books are held in Glasgow University Archives.

57. *Life of Robert Owen*, p. 139.

58. *Buchanan Family Records*, Capetown: Printed for private circulation, 1923, p. 1.

59. Rusk implies that Buchanan was a preacher before he moved to New Lanark, though his evidence for this is unclear (see R. Rusk, *A History of Infant Education*, London, 1933, p. 136.).

60. *Life of Robert Owen*, pp. 138-139. Buchanan's predecessor whom Owen characterised as 'obstinate' had been appointed by David Dale twenty-three years previously. See J. Butt, 'Robert Owen of New Lanark: his critique of British Society', p. 20.

61. *Life of Robert Owen*, p. 235.

62. W. Allen, *Life of William Allen with Selections from his correspondence* (3 vols.) (London, 1846), Vol. 1, pp. 183-209, 215.

63. *Ibid.*, pp. 222, 244, 344, 355, 356; Vol. 2, p. 266.

64. *Ibid.*, p. 237.

65. *Life of Robert Owen*, p. 235.

66. Quoted in J. Butt, 'Robert Owen as businessman', in S. Butt, *Robert Owen: Prince of Cotton Spinners*, p. 201.

67. The New Lanark Cash Book is held in Edinburgh University Library. The amounts have been re-calculated to the nearest pound.

68. See F. Podmore, *op. cit.*, p. 157. W. Davidson's *History of Lanark and Guide to the Scenery* (1828) reports that dancing was still taught even after the schooling at New Lanark had reverted to the 'British and Foreign system'; cited in Harrison, *Robert Owen and the Owenites in Britain and America*, p. 162n.

69. For payments to Whitwell, see the New Lanark cashbook.

70. 'The single thread which runs through all of Owen's ideas, colouring them and imparting their direction to them, is his humanity'. S. Pollard, 'Introduction' to Pollard & Salt, *Robert Owen: Prophet of the Poor*, p. x.

2

Manners, Morals and Mentalities:
Reflections on the Popular Enlightenment of Early Nineteenth-Century Scotland

J. V. Smith

There are circumstances, which seem, at the present moment, to render it the duty of every friend of society, to watch over the sentiments of the lower classes with peculiar anxiety, and to interpose the whole weight of his talents in giving them their proper tone. The truth is, that various causes have combined to bring us rather prematurely to that perilous crisis in the history of the world, in which public opinion acquires paramount force before it has become sufficiently enlightened to be safely trusted.

(Rev. Henry Duncan of Ruthwell, 1821)[1]

1. Introduction

REV. Henry Duncan of Ruthwell is nowadays chiefly remembered as the originator, in Scotland, of popular savings banks, an achievement for which he was eloquently reviled by William Cobbett, who charged him with wishing to transform the working classes into pseudo-capitalists.[2] An enthusiastic disciple of Adam Smith and staunch opponent, with Thomas Chalmers, of legal assessment for poor relief, it is little wonder he became a target for the barbs of that indefatigable adversary of 'Scotch feelosophy' and all its works. He was, though, an undoubtedly able man whose talents were diverse and whose interests ranged widely: antiquarian, painter, natural theologian and prominent member of the evangelical party in the Church of Scotland, as well as political economist and practical philanthropist.[3] He is also of some interest to the historian of education.

During his early years as minister of the sequestered Dumfriesshire parish, immediately after the turn of the eighteenth century, he endeavoured, though with minimal success, to organise adult classes in scientific subjects, particularly astronomy. Undeterred, and believing firmly that scientific study revealed God's purposes in nature, he consecrated Sunday afternoons to 'conversational lectures on the works of God', but again success largely eluded him; local religious sentiment was as yet unreceptive to natural theology, and he found himself accused of desecrating the Sabbath. However, a parochial library which he inaugurated was accorded a more favourable reception.[4]

A definite advance came in 1807 with the launching of *The Scotch Cheap Repository*, a popular periodical consisting mainly of moral tales aimed at 'exciting a taste for reading and diffusing useful instruction among the vulgar'. Two years later, with financial backing from a brother established in commerce at Liverpool, he started *The Dumfries and Galloway Courier*, dedicated to the furtherance of the evangelical cause but also serving as an outlet for many of Thomas Carlyle's early literary efforts and widely regarded as a vehicle 'for the most advanced thought of the day'.[5] The conspicuous strand of natural theology in his thought received fullest expression in *The Sacred Philosophy of the Seasons* (1837) which set out to illustrate 'the perfection of God in the phenomena of the year' and was dedicated to the proposition that 'True Science (is) the Handmaid of Religion'.[6]

In combining advocacy of popular adult education with broader philanthropic goals, as well as adherence to an evangelical species of natural theology, Duncan may fairly be claimed as a typical figure of what L. J. Saunders termed the movement for popular enlightenment in early nineteenth-century Scotland.[7] Saunders himself discussed the characteristics and tendencies of this movement by reference to the efforts of three representative individuals, George Miller of Dunbar, Samuel Brown of Haddington and Thomas Dick of Methven (subsequently Broughty Ferry).[8] Two of these, Miller and Dick, wrote books on natural theology (in Dick's case several), and all three established libraries for the use of working people. Above all, their work as adult educators was, like that of Henry Duncan, dominated by a desire to see the 'sentiments of the lower classes' acquire their 'proper tone'.

The salient intellectual feature associated with these writers and educators was a blending of 'Enlightenment' scientific interests[9] with evangelical Christianity. The natural theology, which was the offspring of this union, was regarded as the most appropriate basis for the 'diffusion of useful knowledge'. Indeed, the cardinal importance accorded to natural theology of a suitably enthusiastic temper led to a blurring of the distinction between scientific education and Christian missionary work: the science expounded by George Miller in his *Book of Nature Laid Open* (1826) was 'intermixed with moral reflections calculated to excite devotional feelings',[10] while Thomas Dick repeatedly proclaimed that sermons and religious tracts ought to make more frequent use of scientific subject matter.[11]

The primary concern of the present essay is to explore, more comprehensively than Saunders did, the relationship between the intellectual resources of the educational movement represented by campaigners such as Miller, Duncan and Dick, and the appointed practical task of channelling the sentiments of the lower classes in approved directions. Initially, however, it will be necessary to discuss briefly Saunders' own treatment of popular enlightenment and then to examine why the condition of the lower strata of society was a matter of such overwhelming concern to adult educationists.

2. 'A age of philanthropy and good will to all men'?

For Saunders, the spread of popular enlightenment was, in many respects, a natural outgrowth from existing educational facilities.[12] By the late eighteenth century (earlier in many areas), there was a well-consolidated network of parochial and burgh schools in the settled countryside and small towns of low-land Scotland. In districts such as Lothian and lowland Perthshire, the con-sequence was a peasantry and working population which was essentially literate — often in a more than merely basic sense — and thus well-placed to take advantage of additional educational opportunities. 'In the circumstances,' wrote Saunders, 'the educational problem could present itself as one of quality rather than quantity . . . and the optimistic tradition of the later eighteenth century could anticipate a continuous and inevitable advance of popular enlightenment and virtue.'[13]

Optimism indeed there was among those 'friends of society' who clamoured for the diffusion of knowledge, including scientific knowledge, among the people. Thomas Dick, writing in 1814 to the editor of the London *Monthly Magazine* from the small Perthshire weaving town of Methven, where he was Secession Church Schoolmaster, indulged the hope that 'the period is fast approaching when the ignorance and superstition of former ages shall be dis-pelled and the gates of the temple of science thrown open to all'.[14] Just as often, there was anxiety lest stray sections of the populace enter the temple unsuper-vised by the wrong gates — or even worse, head off in search of different temples altogether. Adult education, in the eyes of its 'benevolent' and 'philan-thropic' promoters was to be as much concerned with the negative task of counteracting existing (and it seemed growing) evils among the lower orders as with paving the way for unlimited progress. George Miller described his *Monthly Monitor and Philanthropic Museum* (1815) as a 'Cheap Repository for Hints, Suggestions, Facts and Discoveries Interesting to Humanity' but was also quite explicit that its aim was to 'Prevent the Commission of Crimes' and to 'Counteract the Baneful Effects of Pernicious Sentiments'.[15]

Key words in contemporary accounts of individuals and their motives were 'benevolent' and 'philanthropic', and these terms were also employed liberally, and without apparent irony, by Saunders. Thus, describing the historical ecology of popular enlightenment in East Lothian, he wrote: 'In a town like Haddington, there would be a small circle of the benevolent or enthusiastic who received the new learning as it spread and spread it in their turn';[16] while in a similar vein, George Miller was portrayed as a man of 'benevolent and diffuse enthusiasms'. A mid-nineteenth-century commentator, J. W. Hudson, reviewing the progress of adult education during the first half of the nineteenth century, felt certain he was living in 'an age of philanthropy and good will to all men. The middle classes vie with the rich in providing the great and good work of education.'[17] Yet nineteenth-century patterns of usage suggest that 'benevolence' or 'philanthropy' as imputed characteristics of individuals should not be taken at face value: something more than a spontaneously generated glow of disinterested benignity seems indicated. 'Benevolent' persons invariably belonged to particular social groups (middle or upper class), exercised their 'benevolence' upon persons from different social strata (the lower orders) and operated through an identifiable set of institutions (philanthropic and educational societies of various kinds). Among the more important social connotations carried by the terms are the following: (a) they imply an order of society in which those who perform good works are sharply differentiated from potential beneficiaries; (b) this division is a permanent and indeed natural one; (c) advantages accrue to the 'benevolent' themselves as well as their beneficiaries — especially in terms of enhanced status within their local communities.[18]

It is clear from the writings of Dick, Miller etc. that the movement for popular enlightenment was conducted against a background of a clearly demarcated 'map' of society. The 'map' in question embodied basically conservative, typically eighteenth-century assumptions and was couched largely in the language of ranks, orders and degrees. For Thomas Dick, the principle of subordination of ranks was divinely sanctioned and formed the basis for moral action: 'On the divinity of rank . . . is founded a great proportion of those moral laws which God hath promulgated . . . for regulating the inclinations and conduct of mankind.'[19] The social vision of Dick or Miller resembled, in many respects, that of Hannah More and the English Clapham Sect educators[20] — there was the same anxiety 'not to abolish the distinction between rich and poor or to shatter the traditionalist theory of orders, ranks and degrees, but rather to justify both by introducing a new leaven of righteousness'.[21] However, the standard-bearers of popular enlightenment in Scotland exhibited a more wholehearted faith in the effectiveness of education than did Mrs More, who recorded that she 'allow(ed) of no writing for the poor'.[22] Such a position would have made less sense in Scotland with its Presbyterian tradition and established pattern of parochial and burgh schools. But the higher 'base-line' from which educational debate in Scotland began should not blind us to similarities between the problems faced by educators such as George Miller and Hannah More; nor, despite important differences, to common features in the responses made.

3. Education: 'the surest and most powerful instrument for the protection of society'

The educational thinking of Miller, Duncan and Dick was firmly grounded in assumptions and habits of thought appropriate to an ordered pattern of rural or small town life — one which offered some scope for upward mobility to a limited number of talented individuals but remained largely undisturbed by that heightening of aspirations and restless, competitive ferment typical of modern industrial societies. Yet the changes in Scottish society to which the philanthropically minded educators responded were those which heralded the transition from that older 'localised' world to one recognisably 'modern'. Between about 1790 and 1840, in Scotland, expansion of commercial and industrial activity, increase and re-distribution of population and urban growth occurred rapidly and on an unprecedented scale.[23] The process was uneven and impinged on different areas to differing degrees; and it is in the interests of perspective to recall that during the 1820s Scotland was still preponderantly an agricultural nation.[24] Nevertheless, it was amply apparent to observant contemporaries that society was experiencing a metamorphosis which was, as Rev. Henry Duncan wrote, 'without an example or parallel in the history of past ages'.[25] The progress of science, important breakthroughs in technology and the burgeoning of commerce engendered, especially among newly prosperous bourgeois groups, a manic optimism which at times passed into utopianism. Yet equally visible and profoundly disquieting was the misery occasioned by the growth of a demoralised and impoverished population in the poorer districts of the cities and manufacturing towns. 'Lowland Scotland, which was in contemporary terms a very successful industrial economy, paid a heavy price, in terms of deprivation, suffering and social tension, for its achievements.'[26] While new opportunities for advancement opened up for groups such as millwrights, whose skills were relevant to new developments in technology,[27] other, formerly prosperous groups of workers experienced a catastrophic decline in fortune. Handloom weavers (whose wages declined from roughly 30s-40s per week during the final decade of the eighteenth century to around 4s-8s per week when the Assistant Handloom Commissioners made their investigations in 1838) are, of course, the classic case.[28] But their plight was far from unique. In Dundee, for example, flax-dressers, bonnetmakers and tanners all suffered disastrous reversals of economic fortune during the first four decades of the nineteenth century.[29]

Dramatic increase in population accompanied by wholesale migration dislocated the calm rhythms of that traditional order of society which supplied, for the spokesmen of popular enlightenment, a stable background of taken-for-granted assumptions. After a fairly steady growth during the eighteenth century, population soared from approximately 1.5 million in 1790 to over 2 million in 1841.[30] Redistribution was as significant as overall growth, the influx of hordes of country people (and later Irish) into the industrial towns creating problems with which the existing civic machinery was unable to cope. As a result, the social framework was subjected to drastic stresses and strains which at times seemed to threaten anarchy and breakdown.[31]

A further source of anxiety was the circulation of radical political ideas among disaffected elements of the labouring classes. Historians of the period have noted the efflorescence of radical activity which followed in the wake of the French Revolution and the remarkably wide popularity throughout Scotland of Tom Paine's *Rights of Man* — initially among sections of the middle as well as working classes.[32] Thus, paralleling industrial expansion and

rapid social change was a comparable ferment in the world of ideas, a pro-
liferation of attempts to make sense of an emerging industrial society whose
lineaments were as yet only dimly perceived. However, the appearance of
extreme tendencies in France itself, together with the upwelling of patriotic
fervour occasioned by the protracted French wars, cooled the enthusiasm of
the middle classes for thoroughgoing radicalism and aroused a preference
among them for a more cautious, 'Whiggish' reformism.[33]

Analysis of living standards is inevitably a complex, value-laden and inconclusive exercise — yet recent studies of this period are in broad agreement that
there was little, if any, gain in real wages for most workers until around mid-
century. 'The decisive process of industrialisation which occurred in Great
Britain in the eighteenth and nineteenth centuries, seems, at least in its crucial
earlier phases, to have needed a large pool of reasonably docile and relatively
cheap labour.'[34] Needed, that is, if there was to be no drastic reconstruction of
society in the manner sought by hardline radicals, a development which would
have run directly counter to the interests of those groups who were riding the
crest of the commercial and industrial wave. It is no surprise, therefore, that
awareness of the nature of these interests and a desire to protect them characterised those theoretical attempts to grasp the essence of industrial society
which emanated from middle-class thinkers. As Mandrou (following Gramsci)
has written:

> Whoever has thought about the place occupied by intellectuals in societies, whether ancient
> or modern, has seen that they fulfil a specific function — broadly that of developing ideology.
> . . . (A)lthough the intellectuals, discoursing and discussing, play a role which is doubtless
> not so fundamental as that of the production of goods and services . . . what they have to say
> matters a great deal in relation to that social regulation, the need for which is appreciated by
> every society.[35]

If Mandrou's observation is taken seriously, it is unsatisfactory to select for
attention only those thinkers whose work has 'stood the test of time'; the
articulation of vital interests has frequently been the business of 'provincial
intellectuals' whose literary effusions no longer receive serious academic consideration 'in their own right'. However, such neglected tomes may well be of
great interest to anyone concerned with understanding the intellectual
weapons wielded by social groups in furthering their own interests. They also
merit attention as examples of what happens to 'metropolitan' ideas when
these are disseminated (and reworked) in more restricted settings. Indeed the
distinction between the formulation and diffusion of ideas, though it has a
rough utility, is a somewhat artificial one: assimilation of new ideas by a
particular social group invariably involves a modification of the ideas themselves, which carries over into subsequent transmission.

The veracity of the above claim is supported by the evidence relating to
political economy. Complex formulations of its subject matter were simplified
by popularisers such as J. R. McCulloch in such a way as to demonstrate a
more obvious congruence between the entrepreneurial ethos of the manu-

facturing classes and the essential nature of economic activity.[36] Somewhat debased and attenuated versions of the subject were also transmitted to the working class to serve as 'a code of "correct" ideas within which [their] aspirations for reform were to be contained'.[37]

One of the best known attempts, in Scotland, to grapple intellectually and practically with the problems thrown up by industrialisation was that of the leading evangelical churchman, Thomas Chalmers. Chalmers was himself an untiring proponent of simplified political economy for the workers and was 'confident that a lecturer of any talent at all, might, upon this subject, carry the most crowded amphitheatre of plebeian scholars along with him'.[38] His overall position was really Janus-faced: the crusade on behalf of political economy aligned him with the aggressive forces of capitalist development; yet his vision of social order was firmly rooted in his experience of the older Scotland which was suffering erosion by that same industrial capitalism. 'His eighteenth-century ideal of small town, small business life, order and mutual respect meant that the implications of a period of economic dislocation and the new type of production evaded him.'[39] The celebrated experiment he conducted in St John's parish, Glasgow aimed to introduce into a large-scale urban setting, with mobile population and widespread destitution, a 'localised' pattern of social relationships similar to that with which he was familiar from his own childhood and youth in Fife.[40]

Adult educationists like Miller and Dick reacted to perplexing features of their era in a manner akin to that of Chalmers. Combined with belief in the possibility of almost unlimited progress was a tendency to fall back on safe and familiar images of social order. Rev. Henry Duncan gave eloquent expression to this dual sense of optimism and uncertainty:

> (W)hatever may be the difficulties and embarrassments of a period which is without an example or a parallel in the history of past ages — however hazardous it may be to steer the vessel of human society through an untried ocean, where there is no beacon to warn or landmark to guide, it is a voyage, the risks of which we must resolve manfully and cheerfully to sustain . . . We have now passed that point which no other people who ever navigated the sea of time were able to reach; *and we are fast approaching the shores of those new regions in which the universal diffusion of knowledge shall prove to be the surest and most powerful instrument for the protection of society.*[41] (My emphasis)

But a further problem remained: what kind of knowledge was best fitted for securing social order? Duncan, like Chalmers, felt that political economy was an obvious candidate since it appeared to tackle the most pressing problems directly: for example, by demonstrating 'objectively' that strike action could never better the living standards of the workers.[42] But this very directness could also prove disadvantageous since it alerted many working men to the inherently political nature of economic problems. Political economy, in other words, was too transparently ideological. As Tyrrell remarks, 'It was almost inevitable that the popularisers of orthodox political economy would be regarded as employers' spokesmen sheltering behind a facade of religious, scientific and philanthropic notions.'[43]

However, Henry Duncan and other apostles of popular enlightenment also argued, as we have seen, for a scientific education founded on natural theology. This strand of thought overlapped both with the campaign to popularise political economy and with the more formal scientific education provided by the mechanics' institutes from the early 1820s. In the latter case, the approach adopted was one which, on the whole, favoured the presentation of scientific subject matter free from all religious or political trappings — the curricular emphasis being placed squarely on uncontroversial topics in chemistry, natural philosophy and mathematics. Contrastingly, the advocates of natural theological science inclined more to astronomy and natural history, since these subjects yielded a copious supply of examples illustrating God's benevolent design in nature. Their educational outlook was, one might say, less austerely cognitive than that associated with the early mechanics' institutes — George Miller in his popular magazines, and even a more systematic writer such as Thomas Dick, made a more obvious appeal to heart as well as head. The contents of Miller's *Cheap Magazine*, for example, were designed to avoid 'a tedious continued seriousness' without 'bordering too much on lightness and frivolity'.[44] Each issue was a miscellany of moral tales and verse interlarded with items of scientific interest, brief biographies and domestic hints. Domesticity, indeed, was a major recurring theme in Miller's periodicals, and before examining the putative advantages of natural theology as ideological tranquilliser, it is worth examining more closely the emphasis on home and family which typically accompanied this educational standpoint.

4. Reading, refinement and the 'happy fireside'

A good deal of the 'useful knowledge' purveyed by the *Cheap Magazine* and the *Monthly Monitor* was either non-scientific or only marginally scientific: typical topics were the cultivation of cottage gardens, remedies for accidents in the home, and general matters of domestic economy. The scientific material which did appear was often related to a domestic setting and reading itself was represented as an activity most appropriately engaged in within the family circle (the *Cheap Magazine* was subtitled the *Poor Man's Fireside Companion*).[45] The felicities of familial harmony were frequently extolled and well-regulated family life sometimes served as a metaphor for harmony in society at large — the difficulties parents faced in coping with intractable offspring being likened to those of the civil authorities when confronted by political unrest. A similar emphasis may be discerned in the writings of Henry Duncan. His *The Young South Country Weaver* recounts the adventures of William, a young weaver from the vicinity of Dumfries, who sets off for Glasgow to make his way in the world. In this story, Duncan contrasts the sterling virtues of traditional Scotland (as exemplified by William) with the vice, discontent and political unrest of the industrial belt. Having arrived in Glasgow, William lodges with his paternal uncle and family, and soon discovers the household to be a hotbed of political radicalism.

In one colourful scene Daniel (William's cousin), intoxicated with the radical oratory he has just heard at a political meeting, openly defies his father in the name of equality. A dangerous fight breaks out between father and son during which a likely fatality is prevented by William's timely intervention. The moral is driven home forcefully by Duncan: fathers who flirt with the philosophy of social levelling must expect indocility from their own children.[46]

The desirability of orderly family life, guaranteed by training children, from the outset, in habits of subordination, is a vital ingredient of the social 'message' disseminated by Duncan, Miller and Dick. Reading itself forms an integral part of the same set of values: as a hearth-centred activity, it provides a focus for positive family recreation. It is also an antidote to unproductive (and therefore potentially dangerous) ways of passing the time. The avoidance by Miller of difficult, technical reading matter and the emphasis on variety and relative simplicity is thus at one with his general aim of strengthening the domestic domain in peasant and working-class life. A home-centred lifestyle is held up for moral approval and is simultaneously seen as the embodiment of 'refinement' and 'civility': the moral life is roughly equated with the well-mannered life. By contrast 'vice', 'profligacy' and 'coarseness' are associated with gregarious conviviality — the world of tavern, fair and open air sociability.[47]

Clearer illustration of the way a publisher such as Miller sought to implant 'enlightened' habits of mind among his readers may be gained by examining a typical moral tale, 'The Beacon or the Execution Improved: An Humble Attempt to Check the First Approaches to Vice', which appeared in the first volume of the *Cheap Magazine*.[48] Authorship was imputed to a pseudo-nymous 'Observant Pedestrian' (probably Miller himself). Pedestrian, during the course of a summer evening stroll, taken prior to 'lighting a candle to resume my reading', pauses in the churchyard to meditate; as he comments, 'I seldom return from my excursions without being somewhat benefited by the observations I am accustomed to make on men and things.' On this occasion, however, his moral musings are interrupted by his becoming aware of four youths busily helping themselves to beans in an adjacent field. Being convinced that 'it is better to prevent crimes than to punish them', he decides to intervene to 'check some early blossomings of wickedness in the bud'. One of the guilty juveniles, Thomas Bragwell (subsequently revealed as the primary instigator) takes nimbly to his heels at Pedestrian's approach; the remaining three, David Doubtful, Will Candid and John Careless, remain and soon find themselves subjected to intensive interrogation concerning their homes, habits and upbringings. On the basis of their replies, Pedestrian draws a number of conclusions about the moral consequences of different patterns of child rearing. Lack of attention by parents to ensuring their children grow up in proper subordination, allowing them to acquire time-wasting and unproductive habits such as loitering in public places, unwillingness to enforce regular church attendance — negligence of this kind, Pedestrian avers, had clearly rendered the boys acutely vulnerable to evil influences. The appearance of

Temptation, in the guise of Thomas Bragwell, had launched them on the first stages of careers which, if unchecked, could be expected to lead to misery, destitution and early death. Indeed, Pedestrian points to the close parallel between the course on which the boys had embarked and that of MacDonald, Sutherland and MacIntosh, three of the Edinburgh Tron Rioters who had recently perished on the gallows.[49] The talk concludes with the suitably contrite miscreants accepting Pedestrian's advice to remain at home on Sabbath evenings to peruse the edifying contents of the *Cheap Magazine*.

The story thus emphasises the importance of well-regulated family life and the need to 'train a child in the way he should go'. The dangers of loitering and unprofitable use of time also receive attention, and the fact that the boys' crime is theft underlines the sanctity of private property. An additional feature is Miller's introduction of homespun natural theology into a fictional setting.

In the midst of a previous misdemeanour, the young delinquents had been interrupted by a thunderstorm of such awe-inspiring intensity that even the unregenerate Bragwell had been moved to declare that such a sublime display of natural power must surely be the work of God. Mention of this incident is seized upon by Pedestrian as a pretext for arguing that the ubiquity of God in nature is not difficult to demonstrate. He notices a beanstalk in Will Candid's hand, and this serves as the starting point for an excursion into elementary natural theology which concludes as follows: 'By these observations on a bean stalk, you see my young friends, that there is no need for waiting on the loud roaring thunder and vivid lightning to convince the unbeliever that there is a God. No, the mild and silent as well as the rough and gloomy operations of Nature, speak for the existence of a Deity.'

Evidence drawn from nature is thus employed by Miller to bolster and reinforce more conventional Christian teaching. Firstly, additional grounds are supplied for believing in God's existence. Secondly, recognition in nature of the 'nice adaptation of every minute circumstance to the end it was intended to accomplish' confirms God's wisdom and beneficence, and encourages resignation to Providence.

In building up a more detailed picture of the way natural theology could be deployed in an attempt to neutralise social and political discontent, the works of Thomas Dick are invaluable sources. Dick was the author of a number of substantial volumes dealing with scientific, religious and educational subjects[50] and, although not an original thinker, he treated his topics systematically and comprehensively from the perspective of natural theology. Consequently his writings yield important insights into the structure and workings of a 'world view' which was shared by many other adult educationists.

5. Harmony in nature and society

Dick is now best known for suggesting the establishment of literary and scientific institutes to cater for the working classes — a plan which preceded by several years the appearance of the first mechanics' institutes.[51] He also merits attention as an early author of popular scientific works. His first (and best-known) book, *The Christian Philosopher* (1823), immediately went into a second edition and had run through eight sizeable editions by 1842; like several of his subsequent works it proved extremely popular in the United States and also enjoyed the distinction of being translated into Welsh.[52] A contemporary went so far as to claim that Dick was 'the man who has done more than any man we know to popularise science among the people',[53] and among those who claimed to have been directly influenced by reading his works were the eminent American astronomer E. E. Barnard[54] and the Scots missionary, David Livingstone. During his speech of reply when the freedom of Dundee was conferred upon him, in 1857, Livingstone remarked that reading Dick's *The Philosophy of a Future State* had influenced his decision to become a Christian missionary.[55]

To the writer of his obituary in the *Dundee Advertiser*, Dick's works stood 'unequalled among the publications of his time as antidotes to popular scepticism',[56] and it is to a consideration of the intellectual resources which Dick brought to bear on this task and the closely related one of ensuring social harmony that we now turn.

Astronomy was the branch of science which Dick did most to popularise, and it was this subject which supplied him with his preferred models for the interpretation of social and educational questions. In *The Philosophy of Religion* he affords us a characteristically vivid glimpse of the way astronomical imagery provided him with a standard by which to judge the moral and political health of society:

> Suppose the principle which unites the planetary globes to be dissolved and the planets to run lawlessly through the sky — suppose the planet Jupiter to forsake his orbit, and in his course to the distant regions of space, to impinge against the planet Saturn and to convulse the solid crust of that globe from its surface to its centre, to disarrange the order of its satellites, to shatter its rings into pieces and to carry the fragments of them along with him in his lawless career . . . In such a scene, we should have presented to our view a spectrum of physical confusion and disorder; and it would form an impressive emblem of the state of rational beings, whose moral order is completely subverted.[57]

Ideals of harmony and regularity clearly afforded Dick great emotional satisfaction, at once moral, aesthetic and religious. Conversely, disharmony in any shape or form was a source of profound anxiety and for him represented ugliness and danger. Thus, despite an obviously warm humanitarian concern for the sufferings of the poor, Dick remained strenuously opposed to independent working-class political activity, since this seemed to threaten social chaos. Exquisite celestial order was sharply contrasted with the sordid sublunary ugliness of ordinary human affairs. History (other than sacred history) was therefore viewed largely as a depressing catalogue of 'perfidy, avarice, injustice and revenge; of wars, rapine, devastation and bloodshed . . .'[58]

Dick's sense of social order was finely graded and resembled closely the venerable notion of the 'Great Chain of Being' described by Lovejoy.[59] Man occupied a fixed place on a continuous ladder or scale of existing beings which extended upwards from the very lowliest of creatures to God himself; below man was the teeming diversity of the animal world, above him the more rarified orders of superior intelligences. The whole structure was a single entity and depended for its continued existence on every position being occupied; the appearance of gaps in the chain threatened total collapse. Within the range allotted to man, the various ranks of humankind occupied their respective positions in accordance with the decrees of Providence.

Together with astronomical models, this hierarchical vision of the world was of fundamental importance in moulding the categories of thought with which Dick (as well as other, like-minded representatives of popular enlightenment) operated when analysing social and educational problems. A passage from *The Philosophy of Religion*, describing the supposed turmoil which would ensue were the 'Great Chain of Being' disrupted, suggests that this imagined possibility was very real to Dick and helped supply a cognitive basis for his negative feelings about independent working-class political action. Here, as always in his writings, Dick exudes a naive intensity — there is a total absence of irony or humour of any kind, his heart is plainly visible on his sleeve and he addresses the reader with unrelenting earnestness:

> Suppose the lower animals to rise up in indignation against man, and, to swell the horrors of the general anarchy — suppose the superior orders of intelligencies to mingle in this scene of confusion, to exert their high physical and intellectual powers in adding fuel to those malevolent principles and operations, and in attempting to drag other intelligencies of a still higher order from their seats of bliss — suppose all these intelligencies actuated by an implacable hatred of their Creator, combined to deface the beauties of the material creation . . . such a state of things . . . would form a perfect contrast to moral order . . .[60]

In seeking for a principle of unity and harmony in human society, Dick had further recourse to the planetary system as a metaphorical resource. Material objects are attracted by gravitation; the analogous principle in social life is Love, which is thus the binding force which holds the social hierarchy intact. To be motivated by love, in Dick's sense, is to recognise and act in accordance with the corresponding network of reciprocal obligations. Departure from this pattern of conduct leads to *selfishness* or *malignity*, which in any relationship between individuals is manifested in *pride* or *insubordination*, depending on their respective stations.[61]

Dick's comparison between love and gravitation follows the lead of Scottish Enlightenment thinkers of the eighteenth century, such as Hume and Smith — though they used the term 'sympathy' rather than 'love'. For Adam Smith sympathy, like gravity, decreased with distance and was thus greatest among small groups of men characterised by division of labour but unified by a common purpose.[62] Dick (like Miller and Duncan, as well as Chalmers) thought likewise: confronted by the disruptive consequences of industrialisation and urbanisation he appealed to an idealised image of the old 'sympathetic' society of Lowland Scotland.

There was, of course, nothing new in using the Newtonian cosmos as a source of social imagery; it had contributed, for example, to the Panglossian optimism of the England of Soame Jenyns — the outlook which Basil Willey designated 'Cosmic Toryism'. In the latter case, one was presented with a God who clearly 'loved abundance and variety better than happiness or progress . . .'[63] Dick and the popular enlighteners, however, did believe in progress, and there was an obvious tension in their thought between static and progressive components. There are good grounds for supposing that, by the second and third decades of the nineteenth century, the Newtonian cosmos and the 'Great Chain of Being' were, in any case, becoming less plausible as sources of social imagery. The new industrial order required more appropriate scientific underpinning, models which emphasised continuous but orderly change rather than static harmony. For such a purpose, the biological sciences (especially physiology) offered more convincing metaphors than did astronomy.[64] Also, large-scale migration from the countryside to the manufacturing towns meant that the growing ranks of the urban working class were removed from the kinds of community in which it could plausibly be claimed that the norms regulating social life were divinely ordained and universally valid. 'They were planted instead in a form of community in which the officially endorsed norms so clearly [were] of utility only to certain partial and partisan human interests, that it [was] impossible to clothe them with universal and cosmic significance.'[65] The retention by the popular enlightenment educators of the older imagery is presumably attributable to their inability to perceive the new industrial world except in terms of categories derived from the small-scale, 'sympathetic' society with which they were familiar from early experience.

6. Christian Philosophy and the limitations of 'pure piety'

The uneasy co-existence of conservative and progressive elements in Dick's thought imparted a distinctive style of exposition. There is an undeniably manic-depressive quality about much of his writing, a regular oscillation between rapturous anticipation of limitless future progress and sombre musing on the folly and wickedness of man, as revealed by history. Nature does indeed display the wisdom and beneficence of an omnipotent Deity — but in our own world, at least, there are flaws which seem to mar the grand design. These Dick explains in much the same fashion as Bishop Burnet (with whose work he was familiar) had done more than a century earlier — by regarding them as proof that this particular world is indeed a fallen world.[66] The pendular swings from elation to despair and back again result from an unresolved tension between enlightenment rationalism (with its belief in the perfectibility of man) and fundamentalist piety, with its stress on man's fallen condition.

The cultivation of an urbane rationalism, sympathetic to scientific learning, had characterised the Moderate party in the Church of Scotland during the heyday of the eighteenth-century Enlightenment.[67] Early in the nineteenth century, interest in science together with associated aspects of Enlightenment thought (notably political economy) began to 'catch on' among evangelicals and dissenters — yet in association with a more earnest and emphatically scriptural attitude of mind than was typical of moderate ministers, with their deeply engrained distaste for 'enthusiasm'.[68] In these circumstances natural theology became attractive to progressive evangelicals and dissenters as an appropriate system for reconciling rationalism and piety — though, as was noted in the case of Henry Duncan's early ventures, the resulting blend of science and piety was not always appreciated by local congregations. Dick, though never neglectful of scriptural revelation, was led through his attach-ment to natural theology to argue forcefully and frequently that Christians, hitherto, had unduly neglected the vital evidence of God's existence and characteristics revealed in nature.[69] As a result, he arrived at conclusions which were greeted coldly by those evangelicals who wished to allocate reason a comparatively minor part in Christian thought.

This tension was apparent in the reaction of the *Edinburgh Christian Instructor* (the leading organ of the evangelical party in the Church of Scotland) to the first edition of Dick's *Christian Philosopher*. Dick maintained that the natural sciences, since they illustrate the power, wisdom and goodness of God, deserved to feature more frequently as the subject matter of sermons. In addition, there should be a heavy emphasis on the sciences during the course of training for the ministry. 'That man's religious devotions are much to be suspected,' wrote Dick, 'whatever show of piety he may affect, who, in attempting to form some adequate conception of the object of his worship, derives no assistance from the sublime discoveries of astronomical science.'[70]

This was too much for the *Edinburgh Christian Instructor:* 'To Mr Dick's plan of uniting religion with science, we can by no means give our assent. A lecture on a weekday evening, upon the plan proposed by him might be proper and useful; but the Sabbath ought to be devoted to higher themes and to matters that will come more touchingly home to the conscience than aught that science can afford.'[71] In subsequent editions of *The Christian Philosopher* Dick added a disclaiming footnote, to the effect that he had been misunder-stood and declaring that he had no wish to denigrate traditional piety. Never-theless he continued, in his later works, to champion the same species of *rational piety* argued for in *The Christian Philosopher.*[72]

The tension between rational and 'pure' piety also influenced Dick's views on the education of children. As Hamilton has noted, early nineteenth-century Scotland witnessed a growth of interest in teaching through 'explanation' and learning through 'understanding'. Although not new, the emphasis on under-standing was given added impetus by the absorption of rationalist tendencies into the evangelical consciousness — in particular the belief that virtue might result from the cultivation of reason.[73] Dick, with his rationalist leanings, naturally sympathised with this tendency. His thoughts on education in infancy and later childhood were expounded at some length in *The Mental Illumination and Moral Improvement of Mankind* (1836), where he gave vent to his dissatisfaction with the neglect of understanding and the corresponding over-emphasis on rote memory in contemporary teaching practice: 'The effects of memory . . . especially when exercised in the retention of mere sounds and terms, are, in general, attended with painful sensations; and when these sensations are long continued, they frequently produce a disgust of the objects and employment of education.'[74] Yet the inculcation of pious habits was commonly thought to be fostered by requiring children to learn by rote, at a precocious age, large chunks of the Bible or the Shorter Catechism.

7. The Diffusion of Useful Knowledge: the 'solemn stillness of science' or Watt's 'noble engine'?

The movement for popular enlightenment through natural theology preceded but also ran parallel with the more formal scientific adult education provided by mechanics' institutes. Despite the considerable overlap in personnel and subjects taught, sufficient difference in emphasis may be identified for an exercise in comparison to be worthwhile. Both overlap and difference of emphasis may usefully be highlighted by examining Thomas Dick's reservations concerning the curricula of the institutes.

After settling in Broughty Ferry (Dundee) in 1827 as a full-time writer and popular lecturer, Dick began a lengthy involvement in the affairs of the local mechanics' institute, the Watt Institution. In an address to the members, delivered in December 1829, he was critical of the curricular programme which had prevailed at the institution since its inauguration in 1824. He was 'most anxious . . . that the range of study in mechanics' institutes should be enlarged, so as to embrace, not only the whole of moral and political science, but those fundamental principles of religion, in the belief of which all mankind concur'.[75] He had made substantially the same point in his earlier plea for the establishment of popular scientific institutes[76] and was to return to a more thorough consideration of it in *The Mental Illumination and Moral Improvement of Mankind*.[77] He disapproved, firstly then, of the secular, 'value-free' approach to scientific study which typified the larger institutes and, secondly, of the circumscribed curriculum of mechanics, chemistry and mathematics, justified ostensibly on grounds of practical utility.[78]

The sponsors of mechanics' institutes were as eager as Dick, Miller and the like that adult education should be effective as a 'social sedative'.[79] Some interest attaches to why a curriculum based on 'value-free' science should have been thought likely to prove successful in this respect — perhaps even more so than one focusing on natural theology or political economy. Chemistry or mechanical philosophy had obvious advantages over political economy in being less obviously tinctured with ideology; the subject matter was almost certain to be considered 'objective' by working men, even if somewhat tedious. Since scepticism and downright atheism were far from unknown among radical elements of the working class, natural theology might also appear less authoritative than secular science. On the other hand, natural theology drew largely on subjects such as astronomy and natural history which exerted greater imaginative appeal than, say, elementary hydrostatics. The difference in appeal of 'value-free' and natural theological science to their respective advocates may be illuminated by examining the rhetoric of justification offered in each case.

In 1826, a course of lectures on natural history was delivered at the Stirling School of Arts by Mr Macome of Paisley, and at the conclusion of the final lecture, the vice-president of the School's committee, Rev. Bennie, congratulated the lecturer in the following terms:

> The subjects you have illustrated, though not immediately connected with natural philosophy, have all been extremely interesting . . . There is one respect in particular in which I think you are entitled to unqualified commendation: in traversing those wide regions of science which you had selected as the subject of your observations — in explaining the *sublime* phenomena they exhibit . . . and the *beautiful* harmony which we everywhere discern in the system of the universe, you have never neglected to lead the thoughts of your hearers to the supreme invisible Being by whom the mighty system was created and arranged.[80]

Like Dick, Rev. Bennie saw the purpose of scientific education as leading the student 'through nature to nature's God'. To embark upon studies of this kind was to transcend the squalid business of faction fighting and party disagreement:

> There is a calm *dignity* in these pursuits which should breathe a corresponding *tranquillity* in the heart. It is *truth* alone, *sublime, beautiful truth* which we are anxious to discover; and whilst rival parties on the wide theatre of the world are bitterly contending for opinions and rights . . . we withdraw from the turbulent and noisy scene to *meditate* on the mysteries of *nature* . . . In the august temples of science, the sounds of violence are never heard; there a *solemn and perpetual stillness* reigns.[81] (My emphasis)

Rev. Bennie's address, I think, conveys well the blend of moral, religious, aesthetic and intellectual satisfactions which the natural theological world view afforded its adherents — and which they were eager to transmit to at least the more articulate sections of the working class. The mood was contemplative rather than dynamic, as is apparent from the way words such as *tranquillity, dignity, meditate*, etc. are used, and the attitude to nature, though scientific, has an almost Wordsworthian flavour.[82] The feeling conveyed is not in accord with either the acerbity of political contest or the bustle of industry and commerce. Compare now the following extract from Andrew Ure's panegyric on James Watt, delivered at the Andersonian Institution, Glasgow in 1824:

> How truly did Bacon declare 'Knowledge is Power!' The knowledge of the laws of nature arms our feeble hands with her most gigantic forces! How many populous and flourishing cities and towns have been created by the genius of Watt! What were Birmingham, Manchester, Nottingham, Leeds, Preston, and Glasgow before his engine gave them vitality?[83]

In contrast to the rhetoric of 'solemn stillness', the tone here is dynamic and resonates with the aggressive, expansionist mood of early industrial capitalism. Addresses to mechanics in this vein do not generally exhort students to scrutinise the 'Book of Nature' for evidence of divine wisdom and power: instead they are urged to scan its pages in order to understand 'the movements and principles of that *noble engine which gives life and motion to all their operations*'.[84] (My emphasis.) The prevailing secular tone in no way reflects anti-religious feeling, merely that the intellectual and emotional centre of gravity lies in a different place. The stress is on *man's* ingenuity in applying the laws of nature rather than *God's* ingenuity revealed through the laws of nature.

This approach to adult education, linking scientific progress primarily with future prospects for technological development, operated with its own thoroughly un-Wordsworthian notions of sublimity, expressed here in the arrogantly optimistic prose of Andrew Ure:

> (U)nder its [the steam engine's] auspices and in obedience to Arkwright's polity, magnificent edifices, surpassing far in number, value, usefulness and ingenuity of construction the boasted monuments of Asiatic, Egyptian and Roman despotism, have, within the short period of fifty years, risen in this kingdom to show to what extent *capital, industry* and *science* may augment the resources of a state while they meliorate the conditions of its citizens.[85] (My emphasis)

The rhetoric associated with the secular science of the mechanics' institutes and related publications set before working-class audiences and readers the vision of a future dominated by the triumphant onward march of science, technology, and capitalist industry. Mutually reinforcing advances in these areas formed the core around which other aspects of Progress, whether moral, material or political, would be centred. By constant repetition of this message, links might be forged, in the artisans' minds, between the key ideas of scientific progress, technological development and (capitalist) economic growth, so as to confer the rationality ascribed to science upon this cluster of ideas as a whole. Since technological processes were explicable in terms of scientific principles, it could be claimed (plausibly, but incorrectly at this period) that a grounding in the physical sciences formed a necessary basis for improvements in technology.[86] The scientific rationality with which technological development thus became invested could, by virtue of the further link between technology and industrial expansion, be employed to justify economic growth and the progress of capitalism itself.

Viewed in this light, the mechanics' institute movement may be regarded as an early attempt to disseminate a body of ideas which has more recently been termed the 'ideology of industrialisation'.[87] Central to this is the belief that technological development possesses an internal, objective logic which determines a unique sequence of historical stages. Technology itself is regarded as politically neutral, with the important result that political and moral aspirations must be framed 'around the edges', as it were, of the inevitable advance of scientific-technological-economic progress. Moral or political thinking which disregards this injunction may then be stigmatised as 'unscientific', 'irrational' or (more mildly) 'unrealistic'.

Those who, in mechanics' institutes and elsewhere, preached the gospel of progress through capitalist industrial development had good reasons for doing so. If the Industrial Revolution was to prove successful, in the sense of being irreversible, it was necessary for working-class common sense to be transformed so as to 'echo', in an informal fashion, the more precise thought processes characteristic of the physical sciences. Popular culture was in other words seen to be crucially deficient in relation to the demands of the machine age, while at the individual level the implication was that a new consciousness required to be forged — a mentality more in harmony with the requirements of the emerging industrial world. One aspect of this, highlighted by E. P. Thompson, concerned the need for changes in the inward notation of time.[88] But the psychological reshaping had to be more comprehensive than this. More than seventy years ago, Veblen noticed that 'In the modern culture, industry, industrial production and industrial products have progressively gained upon humanity until these creations of mass ingenuity have latterly come to take the dominant place in the cultural scheme . . . Hence men have learned to think in the terms in which technological processes act.'[89] More recently, the need for such mental remoulding has received considerable attention in connection with industrial developments in Third World countries.[90]

During the period dealt with here, education in 'value-free' science seemed, from the perspective of its sponsors, an appropriate vehicle for inculcating, among at least the higher echelons of the labour force, such a new array of cognitive and emotional responses. The subjects taught (mechanics, chemistry, mathematics) involved initiation into cognitive styles which formed an important aspect of the consciousness associated with technological production.[91] In the affective realm, impressive or curious displays of scientific ingenuity could induce a sense of awe at the power released by new technical developments, thus fostering an almost 'romantic' conception of technology as well as engendering faith in salvation through science.

In terms of the gradual trend towards the establishment of a 'scientised' common sense, echoing in less precise forms the thought patterns of scientific rationality, the secular science of the mechanics' institutes represented a more 'advanced' position than natural theology.[92] The physical sciences taught at the institutes were linked firmly, at the level of rhetoric, at any rate, with the idea of technological progress, whereas for a writer such as Dick this connection was more tenuous. Despite his undoubted enthusiasm for advances in the useful arts, Dick's science was, as we have seen, essentially contemplative, attention being concentrated on nature as the embodiment of God's design, rather than on the man-made world of machinery and industrial processes: 'One *subordinate* use of the knowledge derived from this science [natural philosophy] is to enable us to construct all those mechanical engines which facilitate human labour . . . A still nobler and higher use to which philosophy is subservient, is to demonstrate the wisdom and intelligence of the great First Cause of all things.'[93] (My emphasis.) And when reflecting on the benefits likely to result from the progress of steam navigation, Dick's first thought concerned not the furtherance of commerce but the ease with which it would be possible to distribute bibles to all the inhabitants of the world.[94]

We may further note that both 'value-free' and natural theological science functioned as vehicles for the cultural assertiveness of middle-class sub-groups. Promoters of mechanics' institutes were frequently men with commercial or industrial backgrounds, who might reasonably be expected to favour the 'value-free' approach to science, while a substantial proportion of the lecturers offering scientific courses grounded in natural theology were ministers of evangelical or dissenting persuasion.[95] The 'new men' instrumental in the development of industry in Scotland were themselves frequently dissenters or evangelicals[96] and we might therefore expect the more forward-looking ministers to have aligned themselves with the cultural proclivities of their religious constituents. But, in addition, clergymen as a group had their own vested interest in maintaining the influence of religious knowledge, and the two interests could most readily be harmonised through the medium of natural theology.[97]

8. Useful Knowledge: eradicating 'hallucinations of the human intellect'

Despite the differences between adult education emphasising natural theological and value-free science, the many similarities must not be under-rated. At the most general level both strategies aimed to channel, in safe and 'rational' directions, the intellectual energies of the working class (or at least its more articulate sections). Both approaches to science also operated with closely similar conceptions of the nature of knowledge.

Knowledge was seen to consist of aggregations of discrete facts derived directly from empirical investigation. This view of knowledge was reiterated with incantatory monotony in the works of writers such as Thomas Dick,[98] in numerous articles appearing in the various mechanics' magazines[99] and in countless lectures and speeches delivered at mechanics' institutes.[100] The cult of the fact went hand-in-hand with antipathy to forms of knowledge which appeared to emphasise *words* rather than *things*. Metaphysical philosophy was thus an obvious target: 'We have an abundance of ponderous volumes on the subject of moral philosophy; but the different theories which have been proposed and discussed and the metaphysical mode in which the subject has been generally treated have seldom led to any practical results.'[101] Interestingly, Dick's empiricist outlook carried over into the religious sphere; he treated speculative theology with the same contempt as he heaped on metaphysical philosophy, and the term 'biblical empiricism' may not inappropriately be coined to describe his theological stance, since he was 'disposed to view the Revelations of the Bible rather as a series of important *facts* [my emphasis] from which moral instructions are to be deduced, than as a system of metaphysical opinions . . .'[102]

Popular enlighteners and patrons of mechanics' institutes alike saw little educational value in imaginative literature (with the sole exception of moral and religious tales, if these could properly be termed 'literature'), especially so far as the working classes were concerned.[103] In Dick's case this was expressed, at its most basic, in opposition to nursery rhymes or fairy stories for children: 'When the young mind is just beginning to expand, instead of being irradiated with the beams of unadulterated truth, a group of disturbed and unsubstantial images, which have no prototypes in nature, is presented to the view of the intellect.'[104] And in a similar bout of splenetic literal-mindedness he dismissed the novels of Sir Walter Scott on account of their tendency to 'distort and caricature the facts of real history' and 'to excite admiration of the exploits and malignant principles of those rude chieftains whose names ought to descend into everlasting oblivion'.[105]

For adult educationists in the van of 'The March of Mind' scientific standards were the very incarnation of rationality; and scientific knowledge itself seemed almost palpable, progress being measured by the accumulation of ever larger piles of factual information. From such a standpoint, literary studies appeared jejune. Since they did not lead to the steady, cumulative growth of empirically verifiable knowledge, they were deemed to be unprogressive and sub-rational.[106] That they might lead readers to develop qualitatively new insights into human problems eluded the understanding of the fact worshippers.

There was, in any case, a widespread feeling that the plebeian mind was by nature volatile and irrational — a condition for which scientific education, of one kind or another, was thought to be appropriate medicine. Thomas Chalmers, whose own preference was for the 'science' of political economy, claimed that lectures on this subject would 'go far to dissipate all those conditions of imagination which excite the fiercest passions of the vulgar and are in fact the chief element of every popular efflorescence'.[107] Exposure to *fiction*, on the other hand, was likely to overheat the imagination and result in uncontrolled responses.

If literature was not fit educational fare for the workers, the enlighteners were equally adamant that the existing culture of the people was thoroughly anachronistic in an age of rapid scientific and commercial progress. A scientific education, wrote Dick, would eradicate those 'hallucinations of the human intellect' which prevailed among the lower classes.[108] The scientific institutes for which he argued during the second decade of the nineteenth century offered a constructive alternative to 'those hours spent in listlessness, foolish amusements and the pursuit of dissipation; and the habits of order, punctuality and politeness which would prevail in such associations would naturally be carried into all the other departments of life and produce the corresponding effects'.[109] In essence, the educational programme recommended by Dick represented a full-scale assault on popular culture. He was not merely concerned with knowledge in the narrow sense of subject matter, but took a particular interest in what would now be termed the 'hidden curricular' aspects of his proposals. The manners and morals of the lower classes were, for Dick, an affront to Christian decency, and scientific education seemed to afford a means for effecting their much needed reformation. Scientific study demanded systematic patterns of thought and behaviour, favourably compared by the reformers with what appeared a prevailing disorderly impulsiveness. To function effectively, scientific institutes would require those attending to exercise a degree of emotional restraint, and exhibit a formality of conduct not typically associated with rival places of resort, such as the public house. And once embarked upon a course of scientific study, the working man would be in large measure removed from the circumambient temptations and immorality of the lower-class neighbourhood. Thus, to an adult educator such as Dick, intellectual development, moral reform and progress in civility were inextricably interwoven: mentality, morals and manners were to be simultaneously transformed by the same educational process. Further, it was hoped that the beneficial effects on individuals of a more rational (and hence more civilised and moral) lifestyle would become apparent to increasing numbers of working men — thus leading to a gradual metamorphosis of popular culture as a whole.

9. Culture, mind and reason

In his discussion of English working-class schooling during the period 1790-1840, Richard Johnson remarks that 'for the bourgeois observer, the problem with working people was their *obstinately ungovernable behaviour*. They refused, before his very eyes, to conform to what liberal theory and a promise of progress prescribed. They transgressed the values by which he himself sought to live his life.'[110] The natural theology of the popular enlightenment and the 'value-free' science of the mechanics' institutes (not to mention lecture courses on political economy and other 'improving' subjects) represented differences of emphasis within a more general educational crusade against the traditional culture of the people. The study of folklore might be of absorbing significance to genteel antiquarians but, to a man like Thomas Dick, the sooner such nonsense was dead, buried and replaced by a rational, scientific outlook the better. Popular culture with all its deadweight of ignorance, immorality and sheer bovine stupidity posed a major obstacle to the creation of a truly rational society.[111] It was also of course a 'reservoir' of attitudes, assumptions and beliefs which potentially could be mobilised to threaten and challenge the cultural hegemony of the dominant classes. As Johnson indicates, 'One way of viewing the social history of the whole period from the 1790s to the mid-1840s is as an extended war over winning of consent, a prolonged crisis in hegemony . . .'[112]

The campaign to extirpate popular culture had, as we have seen in the previous section, its psychological dimension: a new, rational culture would require the fashioning of new rational human beings. As it was, the educational reformers operated with a partially explicit 'psychology' of the lower orders, a set of assumptions about the way the lower-class mind functioned in its unredeemed condition. There has already been occasion to mention the presumed volatility or excitability of the masses. It was also widely believed that working people were, by and large, 'concrete thinkers' whose minds were ill-equipped to deal with abstract issues. Rev. Andrew Thomson (editor of *The Edinburgh Christian Instructor*) averred that 'the lower orders were necessarily so much occupied by matters of sense that when they seek for recreation they do it in a sensual way'.[113] To Dr Thomson (who was a director of the Edinburgh School of Arts) it was the business of mechanics' institutes to provide the workers with alternative pursuits 'above the grossness of sensuality' which would train their minds in 'sobriety and correct deportment'.[114] In Thomson's view, the shift from 'sensual' to 'rational' thought was indissolubly linked with a parallel shift in manners from boorishness to refinement.

Earlier, George Miller's zealous propaganda on behalf of orderly domesticity was discussed in the context of the wider dissemination of bourgeois values. The virtues of family life were contrasted favourably (by Miller) with the evils of unregulated gregariousness. Thomas Dick felt similarly: 'There is nothing more grating to the man of intelligence,' he wrote, 'than the foolish and trifling conversation which prevails in the various intercourses of social life . . . and in convivial association, the ribaldry and obscenity, the folly and nonsense and the laughter of fools . . . are a disgrace to our *civilised* conditions and to our *moral* and *intellectual* nature.'[115] (My emphasis.) Once again, intellectual development is seen to be inseparable from parallel improvements in manners and morals. Conversely, eradication of the immorality and incivility associated principally with popular culture[116] could also be expected to bring about an improvement in intelligence. Dick was quite clear about the personality characteristics which accompanied a developed intellect: 'For the individual whose happiness chiefly depends on intellectual pleasures, retirement from the bustle of the world is often the state of his highest enjoyment.'[117] The most appropriate setting for the satisfaction of social impulses was the home, not the tavern or street corner: the man of refinement and intellect was very much a *private* person. And Dick, echoing Miller, went on to bequeath us the following vision of marital bliss: 'How delightful an enjoyment it is, after the bustle of business and the labours of the day are over, when a married couple can sit down at each corner of the fire, and with mutual relish and interest read a volume of history or popular philosophy and talk of the moral government of God, the arrangements of Providence and the wonders of the universe.'[118]

Later sections of this essay have been principally concerned with identifying the more important psychological implications of the campaign for 'diffusion of useful knowledge'. Three major psychological dimensions have been identified, which parallel the intended replacement of traditional popular culture by bourgeois norms and values:[119]

(1) volatility, lack of purpose ————————→ stability, purposefulness
(2) gregarious sociability ————————→ restricted sociability, 'private' personality
(3) sensuality, concrete thought ——————→ abstract thought, scientific rationality
     (roughly: stupidity ————————→ intelligence)

At this point a host of fascinating questions concerning the relationship between individual psychology and the nature of society clamour for attention. In his classic work *The Civilising Process*, Norbert Elias claimed to detect a clear, long-term relationship, in post-Renaissance Europe, between increasing civility in social relations and the growth of tighter affect controls at the individual level. He maintained that 'feelings and affects are first transformed in the upper class and the structure of society permits the changed affect standard to spread slowly through society'.[120] It is impossible here to produce even a bare summary of the arguments and evidence adduced by Elias. It must suffice to remark that, to the present writer, the efforts of educators such as Dick, Miller and Duncan appear to have been directed towards effecting a similar kind of cultural-cum-psychological transformation. If this suggested link is at all valid, the contents of the present essay may perhaps be regarded as a 'detail' from a much larger picture, as yet far from complete, whose broad design has been sketched out by Elias.

Conclusions

The movement for popular enlightenment through natural theology was one aspect of a wider campaign in which the 'universal diffusion of knowledge' was to 'prove the surest and most powerful instrument for the protection of society'. This campaign involved an aggressive onslaught on a popular culture which was regarded as anachronistic in the age of the 'March of Mind'. In the long term, traditional popular culture was destined to be gradually replaced by a common sense which echoes, in many respects, key features of scientific rationality. Natural theology represented a significant move in this direction, but because of its overriding religious concerns it still accorded science only limited autonomy. The 'value-free' science of the mechanics' institutes embodied a more thoroughgoing naturalisation of science (and common sense) and also emphasised those interconnections between science, technology and economic growth which are central to the ideology of industrialism. Any drive towards the transformation of culture has its psychological corollaries: scientific adult education would, it was hoped, bring about significant changes in human nature. Changes in mentality would also go hand-in-hand with moral regeneration and the reformation of manners. Details of the changes to be wrought varied according to the particular educational strategy adopted, for example, whether it derived its intellectual inspiration from natural theology or value-free science — but there was, nevertheless, much common ground.

NOTES

1. Rev. Henry Duncan, *The Young South Country Weaver* (Edinburgh, second edition, 1821), p. 58.

2. Anon, *Commemoration of the Centenary of the Death of Rev. Henry Duncan DD* (Dumfries, 1946), p. 15.

3. Rev. Henry Duncan was born at Lochrutton, Dumfriesshire, in 1774, the third son of the parish minister there. He studied at both Glasgow and Edinburgh universities and during his final two sessions at Edinburgh was a member of the Speculative Society. At this time he became friendly with Henry Brougham with whom he corresponded for the rest of his life. After becoming minister of Ruthwell in 1799 he became involved in a number of philanthropic causes (including the anti-slavery movement) and contributed articles on geological and antiquarian subjects to learned journals, William Anderson, *The Scottish Nation* (Edinburgh, 1870), Vol. 2, pp. 90-92. After attending a Quaker meeting, he underwent a profound experience of 'conversion' and became a staunch adherent of the evangelical party within the Established Church, Sophy Hall, *Dr Duncan of Ruthwell: Founder of Savings Banks* (Edinburgh, 1910), p. 42. Despite a plea to him to remain in the Established Church, in 1843 he joined the Free Church, Rev. Thomas Brown, *Annals of the Disruption* (Edinburgh, 1893), p. 384.

4. Sophy Hall, *op. cit.*, p. 40.

5. *Ibid.*, p. 51.

6. Rev. Henry Duncan, *The Sacred Philosophy of the Seasons* (Edinburgh, 1837), p. 341.

7. See L. J. Saunders, *Scottish Democracy: 1815-1840* (Edinburgh, 1950), pp. 248-258.

8. See Saunders, *op. cit.*, pp. 252-253, for Miller; pp. 254-256, for Brown; pp. 256-258, for Dick. Miller, Dick and Brown (like Duncan) all supported the anti-slavery movement and were involved in other philanthropic and religious causes. For the relationship between the efforts of (and alleged conflict beween) Miller and Brown in East Lothian, see L. G. Durbridge, 'Samuel Brown and George Miller: A Mystery', *Library Review*, 23, 1971/72, pp. 131-134. D. Gavine, 'Thomas Dick, LLD, 1774-1857', *Journal of the British Astronomical Association*, 84, 5, 1974, pp. 345-350, gives a useful assessment of Dick's contribution to astronomy.

9. For distinctive features of the Enlightenment in Scotland, see A. Chitnis, *The Scottish Enlightenment: a Social History* (London, 1976), *passim*.

10. George Miller, *Popular Philosophy or the Book of Nature Laid Open upon Christian Principles and Agreeably to the Light of Modern Science and the Progress of New Discovery* (Edinburgh, 1826). p. (i).

11. For example: Thomas Dick, *The Christian Philosopher* (tenth edition, Glasgow, 1846), Vol. 1, pp. 124-126 and *The Philosophy of a Future State* (new edition, Glasgow, 1862), pp. 134-137. (*The Christian Philosopher* originally appeared in 1823 and *The Philosophy of a Future State* in 1828.)

12. L. J. Saunders, *op. cit.*, p. 251.

13. *Ibid.* For growth of libraries in Scotland, see W. P. Aitken, *A History of the Public Library Movement in Scotland to 1955* (Glasgow, 1971), pp. 1-52 and P. Kaufman, *Libraries and their Users: Collected Papers in Library History* (London, 1969), pp. 134-169.

14. Thomas Dick, letter to the editor of the *Monthly Magazine*, 37 (1814), p. 219.

15. *The Monthly Monitor and Philanthropic Museum*, 1 (Haddington, 1815), p. (i).

16. L. J. Saunders, *op. cit.*, p. 251.

17. J. W. Hudson, *History of Adult Education* (London, 1851; 1969 re-print), p. (v).

18. For example, 'They [i.e. historians of abolitionism] would do well to consider the way in which the whole complex of philanthropic societies, including anti-slavery organisations, was part of the mechanism to preserve the standing of the leadership of each British community . . .', C. Duncan Rice, 'Abolitionists and Abolitionism in Aberdeen: a test case for the nineteenth-century anti-slavery movement', *Northern Scotland*, 1, 1, December 1972, p. 81. See also discussion of Andrew Combe in Roger Cooter, 'The power of the body — the early nineteenth century', in *Natural Order: Historical Studies of Scientific Culture*, ed. B. Barnes and S. Shapin (London, 1979), pp. 77-78.

J. V. Smith

19. Thomas Dick, *The Philosophy of Religion* (Glasgow, 1870; Collins Select Library), p. 99.

20. For details of Mrs More's tracts, see Victor E. Neuburg, *Popular Literature: A History and Guide* (London, 1977), pp. 253-259.

21. Asa Briggs, *The Age of Improvement* (London, 1979), p. 71.

22. Quoted in B. Simon, *Studies in the History of Education: 1780-1870* (London, 1960), p. 133. Compare this with quotation from Henry Duncan's *The Young South Country Weaver;* see note 41 below.

23. John F. McCaffrey, 'Thomas Chalmers and social change', *Scottish Historical Review*, 60, 1, April 1981, p. 32 and pp. 38-40. See also, B. Lenman, *An Economic History of Modern Scotland* (London, 1977), pp. 102-103.

24. T. C. Smout, *A History of the Scottish People* (London, 1969), p. 241.

25. Rev. Henry Duncan, *The Young South Country Weaver* (Edinburgh, second edition, 1821), p. 60.

26. B. Lenman, *op. cit.*, p. 156.

27. See, for example, S. G. E. Lythe, 'James Carmichael: millwright, 1776-1853', in *Three Dundonians*, Abertay Historical Society Publication No. 13 (Dundee, 1968), pp. 1-7.

28. B. Lenman, *op. cit.*, p. 119.

29. Carol S. Bebb, The Chartist Movement in Dundee, unpub. B.Phil. thesis, University of St Andrews, 1977, pp. 75-113.

30. J. McCaffrey, *op. cit.*, p. 39.

31. *Ibid.* For the special case of Dundee, see Bebb, *op. cit.*, pp. 52-70.

32. W. Ferguson, *The Edinburgh History of Scotland, Vol. IV, Scotland: 1689 to the Present* (Edinburgh, 1968), pp. 250-260. Those most influenced by Paine and revolutionary ideas during the 1790s were drawn largely from 'the ranks of the urban artisans and lower middle class and some of its best leadership from eccentric elements in the upper middle class', Smout, *op. cit.*, p. 220 and also pp. 442-443. By the second decade of the nineteenth century, however, such doctrines were typical of many working class radicals. In 1834 *The Scottish Guardian* wrote: 'Neglected in their youth, great multitudes of the operatives of Dundee are growing up hostile to those institutions by which they never benefited . . . The ambition to be politicians has come upon them in their days of ignorance . . ', quoted in Bebb, *op. cit.*, p. 35. For radical nationalist sentiment, see James D. Young, *The Rousing of the Scottish Working Class* (London, 1979), pp. 52-53.

33. See, for example, A. Tyrrell, 'Political economy, Whiggism and the education of working class adults in Scotland, 1817-1840', *Scottish Historial Review*, 48, 1969, pp. 151-165.

34. B. Lenman, *op. cit.*, pp. 165-166.

35. Robert Mandrou, *From Humanism to Science: 1480-1700* (London, 1978), p. 11.

36. A. Tyrrell, *op. cit.*, pp. 151-152.

37. *Ibid.*, p. 154.

38. Thomas Chalmers, *Christian and Civic Economy of Large Towns* (Edinburgh, 1821), Vol. 3, p. 394.

39. J. McCaffrey, *op. cit.*, p. 36.

40. Stewart Mechie, *The Church and Scottish Social Development, 1780-1870* (London, 1960), p. 55.

41. Rev. Henry Duncan, *The Young South Country Weaver*, p. 60.

42. Thomas Chalmers, *Christian and Civic Economy of Large Towns*, Vol. 2, chapter 20.

43. A. Tyrrell, *op. cit.*, pp. 164-165.

44. *Cheap Magazine* (Haddington, 1814), Vol. 1, p. vi.

45. The celebration of the domestic sphere, with the fire at its centre, combined with rejection of gregarious conviviality, is typical of many verse and prose items; for example in the *Cheap Magazine*, Vol. 1, pp. 94-95 occurs 'The Happy Fireside':

> Dear Jessie, while the busy crowd,
> The vain the wealthy and the proud,
> In Folly's maze advance;
> Though singularity and pride
> Be called our choice, we'll step aside,
> Nor join the giddy dance.   etc.

The same emphasis is found in the writings of Rev. Henry Duncan. See, for example, his *The Cottage Fireside or the Parish Schoolmaster* (Edinburgh, third edition, 1816).

46. *The Young South Country Weaver*, pp. 49-52.

47. The long-term evolution of the modern family, its relation to the concept of privacy and its gradual 'crystallisation' from an older pattern of public sociability, around the organising concept of 'childhood' formed the central theme of Phillippe Ariès' seminal study, *Centuries of Childhood* (London, 1973), especially pp. 392-399. In a recent extension of the Ariès thesis, R. L. Schnell analysed the part which the concepts of 'childhood' and 'family' came to play as key aspects of middle-class sensibility during the nineteenth century. The earnest desire among middle-class reformers that all strata of society should enjoy a childhood characterised by dependence, protection, segregation and delayed responsibility was one aspect of a more general urge to disseminate bourgeois standards of refinement and civility, R. L. Schnell, 'Childhood as ideology: a reinterpretation of the common school', *British Journal of Educational Studies*, 27, 1, February 1979.

48. *Cheap Magazine*, 1, 1 (1814), pp. 6-31.

49. For details of Tron Riot, see K. J. Logue, *Popular Disturbances in Scotland 1780-1815* (Edinburgh, 1979), pp. 187-190.

50. His major works were: *The Christian Philosopher* (1823); *The Philosophy of a Future State* (1828); *The Philosophy of Religion* (1829); *The Improvement of Society by the Diffusion of Knowledge* (1833); *The Mental Illumination and Moral Improvement of Mankind* (1836); *Celestial Scenery* (1837); *The Sidereal Heavens* (1840); *The Practical Astronomer* (1845); *The Solar System* (1847).

51. *Monthly Magazine:* 37, April 1814, pp. 219-221; 38, August 1814, pp. 23-24; 38, September 1814, p. 121; 39, January 1815, pp. 503-505.

52. A letter exists (dated 27.4.1840) from Robert Griffiths of Caernarvon to Dick concerning arrangements for a Welsh translation of *The Christian Philosopher*.

53. Peter Livingstone, *Lectures on the Genius and Works of Burns and Rev. George Gilfillan* (Dundee, 1852), p. 34.

54. D. Gavine, *op. cit.*, p. 347. For further material on Dick, see 'Portrait Gallery: Thomas Dick LLD', in *Hoggs Instructor* 27.4.1850; W. Norrie, *Dundee Celebrities* (Dundee, 1873), pp. 167-172; *Dictionary of National Biography*, Vol. 5, p. 923; William Anderson, *The Scottish Nation* (Edinburgh, 1869), pp. 705-707; Rev. Robert Small, *History of the Congregations of the United Presbyterian Church, 1733-1900* (Edinburgh, 1904), p. 671. In a letter from Rev. Henry Davies of Penzance to Dick (dated 5.9.1833), Davies wrote: 'Your various publications have been widely read in this part of the kingdom and *The Christian Philosopher* more especially much esteemed.' Dundee City Archives MS GD/X/33/1/10.

55. *Dundee, Perth and Cupar Advertiser*, 25.9.1857.

56. *Ibid.*, 31.7.1857.

57. *The Philosophy of Religion*, p. 21.

58. *The Philosophy of a Future State*, p. 78.

59. See A. O. Lovejoy, *The Great Chain of Being: A Study of the History of an Idea* (Cambridge, Massachusetts, 1936), *passim*.

60. *The Philosophy of Religion*, p. 22.

61. *Ibid.*, p. 100.

62. Christopher Lawrence, 'The nervous system and society in the Scottish Enlightenment', in *Natural Order: Historical Studies of Scientific Culture*, ed. B. Barnes and S. Shapin (London, 1979), p. 32.

63. Basil Willey, *The Eighteenth Century Background* (London, 1962), p. 52.

64. Roger Cooter, 'The power of the body: the early nineteenth century', in B. Barnes and S. Shapin, *op. cit.*, pp. 77-78.

65. Alasdair MacIntyre, *Secularization and Moral Change* (London, 1967), p. 15.

66. *The Christian Philosopher*, Vol. 1, p. 200 and Vol. 2, p. 262. For Burnet, see B. Willey, *op. cit.*, pp. 32-39.

67. A. Chitnis, *op. cit.*, pp. 43-74.

68. A. L. Drummond and J. Bulloch, *The Scottish Church, 1688-1843* (Edinburgh, 1973), pp. 154-155.

69. *The Christian Philosopher*, Vol. 1, pp. 124-126; *The Philosophy of a Future State*, pp. 134-137. It is important to distinguish the evangelical natural religion of Chalmers or Dick from vaguer, less intense invocations of natural theology which were commonplace in the early nineteenth century. Henry Brougham's *Dissertations on Subjects of Science Connected with Natural Theology* (1839), for example, is free from the pious exclamations and earnest evangelising which pervades Dick's works.

70. *The Christian Philsopher*, Vol. 1, p. 22.

71. *Edinburgh Christian Instructor*, 23 (1824), pp. 339-340.

72. For example: *The Improvement of Society by the Diffusion of Knowledge* (Philadelphia, 1841), pp. 295-330; *The Mental Illumination and Moral Improvement of Mankind* (Philadelphia, 1841), pp. 380-390.

73. D. Hamilton, 'The Changing Disciplines of Schooling', Working Paper (Dept. of Education, University of Glasgow, 1978), p. 19.

74. *The Mental Illumination and Moral Improvement of Mankind*, p. 50.

75. *Dundee, Perth and Cupar Advertiser*, 17.12.1829.

76. In one of his communications to the *Monthly Magazine*, he drew a parallel between the work of bible societies and scientific institutes; indeed it seems likely that it was the work of the bible societies which suggested to him the idea of a network of scientific institutes throughout the country. What Dick wished to see was a dual evangelism of science and religion, *Monthly Magazine*, 39, 6, 1815, p. 505.

77. *The Mental Illumination and Moral Improvement of Mankind*, Ch. XV: Mechanics' Institutions, pp. 367-379. See also Section XI, 'On the importance of connecting science with religion', in *The Improvement of Society by the Diffusion of Knowledge* (Philadelphia, 1841), pp. 295-330. Dick's reservations about the secular science of the mechanics' institutes were closely similar to those urged by the evangelicals against phrenologically inspired developments in schooling which, it was alleged, would 'take God out of education'. See Richard Ely, 'The origins of the debate over "secular" instruction', *History of Education*, 9, 2, June 1980, pp. 143-157.

78. In Scotland, the Edinburgh School of Arts in particular was noted for its very narrow curriculum: initially even astronomy was judged to be an unsuitable subject, J. Woodall, The Edinburgh School of Arts: 1821-1851, unpublished Diploma in Adult Education thesis, University of Edinburgh, 1964, p. 12. 'To convey any solid instruction in those branches such as the workman may turn to practical account, requires all the time he has to bestow. It would be very easy to introduce many parts of science which would attract by striking phenomena . . . and would draw together a very crowded audience; but this could not be done without sacrificing objects of far higher value.' From the third annual report of the directors of the Edinburgh School of Arts, reported in *Glasgow Mechanics' Magazine*, 2, 1825, pp. 8-10. At the Dundee Watt Institution, between 1825 and 1829, lectures were restricted to the areas of mathematics, natural philosophy and chemistry, J. V. Smith, *The Watt Institution, Dundee: 1824-29*, Abertay Historical Society publication No. 19 (Dundee, 1978), Chapters 1 and 2. At Glasgow Mechanics' Institution, this pattern was, for the most part, repeated, though there were some lectures on anatomy and natural history from the outset, see R. J. Heydon, The Origins and Development of Glasgow Mechanics' Institution, unpublished MEd thesis, University of Glasgow, 1968, pp. 38-39. It is necessary to emphasise that we are concerned here with curricula at mechanics' institutes only during their first phase (roughly the 1820s).

79. For example: 'It would be expected that the Watt Institution would be the means of promoting virtuous and industrious habits among the working classes by furnishing them with an agreeable and rational mode of employing their spare time . . .' Mr James Brown (flaxspinner), in handbill aimed at soliciting subscriptions for the establishment of Dundee Watt Institution, quoted in J. V. Smith, *op. cit.*, p. 6.

80. *Glasgow Mechanics' Magazine*, 4, 1826, pp. 9-12.

81. *Ibid.*

82. The twin influences of evangelicalism and the 'Romantic' conception of nature on the development of nineteenth-century natural history are discussed in David Elliston Allen, *The Naturalist in Britain* (London, 1978), Ch. 4.

83. *Glasgow Mechanics' Magazine*, 2, 1825, p. 383.

84. Mr Burns in a lecture at Glasgow Gas Workmen's Institution, reported in *Glasgow Mechanics' Magazine*, 4, 1826, p. 171.

85. Andrew Ure, *The Philosophy of Manufactures or an Exposition of the Scientific, Moral and Commercial Economy of the Factory System of Great Britain* (third edition, London, 1861), p. 18. Ure did in fact write one work attempting to reconcile science and religion. This was his *System of Geology* (1829) which was a disastrous failure and appears, in any case, to have been written from opportunistic motives. For an account of Ure's 'combative and rancorous disposition' and its effects on his career, see W. V. Farrar, 'Andrew Ure FRS and the Philosophy of Manufactures', *Notes and Records of the Royal Society of London*, 27, 2, 1973, pp. 299-324.

86. Dr Alastair Durie of the Department of Economic History, University of Aberdeen, in a paper delivered to the Scottish History of Education Society at Dundee University on 16 May 1981, stressed the tenuous nature of the link between technological development and scientific education during the early phase of the Industrial Revolution in Scotland. The one exception appears to have been the chemical industry, B. Lenman, *Integration, Enlightenment and Industrialization* (London, 1981), p. 126.

87. See David Dickson, *Alternative Technology and the Politics of Technical Change* (London, 1974), Ch. 2. The ideology of industrialisation was initially associated with the progress of capitalism. But as Dickson points out, it was subsequently adopted by nominally socialist countries. Lenin, for example, 'decided that the forthcoming "cultural revolution" would require full-scale industrialisation and expansion of machine technology on the capitalist model', p. 54.

88. E. P. Thompson, 'Time, Work-Discipline and Industrial Capitalism', *Past and Present*, 38, 1967, p. 57. In this classic paper, Thompson discusses the development, among labour élites, of a more 'rational' sense of time, *i.e.* one more in tune with the imperatives of capitalist production.

89. T. Veblen, 'The place of science in modern civilization', *American Journal of Sociology*, 2 (1906), reprinted in *Sociology of Science*, ed. B. Barnes (London, 1972), pp. 321-30.

90. Peter L. Berger, Brigitte Berger and Hansfried Kellner, *The Homeless Mind: Modernization and Consciousness* (London, 1974), *passim*.

91. For an extended discussion of technology and consciousness, see *ibid.*, Ch. 1.

92. 'Another possible answer [to the question why value-free science should be thought appropriate as a tool for social control] has the virtue of setting the mechanics' institutes and their curricula in the more general context of educational innovation. They belong toward the end of a chain of cultural innovations leading from Paley on the one hand and Adam Smith on the other, through various strands of natural theology and political economy, always to increasingly naturalistic cosmologies.' S. Shapin and B. Barnes, 'Science, nature and control: understanding mechanics' institutes', *Social Studies of Science*, 7, 1 (1977), p. 55.

93. *The Christian Philosopher*, Vol. 2, p. 9.

94. *Ibid.*, p. 206.

95. Dick himself underwent training for the ministry and was licensed to preach in the Secession Church in 1801. On many occasions, after taking up residence at Broughty Ferry, he was asked to officiate at services of local dissenting congregations. In a letter (dated 30.6.1828) to Dick from Mr George Young (Lochee), the latter referred to Dick as 'Preacher of the Gospell' and claimed to be 'both satisfied and edified by your ministrations'. Dundee City Archives, MS GD/X33/1/6.

Astronomical lectures with a natural theological basis seem to have been especially popular. To take just one example, in 1828, Rev. T. Gray of Pathhead United Presbyterian Church, Kirkcaldy, gave numerous popular lectures on astronomy in Edinburgh. These lectures were 'illustrated by suitable apparatus, experiments etc. and particular attention [was] paid to the evidences afforded in the celestial phenomena of the Divine Power, wisdom and benevolence', *Edinburgh Evening Courant*, 28.1.1828.

96. Drummond and Bulloch, *op. cit.*, pp. 131-132.

97. One of the most influential discussions of science as a 'lever' for cultural and social

assertiveness is A. Thackray, 'Natural Knowledge in Cultural Context', *American Historical Review*, 79, 1974, pp. 672-709.

98. According to Dick: 'All science may be considered as founded on *facts* and perhaps there would be few exceptions to the truth of the position, were we to assert that the most sublime deductions of truths, in every science, when stripped of all their adventitious circumstances, simplified and expressed in the plainest and most perspicuous terms, may be reduced to so many facts.' *The Improvement of Society by the Diffusion of Knowledge*, p. 56. See also *Monthly Magazine*, 37, 1814, p. 220; *The Christian Philosopher*, Vol. 1, p. iv. Dick also suggested that instead of 'foolish inscriptions and devices', scientific facts should be inscribed on dishes, drinking vessels etc., *The Mental Illumination and Moral Improvement of Mankind*, p. 408.

99. See, for example, *Glasgow Mechanics' Magazine*, Vol. 1 (1824), p. 26.

100. For example, J. V. Smith, *op. cit.*, p. 16.

101. *The Philosophy of Religion*, p. 16.

102. *Ibid.*, p. iv.

103. See discussion in R. D. Altick, *The English Common Reader* (Chicago, 1957), pp. 194-198; also J. V. Smith, *op. cit.*, pp. 15-16.

104. *The Philosophy of Religion*, pp. 327-328. Dick also objected to illustrations in children's picture books, where 'The sun and moon are represented with human faces' or 'peacocks, cranes . . . and mice are represented in the attitude of speaking with each other . . .', *The Mental Illumination and Moral Improvement of Mankind*, pp. 92-93.

105. *Ibid.*, p. 329. Dick did, however, respect Scott's powers of narration and wished they could be enlisted in a more specifically Christian cause, *ibid.*, p. 383.

106. As Arnold Thackray has demonstrated, science provided the 'new men' of the early industrial era with the means to assert themselves culturally and to define a new standard of rationality against which the literary and classical learning of older-established groups could be judged and found wanting, see Thackray, *op. cit.* Of classical schooling, Dick commented, 'the absurd opinions of Greek and Roman poets' run counter to the needs of 'a *rational* and Christian education', *The Mental Illumination and Moral Improvement of Mankind*, p. 152. Classical and literary education was thus *sub-rational*.

107. Thomas Chalmers, *Christian and Civic Economy of Large Towns* (Edinburgh, 1821), Vol. 3, p. 406.

108. *The Improvement of Society by the Diffusion of Knowledge*, p. 29.

109. *Monthly Magazine*, 37, 1814, p. 221.

110. Richard Johnson, 'Notes on the schooling of the English working class, 1780-1850', in *Schooling and Capitalism; a Sociological Reader*, eds. R. Dale, G. Esland and H. Macdonald (London, 1976), p. 49.

111. Dick subscribed wholeheartedly to the Enlightenment belief in a unitary standard of rationality: once explain its nature to the ignorant and they would inevitably accept its essential rightness. 'Reason' was thus seen to be 'above culture'. Consequently, all cultural patterns which deviated from 'self-evident' Enlightenment criteria were to be erased. In similar fashion, the Edinburgh reviewers believed that the Gaelic language had to be eliminated before the Highlanders could be 'improved', see *Edinburgh Review*, No. VII, 1804, p. 66.

112. R. Johnson, *op. cit.*, p. 50.

113. Address to the annual meeting of subscribers to the Edinburgh School of Arts, reported in *The Scotsman*, 8.6.1825.

114. *Ibid.*

115. *The Improvement of Society by the Diffusion of Knowledge*, p. 104.

116. Dick (in the manner of Arnold Thackray's men of the Manchester 'Lit. and Phil.') was also concerned to attack the manners, morals and culture of the landed classes.

117. *The Improvement of Society by the Diffusion of Knowledge*, p. 104.

118. *Ibid.*, p. 105.

119. Two of these dimensions are strikingly similar to those employed by the modern personality theorist H. J. Eysenck: (1) corresponds closely to Eysenck's neuroticism-stability axis while (2) resembles his extraversion-intraversion axis. (3), on the other hand, corresponds roughly

to the concept of intelligence as embodied in the notion of I.Q. The similarity is perhaps due to a basic continuity of assumptions, since the industrial revolution, about which psychological characteristics are deemed valuable.

120. See N. Elias, *The Civilising Process* (Oxford, 1978), pp. xi-xviii.

3

'Scotland a Half-Educated Nation' in 1834?
Reliable Critique or Persuasive Polemic?

Donald J. Withrington

1

SCOTLAND a Half-Educated Nation, both in the Quantity and Quality of her
Educational Institutions bears the publication date 1834; but it was still in
preparation late in that year and seems not to have been issued until the early
weeks of 1835. The pamphlet, ninety-five pages long, grew out of the
proceedings at a public meeting held in Glasgow on Thursday 2 October 1834,
a meeting called by the recently formed Glasgow Educational Association.
Many passages in the pamphlet were taken, more or less directly, from the
extensively reported speeches at the meeting printed in the local newspaper,
the *Scottish Guardian*. The authorship of the pamphlet is rather coyly hidden,
from non-local and non-contemporary readers, by its being attributed to 'the
Editor of the *Scottish Guardian*'; indicating, it seems to me, that its author,
George Lewis, was to some extent at least disclaiming direct personal responsibility for every phrase and word and sentence that he wrote — explaining to
those in Glasgow who were already 'in the know' that he was drawing heavily
on what he had heard and reported at the Glasgow meeting.[1]

The *Scottish Guardian* had been founded in 1832 for a very specific purpose.
With the passing of the Test and Corporation Acts in 1828 and of Catholic
Emancipation in 1829, the major civil disabilities of protestant and Catholic
dissenters had been removed; and this inaugurated, in the height of the fervour
for political reform, a movement among protestant seceders and dissenters in
Scotland which is known as the 'Voluntary Controversy' — during which the
voluntaries moved from attacks on the legally-enforced payments of Church
teinds (or of annuity rates demanded in the towns for the support of the Established churches there) to a claim that Christianity only flourished in purity and
vigour when it was entirely unconnected with the state and finally to a demand
for the ending of all state connection with religion and for the disestablishment
of the Scottish Church. The *Guardian* was intended to provide a forum for
supporting and defending the Church against such attacks, in a city and its sur-

rounding area which had long had a very substantial population of seceders and dissenters of all varieties.[2]

The Glasgow Educational Association, founded in mid-1834, was closely tied in to the *Scottish Guardian*, a fierce supporter of the principle of Church establishments, demanding the extension of the parochial school system, holding that it was the duty and responsibility of the state to supply religious and educational services to the people through the media of the national Church and the national school system. The first secretary of the Association was George Lewis: later he was to share that task with another and increasingly well-known member, David Stow. It was founded at a time when, as we shall see, Lord Brougham made it plain that the Melbourne government — dependent on the support of dissenters, particularly urban dissenters, in England and Scotland — was unhappy about further state funding of schooling under the aegis of national Churches and when in June 1834 a bill brought forward in the House of Commons 'to regulate and enlarge the provision for parochial education in Scotland' had been rejected.[3] That bill was presented in parliament by J. C. Colquhoun, MP for Dunbartonshire, and it was Colquhoun who became first president of the Glasgow Association. Colquhoun chaired and took a prominent part in the initial, major enterprise of the Association — 'one of the most numerous and interesting meetings we remember to have seen in Glasgow, of the Friends of Education and of our Religious Institutions' on the subject of 'Extending the Parochial Schools of Scotland',[4] the meeting of 2 October and the basis for Lewis's pamphlet. Meeting and pamphlet alike had twin purposes: to persuade an increasingly hesitant government to fill the gaps in Scottish educational provision by way of additional parochial schools and not through an extension of the voluntary/private system; and to retain, develop and underline the essential connection between all state-supported schooling, of whatever kind, and its supervision and control by the national Established Church. The October meeting was openly partisan and Lewis's pamphlet was no less partisan, a political and ecclesiastical treatise almost as much as it was an analysis of the state of Scottish education in the mid-1830s. When *Scotland a Half-Educated Nation* was issued in 1835, it went almost unnoticed: it was not widely reviewed, and generally it was ignored by the more energetic and lively of the reviewing journals and newspapers — these were in any case mainly supporters of the Liberal/dissenting cause, to whom Lewis's pamphlet was a party piece best avoided. It seems to have lain undisturbed until resurrected in the researches by L. J. Saunders for his remarkable *Scottish Democracy 1815-40* in 1950. It has had only a little attention since then, mainly because of its pithy and arresting title, to some extent because of what Lewis has to say about the need for teacher training. It is still known about rather than known, recognised by its title and not by its arguments; however, before we go on to look at Lewis's thesis, we should give some more attention to the public debates on education and Church matters in 1833-34 and to the Glasgow meeting in October 1834.

2

Hansard, containing the printed proceedings of both houses of parliament, is a good starting point. Parliamentary business was the very stuff of newspapers in the 1830s — column after column was given over to reports from Westminster, and there were letters, commentaries and editorials galore on them in journals and newspapers of every political standpoint: what was said in parliament was news and, with the newspaper commentaries, informed and directed opinion throughout the country. The pages of *Hansard* in our period are well bespattered with debates on the presentation of petitions, debates on bills or on motions for committees of enquiry on Scottish education and related topics.

Early in the 1833 session, for example, two major government figures — Lord Chancellor Henry Brougham in the Lords and Lord Althorp in the Commons — spoke generally on education. Lord Brougham, asking in March 1833 for annual returns on the state of schooling in England and Wales to be made available, declared his object to be 'the improvement of the moral condition of the people by affording them the means of popular education' and later claimed 'they ought therefore to lose no time in giving education a better chance: because in proportion to instilling moral and religious feelings into the minds of the people — especially of the young — they had a better hope of improving their civil condition'.[5] Brougham, calling on statistics about literacy among criminals and others in Russia, Spain, the USA and France, was persuaded that less education brought more criminal violence, an argument countered by William Cobbett in the Commons but upheld fervently by Althorp — 'A great deal lately has been called education, which was only the name of education: and if *real* education (i.e. not reading and writing, but a moral training through the agency of reading) were spread among the people, he believed a great benefit would arise and that it would have a great effect in preventing the increase of crime'.[6] This style of argument continued in the following month, April: Mr Lennard, MP for Malden, was sure that 'without education the mass of Society could not be preserved from corruption and an increase in crime'; and the renowned Radical, Joseph Hume (sitting for Middlesex) noted that, having read the Report on the Poor Laws — the English Poor Law Amendment Act would be passed in 1834 — it 'presented a state of ignorance and crime in the country that ought to be appalling to every person . . . if some speedy and effectual check was not put to the dreadful march of demoralization, no property would be safe'.[7] These are typical comments from one influential source; they can be paralleled in journals and newspapers of all political persuasions, in debates in the General Assembly, in a host of pamphlets. The emphasis was on moral regeneration, on the stabilising of and the securing of its vital principles (for example, the sanctity of property): the increase in crime, of drunkenness, of pauperism could be effectively countered only by the moralising impact of schooling. The General Assembly meanwhile angered Melbourne by a petition it sent in about the government's intention to provide state money for Catholic education in Ireland: Melbourne considered illiberal what Lords Belhaven and Haddington and the Bishop of Exeter accepted as truisms, namely that all state-supported schooling in Britain should (a) have protestant teachers, (b) use the Bible as an essential classbook, and (c) have certain school hours set aside for protestant instruction.[8]

During 1833 this same emphasis, on the need to defeat the brutalising and morally corrupting influences which were at work, comes through strongly in debates on Church reform. Much was said about the need in England to improve Sabbath observance, for instance — usually accompanied by reverent remarks about the good example of Scotland.[9] Scottish debates were centred on the increasingly vexed question of patronage in the national church. George Sinclair (Caithness) believed that the 'tone and temper of the times', in the immediate aftermath of conceding franchise reform for parliamentary elections and in the throes of settling the political reform of the municipalities, had brought the people into total opposition to patronage and to any restrictions on their rights to take part in the election and appointment of their ministers of religion. For him and for many other Churchmen the dangers were painfully obvious: 'Unless we did away with the law of patronage, Voluntary Church principles would become more and more predominant and the safety of that Establishment endangered on which the national happiness and morality of Scotland so materially depended'.[10] Horatio Ross (Montrose) saw the end of patronage as likely to stop that drift away into the seceding churches, who 'had united with the Dissenters in forming a Voluntary Church Association to crush the Established Church altogether'.[11] Colquhoun, in his very first public act in the Commons, supported Sinclair's motion. Thus, just as in the earlier discussions on schooling, and paralleling the arguments which Thomas Chalmers had used in 1819-20 and frequently since for the extension of both churches and schools within the traditional structures,[12] so Sinclair and the others identified Established religion and state-supported schooling as giving the only security they could gain in promoting 'national happiness and morality'. The more the voluntaries attacked state religion, demanding an end to all 'unjust, unScriptural and injurious connexions between Church and State',[13] the more vehemently Churchmen held to and defended the concept and principle of Establishment: it was the Church Evangelicals, led by Chalmers, in the Assembly and other Church courts, in public meetings and in a torrent of pamphleteering all intended to countermand the Voluntaries' attacks, who both led the movement for church reform (for example, promoting the Veto Act in the Assembly to offset the worst excesses of patronage and the Chapel Act to ease some of the internal problems of church extension) and for Church defence — through such agencies as the *Scottish Guardian*. To the Church Evangelicals in particular the necessary identification of national religion and national education was self-evident and the duties of government, any government, to promote both were just as obvious. But a ministry as dependent on the dissenters' votes as was that of Lord Grey (until mid-1834) and that of Melbourne (until late 1834) could hardly agree.

In 1834 the problems of Church patronage rumbled on, tempered to some extent by the fact that the Veto Act and Chapel Act only fully became church laws in May of that year, and it was some time before conflict over the veto was to appear in the secular courts: however, a select committee to enquire into patronage in the Church of Scotland was appointed in February 1834, while in the following year another committee — on church accommodation — was formed. (Neither was to seem very beneficial to the Church in their reports.) But during 1834 the question of the provision of education, in all countries of Britain, became and remained prominent.

In April Lord Brougham introduced a debate on the 'Progress of Education' in the Lords and was mainly concerned to explain why, having argued for a 'Scottish-type parochial system' for England ten years earlier, he would not do so any more.[14] He had not believed in 1818 that voluntary effort, by dissenters and churchmen alike, could have produced such remarkable results: and he was convinced that to legislate a school in every parish would put an end to those voluntary contributions. Government had helped, in making grants of £10,000 to each of the two school societies — the dissenting British and Foreign Schools Society and the anglican National Society: not less that £40,000 or £50,000 had been voluntarily subscribed in addition. Even so, there were destitute areas; and there were schools not offering a 'really useful education'. He therefore hoped to persuade government and parliament to make two grants: further help to the Societies to aid in founding new schools (but not in keeping them going, which was to be done voluntarily) and 'another £20,000 towards the establishment of seminaries or normal schools for the education of those who would be called afterwards to preside over the inferior schools themselves'. But, he confirmed, 'the voluntary principle should however always be adhered to — nothing like compulsion should enter into the system'. In answer to comments that a school system that would really do good in the country must be directly under the influence of the Church of England, Brougham scathingly remarked that it had needed the stimulus of dissent in the 1820s to make the Church move at all in providing schools, for all its millions in wealth and people. This speech was widely reported, but very differently received, in the Scottish press. To the dissenters in Scotland it provided a signal to press on with their attacks, particularly on Church establishments and on Church superintendence of schooling: indeed in May 1834, while introducing to the Lords a petition from Glasgow, from a meeting of 48,600 people, demanding an end to Church establishment in Scotland, Brougham went out of his way to warn the Scottish dissenters against pressing too extreme a view — 'he could not think of leaving 14 millions, he believed he might say 16 millions or 18 millions of persons, wholly without any established or enduring means for the maintenance and support of religion'.[15] To the Churchmen of Scotland, despite these more temperate remarks, Brougham's speech spelled disaster: a sum of £10,000 had been granted for education in Scotland but nothing had yet been done, no doubt because the cabinet refused to allocate it to the Church of Scotland — and this presumption was confirmed some months later, in

October 1834, when the Lord Advocate was reputed still to be having difficulties in getting 'proper parties' to act as go-between the government and the
people of Scotland, for there was no educational society which acted for
Scottish dissenters — there was even the suspicion that the English-based
British and Foreign Schools Society ('entirely ignorant of Scotland') had been
asked to act.[16] Such prevarication, such deliberate avoidance in giving any
additional responsibility to the Established Church in Scotland, the sense
among Scottish Church evangelicals that the distinctiveness of the Scottish
situation was not understood or was being deliberately ignored in order to
avoid any difficulties with the dissenters (and what's more, with the English
dissenters rather than the Scots), all combined to produce an enhanced and
increasingly resentful and determined attachment to the principle of Establishment and to the identification of school extension with Church extension.

In June 1834 the House of Commons gave much time to education.
Roebuck, MP for Bath, had unsuccessfully a year earlier moved a comprehensive bill for a state-supported parochial school system in England and Wales:
'we allow crime and misery to spring up and then attempt, by a vast and
cumbrous machinery, to obviate the mischief; we punish, we do not
prevent'.[17] Roebuck's scheme was to be compulsory for all children aged 6-12
years, was to have elected district school committees which would select and
dismiss masters, supervise the schools and determine the subjects of
instruction: there would be three ranges of school — infant schools, schools of
industry for older children, and normal schools for the instruction of teachers.
But all this had been too much for his listeners: Lord Althorp wanted action
'without the immediate and direct influence of Government'; Joseph Hume
wanted to ensure that no schools that were erected were 'placed under the
domination of any Church; Sir Robert Peel, fierce supporter of Anglican
influence in English schooling, thought that 'in a country like our own, which
was justly proud of the freedom, he doubted whether it ought not to be left
free from control'.[18] A year later, in June 1834, Roebuck moved the setting up
of a committee of enquiry: 'At all times, but more especially at a period of
excitement like the present, it was the duty of Government to watch narrowly
and endeavour to direct the culture of the people . . . to raise the mental and
moral culture of the people . . . His desire was, by affording education to the
people, not so much to raise them from their proper station as to make them
happy and contented in it . . . it was the duty of Government . . . to supply
the people with that knowledge which would induce them to obey' its laws.[19]
Sir William Molesworth (East Cornwall) agreed with Roebuck and said in
what is, in the context of this essay, a significant phrase — 'the education of
the lower classes in this country was as deficient in its quantity as in its quality
. . . the present system was the most incomplete'. And Molesworth went on to
comment on the training and certification of teachers under a government-
sponsored programme: 'The intervention of the State would stamp a new
character and dignity upon a most useful class of individuals, he meant schoolmasters, who . . . would by such a course be regarded as public func-

tionaries'.[20] Lord Morpeth (MP, Kent) held it indispensable to the success of any scheme of public education 'that the Scriptures without mutilation or comment should be its foundation'.[21] The comments on Roebuck's motion were this time generally favourable: he got his Select Committee on Education in England and Wales, which sat for a first session from 12 June to 6 August 1834 and published its initial witness evidence in August — the witnesses including two Scots, Professor James Pillans of the chair of Humanity at Edinburgh University and Lord Brougham.[22]

On 17 June 1834 a Bill to regulate and enlarge the Provision for Parochial Education in Scotland was moved in the Commons, by J. C. Colquhoun,[23] who argued that the parochial system in Scotland had been 'completed' a century and a half before, with the assured provision of one rate-supported school in each rural parish. But population had more than doubled, from one million to 2.3 million; without a corresponding increase in the structure for state schooling, the numbers of schools were no longer adequate. Colquhoun reported researches which showed that one-sixth of the population in Prussia, one-quarter in the state of New York and one-fifth in Holland were at school. The General Assembly committee on education expected that one-sixth should be at school, and in some Lowland parishes this was the case. But in Glasgow the proportion was only one-fourteenth, it was one-fifteenth in Dundee and Perth and reputedly one-twentieth in the Abbey parish of Paisley and one twenty-fifth in Old Aberdeen; in the parishes of Banffshire, Moray and Aberdeenshire — the Dick bequest area — only one-eleventh were at school. In Glasgow 20,000 children were growing up uneducated (and 6000-7000 persons living by crime); in the Highlands one-sixth of the population could not read and a half could not write. 'Scotland ranked high in the estimation of all in the subject of Education: he was sorry to contest that opinion.' The General Assembly estimated that a schoolmaster ought to have at least £40 per annum plus his accommodation: and the incomes of many parochial schoolmasters were not within reach of that sum and those of private teachers generally much worse, to the extent that only 'inferior men' would take up these situations. Colquhoun believed that if they would secure good masters, well paid for their efforts, then there had to be a permanent salary — and that would generally have to come from state and rate aid: it was difficult to see charitable contributions at a level which could maintain the numbers of schools that would be needed. Nor was it enough merely to provide a master — 'without the agency of the parish minister, visiting the people and urging them to send their children to school, they might have little inclination to send them or to resist the many temptations to keep them away or prematurely withdraw them'. Colquhoun's plan would need £60,000 annually — the Edinburgh and Glasgow police cost more than £60,000 a year 'and consider the influence which education had in the suppression of crime: the peace and tranquillity of the country would be preserved'. Joseph Hume and Sir Daniel Sandford (MP, Paisley) urged the appointment of a committee of enquiry;[24] Lord Althorp greatly preferred the grant-in-aid system that had been adopted for

England, and Sir George Strickland asked, if Scotland were to get £60,000 a year for parochial education, then how large a sum would the House be called up to vote for the same purpose to England?[25] Colquhoun, under pressure, withdrew his motion.

3

Curiously enough, on the same day that Colquhoun introduced his bill in the Commons, the *Scottish Guardian* carried a rather belated note on a report on parochial education which had been presented to the presbytery of Glasgow on 6 May. This seems to have made little specific reference to the wider issues which had been in public debate for months past: the report, however, provided comments which undoubtedly were relevant to those issues. There were a group of administrative recommendations: each parish minister was to carry out a full review of the state of education in his parish, this review to be made annually and its report kept by the presbytery in a separate register; help was to be offered to schoolteachers in buying books, maps, etc. for use in the classroom; and the presbytery was to give its support to the schoolmasters' petition on pay. Other recommendations referred to matters of policy: the presbytery approved the 'intellectual system' of instruction, usually associated with Wood's sessional school in Edinburgh, and felt it desirable to 'have some superior method' of training teachers, in a model school for example; the ministers reaffirmed their belief in the vital nature of Bible-reading in all schools; and they sensed a need to review the 'mode' of trial or assessment that was made of applicants seeking employment in the parochial schools — possibly that they should have completed no fewer than two full sessions at college and (interestingly) perhaps also one session of Divinity as a minimum. Hence we can see a group of local clergymen, looking at the weaknesses in the local educational structure, highlighting issues which had been or were being debated in parliament: the kind of academic and professional training which was necessary to improve the quality of instruction; whether or not new advances in educational practice were to be approved; the particular value of moral (Bible-based) instruction; and so on.

The *Guardian* kept educational issues to the fore. On 27 June there was a front-page article on the 'Present State of Education in Paisley'; on 8 July another front-page discussion, this time 'On the Superintendence of Schools by the Church of Scotland', underlining what was to the writer the essential nature of that oversight of all schooling if education was to retain and enhance the moral training that had to accompany the mental in all good schooling. A curious item on page 2 on 5 September announced that Mr. Auld, the teacher of the St. John's Parochial School at Annfield in that parish, was banning the use of the tawse as an experiment. On 3 October the front page was back to more wide-ranging educational topics with an article on Roman Catholic schools in Glasgow. And then, on 7 October, the entire front page and some part of an inner page were taken up with the report of the Glasgow Educational Association meeting on 2 October, on the 'Extension of the Parochial Schools of Scotland'.

J. C. Colquhoun, president of the Association, chaired the meeting and introduced the subject. His concern was not with 'common and mere elementary education which is confined to reading and writing' — four-fifths of the inmates of English and Scottish jails could read and write but it had not restrained them from crime. It was a test of education that it 'represses crime and diminishes vice . . . takes from the enormous mass of human misery and adds to the amount of human happiness'. Those statesmen who said they would adopt the literary part of the parochial system without the religious would turn it into a cheat and a delusion — 'You may produce no transforming effect upon the character and the conduct of the people, and without this your system of education is worthless and does not deserve the name.' Colquhoun then restated points he made in his Commons speech — the need to extend the parish system, particularly in the destitute areas of the Highlands and large towns; the need to remunerate teachers better; noting that the humbler classes in the towns were incapable of paying for the better teaching which they might otherwise ensure they got in voluntary schools; commenting on the large expenditures on prisons while too little was being spent on preventing crime through good moral and intellectual training; that government should multiply and extend, not mutilate or destroy, the parochial system.

George Lewis spoke next, introducing a motion which specifically called on Government to extend the legal parochial school system into all the towns and to ensure the universal education of all the children of Scotland. It was the 'fixed and stationary condition' of both the parochial church and parochial school systems which, 'amidst a rapidly progressive population', had led to 'the decline of that intelligence and piety amongst great masses of her population, in town and country'. Much was owed to charity and private schools and they had done all that could be reasonably expected, yet 'Scotland is still but a half-educated nation'. After a short discussion of comparative statistics, drawing heavily on Colquhoun's speech in parliament and with particular reference to Prussia, Lewis reminded the audience that it was not enough to have sufficient numbers of teachers: 'we must have well qualified teachers' — and yet in the Scottish towns education was 'almost entirely in the hands of private schoolmasters'. For Lewis it was 'a matter of inevitable necessity to the well-being of society' and also to the securing of new-won political privileges that 'there be a great and immediate augmentation of our ancient system of popular instruction'. Finally, Lewis returns to his first point, that close interrelationship of national church and national school which alone gave Scotland her 'intelligence and national worth', in a resounding passage which he then put almost unchanged into *Scotland a Half-Educated Nation*:

In all but our parochial churches and parochial schools, we have lost our nationality. In these alone we survive as a nation — stand apart from and superior to England. These are the only remains we can show the stranger of the ancient excellence of our country — the only memorials of the wisdom and worth of bygone days. These are the only institutions around which linger Scottish feelings and attachments: in the support, extension and improvement of which may yet be rallied all the patriotism and piety of Scotland. It is not enough to preserve these noble remains of our nation from the hand of the spoiler — to preserve them, as the ancient regalia of Scotland are now preserved in her metropolis, to be shown to the curious stranger as things that one had a meaning and a use. The evils of a century's neglect must now be remedied, that, refitted to the altered circumstances of our country, Scotland may again be crowned chief amongst the nations for wisdom, and knowledge and righteousness.[26]

A second motion was introduced by Andrew MacGeorge, local worthy and local historian, insisting that the great purpose in education was not the cultivation of intellect only, but the 'formation of right principles, dispositions and habits', based on the use of Scriptures in all juvenile education. These influences had been much weakened as increased population over-extended the parish schools. 'In the place of sobriety of manners, the virtuous habits and the marked influence of religious truth which distinguished Scotland in former days, we see everywhere an inundation of improvidence, intemperance and crime, great dissolutions of morals, and lamentable ignorance, indifference and error in religion'. For MacGeorge, too, the holy alliance of national church and national school, revived and extended, could alone meet these problems.

The task of speaking to a third motion was entrusted to the Rev. Robert Buchanan, who had been inducted into the ministry of the Tron Kirk only in August 1833, and was one of the original and most active members of the Glasgow Association according to his biographer. The importance of the motion and the obvious effort which Buchanan put into preparing his speech clearly show him to have had the confidence of his colleagues. The motion, noting that it was not sufficient merely to introduce the Scriptures 'in an un-mutilated form into schools', declared that all teachers had to be 'men "sound in the faith" and able to commend right principles to the understandings and hearts of the young'. Recent improvements in the 'art of education' were certainly to be 'engrafted on our parochial schools', but in extending the parochial system 'the ancient platform must be followed, and all the religious securities, devised by the wisdom and piety of our ancestors, be preserved in-violate; without which no system of education can ever deserve or obtain the confidence of the vast majority of the people of Scotland'. Buchanan began his speech with a long, well-researched account of the educational provisions in the First Book of Discipline and of the acts of 1616 and 1633, no doubt drawing on Thomas M'Crie's recently published biographies of John Knox and Andrew Melville,[27] and sketching in the general historical development of the parochial system in the seventeenth century and beyond. Education had to be of a 'Scriptural character' taught by those versed in 'the faith of its great cardinal and saving truths', pledging the people to 'a system by which the national education of Scotland is connected with the doctrines and the superintendence of its national Church'. Buchanan foresaw great dangers if the legislature attempted to weaken or alter that superintendence — it would 'open a door to endless divisions and ultimately destroy all religious securities in our educational system whatever'. The passage with which Buchanan ended a rousing and excellently composed speech recalled Lewis's final sentences in their deliberate emphasis on national identity, national piety, national religion:

> And I hope that the sacred fire which has been this evening kindled, shall spread like the ancient signal fires from city to city, from village to village, over the whole face of the land — that the fervid Christian patriotism of true-hearted Scotsmen will rally round a cause which involves so deeply the welfare of our children, the honour of our country, and the glory of our God.

Buchanan's motion was seconded by David Stow who made two additional points. Firstly, that it was not enough to have the Bible read without explanation in the schools — 'The truth is that unless children are made to understand it, they might as well read a foreign tongue.' Secondly, he refers to the school at Annfield in St. John's parish as providing a standard at which others should aim: it employed Bell's monitorial system, Wood's intellectual system and the moral training and system of Bible lessons of (Stow's) Model Infant School: 'it is thus a juvenile school, not simply for teaching or training *the intellect alone* but for training *the whole man* — physical, intellectual and moral'.

Attached to the three motions was a petition, to be presented by Colquhoun to the House of Commons on behalf of the meeting. This began with a plea for a parallel enquiry into Scottish education to that already in progress on the state of education in England. It noted that 'much and extensive delusion and exaggeration prevail, respecting both the amount and the quality of the education at present going on in this part of the island'; in particular the towns had never 'enjoyed the advantages of the admirable parochial schools' and had largely 'been abandoned to private teachers' who, for the want of their ability to pay fees, 'have left great masses of the poor altogether uneducated or without any education worth the name'; the rich in the towns had the monopoly of the best private unendowed schoolmasters, yet it was the poor — unable to spare their children long for schooling — who 'ought to be provided with the most efficient schoolmasters'. The system of national instruction in parish schools 'is open to receive every improvement in the art of education which modern intelligence may have devised', yet it needed more than that to 'raise its labouring population and restore them to the intelligence and virtuous habits of their ancestors'; enlarged as it would have to be, it would still draw 'its lessons from the word of God'. Finally, the petition claimed that because of the great unanimity in Scotland among dissenters and Christians in all matters of Christian doctrine (they 'have one and the same Confession of Faith'), there would be no practical difficulty in extending the parochial school system under the continuing religious control of the Established Church, since the parish schools had hitherto been attended by the children of dissenters and Christians alike. Hence the extension of the national system of education would not only be supported by 'the numerous adherents of the Established Church but by great numbers of the pious of leading Dissenting denominations'. And 'any attempt to innovate in a matter in which the Scottish nation has always been peculiarly jealous and intolerant of innovation' would find the legislature in 'collision with the firmest principles and best affections of the people of Scotland'; it would 'involve itself in inextricable difficulties, give satisfaction to no party, and defeat its own efforts for extending the blessings of education'. The extension of the means of popular instruction would be 'the choicest fruit which can be gathered from the extended political privileges of Scotland'.

There can be no doubt that, by his own prompting or by others', Lewis must soon have begun to compose his pamphlet, to be put to the printer in the last weeks of the year. Meanwhile he was, of course, still editing the *Scottish Guardian* and being influenced by the news and commentaries he printed. On 10 October, the *Guardian* carried the reprint of a *Scotsman* article, based on moral statistics from France, entitled 'Does mere intellect diminish crime?' — and still more statistics and comments on morality in France appeared on 14 October. On 17 October the 'Past and Present State of the Town of Dundee' was described, and some figures which Colquhoun had quoted about expenditure on the Glasgow Bridewell were challenged in a letter to the editor. On 21 October Lewis wrote a leader to comment scathingly on articles in both the *Scotsman* and the *Glasgow Courier:* both papers had proposed earlier that all religious education should be omitted from schools until such a time as a youth could choose a religion for himself; but now they were recommending not only an intellectual training but a 'moral and religious training' too — and there is the hint of triumph in the *Guardian,* that somehow or other the good sense of the Church Evangelicals' principles will win through.

On 28 October there appeared a notice by the Glasgow Educational Association, announcing a series of fortnightly soirées in the Assembly rooms — 'papers to be read on education in our own and other countries, on the recent advances in the art of instruction and on the various questions connected with the extension and improvement of our system of national education'. Three, perhaps even four, of the series of six were held in time for Lewis to be able to adapt the contents of his pamphlet if he so wished. On 6 November Professor Welsh of Edinburgh University, recently returned from Prussia, was to speak on Prussian schools and on 'the duty of the friends of the Church of Scotland and of the Church itself at this conjuncture, in regard to Education' — in so doing he firmly recommended a thoroughly professional training for teachers through the establishment of Normal schools.[28] On 17 November, the Rev. Robert Buchanan was to address the company 'On the Superintending Power of the Church of Scotland over the Parochial School'. On 1 December the Rev. Brown of Anderston would speak on ' The Religious Securities in a National System of Education'. Finally, though it was as late as 15 December, the Rev. J. G. Lorimer would review 'The Services which the Church of Scotland has rendered to the Cause of Education in every period of her History'.

On 4 November there was a front-page article on Roman Catholic schools in Glasgow which included the demand that 'only those sound in the faith' (that is, protestants passed as fit to teach) should have the responsibility of teaching in any school; and a leader chided a St. Andrews professor for having said that schoolteachers should be 'freed from the domination of presbyteries' and should be more openly elected to office as well as being subject to periodic review. Church superintendence over and control of schooling was clearly a matter of anxiety to the *Guardian* writers and readers. On 7 November the Rev. Robert Burns of Paisley, convener of Glasgow presbytery's committee on parochial education, was reported to have received a request from the Lord Advocate 'for statistical returns of the state of education in Scotland', and he wanted speedy replies 'before the supplies were made up, in order that as liberal a grant as possible be made to Scotland'. This enquiry — the results of which were to be published in 1837 — at least showed some government awareness of the need to have more up-to-date information about Scottish schooling: it was not, of course, anything so grand as the select committee, able to call witnesses and to make a report, which Lewis and others wanted (in parallel to the one Roebuck had gained for England).

November and December saw much evidence in the *Guardian* of activity in matters of Church extension, the setting up of subscriptions for additional church accommodation in the city — with £20,000 promised by 9 December, and news that £80,000 in all was needed. On 2 December it was reported that the Marquis of Bute had just designated an entirely new parish on his lands, with all the burdens on it to be borne by him: 'were this generally imitated by the nobility, Radicalism and Voluntaryism, those twin enemies of our country's peace and prosperity, would be ere long extinct . . . The extension of the Church is the death of Voluntaryism.' A similar extension of the parochial school system would kill off at least the worst of the voluntary schools. Church reform-from-within was in the air too, and twice in these months there was discussion of the eldership and the need to make it a more active force again. On 9 December, in a leader which warned that for all its efforts voluntaryism could never fill the gaps in church accommodation, Lewis added, 'and the same thing is true of voluntary education': the reform and revitalisation of church organisation and of parochial schooling would march together.

4

That indicates the background to the making of Lewis's *Scotland a Half-Educated Nation:* it is clear that the pamphlet reflects very closely many of the general educational arguments that we have noticed, that it draws very heavily on the Glasgow Association meetings and is compellingly influenced by the Church Evangelical flavour of the *Scottish Guardian* and its contributors. But how was the pamphlet laid out, and does it introduce arguments which we have not met already? The text is in nine sections: an introduction and then eight parts with the following self-explanatory subtitles — (i) the past fame of Scotland as an educated nation; (ii) The present state of education in Scotland, in quantity and quality; (iii) The state of education in the towns of

Scotland; (iv) Shall we trust any longer to the voluntary school system?; (v) What ought the legislature to do?; (vi) Recent improvements in education; (vii) Practical difficulties; (viii) Religious securities. An appendix of four items is attached: a report of the French minister for public instruction in 1834; a report on the designation of new parishes in the city of Aberdeen (sharply criticised in the *Guardian* of 21 November for being much too large, two containing over 3,000 and three containing over 4,000 souls); a copy of the resolutions and petition agreed to at the meeting of 2 October 1834; and a note on the state of mechanics' institutes in Scotland.

The introduction notes that it is important always to judge Scotland in comparison with other nations ('Measuring ourselves by ourselves, we are not wise', says the quotation on the title page) and necessary to 'shake the national satisfaction with the present condition'; a main aim of the pamphlet is confirmed as pleading ' a case for the Parliamentary enquiry that we solicit'. The next section (past fame) leans heavily on Buchanan's speech at the October meeting but it also takes in data about school provision from Brougham's enquiry of 1818 and from Colquhoun's speech in the Commons in June. It ends with a characteristic Lewis argument: 'We are vain of our past fame as an educated nation . . . but we are the degenerate descendants of a noble ancestry . . . Our ancestors rise up to condemn our neglect. Prussia has risen up to condemn us. Even infidel and Popish France is providing elementary instruction for her population . . . but Scotland is still dreaming of abundance in the midst of destitution.'[29] In the following section (present state) there is much use of the statistics brought together earlier by Colquhoun, and discussion of the proportion of a population which ought to be at school (and the proportions who were at school in the Highlands and rural Lowlands). Lewis criticises the quality of private schoolteaching — 'moral and intellectual training, the development of understanding and the heart, is unattempted and unknown', and calls for the 'immediate interposition of government, not only for the planting of new schools but for elevating those already planted'. He then moves on to another Church-Evangelical point: 'It was not our parochial schools alone, nor our churches alone, but it was the clergy, the schoolmasters and the eldership of Scotland leagued together in the same holy enterprise which obtained for Scotland its ancient educational pre-eminence.'[30]

In his commentary on 'Education in the towns' Lewis again brings in Brougham's and Colquhoun's findings and also the Dick Bequest report, newly published entries in the *New Statistical Account* and other surveys of individual parishes. The author strains again to have his statistics match his predilections: in the previous section he struggled to explain away apparently anomalous returns from some Perthshire and some North-East parishes;[31] in this one the attendance returns for manufacturing districts in Greenock and Paisley seem too high,[32] and he therefore argues that 'It is vain to conceal that the solitary fact of a certain amount of school attendance gives us very little information: show us the schoolmaster . . . and we shall know what the education he gives is worth'. And this leads on neatly into an attack on the voluntary system which

> in town and in country, in schools as in churches, gives those whom Providence has blessed with abundance a monopoly of the best schoolmasters for their children but leaves the poor man with nothing but the dregs . . . Our churches and schools are open, but only to those who can pay for them . . . If the nation will not pay for the schoolmaster to prevent crime, it must pay tenfold for the repression of social disorder and for coercing an unhappy, dissolute and reckless population.[33]

The next section, specifically on the efficiency of voluntary schools, is dominated by a discussion of Brougham's change of heart, from 1818 when he favoured a fully fledged system of state-supported schools to 1834 when he opposed giving more than the most modest aid to set up new schools but was ready to press for £20,000 for the establishment of Normal schools and for 'useful libraries'. Lewis has to admit that he welcomes the proposal to give government sponsorship to teacher training: 'it is to raise high the quality of education by raising higher the respectability of the schoolmaster'.

In arguing for action by the legislature — if it were to do nothing else it should raise parochial schoolmasters' salaries in order to attract better men to the profession — Lewis was adamant that government should not believe its task was only to provide schooling for the poorest. The national Church and the national schools were in Scotland for rich and poor alike: 'in any national system the Government must therefore have an eye to bring all classes into the same school'.[34] This traditional emphasis on community schooling was necessary for success in Scotland: 'if schools are erected only for the poor, the poor will despise pauper schools'.

The sixth section on 'Recent improvements' is a much more extended discussion than is to be found in the other sources we have looked at of matters of classroom innovation. Extracts had been sent to Lewis from the Advocates' Library in Edinburgh of some of the Wodrow Mss there, including returns made in the early 1700s by presbyteries in and near Glasgow, and Lewis was greatly surprised by the 'modern' ring of the comments he read — on the value of making school enjoyable, of using Comenius-style pictures in teaching to read, on the liberal attitudes to choice of curriculum, etc. Typically and erroneously, Lewis blames the fact that these innovatory and liberal ideas did not apparently come as a direct inheritance to the 1830s on the restoration of patronage in the Church in 1712 and its continuation since. Only with the appearance of David Stow's infant moral training system, combined with the training programmes of Wood and Wilderspin, had there been a comparable improvement in the classroom, and in a few years Britain could have 'a style of intellectual, moral and religious education . . . superior to any that exists in Prussia or in any country in the world'. Such a regeneration would depend on the establishment of Normal schools, offering the teacher 'an education as truly professional as the lawyer, the doctor or the divine'. Lewis agreed with Professor Welsh's judgement at his talk at the Glasgow Educational Association's soirée: once a Normal school had been erected and had been 'brought into shape and established on sound principles by the Church', then government would be ready with building grants and endowments for its 'efficient and permanent maintenance'.[35] And the Association meant to proceed to establish a Normal school as soon as possible.[36] Lewis's antipathy to voluntaryism and his dedication to bringing back the whole people of Scotland into their national Church and their national schools come to the fore yet again:

> The re-edification of the schools of Scotland is a work which should go hand in hand with the re-edification of the Church itself; and by anticipating the Government in both, we shall best secure the assistance of Government in behalf of both. These are the true Scottish questions; and for effecting these objects all parties in the Church may unite their strength.[37]

The main 'practical difficulties' discussed by the author are, firstly, the problem of finance and, secondly, the question of compulsory school attendance. There is no doubt in Lewis's mind that money *could* be found by government through taxation to fund the extension and improvement of parochial schooling — 'it is the *will* alone that is wanting'. So far as ensuring attendance at school was concerned, while rural parishes would accept a law in the matter, 'in the towns it would be impossible to enforce'. One helpful action that government could take would be to demand certificates of school attendance from all candidates seeking appointments in government service; other employers might follow such a lead. But, once again, Lewis's ultimate solution was to be found in the unstoppable force created by Church and school working together:

> We must look not to a *legal*, but to a *moral* force — not to our Legislature but to our religious institutions . . . The habit of school-going, at one time almost universal in the rural parishes of Scotland was due, not so much to any enactments either of church or state on the subject, as to the continual visitation of the pastor and elders . . . To the extension, therefore, of the churches, and multiplication of the pastors and elders of Scotland, do we look again for the revival of that moral influence which, both in the town and country, will do more to counteract the evils of the factory system than any law which the Legislature can enact or the magistrate enforce.[38]

In the final section, the outline which Lewis gives of the needed 'religious securities' follows what we have seen in Buchanan's speech to the Glasgow meeting. If religion were not taught specifically in the schools, but left — as the *Scotsman* and its supporters would prefer — to the whims of parents and to the clergy, that would be, 'in present circumstances, tantamount to leaving the children of the poor without any religious education whatever'. He then goes on:

> Lay deep and strong in the hearts of the youth of Scotland the foundation of New Testament doctrines, and when they grow up to manhood they will walk in the path of Christian duty . . . This is the moral and religious training which all the youth of Scotland once had from their parents, teachers and pastors: and it is the only moral training which will again empty the jails and bridewells of Scotland and work out the peace and harmony of society.[39]

5

What, then, are we to make of *Scotland a Half-Educated Nation?* It begins, gently enough, with a plea for better provision of schools to ensure that, at a time when 'the political privileges of the mass of our countrymen have been enlarged', there would be available to all 'the means of sound popular instruction' in order to safeguard 'the right use and secure possession of those very privileges'.[40] As the argument in the pamphlet develops, there is greater concentration on the particular value of 'sound moral training' as security against the ever-increasing tide of criminality, intemperance and indolence and against the evils of radicalism, intolerance and indifference to religion which would otherwise rock the foundations of society; that security, it is then claimed, depends immediately and ultimately on the resurgence of Church influence in all aspects of the living of the people and particularly in the instruction of the youth — voluntaryism, tainted with radicalism, antagonistic to those cornerstones in the fabric of social stability, national Established religion and national Church-influenced schooling, could never in any case meet the anticipated demands of the people for universal education of intellectual quality enhanced by an assured moral instruction. As we have seen, as the author develops his theme, it is on what he considers the crucial association of Established Church and national schooling that his special emphasis is laid, and then overlaid with an appeal to patriotism and tradition. The identification of the hoped-for regeneration in education, to regain once more the national prowess of a past age, with a necessary renewal of the attachment of the people to the Church, is a gradually more strident theme in the pamphlet — which takes on more and more the flavour of a polemic on behalf of Established religion in the contemporary battle between voluntaryists and the state-supported Church. It is certainly not by chance that in the very last sentence of his pamphlet, when he returns momentarily to the question of the newly enlarged political franchise, Lewis — in contrast to his introductory comments — brings in the real motivation that lies behind his analysis:

> Under what other auspices, then, but those of the friends of the Church of Scotland, should the enlarged political privileges of the community be now converted into the means of re-building and renovating the moral institutions of our country, and carrying forward Scotland in the career of moral improvement?[41]

Make no mistake about it, *Scotland a Half-Educated Nation* is and was intended to be a partisan statement on behalf of the Established Church in a period when it was under severe attack. For those committed to Church defence — stung into action by the voluntaries, secularists and radical-atheists, and themselves aware that reform was needed and more energetic policies had to be pursued if the Church was ever to 'regain the affections of the people' — the traditional Church supervision of schooling became a vital issue, to be saved in the first instance and then to be extended, and so in the end to provide a greater security for the Church itself.

But this is not to say that Lewis and his fellow-Churchmen whose comments form the basis of the pamphlet were not also anxious — as were so many others, with different views — about the state of Scottish education. Government after all had promoted a royal commission into the Scottish Universities (1826-30) and was in 1834-35 seriously considering legislation on them,[42] and successive governments had sponsored surveys of educational provision in an attempt to have data to hand on which they might, if necessary, take legislative action.[43] The information that was readily to hand, and which was used by Lewis, Colquhoun, Buchanan and others, was generally incomplete, often out of date, sometimes difficult to interpret. It was used, increasingly, by all parties to argue their own cases — thus Lord Brougham and Colquhoun can be seen drawing on the same evidence in order to support or to deny the efficacy of private adventure schools. Lewis in our pamphlet is no exception. He tends to draw a much more generous, even idyllic, picture of later eighteenth-century education — when he saw the Church in good heart and in good control of schooling — than was really warranted; he says nothing in effect about the numbers and quality of urban subscription academies and schools, though we know most of them asked for Church inspection and superintendence; he gives what we now can judge to be a very grudging view of the quality of much of the adventure and private schooling that was available — for instance the 1838 returns show a substantial number of private schoolteachers who were graduates or who had completed sessions at one of the colleges.[44] The data on which Lewis and the others drew were, however, what was available to them and we should not criticise them for not having to hand better and fuller information. They were, however, often pretty cavalier in their interpretations, frequently looking for party points to make, and concerned, when uncomfortably awkward data appeared (as in the literacy figures), to explain the problem away or to ignore it. But Lewis is not more culpable here than many other of his contemporaries.

Persuasive polemic? — yes: well written, pithy and sharply argumentative at times, attempting always to provide evidence for its statements; but undoubtedly partisan, increasingly dominated by the special interests its authors had in Church defence. Reliable analysis? — certainly it attempts to use the data which were available, and much of the evidence, as drawn from Brougham's reports, Colquhoun's survey, the *Moral Statistics of the Highlands and Islands*[45] and other sources, is reported correctly enough; but the analysis is often wayward, the evidence is strained in order to support a hoped-for outcome, presumption and assumption often overtake and submerge deduction. Certainly, the reader who does not keep clearly in mind the background to the making of the pamphlet, its identity with the *Scottish Guardian* and with that energetic group of Glasgow Church-evangelicals who formed its arguments and penned them, will not gain all that he might otherwise do from the book — and could very well be misled too.

NOTES

1. George Lewis was born in Glasgow in 1803, son of a merchant there, and he was in turn a student at Glasgow, Edinburgh and St Andrews Universities. He was licensed to preach by the presbytry of Glasgow on 11 June 1828 but did not enter the ministry until 1837 when he became assistant and successor to Rev. William Thomson in the Middle Parish, Perth, when Thomson had reached the age of 63. In the meantime Lewis had become editor of the *Scottish Guardian*. In February 1839 he was presented by Dundee town council to the new city parish of St David's and was admitted in June, remaining there until the Disruption in 1843 when he became the first minister of the Free St David's. In 1849 he was translated to East Lothian, to the Free Church at Ormiston: he resigned the charge in 1865 and died in January 1879, aged 75. It may be of interest to add that William Thomson lived to go out at the Disruption, to take up a Free Church ministry in Perth and to survive until 1863, when he died aged 90.

2. Statistics gathered in 1819 by James Cleland, city chamberlain in Glasgow, showed that even as early as that year only half the families in Glasgow were in attachment to the Established Church, the other half attending a wide range of presbyterian seceder, protestant dissenter and Roman Catholic churches. It is hardly to be doubted that by 1834 the non-Established churches could claim the adherence of more than half the population in the area.

3. *Hansard's Parliamentary Debates*, 3rd ser., vol. xxiv, cols. 514-518.

4. *Scottish Guardian*, Tues., 7 Oct. 1834.

5. *Hansard*, vol. xvi, cols. 633, 637.

6. *Ibid.*, cols. 4, 5.

7. *Ibid.*, vol. xvii, col. 594.

8. *Ibid.*, vol. xviii, col. 1355.

9. E.g. *ibid.*, vol. xvi, col. 1232.

10. *Ibid.*, vol. xix, col. 706.

11. *Ibid.*, col. 707.

12. E.g. his speech at the opening of two parochial schools in the parish of St John's, Glasgow, in 1820: William Hanna, *Memoirs of the Life and Writings of Thomas Chalmers, D.D.* (Edinburgh, 1851), vol. ii, pp. 238-246.

13. Quoted by Lord Brougham: *Hansard*, vol. xxiii, col. 845.

14. *Ibid.*, vol. xxii, col. 843 *et seq.*

15. *Ibid.*, vol. xxiii, col. 845.

16. *Scottish Guardian*, leader, Friday, 10 Oct. 1834.

17. *Hansard*, vol. xx, cols. 141-163 (esp. 152).

18. *Ibid.*, cols. 167-168, 171, 172-173.

19. *Ibid.*, vol. xxiv, cols. 127-129.

20. *Ibid.*, col. 131.

21. *Ibid.*, col. 136.

22. *Report of the Select Committee on Education*, Parl. Papers, 1834, vol. ix, pp. 30-57 (Pillans), pp. 220-225 (Brougham).

23. *Hansard*, vol. xxiv, cols. 514-518.

24. *Ibid.*, col. 518.

25. *Ibid.*

26. Lewis, *Scotland . . .*, p. 75: the differences in the texts are minor but the version in the pamphlet is slightly more incisive and reads rather better, and that has been quoted here.

27. The biography of Knox first appeared in 1811, that of Melville in 1819: both books went into later editions and were reprinted. M'Crie's scholarship was always admired, even if it was not always comfortable to have such an astute and careful historian as a prominent minister of the Original Secession Church.

28. Lewis refers to Welsh's lecture in the pamphlet (p. 75). His visit produced swift reaction from the Glasgow Association. On 21 November the *Guardian* reported that the Association was to send 'two young men' to Prussia to study the school system there; and on 23 January 1835 the paper carried a notice that, 'having it in view to establish in Glasgow or neighbourhood a

Seminary for the Training of Teachers', the Association wished to appoint a 'gentleman of liberal Education, decided Christian character and a member of the Church of Scotland' to visit schools in England and Germany before his probable appointment as head of the Normal school — it was intended that he should engraft 'whatever is excellent in the modes of tuition in England and Germany on the Scriptural and Protestant principles of the venerable Parochial Schools of our native land'.

29. Lewis, *Scotland* . . ., pp. 20-21.

30. *Ibid.*, p. 30.

31. *Ibid.*, pp. 27-28, 31-32.

32. *Ibid.*, pp. 37-39.

33. *Ibid.*, pp. 43-44.

34. *Ibid.*, pp. 54-55.

35. *Ibid.*, p. 75. In effect this was the policy being hesitantly outlined by Brougham during 1834 — in a speech in the Lords in April (*Hansard*, vol. xxii, cols. 843-849) and in his evidence to the Select Committee on Education in England and Wales in the summer of that year, in the *Report* printed for the Commons in August (PP 1834, vol. ix). Lewis seems to have concluded that there was no likelihood of a Liberal government providing the monies needed for a wholly state-supported extension of the parochial school system, although there were good indications that grants-in-aid might be made: subscription schemes for school extension, similar to those already in being for Church extension, might therefore be necessary.

36. See note 28.

37. Lewis, Scotland . . ., p. 75.

38. *Ibid.*, pp. 80-81.

39. *Ibid.*, p. 84.

40. *Ibid.*, p. 3.

41. *Ibid.*, p. 89.

42. The government had had it in mind to legislate soon after the report was published in 1830. Eventually in early 1835 it became known that the Lord Advocate was preparing a bill, only for him to be overtaken by two Liberal-radical MPs, Bannerman of Aberdeen and Oswald of Glasgow, who each introduced a bill for the colleges in his own constituency. These reforming proposals contained clauses which effectively would have excluded the Established Church from any responsibility for and from most of its influence in the universities, even over appointments in divinity. The cry 'the Church in danger' went up, and the Church-Evangelicals went furiously to work to see that the bills failed: and it was the religious implications of the reforms, not the proposals for changes in curricula or teaching or in large part in administration, which caused the furore.

43. Such as the enquiry ordered on 9 July 1834, when directions were given by the House of Commons for the gathering of returns from presbyteries of information on: each parish, its extent and population; the numbers of children under 5 who have been taught or are learning to read, how many of each sex aged 5-15 have been taught to read or are learning to read, and how many have been taught to write or are learning to write; the number of parochial schools and the number of instructors, their salaries, school fees and other emoluments, the least and greatest numbers of scholars of each sex within two specified half-years, what branches of education are directed to be taught, what are usually taught, and what others might conveniently be taught; and a similar group of questions for all non-parochial schools in each parish. Abstracts of the returns from this survey were ordered to be printed on 21 March 1837 (PP 1837, vol. xlvii).

44. This was a much more extensive and informative report than that provided by the survey of 1834, with elaborate answers being provided by the parochial and non-parochial schoolteachers. The returns were published in 1841: PP 1841, vol xix, 64, with 312 large pages being given over to parochial schools and 789 to the data derived from non-parochial schools.

45. This was published in 1826 from a survey carried out in 1823-24 by the Inverness Gaelic Society. Its main finding was that literacy in English was poor in Gaelic-speaking areas and very good indeed in others (e.g. Orkney and Shetland) where there was no greater provision of schools. Lewis also made use of the reports on Highland schooling made by the General Assembly's Committee on Education which was active in gathering data in the early 1830s.

4

Scottish Schoolmasters in the Nineteenth Century: Professionalism and Politics

Douglas Myers

What the profession requires is emancipation — Emancipation at once from internal jealousy, and from external domination and interference . . . The School has too long been under bondage to all and sundry influences — educational to ecclesiastical polity; the schoolmaster to the clergy in particular.

> (An anonymous schoolmaster writing in the *Scottish Educational and Literary Journal*, 1855)

Our duty now is, Gentlemen, to make the Government acquainted with our objects, and the provisions of our Charter; and we must assert our right to have a voice in the educational arrangements of the country, and a much larger share in the management than we have hitherto enjoyed — to have the schoolmaster placed at least on a level with the clergyman in respect of all matters in which education is concerned.

> (James Bryce, presidential address to the Educational Institute of Scotland, September 1853)

The object of the Privy Council grants is to effect the education of *a class;* the object of the parochial schools was to overtake the education of *the people.*

> (A. C. Weir to the Argyll Commission, 1865)

THE history of the teachers of Scotland in the nineteenth century is especially notable in two respects: first, for the effort they made to attain the power and status of an independent profession, and second, for their attempt to formulate and promote an independent position on national education policy. That they were able to pursue these twin ambitions with a remarkable degree of commitment, skill and clarity was due in large part to the established rights and reputation Scottish teachers enjoyed at the outset of the period. As control and direction of education, in Britain and elsewhere, shifted from the churches and voluntary groups to the state, only in Scotland were teachers in a position to make a serious bid for occupational and political autonomy and influence. Their failure to achieve either of their main objectives says a good deal about the problems the teaching occupation generally has faced and about the difficulties it has encountered in trying to define and maintain a socially and politically realistic and viable role for itself.

1

At the beginning of the nineteenth century Scottish teachers owed their eminence and prestige to the existence of a national educational system and tradition developed over the previous two-and-a-half centuries. Although it had existed as little more than a declaration of intent for a lengthy period after the Scottish Reformation, legislation during the seventeenth century — culminating in the 1696 Act (eleven years before the union with England) — had put flesh on the bones. Together with the long-established Scottish universities, this nationwide system of parochial and burgh schools gained for Scotland an international reputation for educational excellence which that country has retained — deservedly or not — to the present day.

During the second half of the eighteenth century, when it flourished most effectively, the Scottish national education system consisted of about 900 parochial schools and 80 to 90 burgh schools. These schools, established in law, were maintained and supervised by the Church of Scotland in partnership with those who paid taxes toward their support (in the country the landowners, called the heritors, and in the towns the burgh councils). This school system embodied an educational tradition which, although often exaggerated and romanticised, certainly emphasised accessibility, general education, and social mobility, in significant contrast to the exclusivity, narrow curriculum, and more rigid social stratification that characterised English educational attitudes.

In the parochial schools, schoolmasters enjoyed several rights and privileges which conferred on them a unique degree of independence. First, through their connection with the established church and their recognition in legislation by the state, parochial schoolmasters occupied an official status possessed by few other occupations. As one nineteenth-century writer observed, the Act of 1696 had regarded education as 'intimately connected with the Church yet, in some respects, distinct from it' and, in its treatment of schoolmasters, had taken an important step 'towards the elevation of the teacher to the position of an independent servant of the commonwealth in direct relationship to the civil power'.[1] Secondly, parochial schoolmasters were guaranteed, under law, accommodation — a small house and garden — and a basic income, augmented by the fees of parents and, often, by payment for various additional duties such as acting as clerk for the parish session. These provisions, while modest, were certain and, in a country as poor as Scotland, ensured the teacher a position of considerable respect and status in the community. Finally, and most important, the parochial schoolmaster in Scotland, while supervised and directed by the minister and the local heritors, enjoyed security of tenure, holding office under the law on the basis of *ad vitam aut culpam*. This feature of his position deserves detailed consideration.

In order to dismiss a parochial schoolmaster in Scotland, lengthy due process had to be followed. Specific complaints on the grounds of gross misconduct (for example, immorality, or cruel and improper treatment of children) or neglect of duty (absence from school over an extended period, mismanagement, inefficiency) had to be presented to the presbytery — the local council of clergymen — by the minister, heritors or elders of the church. The presbytery would then give notice to the parties involved (the complainants and the teacher) and would conduct an official hearing on the matter at which both sides could present witnesses and argue the case. The presbytery could censure or suspend the teacher or order his removal from the office of parochial schoolmaster, such latter decision having the force of law (to be carried out by the sheriff if necessary). The schoolmaster could only appeal beyond the presbytery on the technical grounds of improper procedure, in which circumstance the appeal could proceed through the higher courts as far as the House of Lords.

The cases on record make absorbing reading.[2] A good example of the atmosphere and procedure in a straightforward case of gross misconduct is the trial of John Byers, a parochial schoolmaster in Roxburgh, who was charged with habitual drunkenness in 1819. On July 3 1819, Byers was given notice by the officer of the Presbytery of Kelso that a complaint had been laid against him by 'his Grace James Duke of Roxburgh, Robert Kerr, Esq. of Chatto, and the other Heritors of the Parish of Roxburgh'. The complaint read that, whereas, under the laws of Scotland, a schoolmaster 'should be diligent and attentive in the discharge of the duties of his office, and a person of fair character and reputation, having a sober, religious, and christian [sic] deportment not addicted to vice and immorality . . . [Byers] . . . in place of shewing a pious moral example . . . has for several years past . . . betaken himself to the immoral and vicious habit of drinking, amounting almost to total intoxication, which has rendered him totally unfit to discharge the duties of a Schoolmaster . . .' Byers was informed that the Presbytery would hold a hearing of the case on July 13, and was furnished with a list of the witnesses who would appear against him.

At the hearing, a succession of witnesses testified that Byers drank habitually, had several times suffered hallucinations, occasionally struck his wife (once he threw a full tea-tray out of the window), sent pupils regularly to buy him whisky and often fell asleep in the school smelling of drink, did not attend the parish church, and failed to perform the duties of the parish session clerk. Over the objections of his 'Agent', the testimony of adults as to what their children told them had happened was accepted by the court as admissible, on the grounds that 'Parents have no other means of ascertaining the conduct of their Children's Teachers . . .' The testimony of the children themselves was taken, although the evidence of one Margaret Huggan, aged eight, was declined on account of 'her tender years and appearance'. At a further hearing on August 24, 1819, Byers was able to present witnesses who testified on his behalf, but to no avail, since sentence of deprivation was passed and carried out later that same year.

A similarly clear-cut case of neglect of duty was that of John Miller, a schoolmaster in the Presbytery of Peebles. In November 1839 a complaint was presented to the Presbytery charging Miller with 'having for a long period neglected to open and teach the school, and with having recently removed from the parish altogether with his family and furniture to Edinburgh', despite entreaties to stay and teach. At its January meeting in 1840 the Presbytery approved of the terms of a libel charge specifying that Miller had kept the school closed for three months in 1839, had moved to Edinburgh without permission from the parish or presbyterial authorities, and had sent an unauthorised and 'irresponsible person' from Edinburgh to teach in his stead. In this case, Miller, unlike Byers, decided not to fight it and the March meeting of the Presbytery received and accepted a letter of resignation from Miller and dropped the proceedings against him.

Inefficiency or incompetence, of course, were more difficult to ascertain and, doubtless, complainants and Presbyterial Courts tried to frame the libels against schoolmasters in the clearer terms of gross misconduct and neglect of duty as much as possible. In all the cases listed in the parliamentary returns, only five referred to 'inefficiency' or 'mismanagement' in the charge. The most significant of these cases concerns John Inverarity, the schoolmaster of Lochmaben, who in August of 1842 was complained of to the Presbytery in the following terms:

> That the petitioners have no cause of complaint against the said John Inverarity as a competent scholar, but they have much reason to complain, and do complain of his 'neglect of duty' as a parish schoolmaster, arising from his inability to communicate to his pupils that instruction which he is bound to give, his total want of system in the school, his want of discipline, his perfect indifference whether his scholars attend to or benefit by his instructions or not, and great waste of energy.

The Presbytery sent a committee to visit Inverarity and discuss the complaint with him. The schoolmaster, after some hesitation, decided to reject the charges and to fight any libel action that might be brought against him. He engaged a Mr. Baird, a 'writer in Lockerbie' (that is, a solicitor) to act as his agent and sent a letter to the Presbytery in which he denied the charges and declared loftily that 'I have always been taught to consider efficient teaching as the sole prerogative of the Father of Lights, who teacheth savingly and to profit: and, therefore, to ascribe such epithets as efficient and effective to any mere instrument, must be regarded as nothing less than an impious surrogation of the honours righteously belonging to the Eternal.' This tone can scarcely have endeared him to the Presbytery, which overruled Baird's basic defence that the charges were not relevant to 'neglect of duty', but to 'inefficiency' and that 'a charge of inefficiency is not one of those charges which the Presbytery can be called upon to make the foundation of a libel', and announced its intention to frame a proper libel against Inverarity. In December 1842, the heritors of the parish declared their support of the Presbytery and agreed to sponsor the libel. The formal charge, which was presented to the Presbyterial Court in June 1843, was a detailed and convincing indictment of Inverarity on the grounds of inefficiency and neglect of duty. In August of 1843 the Presbyterial Court heard full arguments relating to the validity of the terms of the charge, overruled Baird's objections again, found the libel 'relevant in all its articles' and called for the complainants to present the evidence of their charges on the first Tuesday in September.

Unfortunately, the case was suspended at this point. At the end of the August hearing the heritors' agent had requested that 'in consequence of the appointment of Mr. Inverarity to a Church in Leith, proceedings . . . might be postponed', and in April of 1844 the presbyterial clerk reported that Inverarity had resigned 'in consequence of his appointment to the Presbyterian chapel at Longtown'. As far as one can judge on the basis of the material available, the heritors and presbytery in this case were prepared to pursue their libel on the grounds of inefficiency and neglect of duty to a verdict. It seems extremely likely that this verdict would have gone against the defendant, but there is no way of knowing whether it would have been upheld by the higher courts as being valid. Either way, it would have been a valuable test case on the issue of efficiency and parochial tenure.

The parochial schoolmaster's security of tenure was a matter of considerable controversy in the eighteenth and nineteenth centuries. Certainly the teachers themselves, and many others as well, were emphatic in support of this protection and its beneficial influence. 'Security of office, independence of local control, and a decent remuneration, have made the parish school the lever that has raised Scotland to her present pinnacle of greatness as an educated country,' wrote one.[3] Others, particularly the clergy responsible for the supervision of the schools, saw security of tenure as making it impossible to get rid of incompetent teachers; it was agreed on all hands that the absence of any pension provision, which forced schoolmasters to cling to office into extreme old age, was a serious flaw in these educational arrangements. While it is true that incompetence, then as now, was a difficult charge to prove conclusively in teaching, the records seem to indicate that where due process was followed, serious substantiated complaint against a schoolmaster usually resulted in his vacating the office.

The available records show that between 1791 and 1853, 139 charges were brought against schoolmasters, the great majority (94) on grounds of gross misconduct. Of the total, 106 resulted in the schoolmaster vacating office (81 verdicts to remove the schoolmaster, 23 cases in which the schoolmaster resigned before the verdict was reached, and two retirements). There were 17 suspensions, rebukes and admonishments; three 'not proven' verdicts; and only one outright acquittal. During that period, three schoolmasters launched appeals against their verdicts, one of which went ultimately to the House of

Lords for judgement, and all of which were successful.

Doubtless it was time-consuming and troublesome for the authorities to have to go to such lengths in order to dismiss a schoolmaster, but it seems clear that despite its drawbacks this unique protection for a schoolmaster did much to make his office a highly coveted and respected position. About half of the parochial schoolmasters had attended university and almost all were men of standing and influence in their communities. Looking back from a much changed situation in mid-century, one observer noted regretfully: 'We begin to miss our old kings among our teachers, those spirited old men whose native force of character and talent had never known a check; who amidst the undeniable degradation of the schools in many parts of the country, lent such a lustre to the profession that all men spoke well of it'.[4]

The burgh schoolteachers of Scotland were even more prestigious than the parochial schoolmasters, although their positions lacked either the guaranteed income or the security of tenure that characterised their parochial colleagues. The burgh schools attracted teachers of high academic background because of the wider curriculum they offered, the higher fees they charged, and the fact that rivalries between the burgh councils and the Church of Scotland frequently left them a large degree of independence. The burgh teachers, in terms of scholarship, income, and social position were, in fact, the most distinguished and influential group of Scottish teachers.

It was this group of a thousand or so parochial and burgh schoolmasters which constituted the official teaching staff of the legally established national education system of Scotland. They were by no means the only teachers in Scotland, however — indeed, they were a minority. By 1800 there existed about two thousand other schools of the various types so familiar to nineteenth-century historians of education — dame schools, private adventure schools, denominational schools, town academies, and so on. But it was the parish and burgh schools and their schoolmasters which set the tone and example for all the rest. It was that established system that created a Scottish national educational ethos with several distinctive characteristics: that education was a public/state as well as an individual/voluntary responsibility; that a basic education for literacy and godly upbringing should be readily available to all; that students of talent — the 'lad o' pairts' — should have access to a broader and longer education, sometimes including university; that the dominie and burgh schoolmasters occupied positions of importance and were entitled to a considerable degree of protection and respect.

As mentioned above, the Scottish education system probably reached its zenith during the mid-eighteenth century. The combination of public and private schools just described met the educational needs of a relatively stable, frugally prosperous, and largely presbyterian agrarian/village society to a much higher degree than in most other countries. In the late eighteenth and early nineteenth centuries, of course, this favourable situation deteriorated. There is no need here to detail the familiar phenomena of industrialisation, population explosion and shift, rapid urbanisation, and social dislocation and disintegration, except to say that they all occurred with devastating effect in Scotland. The national school system began to decline rapidly. Parish schools established to accommodate 50 to 100 students — perhaps with an assistant schoolmaster if the upper figure was reached — could not cope with thousands, and there was no state mechanism to establish new parochial schools. Though the Church of Scotland, other denominations, and various voluntary groups attempted to meet the new needs (about 2000 additional independent schools were established between 1800 and 1850), by 1834 the Rev. George Lewis of Dundee could write a startling exposé of educational conditions entitled *Scotland a Half-Educated Nation: Both in the Quantity and Quality of Her Educational Institutions.*[5]

Three developments during the first half of the nineteenth century deserve special mention, however, because of the particular impact they had on Scottish teachers. The first of these was the development of a whole new range of occupations which aspired to and sometimes achieved what is commonly referred to as 'professional' power and status. Most of these occupations went through several stages on the way — self-consciousness; self-organisation; official recognition through a Royal Charter from the Crown; and, finally, self-government granted by parliamentary legislation. As we have seen, the parochial and burgh teachers of Scotland already possessed some of these 'professional' advantages to a degree. The economic and social pressures of the nineteenth century, however, threatened to diminish their traditional prestige and influence, and they were keenly aware of other occupational groups whose fortunes seemed to be on the rise. By mid-century Scottish teachers were prepared to try to emulate them.

A second development of fundamental importance to Scottish education and teachers was the intervention of the central government in education, beginning in the 1830s and increasing rapidly thereafter. But the central government that took action in 1833, in contrast to the one that had established the Scottish national education system in 1696 and before, was essentially an *English* government, of course, not a *Scottish* one. One of the ironies of this nineteenth-century government intervention was that, while the Scottish system and tradition were frequently used as an admirable example and justification for government action, the assumptions used and means chosen were very un-Scottish indeed. For example, the English assumption was that the elementary school was exclusively a school for the poor, for the labouring classes, with a correspondingly restricted curriculum. Scottish parochial schools, however, drew from a wider social spectrum, offered a broader curriculum and even enabled talented students to go to university. Nevertheless the English assumptions, criteria and mechanisms were now applied to Scotland with very little if any adaptation.

Of particular concern to the Scottish schoolmasters was the fact that the pupil-teacher system, introduced in 1846, created an apprenticeship/normal school system of training teachers for working-class elementary schools; the notion of an elementary schoolteacher with a university background was of course quite outside the context of English educational assumptions. Yet the pupil-teacher system was applied in Scotland as well as in England, and Scottish schoolmasters feared that the quality, the status and the prestige of the new teachers would be inferior, that they would suffer from 'a want of an enlarged general education, and . . . liberality of mind, comprehensiveness of view, and improvement of all the faculties which are imparted by a mixed education'.[6] Moreover, the wider implications of the Anglicising tendencies of central government intervention in Scottish education were not lost on Scottish teachers and others. James Bryce, one of the leading burgh school-masters of his day, contended that by 1853 the new educational system estab-lished and directed by the Privy Council in London had 'paved the way for an assimilation of Scotland to England'.[7] This question, in fact, became *the* leading public political issue of the early 1850s in Scotland.[8]

Most Scots were not ardent nationalists during this period. On the contrary, prevailing opinion amongst public men and politicians, commercial and industrial leaders, and the press was enthusiastically North British in tone (the main nationalist organisation of the time, for example — the National Association for the Vindication of Scottish Rights — received very little influential and not much popular support). But the education question was different. Most Scots recognised it as a genuinely distinctive national tradition and, by mid-century, were increasingly aware of two things: the old Scottish system of parochial and burgh schools, complemented by other types, was hopelessly inadequate to cope with contemporary educational conditions; and the new government system of grants to religious bodies, inspection, and pupil-teachers was threatening to destroy the very qualities that made the Scottish tradition distinctive. By 1850 a very sizeable body of opinion in Scotland was convinced that major legislative reform of Scottish education along traditional Scottish lines was urgently required. An intensive political campaign to accomplish this was launched which received massive popular support. As Lord Advocate James Moncrieff later recalled, the national educa-tional reform issue 'was one of the few political questions which impressed itself on my emotions as well as my convictions'.[9]

Finally, the third development of special concern to Scottish teachers was the schism which occurred in the established church, again at mid-century. For a society in which the Church of Scotland had played such a central and per-vasive role in all aspects of national life, the social, political and psychological impact of the Disruption in 1843 was profound. For parochial schoolmasters the impact was direct because the walkout of about half the Church of Scotland's clergy to form the Free Church of Scotland put a similar decision of conscience squarely before each of them. A large number of parochial school-masters left the protection and security of their positions to become Free Church schoolmasters and, during the decade following the Disruption, that denomination built an independent system of nearly 700 schools. For Scottish teachers, all this threw into sharp relief questions concerning the nature of the teacher's position and his relations to church, clergy and government.

2

The Educational Institute of Scotland was officially established in September 1847. There had long existed to some degree a corporate sense and identity amongst parochial and burgh schoolmasters dating back to the seventeenth-century legislation that gave them official existence. From time to time during the eighteenth century local associations of such teachers had existed briefly. Occasionally, the parochial teachers had even petitioned the General Assembly of the Church of Scotland for improvements in salary and living conditions.

This identity received a significant boost with the legislative establishment of the Burgh and Parochial Schoolmasters' Widows' Fund in 1807. The purpose of this organisation was limited to overseeing the collection and disbursement of relief funds, but it nonetheless provided the first national structure for teachers, and its meetings enabled schoolmasters from various parts of the country to discuss more general matters as well. Out of this, too, grew the Scottish School Book Association, in 1818, which aimed to produce and improve school texts. It did so well at this that it was able to offer bursaries to the sons of schoolmasters. It was taken over by the publisher William Collins in the 1880s.

But although the EIS drew upon and profited from these precedents, it was a radical innovation in Scottish teacher organisation. As already mentioned, a number of other occupational groups were organising themselves and asserting their independence during this period, and teachers were no exception. In 1840 the Ulster Teachers' Association was formed and in 1846 the College of Preceptors in London. But, as it turned out, the EIS was by far the most ambitious, vigorous, and successful of British nineteenth-century teachers' organisations.

The initial impetus came from the élite of the Scottish teachers, the burgh school and academy teachers in Glasgow and Edinburgh. After a series of communications and meetings in late 1846 and early 1847, this group passed a series of resolutions advocating the establishment of a national organisation. They also had printed 2300 copies of their resolutions and, together with an accompanying letter written by their acting secretary, George Ferguson, sent them out to teachers across the country, urging them to organise local meetings to consider the idea and to send back a response by May.[10]

The emphasis in Ferguson's letter was very much on the poor economic position and low status of Scottish teachers. The schoolmaster, Ferguson declared, was 'unnoticed by the great and regarded as an inferior by the middle-classes . . . he alone has not participated in the general prosperity'. Partly this was due to the teachers' own timidity and apathy because, 'while the members of every other liberal profession have broken through the trammels which formerly fettered them', teachers 'have rested satisfied with the empty praise which has been liberally bestowed upon them'. The remedy was precisely to emulate these other rising occupations in a unified and energetic way. Take, for example, the surgeons. Surgeons were a favourite model for the EIS leaders, probably because of the social distance they had come from their early eighteenth-century association with barbers to their nineteenth-century challenge to the physicians at the top of the medical pecking order, and perhaps too because of their Scottish connections. The surgeons, Ferguson pointed out, had taken several definite steps. First, they had 'adopted the necessary means of improving their professional skill'. That had enabled them to present 'a strong and well merited claim' for public confidence and respect. Having achieved that, they were then in a position to apply for and receive official recognition and power as a 'separate and independent body', controlling the licensing and behaviour of its members. There was no reason teachers could not adopt exactly the same strategy with exactly the same results. Their knowledge and skills, Ferguson maintained, were 'not inferior to the surgeons' and it would be difficult to show why schoolmasters 'should not fix the standard of professional attainment, license their own members, and regulate the matters which concern their peculiar duties and interests, as well as the Physicians, Surgeons, Clergy, Lawyers or any other professional body'.[11]

This appeal, with its emphasis on the economic and status concerns of Scottish teachers, received an immediate and strong response. By May 1847, favourable replies had been received from all but 15 Scottish presbyterial districts. On September 18 over 600 delegates met in the Edinburgh High School for the inaugural assembly of the EIS.

Although Ferguson's letter had stressed what might be termed the narrow occupational concerns of the Scottish teachers, it is worth noting that he had also appealed to their wider educational and public interests as well, both in terms of raising the attainments and skills of teachers and in terms of fulfilling a responsibility 'to devise the best means of improving the education in the country'. This last was, of course, a reference to the growing political controversy about national educational reform. It was this broader political concern, in fact, that provided the main focus for the inaugural address of the first EIS president, Dr. Leonhard Schmitz.[12]

Schmitz began by outlining the familiar grievances of low income and status and calling for a determined effort by teachers to take steps similar to those taken by other occupations in achieving professional status and influence. But most of his attention was devoted to the national education question. The government, he noted, was adrift and confused, intimidated by 'certain powerful parties in the State' and discouraged by the failure of the 'ill-digested plans it has proposed from time to time'. Here, then, was a splendid opportunity for the teachers of Scotland. Unlike the Ulster Teachers' Association (which was too small) or the College of Preceptors (which was too narrowly class-based), the teachers of Scotland had formed a 'truly national association of teachers of all denominations in the country' which could exert a powerful influence on national educational policy. That policy, Schmitz contended, should be based squarely upon the principles embodied in the parochial and burgh school system, suitably adapted to contemporary conditions:

> Scotland was the first country in the world in which a regular system of education was established . . Scotland also is the first country in the world that has a National Association of all her teachers, resolved and determined to provide their country with the best system of education they can devise and to accomplish an object which several successive governments have been unable to arrive at.[13]

It is clear, then, that the founders of the EIS had two explicit aims, one narrow and one broad, one professional and one political. This is not to say, however, that there was unanimity on these aims or agreement about how to achieve them. Given the tenor of the times, an organisation which cut across denominational and other lines was bound to experience internal tensions. Although the EIS received widespread support from Scottish teachers, its membership comprised several distinct groupings of interest and attitude (the membership was reported as 1300 in September 1847 and had risen to 1700 by the next annual meeting; by 1852 there were 65 local associations with close to 2000 members, which probably amounted to perhaps one-third to one-half of all those engaged in some sort of teaching in Scotland, and certainly it represented the most active and ambitious segment of the occupation).

The burgh and higher level teachers — about a quarter of the total — formed the most energetic and influential group. During the first ten years of its existence, three of the EIS presidents were rectors (headmasters) and four more were burgh schoolmasters. They were the élite of the occupation — well-educated, talented, independent, prosperous, respected. They had taken the lead in establishing the organisation and they defined, articulated and fully supported both its professional and its political objectives.

The parochial schoolmasters — something over one-third of the total membership — constituted the second most powerful group in the EIS. Their position on the aims of the EIS was more ambivalent. They were, on the one hand, strongly sympathetic to the professional aspirations of the organisation. They had enjoyed a measure of independence traditionally and they were concerned to restore what they saw as a serious decline in their economic situation and social status. They were, however, much more cautious about the political aims of the EIS. The Church of Scotland saw most of the proposed schemes for national education reform as threatening to its rights and privileges and, along with the conservative country lairds, consistently opposed legislative action. The parochial schoolmasters, therefore, although somewhat restive under clerical control, were loyal to their church and were reluctant to involve the EIS in the public political controversy on national education. At the very first assembly, in fact, immediately after Schmitz's exhortations about educational reform, the parochial schoolmasters' leader, William Knox, sounded a warning note: 'No difference of opinion has ever been entertained with regard to the objects which this institute had in view . . . There were, however, great doubts entertained as to the best means by which these objects could be accomplished'.[14]

The rest of the membership was made up of a variety of denominational and independent elementary schoolmasters, the largest single group being Free Church teachers. This group was much less cohesive and influential. Their economic situation was more precarious and they enjoyed none of the legal rights and protections of the parish teachers. Certainly they supported the professional aims of the Institute, and a number of them were outspoken advocates of sweeping educational reform.

Besides these internal tensions, the EIS also had to contend with a generally cool and sometimes hostile external response. Several groups were unlikely to welcome its appearance or activities. The patrons and managers of Scottish schools, especially the country heritors, were not anxious to share their control of those institutions. Nor would they be enthusiastic about the improvements in salaries and facilities which would inevitably increase their financial obligations. The clergy (especially of the established church but of the other denominations as well) would be reluctant to relinquish what they saw as a special supervisory responsibility over teachers. The Rev. R. Candlish, head of the Free Church Education Scheme, for example, emphasised the 'very strict attention which is paid to the religious and spiritual qualifications of the teachers'. He declared that he would 'dread above all things a mere scheme to encourage young men to give themselves to the office of teaching, if it were not connected with proper guarantees to secure their religious and spiritual character'.[15] Finally, the government could be counted on to ignore or oppose any claims which would further complicate its development of an education system to deal primarily with English conditions.

Some indication of the strength of this opposition is illustrated by an indignant letter to *The Scotsman* in 1850 in which the writer warned this 'Infant Hercules' to 'strike a lower pitch at its meetings' and to avoid 'insulting any sincere labourer in the cause of education' — presumably a reference to school managers or clergymen. 'The imaginings even of a charter [the EIS was seeking a Royal Charter at the time] constituting this most numerous, and irregular, and irresponsible body, a tribunal of educational qualifications . . . is a symptom of alarm enough to render it doubtful what may be tried next'.[16] As the president of the EIS put it several years later:

> We have no open declared enemies — but assuredly we have no friends; and at the present moment, many would rejoice at our fall.[17]

During the first few years of the Institute's existence, its leaders concentrated their efforts on its occupational functions and objectives. This was partly a matter of necessity and partly a matter of strategy. Other occupations had based their claims for professional power and status on a demonstrated capacity for self-organisation and self-improvement. The founders of the EIS had those models very much in mind. An elaborate and rigorous system of examinations across a wide variety of subjects was set up. Different ranks of membership — based on qualifications, experience and competence — were established. Lectures, discussions and exhibitions on educational subjects were conducted locally and nationally, and a journal was launched.[18]

Besides a concern for the improvement of the quality of Scottish teachers and education, the leaders of the EIS were also motivated by the desire to establish the EIS as the licensing body for Scotland — the ultimate mark, they saw clearly, of a self-governing independent profession. As Schmitz put it in 1848, reporting that the exam and diploma system had been established:

> Up to the present moment I am not aware that either a public body or private individual has ever applied to the Institute to recommend a teacher; but I hold that we shall not have fulfilled our mission until the time arrives when no public or private body of individuals will employ a teacher who is not sanctioned or recommended by the Educational Institute.[19]

The difficulty was, however, that without official recognition and sanction that situation was unlikely to arrive.

The EIS leaders seem to have hoped that a Royal Charter, similar to those often granted to other occupations aspiring to professional status, would confer such recognition and sanction. At any rate, in proposing the terms of such a charter, they included a clause which would have made it 'indispensable for the applicants to produce the Certificate or Diploma of the EIS' in order to be hired as a schoolmaster in a school supported by public funds.[20] The clause was withdrawn as a result of public criticism and of legal opinion, which advised that only parliament, not the Crown, could grant such monopoly power.[21]

Without such sanction, of course, the value and desirability of the EIS certificates were severely diminished. The problem was rendered even more serious by the fact that the EIS certificates were in direct competition with another set of qualifications — the government certificates granted by the Privy Council to successful pupil-teachers and normal school graduates. Not only were these certificates regarded with increasing favour by school managers when hiring teachers, but they also involved grants of money to the holders. By 1855 there were over 500 such certificate holders in Scotland; by 1865, over 1500.

This rival system threatened to render the EIS diplomas irrelevant and useless, and also represented the advance of another aspect of English influence on Scottish education. 'In both . . . England and Ireland,' observed James Bryce, 'those who are instructors of the lower classes are a totally distinct set of men with whom the teachers of the upper and middle classes have no contact and even fewer sympathies. To set up a like distinction in Scotland is the manifest tendency of these provisions.'[22] That same Anglicising influence was evident in the Privy Council's response, in 1855, to an EIS request for recognition in Scotland of the Institute's diplomas as necessary qualifications for teaching. The secretary, R. R. Lingen, replied that the Committee was responsible for certifying 'those teachers in elementary schools for the labouring classes' and could not 'delegate this duty to any independent Board by accepting its diplomas'.[23]

On several occasions clauses recognising the certificates of the EIS were included in the Scottish educational reform bills proposed during the 1850s. On each occasion the clause was struck out during the committee stage; in any case, all the bills were unsuccessful.

The failure of the EIS to gain sanctioned recognition for its certificates had a serious effect on its growth in membership. The original influx of members, of course, was not subject to the entrance examination requirements but, after several postponements, the system was instituted. As a result the Institute grew very slowly; only a few ambitious teachers every year were willing to submit themselves to the rigours of the EIS exams with no other incentive than the honour of success. The Institute was not enlisting into its ranks 'that number of young promising and aspiring teachers, which we had anticipated', lamented one EIS president.[24] Indeed, concern began to be expressed at the 'rapidity with which its own ranks are thinning'.[25]

Rival associations of government-certificated teachers began to be formed; in 1856 one such group of teachers in Aberdeen requested admission without examination to the EIS, pointing out that such a policy would give the Institute a 'considerable addition of numerical strength'.[26] Although no official policy change seems to have occurred, local EIS branches in the 1860s were recognising the government certificate as sufficient qualification for membership. By 1871, in fact, the Institute's president was advising his colleagues to 'cling less tenaciously to the hitherto vain hope of being recognized as the great licensing body for teachers in Scotland'.[27]

3

A major reason the leaders of the Institute tried to concentrate on the professional objectives of the organisation was that those objectives commanded the widest support amongst the various levels and types of schoolmaster in the membership. The burgh and higher level teachers who played such an active part in establishing the Institute hoped that by avoiding controversy and emphasising common occupational interests at first, a solid united base could be created from which the EIS could address itself to broader questions of public educational policy — in particular, the question of national educational reform.

The context of the period, however, made such limitation extremely difficult. As described above, the years 1850-1856 were ones of intense public agitation and political activity on the Scottish education question. In 1850, the National Education Association was formed to campaign for legislative reform of the Scottish school system. Its leadership was distinguished,[28] its activities numerous and effective and its influence powerful.

During the period, four major legislative proposals regarding Scottish educational reform were presented in Parliament — in 1850, 1851, 1853 and 1854. All these proposals had similar characteristics — control and management by a national Scottish Board of Education; parochial schools and denominational schools to be given public support if they would allow inspection and open attendance; new public schools, under heritors' or rate-payers' control, to be established where necessary; and, most important to teachers, the traditional rights and protections of the parochial teachers to be applied to all.

Every one of these four Scottish Education bills won support from the majority of Scots MPs. On the first two, in 1850 and 1851, that majority was a slim one. Between 1851 and 1854, however, an extraordinarily vigorous public controversy on the subject took place. As a result, by the time the next two bills were considered in 1854 and 1855, Scottish public and political opinion had shifted heavily in favour of reform. The Scots MPs voted better than two to one for the bills. Despite this impressive Scottish support, however, none of the bills passed. This was a source of great indignation in Scotland. As *The Scotsman* put it:

> No such thing as the rejection of a Scotch Bill supported, like the Lord Advocate's measure, by a sweeping majority of the Scotch members, has happened since the Reform Bill. Here is a grievance at last — substantial, irritating, humiliating.[29]

Nonetheless, the result stood. Scottish educational legislation had to wait for two more unsuccessful attempts, a Royal Commission, and the passage of an English Education Act in 1870. When at last it did come, it was substantially less Scottish in character than the proposals put forward in the 1850s.

It is not surprising that, despite their best intentions, the leaders and members of the EIS found it extremely difficult to keep such political questions from intruding upon their activities and deliberations. Even the question of their professional power and status, of course, had significant political implications. But the national education question, from Schmitz's first presidential address and Knox's rejoinder, kept coming up. Many of the leading and executive members of the EIS were involved prominently in the reform controversy outside the Institute and it was difficult for them to set their views on the subject aside when dealing with issues affecting schoolmasters. *The Educational Journal*, for example, which was intended to be scrupulously non-controversial, seemed always to contain references or articles which gave offence to one side or the other. Every presidential address seemed to do like-wise. Finally, local associations from various parts of the country kept sending in resolutions on the subject. By 1853 the issue could no longer be ignored; it proved, however, to be almost impossible for the EIS to deal with.

In May of 1853 a special sub-committee was appointed representing the constituent groups in the EIS. After a series of meetings it became evident that there existed a basic split between the parochial schoolmasters and the others. The position that the former took, throughout the months of meetings and discussions that followed, was not couched only in terms of the legitimacy of the EIS considering the subject at all; they argued that no such provision had been made in the original constitution and charter and that, in any case, considera-

G

tion of the subject 'would at once lead the Institute into the arena of political agitation'. EIS members would 'lose their literary, to put on a political character; thereby drawing upon themselves the jealousies of both the community and of the government'.[30]

The advocates of EIS involvement in the national education issue argued, as James Bryce did in his presidential address of that year, that the education question was of such magnitude and importance that the teachers simply could not stay aloof any longer. 'The time has arrived,' he declared, 'when the parochial system must be readjusted, in conformity with the social changes of late years.' These readjustments would necessarily have profound effects on Scottish teachers, but was 'any man so sanguine,' Bryce asked, 'as to imagine that this Institute will be consulted in respect of such changes, or that the advice of any practical teacher will be taken?' It was necessary, therefore, for the Institute to take a clear position on the issue and to promote it vigorously — 'management, control, status, will not be offered to us'.[31]

After long debate the 1853 general meeting did in fact pass a series of resolutions in favour of national educational reform, but by so narrow a margin — 43 to 39 — as to thoroughly dishearten the advocates of direct, independent political action. In order not to split the membership further the executive decided to ask the Lord Advocate for an opinion on the matter, although a lawyer consulted by the EIS earlier had had no doubt that the issue was a legitimate one for EIS deliberation and action. Moncrieff's opinion, however, had a further dampening effect on the activists, the more so because he was a leading advocate of educational reform. The Lord Advocate's view was that, although the issue was not one within the scope of the Institute's original purposes, it could certainly discuss and pass resolutions on the subject if it wished. At the same time, the Lord Advocate felt it would be 'clearly illegal to employ any [Institute] funds in carrying out the measures contemplated by them'. Finally, Moncrieff strongly advised the EIS 'to abstain from introducing and discussing contraverted public questions, inasmuch as these are matters . . . very likely to impair or destroy its usefulness'.[32]

A further attempt to deal with the issue was made in 1855 but, again, stalemate was the result. As the furore of the '50s subsided, the EIS confined itself to taking very specific and restricted positions on proposed educational legislation. Indeed by the late 1860s, when legislative action was again being considered, *The Scotsman* was able to express criticism of the Institute's attitude to the national education question, on very different grounds from previous critics:

> They have never grasped or even looked at the question in its entirety, or in its general principles, but have merely kept 'pottering' over it with a general inclination to conclude that whatever is, is right, and that whatever is new is doubtful.[33]

In fact, the EIS was quite forthright in its support of the 1869 Bill and its opposition to the 1871 and 1872 Bills. But the newspaper's sense of the schoolmasters' growing caution and timidity on such matters was not far off the mark. Certainly, those characteristics were very different from those the founders of the EIS had hoped for.

Despite a remarkable degree of sophistication, vigour and unity, the leaders of the schoolmasters of Scotland in the nineteenth century were unable to attain either of their goals of professional independence or political influence. Although this was precisely the period in which a number of other occupations claimed and received such power and status — including the crucial power to license — even their allies on the national education question were not prepared to support such recognition for teachers. Ironically, by 1872, the schoolmasters in Scotland had suffered a dramatic reduction in their traditional independence, security and influence.

Until 'teacher militancy' arose in a new guise and context in the mid-twentieth century, the experience of Scottish teachers after 1872 was much like that of their counterparts in England and North America. Instead of the *reality* of professional power and status, Scottish teachers — like the rest — had to content themselves with the lofty but insubstantial *rhetoric* of professionalism. Only when a new analysis of the occupational realities of teaching emerged — combined with a more searching scrutiny of the concept and values of 'professionalism' itself — did teachers generally begin to develop other forms and means of collective action. Nonetheless, the unique experience of nineteenth-century Scottish teachers in their struggle to maintain and strengthen their traditional position remains a remarkable and illuminating episode in the history of the teaching occupation.

NOTES

1. A Layman (S. S. Laurie), *The Present Aspects of the Scottish Education Question* (Edinburgh, 1856).

2. *Parliamentary Papers, 1837-38*, VII, pp. 437-450; and *1854*, LIX, pp. 65-244.

3. A Parochial Schoolmaster, *A Plea for the Parish Schools* (Edinburgh, 1867).

4. Milligan, W., *The Present Aspect of the Education Question in Scotland* (Edinburgh, 1857).

5. Lewis, George, *Scotland a Half-Educated Nation: Both in the Quantity and Quality of Her Educational Institutions* (Glasgow, 1834).

6. Bryce, James, 'The Minutes of Council Viewed in Connection with Scottish Conditions', National Association for the Promotion of Social Science, Transactions, 1861.

7. Bryce, James, *Address at Annual Meeting of EIS*, 1853. James Bryce was a member of a remarkable Scottish-Ulster schoolmastering family. His eldest brother, Reuben John, was a Glasgow graduate, the minister of a Presbyterian church in Belfast and, simultaneously, the headmaster of the Belfast Royal Academy for 54 years. R. J. Bryce wrote and lectured on educational topics — he was the main speaker at the founding meeting of the Ulster Teachers' Association in 1840 — and received an LL.D. from Glasgow. Another brother, Archibald, was the rector of the Edinburgh Academy. James himself won the Blackstone Prize for Greek at Glasgow and taught science and mathematics at the Glasgow High School. He was an eminent geologist, a Fellow of the Geological Societies of Dublin and London, and an LL.D. from Glasgow. He was president of

the EIS in 1852-53. His son was the well-known late nineteenth-century scholar and Liberal politician, James Viscount Bryce.

8. Myers, J. D., 'Scottish Nationalism and the Antecedents of the 1872 Education Act', *Scottish Educational Studies*, Winter, 1973.

9. Moncrieff, James, *An Educational Retrospect* (Glasgow, 1886).

10. George Ferguson was a graduate of Edinburgh University and the Classics Master at Edinburgh Academy. In 1847 he was appointed Professor of Humanity at King's College, Aberdeen, which later awarded him an LL.D. Despite his university position, he remained EIS secretary until the 1860s.

11. Belford, A. J., *Centenary Handbook of the Educational Institute of Scotland* (Edinburgh, 1947).

12. Dr. Leonhard Schmitz was a Ph.D. in Classics from Bonn who had come to Britain in the 1830s and who, in 1845, had been appointed Rector of the Edinburgh High School, a post he held for 21 years. In the 1860s, Schmitz held university posts in England. He was a Fellow of the Royal Society and received LL.D.s from Aberdeen (1849) and Edinburgh (1886).

13. *Edinburgh Evening Courant*, September 20, 1847.

14. *Ibid.* William Knox was an outstanding example of the parochial schoolmaster. He began teaching in Yetholm at age 16 and was parish schoolmaster in St. Ninians, near Stirling, for fifty years. His school and students had a high reputation and he was an influential figure in the community. He was treasurer of the Burgh and Parochial Schoolmasters' Association and of the Scottish School Book Association for many years and was elected the second president of the EIS. Glasgow University awarded him an LL.D. in 1863.

15. Candlish, R., *Speech on the Sustentation of Schoolmasters* (Edinburgh, 1846).

16. *The Scotsman*, September 24, 1850.

17. Robertson, A. D., *Presidential Address*, 1854.

18. *The Scottish Educational and Literary Journal* was a serious, well-written publication, but its expense proved prohibitive after four years.

19. EIS, *Proceedings*, 1848.

20. EIS, *Proceedings*, 1848.

21. A Royal Charter was granted in 1851. It merely noted that one of the functions of the EIS was to assess and signify the acquirements of teachers but compelled no one to notice or require this.

22. Bryce, James, *NAPSS Transactions*, 1861.

23. EIS, *Minute Book*, 1855.

24. Gloag, James, *Presidential Address*, 1856.

25. Burton, R., *Presidential Address*, 1859.

26. EIS, *Minute Book*, 1859.

27. Belford, *op. cit.*, p. 87.

28. The principal of St. Andrews was the first president of the NEA; the vice-presidents included two provosts (mayors), two MPs, two professors, and two teachers — Leonhard Schmitz and another prominent burgh teacher.

29. *The Scotsman*, May 17, 1854.

30. EIS, *Minute Book*, 1853.

31. Bryce, James, *Presidential Address*, 1853.

32. EIS, *Minute Book*, 1854.

33. *The Scotsman*, September 22, 1869.

5

A Reinterpretation of 'Payment by Results' in Scotland, 1861-1872

Thomas Wilson

THE period 1861-1872, although crucial to an understanding of future educational developments in Scotland, has largely been ignored by historians. This essay attempts to remedy the deficiency, and cast new light on the period. It is divided into three parts. In the first, the extent of our present understanding of the background to payment by results is critically examined. It is suggested that the general histories of education offer an inadequate account, and so the second section aims to give a clear and accurate narrative of events. The third section is critical and interpretative: drawing on the primary evidence available, it attempts to explain why payment by results, destined for Scotland in 1861, was delayed for over ten years. It is concluded that the long delay in implementation cannot be seen solely in terms of education. Rather, a complex series of political and economic factors hold the key: these varied in force at different times and involved such considerations as the fate of alternative legislation and the power of the Scottish MPs.

1

The Scotch Code, 1873, introduced payment by results to Scotland. Its arrival had not been altogether unexpected. The Revised Code of 1862, which introduced payment by results to England and Wales, had been intended to apply to Scotland. However, its suspension in 1862, and only partial implementation in 1864, had led teachers to hope that Scotland might be spared the full rigours of its effects. The 1872 Education Act, however, finally ensured that Scotland too would receive Privy Council grants only by 'results'. Thirty years later, one of the Scottish inspectors stated in his memoirs that the Revised Code

> . . . even in its merely formal application to Scotland did great harm, and retarded, if it did not in some important respects actually throw back Scottish education by ten or twelve years.[1]

Judgements of this sort were anticipated in the 1860s. It was a time when teachers and their organisations, as well as other individuals and groups with a legitimate interest in education, were most vocal in their views. The Revised Code produced such opposition that education was discussed at public meetings, brought to the attention of Members of Parliament and the Government by petitions and deputations, and before the public in pamphlets and the press. Yet, Scottish historians of education have generally ignored the years 1861-1872, giving more attention to the post-1872 period when payment by results was actually in operation. This is perhaps not surprising, but in many respects the uncertain years preceding the arrival of the Code were formative ones. Individual examination in the 3 R's, based on the Standards, had been introduced. The stress on the basics had been established, and the teacher's competence, if not his salary, was measured by his results. Similarly, two books, still in use today, made their first appearance in 1864 — the attendance register and the school log book. Again, this was a period of growing power for the Inspectorate, a body which continues to exert considerable influence on the shape of education: it could even be argued that, as a result of this increased power for the Inspectorate, the development of teaching as an autonomous profession was hindered, since teachers became more subject to external direction. Behind all of these developments can be detected the concept of 'efficiency', which was more fully expressed in the Revised Code itself.

No detailed study of the Revised Code in relation to Scotland has yet appeared, although the Code and its principle of payment by results have been thoroughly investigated in their application to England.[2] For information on the period 1861-1872, therefore, the general histories of education are the only readily available source. Unfortunately, critical discussion or analysis of events is not a feature of these histories: they aim only to give a narrative account of events and it soon emerges that important questions connected with Scotland and the Revised Code have never been asked, let alone answered. More fundamentally, even by their own narrative standards, the value of the general histories is somewhat dubious. An examination of Strong,[3] Morgan,[4] Knox[5] and Curtis[6] reveals that, not only do they fail to consider the Revised Code from the Scottish point of view, but, by apparently regarding Scotland in the same light as England in relation to the Code, they also fail to give an accurate record of events.

Curtis may be excused a lack of detailed treatment in a chapter lasting 43 pages, in which he relates Scottish educational developments from Columba to the 1872 Act. Yet, when his object is to give correct factual information, and he writes:

> The Revised Code was intended to apply to Scotland. The parochial schools, with a wider and more liberal tradition than the English elementary schools, resented its introduction bitterly, and in 1864 the most injurious part of the Code, payment by results, was withdrawn . . .[7]

he fails even in this aim. The reader, knowing from Curtis's own account that the Revised Code was introduced in England in 1862,[8] would assume that Scotland's grants had been subject to the Code for almost two years, rather than the actual period of six weeks.

Knox is equally unreliable:

> In view of widespread protests it was agreed in June 1864 to suspend the financial provisions of the Revised Code pending the appointment of a Royal Commission to inquire into the schools of Scotland.[9]

The unwary reader is again left with the impression of the Code in operation from 9 May, 1862[10] until June, 1864. He might pause, however, to wonder why the 'breathing space' which Knox refers to later in his account lasted for ten years — assuming that he realised it ended in 1872.

James Scotland, writing in 1969, is more accurate in his account, but he leaves a number of questions unanswered. He says, 'In Scotland it [the Code] was introduced on 4 May, 1864.'[11] No mention is made of the fact that it was originally intended for Scotland in 1861, or why it did not come into effect at that time. After a brief account of the provisions of the Code, James Scotland states:

> In Scotland, however, it did not come into full operation. A Circular issued on 11 June, 1864, five weeks after the introduction of the Code, suspended it as far as payments were concerned until 30 June, 1865, though individual examination was retained. Thereafter this suspension was renewed annually . . . that is until 1872.[12]

Unlike his predecessors, Scotland draws on the Minutes of the Committee of the Privy Council on Education to explain why these annual suspensions occurred:

> To allow time for measures to be taken upon the Report of Her Majesty's Commissioners appointed to inquire into the schools in Scotland.[13]

Alternative explanations, based on a wider range of evidence, are not considered. Clearly the various changes of policy and the reasons behind them invite closer examination. A necessary preliminary, if the errors of the general histories of education are to be avoided, is a careful and detailed narrative of the events leading up to the introduction of payment by results.

2

In 1833 a Radical MP, J. A. Roebuck, proposed a Bill to set up a Committee to inquire into the means of establishing a national system of education for England and Wales. The Church of England and the Nonconformists resented government interference in elementary education, which, between them, they largely controlled, and religious controversy ensured that the Bill failed. This attempt, however, prompted State intervention in education, for, one month later, Parliament voted £20,000 for the provision of schools in England and

Wales. The religious difficulty was avoided, for the aim was simply to aid the work of the two main voluntary societies: the National Society and the British and Foreign School Society,[14] each of whom received £10,000. In 1834 the scheme was extended to Scotland, and £10,000 was made available to the Church of Scotland.

In 1833, therefore — the year of Roebuck's proposed Bill — State aid to education was established. As a result, however, of the entrenched position of the religious bodies, the principle behind state intervention in elementary education was laid down: namely it was an aid to local voluntary effort and that alone. Thus, unless one-half of the cost of building a school was met by local subscription, no grant would be made. Parliamentary grants, therefore, would only stimulate local effort. They were not a substitute for it.

Despite the existence of these guidelines, there was mounting criticism of the system of grants in Parliament, and a Committee of the House was set up to inquire into State aid to the voluntary societies. It reported in 1838, and urged that more schools and teachers were needed, and proposed an increased grant to the voluntary societies. The Whig Government, however, was not satisfied with the voluntary system, and wished to exercise greater control over the use of the Parliamentary grants. As a result Sir John Russell introduced a plan for education. This provided not only for a special Committee of the Privy Council, with the Lord President as Chairman, to administer the grant, which was now also to aid the maintenance of the schools, but also for government control in the form of inspection of these aided schools.

The real work of the Committee of Council of Education was left to its Secretary, Dr. Kay (later Sir James Kay-Shuttleworth[15]) and the new inspectors. Kay-Shuttleworth knew that little improvement in elementary education would come about without the consent of the religious bodies, who guarded their control over their respective schools jealously. Unless they accepted the grants, little could be achieved educationally, while if they did not accept government 'interference' in the form of inspection, there would be no grant from the Committee. As a result Kay-Shuttleworth worked closely with the Churches. A concordant with the Church of England ensured that inspectors would only be appointed after consultation with the Archbishop, and soon after the Nonconformists gained a similar right. Thus, denominational inspection was established in England in 1840. In Scotland the position of the Established Church with regard to education was respected, and the Education Committee of the General Assembly was consulted by the Committee of Council.[16] The method of inspection also reflected the importance of the religious bodies, for it was based on co-operation and advice, rather than direction.[17]

The early inspectors' reports showed that the standard of elementary education was generally poor. Kay-Shuttleworth was keen to improve the situation, and, under him, grants were made available for school furniture, teaching apparatus and teachers' residences. Gradually, therefore, the condition of the schools was improved. One important area, however, had not been tackled — the quality of the teachers.

Impressed by the schools in Holland and Switzerland, and with the Normal Schools of Stow and Wood in Scotland, Kay-Shuttleworth was determined to improve the quality of teaching, by replacing the mechanical monitorial system with the class system. His proposals, approved by the Committee of Council, led not only to a rapid increase in the Parliamentary grant but also to an extension of state intervention in education.

The Annual Grants, 1846-1861

The minutes of 1846 set out the details of the new provisions.[18] By these, managers of schools were allowed to select boys and girls of 13 years of age, and apprentice them to be trained in the art of teaching. Their own instruction was to progress at the same time, since the teacher had to give them one and a half hours' tuition each day. The State paid the apprentices' stipend, and continued to do so for five years, provided they passed an annual examination, set by the inspector. These pupil-teachers could win, by public examination, a Queen's scholarship to one of the Normal Schools under inspection. At the end of the period there, they would gain a Certificate of Merit. These certificated teachers had their salary augmented by the Government, the amount depending on the grade of the certificate. The teachers who taught the pupil-teachers had to be certificated and were paid by the State for teaching them. Teachers already in service were encouraged by the inspectors to sit and gain the certificate. The financial advantage meant that many availed themselves of this opportunity.

Thus the Government hoped to obtain not just more teachers, but a better-trained force. To facilitate this, the Normal Schools, which had previously only received building grants and had been dependent on fees, now received money for every Queen's scholar. Hence the Minutes bearing on elementary and Normal Schools, which had previously been kept apart, were practically merged, and the two institutions were seen as different parts of the same system.

With increased grants, the power of the Inspectorate over the schools increased, although the guiding principle was still encouragement rather than direction. This was reasonably successful, for poor organisation and unsatisfactory methods in schools began to disappear, as the inspectors' reports in the post-1846 period show. Whether these improvements were due to the guidance of the inspectors, or the fact that schools which failed to fulfil the regulations were not accepted for grants, is open to argument.

Throughout this period, the State continued to encourage self-help. Augmentation grants and grants to pupil-teachers were dependent, not only on certain conditions as to school premises, but also on voluntary effort raising two-thirds of the sum, and of this two-thirds, one-half had to be in the form of local subscriptions, excluding fees.

In Scotland, the Annual Grants did not come into effect until 1848. The parish schools were relatively slow to enter the system. This may have been due to the fact that the schools could not meet the Committee of Council's conditions, or that they were unable to take advantage of the grants because of the clauses insisting on voluntary effort. The growth of Free Church schools, however, caused the number applying for grants to rise.

The Education Office also increased in power. An Order of Council of 1856 raised the Committee to the status of an Education Department. With this increased power, the need for greater accountability was highlighted. Since the Lord President, Earl Granville, sat in the Lords, a new position, that of Vice-President, was created. This was a political appointment, the holder being a member of the Cabinet, and a member of the House of Commons. Thus the Vice-President was accountable to the House for the working of the Education Department.

During the 1840s, although reports from the English inspectors had shown improvements in organisation and methods, they had also highlighted certain weaknesses in the elementary schools. Irregularity of attendance and the early leaving age of many pupils came to light, as did the disturbing fact that children in poor but populous areas were receiving no education, or a very limited one. These areas were excluded from participation in the Government grants, because they were unable to find local subscribers prepared to put up the required two-thirds and fulfil the other conditions which governed the issue of grants. It was to aid these schools, while encouraging more regular attendance, that a Capitation Minute was introduced. The grant introduced by this Minute did not, however, extend to Scotland.

By a Minute of 2 April, 1853,[19] the Committee of Council gave a capitation grant to schools, ranging from 3/- to 6/-, depending upon the number and sex of the scholars, providing that they had attended 176 days in the year ending on the date of inspection. The managers were required, however, to spend at least seven-tenths of the whole school income, although the strict requirements, pertaining to school buildings, were somewhat relaxed. One condition, however, still operated to exclude the poorest schools. To be eligible, the income of the school in the preceding year from endowments, subscriptions, collections and school pence (fees), had to amount to 14/- per scholar in schools for boys and 12/- for girls, without including the annual value of the teacher's house or other school buildings. The result was that not only were poor areas still unable to apply, but a large number of schools, already receiving all the grants available, took advantage of the Minute. As a result, the capitation grants, which had been designed to aid poor schools, were abused. Indeed, not only did schools receiving a sufficient amount of Government money apply, but managers took advantage of the clause which allowed seven-tenths of the capitation grant to be recognised as equalling voluntary contribution. They, therefore, substituted the money from the capitation grant for contributions which should have been paid out of their own pockets. Thus a minute, which was enabling, not obligatory, and intended for needy schools, was used as a substitute for local effort in wealthy areas. What was more, it became apparent that the whole system of Privy Council grants was based on two conflicting principles — one requiring voluntary effort, and the other almost encouraging its absence.

By 1860, Government grants had increased tremendously, both in terms of money and range. They took two principal forms — grants to Normal Schools, including the Queen's scholarships, and grants to elementary schools, under their various headings of book and apparatus grants, augmentation grants to the teacher, stipends to pupil-teachers, and gratuities to the masters for teaching pupil-teachers. So complex, in fact, were the conditions governing the issue of grants, that, to simplify the regulations and clarify the position, a codification was drawn up in 1860, covering grants to both elementary and Normal Schools.

The volume and scope of the grants had so increased that, from £20,000 in 1833, the Education budget had risen to £668,000, when Robert Lowe took office in 1859. When so much money was spent, the deficiencies in the education provision, revealed by the annual reports of the Committee of Council, led to criticism of the whole system in Parliament. There was, however, concern over the number of illiterates in the country, and the debates in Parliament show that many MPs wished a greater proportion of the population to gain at least the moral and religious benefits of elementary education.[20] At the same time, there was a great and increasing demand to cut the expenditure on education, particularly after the costly Crimean War. To attempt to solve these seemingly irreconcilable objectives, a Royal Commission was appointed in 1858.

The Newcastle Commission, 1858-1861

The Royal Commission, under the Chairmanship of the Duke of Newcastle, was set up on 30 June, 1858. Its remit was 'to inquire into the present State of Popular Education in England and to consider and report what measures, if any, are required for the Extension of sound and cheap elementary instruction to all classes of the People'.[21] The Report was issued in 1861, and, on the whole, it was optimistic. It praised, for example, the certificated teachers, and stated that they were much superior to their uncertificated predecessors. Trained teachers were said to be more efficient than untrained, and the pupil-teacher system was also commended. No large district, the Commissioners said, was entirely without schools, and the majority of children were in attendance at some point.

The Commissioners were men of their time, and therefore accepted that children would leave school at an early age, to meet the needs of the labour market — boys when they were 10 or 11, and girls, at the most, at 12 years. Given this, however, too many pupils left school unable to read, write or count. The teachers, despite the advances that had been made, were partly at fault. Inspectors in their reports, and the observations of the Assistant-Commissioners, had shown that the younger and weaker pupils were neglected, and too much higher work was done at the expense of the 3 R's. Irregular attendance also contributed to this disappointing result of twenty years of state-aided popular education.

The Commissioners, therefore, made recommendations to improve the education of boys and girls, during the years when it was expected that they would be at school. It was proposed that the grant system should be twofold. Grants should be paid by the State according to the attendance, staffing and general efficiency of the school. A second grant was to depend on the number of children who passed a yearly examination in reading, writing and arithmetic, and would come from an Education rate, levied locally. Thus State aid would be simplified. There would now be a unified grant system, based on attendance and the inspectors' report, rather than the numerous grants which had been previously in operation. This would reduce the workload of the Education Office by simplifying the distribution of grants.[22]

The local grant, the Commissioners claimed, would ensure that the basics were attended to, and the State maintenance grant would be an incentive to attendance. Furthermore, the grant earned by 'results' would aid those areas which had gained little in the past from the State, since local voluntary effort had not been sufficient for them to qualify.

The Commissioners highlighted the two conflicting principles of State aid, namely, demanding voluntary effort on the one hand, and almost discouraging it on the other, by the system of capitation grants. As has been shown, by demanding voluntary subscription, poor areas suffered, while wealthy areas, quite able to provide for themselves, exploited the system. In effect, the annual grants from 1846 had failed to deal with the worst areas and were extremely expensive into the bargain. These problems, the Commissioners hoped, would be solved by their two-tier system of grants.

The Government considered the recommendations made by Newcastle, and produced a revision of the 1860 Code. This was outlined by the Vice-President of the Committee of Council, Robert Lowe, in the House of Commons on 11 July, 1861, and issued by a Minute of 29 July.[23]

The Revised Code

The Revised Code abolished grants for school books, maps and apparatus, teachers' augmentation grants, pupil-teachers' stipends, scholars' capitation grants, teachers' pensions and certain payments to training colleges. These were replaced by an annual grant for each school, payable to the managers.

The managers were to make their own bargain with the teachers in respect of salary. However, the Privy Council stipulated that these teachers had to be certificated, and that one pupil-teacher or probationer had to be engaged for every thirty pupils in average attendance above the first fifty. The pupil-teachers' stipend was also to be paid by the managers, and the contract of indenture was to be between manager and apprentice.

The new capitation grant was to be at the rate of 1d. for each attendance of the child above 100 attendances (or 50 complete days), and each child, for whom the grant was claimed, had to be present 16 times within 31 days, prior to inspection.

To remedy the defects of irregular attendance and poor teaching, the principle, on which the grant would be given, was to be payment by results. One-third of the grant claimed per pupil could be lost if the scholar failed to satisfy the inspector in reading, writing and arithmetic. No child who failed to make the required number of attendances could be presented, and absence on the day of the examination meant forfeit of the grant for that child. The examination was to be based on a Table of Standards, and this was laid down by age. The total amount paid, however, could not exceed the fees and subscription together, or 15/- per child.

Unless the inspector was satisfied with the state of the school building, materials and the quality of instruction in subjects over and above the 3 R's, deductions from the grant earned could be made, at the rate of not less than one-tenth and not more than one-half of the grant claimed. The grant to Normal Schools was also considerably reduced by the new Minute.

The reaction to the Revised Code was immediate and considerable. The Code, stated Kay-Shuttleworth,[24] although purporting to be the result of the Report of the Royal Commission, was totally unrelated to its recommendations. The Commission had recommended two grants: one a maintenance grant given by the State to aid schools, the other raised by a local rate, to be earned by results in the 3 R's. As a result of the supposedly religious difficulty, which an Education rate would cause, this scheme was dropped. However, the proposal that some of the grant should be earned by results was retained, and indeed extended, so that effectively no grant would be forthcoming from the Committee of Council without its being earned. Thus the principle on which all former grants had been given, namely distributing public money to pay for the means of education, was to be replaced by a system which paid only according to results. To equate educational results with achievement in the 3 R's, maintained Kay-Shuttleworth, was not education in the true sense. Substituting an individual examination for general inspection, and making the grant totally dependent on this, would bring disastrous results. All that had been achieved in twenty years would be sacrificed, if the Code was implemented, since its sole object was to cut the education budget. For him it was not a revision, but a 'disastrous revolution'.[25]

In one sense Kay-Shuttleworth and the other critics of the Code were wrong in regarding it as a revolution. The Revised Code did not invent payment by results, for this had been attempted when the first capitation grant had been made in 1853, but soon abandoned, since uniformity of inspection seemed impossible to attain. Thereafter the inspector recorded only an indication as to how well the subjects were taught.[26] Grouping by age, instead of by class, had also been part of this earlier scheme. Indeed, the augmentation grant, the pupil-teachers' stipend, the award of the Queen's scholarship, as well as the certificate with its monetary value depending on the grade achieved, had all been awarded on the basis of payment by results.

The outcry, however, from educationists and inspectors in England against the Code, caused Lowe to postpone its implementation until 31 March, 1863, by a Circular addressed to inspectors on 25 September, 1861. So great was the outcry that the Government realised that concessions would have to be made before Parliament would approve the new Minute. Opposition to the Code from at least some MPs was considerable. Sir James Kay-Shuttleworth had argued in a letter to the *Daily News*[27] that, since the Code had never been discussed by the Committee of Council, there should be a Parliamentary inquiry into it. Lowe and Granville, therefore, were well prepared for criticism when they defended the Revised Code in the Commons and Lords respectively, on 13 February, 1862.

In the Commons, Lowe outlined the modifications which the Committee was prepared to make. Scotland, he stated, was to be exempt from the working of the Revised Code 'for the present'.[28] In England and Wales, children under six would not be examined, and a capitation grant of 1d. would be awarded per attendance after the first 200. The clauses, demanding that each scholar had to attend 16 days within 31 days before the inspection, were cancelled. In addition, the inspector had to be satisfied that the state of the school generally deserved the grant before he proceeded to examine the scholars individually in the 3 R's. Schools, however, would only need to employ one pupil-teacher for every forty (instead of thirty) scholars above the first fifty, or one certificated or assistant teacher for every eighty scholars. The withdrawal of grants to Normal Schools was also suspended.

These slight concessions did not abate Parliamentary criticism and the debate continued throughout March. A series of resolutions, moved in the Commons, led to a three-day debate, and Granville had equal difficulty in the Lords. Before any of the resolutions had been taken up, however, Lowe announced on 28 March that the Committee accepted certain of the proposed amendments. These further modifications were defined on 12 April.

A portion of the grant was to be paid, not on results, but on general inspection of the school only. Thus, each school could depend upon a maintenance grant with reasonable certainty. The grouping by age for the Standard examination was abandoned, and replaced by grouping by class. All pupils under six years, who had made 200 attendances, were to earn 6/6d. without being subject to an examination. Those over six would earn 8/-, subject to an examination in reading, writing and arithmetic. A reduction of 1/3d. would be made for every failure. However, before any grant could be earned, the inspector had to be satisfied as to the state of the buildings, had to ensure the register and log book were correct, and that other subjects, chief among them being religion, were being taught. If he was not satisfied, then the reductions, previously outlined, would operate. Reductions would also occur if the specified number of pupil-teachers or assistants had not been employed by the managers. The teachers were protected, however, by having the first claim on any grant earned, and the pupil-teachers the second.

Significantly, Lowe stated that further revisions of and alterations to the Code would be submitted to Parliament before any action was taken upon them. He clearly realised the strength of Parliamentary opposition to the Code and Parliament's sensitivity at the Government's apparent attempt, by use of a Minute, to ride roughshod over it. As a result of these modifications, those MPs opposed to the Code withdrew their resolutions, and it was finally accepted by Parliament on 5 May, 1862. A Minute of the Committee of Council of 9 May put the Revised Code into effect in England and Wales.

Scotland was still subject to the 1860 Code. A Minute of 21 March, 1863, however, extended the Revised Code to Scotland, with effect from 1 April, 1864, although new schools claiming the grant were to be subject to it from 30 June, 1863. A Minute of the same date also issued new regulations for Normal Schools, ensuring that those in Scotland as well as England and Wales were subject to payment by results.

In fact, payment by results did not come into effect in Scotland until the beginning of May 1864, since the reallocation of inspectors' districts was only completed by the end of April. The Code operated fully, however, for only six weeks, for on 10 June, 1864, the new Vice-President of the Committee of Council, H. R. Bruce, announced that a Royal Commission (the Argyll Commission) was to be appointed to inquire into the schools in Scotland. As a result, the Revised Code was suspended for one year. Payment, therefore, was still on the basis of the old Code, although individual examination, based on the Standards, was introduced as intended. This system continued, with further annual suspensions of the Revised Code in Scotland, until 1873. Following the Education (Scotland) Act, 1872, the Scotch Code, 1873, instituted payment by results.

3

Given the sequence of events that has been outlined, it is now possible to move on to consider the reasons for the differing treatment of Scotland and England. In particular, why was the introduction of payment by results to Scotland delayed by over ten years? It has been noted that the general histories are not especially helpful when it comes to matters of interpretation. There is, however, a specialist work which, while not primarily concerned with the Revised Code, does offer suggestions as to why it was not implemented in 1862 as intended — T. R. Bone's *School Inspection in Scotland, 1840-1966.*[29] Bone's approach is more analytical than that of the general histories and, since inspection was vital to the workings of the Code, his comments are of some interest.

After an explanation of the controversy in England which followed Lowe's proposed changes in the education grant, Bone turns to the reaction in Scotland:

In Scotland opposition to the Code was very strong . . . and separate consideration was demanded on two special grounds.[30]

These were educational arguments peculiar to Scotland. One was the tradition of the poor but able boy going straight to the University from the parish school, and the other was the oft-stated claim that in Scotland there was a social mix of gentry and poor in the one school. The clauses of the Revised Code, it was argued, would destroy these hallmarks of Scottish education. Educational arguments against the Code were also expressed in England but they were less nationalistic in character, and Bone states that the need for economy was so great that Lowe was able to defend the Revised Code in February 1862 with only a few concessions and modifications. In the same speech, however, Scotland was exempted from the workings of the Revised Code, for

> Lowe agreed . . . that this system should not be applied to Scotland until he had more information about education there, and the Scottish grants continued to rest on the Code of 1860.[31]

Hence, although the educational arguments of influential men like Sir James Kay-Shuttleworth and Matthew Arnold failed to stop the Revised Code in England, since the arguments for economy were stronger, Bone implies that Lowe acceded to the Scottish educational argument for separate treatment.

Bone does, however, qualify this view, adding that Lowe

> . . . was probably more ready to make this concession in the case of Scotland since payment based on the Revised Code would not have saved nearly as much there as in England, because there were no capitation grants for Scottish schools.[32]

Thus, Bone suggests that Lowe was prepared to accept the educational arguments for separate treatment for Scotland, since in terms of economy little saving would be achieved in applying the Revised Code to Scotland. How tenable is this view?

The educational argument for separate treatment

In his speech to the Commons on 13 February, 1861, Lowe gave a number of reasons for not extending the Revised Code to Scotland. The first point he made was his acknowledgement that the Newcastle Commission had not extended its enquiry to Scotland. Further, he stated, there were many differences between the two countries in the matter of education, and he therefore thought that it would be unwise to extend the Code to Scotland. It does appear, therefore, that Lowe decided not to implement the Revised Code for educational reasons. Before accepting this neat explanation, however, it seems wise to examine whether these arguments alone would have been likely to have convinced Lowe.

Certainly Lowe may have been impressed by the reasoning of the protests from Scotland. The Resolutions passed by the Free Church Teachers' Association, for example, clearly state what Lowe implied:

... the circumstances in which these new arrangements have been introduced form an injustice to the people, and especially to the educationists of Scotland, inasmuch as the Revised Code purports to be the result of the recommendations of the Royal Commissioners appointed to inquire into the state of Education in England and Wales. No such Commission has ever investigated into the working of the Privy Council grants in Scotland, and therefore no new arrangements ought to be forced upon this country until it be ascertained whether they are required.[33]

Similarly it argued that the Revised Code, by paying only for the 3 R's, would wreck Scottish education. Teachers would naturally concentrate on these subjects since they and they alone were the paying subjects. The higher subjects, and any teaching above the top level of the Table of Standards, would die out. Thus, the tradition of boys going to University straight from the parish school would be destroyed.

These appeals may have impressed Lowe, yet his own view of popular agitation, to be made so apparent in the lead-up to the 1867 Reform Act, suggest that they were unlikely to cut much ice. Indeed, when Parliament opened, numerous petitions from the elementary school teachers and Normal School lecturers in both England and Scotland were presented, and these continued to arrive up to and including 13 February, 1862. These, however, were not successful in achieving the withdrawal of the Revised Code in England.

It is, of course, possible to argue that the opposition in England did have some effect upon the Government, since Lowe suspended the introduction of the Code by a Circular of the Privy Council at the end of September 1861,[34] and indeed made concessions on 13 February, 1862. The danger in this argument, however, is to apply too closely the attitudes of the twentieth-century to the mid-nineteenth century. Parliament and the Governments of this period were well used to petitions. Indeed, if one accepts the achievements of Chartist agitation, as a representative example of the effect of the petition, its success was negligible.

The Circular of 25 September, 1861, is a more reliable guide to the Government's motives. It stated that the Code would be suspended until Parliament had time to consider it. Although the educational arguments of men like Arnold and Kay-Shuttleworth failed to stop the Code altogether, their political influence[35] ensured that neither Lowe nor the education office could ride roughshod over Parliament. Indeed, when one considers that the Government was in a precarious position in Parliament,[36] it becomes clear that both debate in the House and tactical concessions were essential.

Thus, in spite of Lowe's statement about the differences between England and Scotland educationally, and thus the need for separate treatment, one must be wary of accepting his explanation at face value since considerations of political strategy were also clearly involved. A deeper examination of Lowe's motives is necessary before we agree with Bone that Scottish educational arguments helped to secure Scotland's exemption from payment by results in 1862.

The economic argument for separate treatment

It is generally accepted that the Newcastle Commission, set up during the Derby Ministry of 1858-1859, was prompted by the rising cost of education.[37] The Palmerston-Russell Government of 1859-1865 was equally keen on economy. Gladstone again became Chancellor of the Exchequer, and followed a policy of retrenchment, exemplified by his Budget of 1860.[38] The Cabinet were generally of the same mind. Indeed, in spite of panic over French ambitions, they accepted Gladstone's objections to a proposed expenditure of £11 million on coastal defences. This shows the strength of demand for economy in public expenditure. Given this climate of opinion, increased expenditure on education was out of the question. In this the Government had public support. Income tax had risen in 1854 to pay for the Crimean War. The war won, economy was the priority.

When the Newcastle Commission was appointed, its remit implied, at least, that the cost of public education should be kept to a minimum.[39] Implementation of their proposals in their entirety, however, would have been unlikely to cut the cost. The Chairman of the Commission, writing to Lord Granville, made it clear that their recommendations would mean additional expense.[40] This clearly was a major factor in ensuring that the Commission's prososals were not accepted. Instead, the Code of 1860 was revised, with the aim of reducing expenditure.

Given this, it seems odd that the Revised Code was not applied to Scotland, as had been intended. Bone's economic explanation for Scottish exemption, which he adds to the educational one, rests on the fact that the capitation grant had never been applied in Scotland, and thus the saving which could be achieved by payment by results would be negligible. This implies that the capitation grants were at the root of the expense in England and that it was these grants which the Revised Code was designed principally to reduce.

However, an examination of the expenditure for 1862, when the grant was at its highest, is extremely revealing. Of the £813,441 expended: £121,627 was spent on augmentation of teachers' salaries; £301,826 on pupil-teachers; £106,451 on building and repairing elementary and Normal Schools; £101,865 on grants to training colleges; and £77,239 in capitation grants, the remainder being made up of inspection, administration and postage.[41] In terms of financial saving, therefore, the capitation grants were negligible. They were not the main cause of the high expenditure on education in England.

In 1862, expenditure by the Privy Council on Scottish education was just over £100,000 — one-eighth of total expenditure. It would appear unlikely that, at a time when retrenchment was so essential, Scotland would still be allowed to gain one-eighth of the total educational grant, when the grant in England was about to be cut by the Revised Code.

Yet, on 13 February, 1862, Lord Granville in the House of Lords, and Lowe in the Commons, both stated in their speeches, exempting Scotland from the Revised Code, that capitation grants had never applied there. This implies that the grants were an important element in the education expenditure, and this is clearly the interpretation that Bone has placed upon these words. It has been shown, however, that capitation grants were almost the lowest item of expenditure. Why, therefore, should both men stress these grants?

To appreciate this, it is necessary to refer once again to the principle upon which grants, from 1839, had been made. It will be recalled that from the outset grants were based on corresponding voluntary effort. Until 1853, this principle, of helping only those who could help themselves, had been adhered to. The grants were at the average rate of one-third of the local outlay on building and supporting elementary schools.[42] The principle was maintained during the 1840s as more grants were added. However, it became increasingly evident that schools in poor areas, because they could not raise the required sum locally, were excluded. It was to help these schools that a Capitation Minute was introduced in April 1853. A measure of voluntary local effort was, however, still required. Not only did this continue to exclude the very schools the capitation grant was supposed to aid, but, ironically, a clause of the minute also allowed managers of schools in wealthy areas to claim seven-tenths of the grant as equivalent to voluntary contribution. This meant that government money was being used as a substitute for local effort. The two conflicting principles on which the system was administered — the one requiring voluntary effort, the other almost encouraging its absence — were subsequently criticised by the Newcastle Commission.[43]

When the Commission's report was considered by the Government, Lowe seized upon this abuse of the principle upon which all grants had been supposedly made, namely as an aid only to local voluntary effort. It was of little importance to him that the capitation grant was the smallest element of expenditure; what was of importance was that its abuse was a damning indictment of the whole system of grants hitherto in operation. The capitation grant had positively reduced local effort, while failing to extend public education to those areas where it was most needed. Thus Lowe had a concrete example of expensive waste with which to attack the whole Privy Council system of grants:

> Hitherto we have been living under a system of bounties and protection; now we prefer to have a little free trade.[44]

In this view he was not alone. It was the mood of the Government, of Parliament, of the country and of the time.

Lowe was a skilled politician; he used the abuse of the capitation grant to discredit the whole system of grants. Given the cost of educational provision, economy would have taken place in England, even if capitation grants had never existed. Clearly, therefore, the lack of these grants cannot explain Scotland's exemption from the Code.

The pressure for economy in the education budget from Gladstone, the Cabinet and Parliament meant that payment by results, or something like it, was almost inevitable. Given Lowe's own view of popular education and political economy, coupled to the prevailing belief of the time in securing value for money, it seems odd that one-eighth of the total Privy Council grant was to be allocated to Scotland, without such a guarantee. This suggests that Lowe had a very good reason for not implementing payment by results in Scotland.

Other possible reasons for Lowe's exemption of Scotland

One possible reason for Lowe's action is that the Government was forced to treat Scotland separately, from political necessity. It is clear from the evidence that important people did champion Scotland's cause. Bishop Terrot signed a letter to Lord Granville opposing the Code, on behalf of the Scottish Episcopal Church Society.[45] The Earl of Dalhousie also objected to details, if not the entire Code. However, it is unlikely that this would have swayed the Government. What was politically of more importance was that a number of Scottish MPs supported the claim for separate treatment. This is significant, for, in political terms, Scotland was powerful. Given the precarious position of the Palmerston-Russell Government, its survival depended as much upon the forty Scottish Liberal MPs as upon the support of the Radicals in Parliament.[46]

There is, however, no evidence to suggest that the Scottish Liberal MPs, or even a group of them, threatened to vote with the opposition unless Scotland was spared the Revised Code. Indeed, we know that Lowe had the support of the Duke of Argyll, who was in complete agreement with the Revised Code.[47] Thus, without hard evidence, it is not possible to argue that political motives influenced Lowe over Scotland. In applying the Code to England, where the Parliamentary battle was a hard one, the concessions he made in no way undermined the principle of payment by results. How, then, can Scotland's exemption be satisfactorily explained?

Lowe's speech in the House of Commons on 13 February, 1862, perhaps holds the answer. Speaking of the deputations from Scotland, he said:

> It had generally been said by those who approached us that there is no objection to revise the Code *per se*, but that Scotland is on the eve of being able to organise a system that will be more acceptable to the people. We have also been informed that the Lord Advocate is contemplating a measure on the subject.[48]

Here we have an indication as to Lowe's real line of thought. The deputations, which Granville and Lowe had received, had argued for a national system of education, based on the parochial system. This is stressed by the London correspondent of *The Glasgow Herald:*

> For some weeks past the opponents of the Revised Code have been mustering strongly in the metropolis and the Government have been met with numerous deputations from various parts of the country. For a week past there have been deputations from Edinburgh and Glasgow, having reference partly to the effects of the New Education Minute, but more particularly to a proposed extension of the system of education in Scotland.[49]

Leading Ministers and members of the Free and United Presbyterian Churches contemplated such a system of national education which would include all denominations, and *The Herald* continued:

> . . . the Lord Advocate is said to have approved of this scheme and promised to do his utmost to promote it.

Lowe was obviously aware of these developments, as was Granville. Both stated in their speeches that there was a general feeling of dissatisfaction with Privy Council grants in Scotland, and Lowe confirmed that the Lord Advocate was contemplating a measure for Scotland.

The proposed measure of national education, and what it would entail, was not lost on Lowe. If the Lord Advocate secured its passing, Scotland would gain less of the Privy Council grants. A national system, which would include all denominations, would be rate-supported, in some form at least. This solution was not open to Lowe in England, where rate support would have been politically impossible, because of the denominational problem which dogged every education question. Lowe clearly hoped — over-optimistically as it transpired — that this problem could be overcome in Scotland. To effect economy in England, Lowe needed payment by results. This was his original solution for Scotland, which consumed one-eighth of the education grant; but, if Scotland were to achieve a national system, then the saving might be even greater.

The Revised Code was devised principally for reasons of economy, and as such Scotland was included. It would undoubtedly have been applied there, had Lowe not been assured that a national system might come about. In his speech he reminded MPs of the success of the Parochial and Burgh Schools Act, of the last session.[50] At the same time, however, he was no doubt aware of the previous failures to achieve such a national system, and the tone of his concession to Scotland made it clear that the Revised Code was still in reserve to make the necessary economy, should the measure fail.

Lowe was a shrewd politician. His speech, justifying his decision not to extend the Code to Scotland, embodied the arguments which had poured out of Scotland in petitions, memorials and deputations against its introduction. None of these, however, was the chief motivating factor. At the core of his speech lies the real answer for his action — Lowe hoped for greater economy (as far as Scotland was concerned) than any system of payment by results could achieve.

At midnight on Tuesday, 18 March, 1862, the Lord Advocate proposed his Bill to improve the education system of Scotland. The stated aim was to assimilate the existing denominational system to the national parochial schools of the country. As *The Herald's* London correspondent had predicted, reaction in Scotland against the scheme was swift.

Even before the Bill had been printed, Dr. Cook, the Convener of the Church of Scotland's Education Committee, condemned it, because it gave no security for the teaching of religion, and would excite greater ecclesiastic animosity than before. The General Assembly unanimously resolved to petition Parliament against the Bill, which they 'viewed with deep regret and alarm'.[51] The Free Church and the United Presbyterians supported the Bill, but wanted important amendments. The Free Church suggested that all new schools should be constituted and managed popularly, as was provided in the Bill for district schools. Similarly the United Presbyterians, meeting in Edinburgh in April, passed resolutions objecting, among other things, to the government of rural schools by the minister and heritors.[52]

What runs through these Resolutions is fierce denominational interest and, in some cases, religious bigotry. Both the Free Church and the United Presbyterians objected to the special provisions for Roman Catholics and Episcopalians. Opposition, however, was not confined to the religions. The schoolmasters themselves were keen for every advantage. A Committee of Parochial Schoolmasters had an interview with the Lord Advocate in April, at which his Lordship promised that clauses, whose effects upon parochial schoolmasters were doubtful, would be amended. The Free Church teachers also pressed for amendments. In addition, the Convention of Royal Burghs voted overwhelmingly against the Bill, and recommended their Committee to take steps to prevent the Bill passing. County meetings displayed the same opposition.

As a result of all this, on 26 May, 1862, the Lord Advocate announced in the Commons that, because of the strength of opposition, he would not proceed with the Bill, but hoped to introduce a new one.

By October, however, it was clear that there was little hope of any new Bill meeting the wide range of opposition. At Greenock on 20 October, Murray Dunlop, addressing his constituents, said that the failure of the Lord Advocate's efforts to settle the education question took all heart and hope from him of a national system being achieved. He blamed his brethren of the Free Church, as much as any, for their failure to sacrifice some of their own special objects for the general good.[53] Thus, in spite of the Lord Advocate's warning that if the measure failed, then the Revised Code would be introduced, teachers, as well as denominational strife, had caused the withdrawal of the original Bill and the decision eventually not to proceed. The measure having failed, therefore, Lowe reverted to his original scheme, and the Revised Code was extended to Scotland by the Minute of 21 March, 1863.[54] Economy was now to be achieved by payment by results.

Yet, on 10 June, 1864, after payment by results had been in operation for just six weeks, the Revised Code was suspended for one year, and a Royal Commission set up to inquire into the state of education in Scotland. If the Privy Council grant had to be cut for reasons of economy, it seems odd that the Government should once again postpone the implementation of the Code. This poses the question why the Government was prepared to take this course of action in 1864. Again it is necessary to look at considerations of political tactics and strategy.

The Museum attributed the suspension of the Revised Code and the appointment of a Royal Commission for Scotland to the departure of Lowe as Vice-President of the Committee of Council. His retirement had been followed by the withdrawal of the Minute of 19 May, 1864 and 11 March, 1864, as well as the concessions for Scotland. As *The Museum* puts it:

> All this is very significant. Every one of these measures has been proposed and urged upon the Government while Mr. Lowe was in office. Every one of them had been stoutly refused. But no sooner is Mr. Lowe out of office than every one of them is granted. It is not difficult to see, then, where the obstruction lay.[55]

At first sight *The Museum's* account seems to be the likely answer to this *volte face* on the part of the Government. For example, the Lord Advocate had been approached before the close of the session of 1863 by some Scottish MPs,[56] requesting that a Royal Commission should inquire into the state of education before deciding whether the Revised Code was best adapted to Scotland's needs. This request was refused on 28 February, 1864, yet on 6 May, when a deputation of MPs again petitioned Granville for the appointment of a Commission and the suspension of the Code, they were given the impression that their request would be granted.[57] The interim had seen the resignation of Lowe, and thus *The Museum* seems correct in suggesting that it was the conciliatory nature of the new Vice-President, H. R. Bruce, which accounted for the concessions.

This view, however, tends to cast Lowe, not only as villain of the educational piece, but also as all-powerful as far as education policy was concerned. This was not the case, as the preceding analysis of the motives behind the introduction of the Revised Code shows. Clearly, Lowe was simply putting into effect the wishes of the Cabinet, and the Chancellor of the Exchequer in particular, for retrenchment in education expenditure. True, Lowe devised the means, but the policy was not his alone. One must, therefore, be cautious in casting Lowe in an all-powerful position over education policy. Indeed, no account which ignores the political developments of the time and fails to view educational matters against this background will stand close scrutiny. To understand why the Government was willing to submit to a Royal Commission in May 1864, after having rejected the same request in February, must involve an examination of the position of the Government in May 1864.

From the outset, the Palmerston-Russell Government had been dependent on Radical votes:

> To retain office they must propitiate the Bright party. They must throw them crumbs occasionally, smuggle little Radical clauses into otherwise good Bills . . .[58]

By 1864, the situation had become worse. The Tories in Parliament were equal in strength to the Whigs and Radicals put together. To alienate the Scottish MPs, therefore, could have proved disastrous for the Ministry. Scotland sent 53 MPs to Westminster, 40 of whom were Liberals, and it is possible, therefore, to suggest that the Government might have been anxious to prevent a defection from its Scottish supporters. For this reason, it may have been prepared to grant a Royal Commission and suspend the Code. If this were the case, why did the Government only agree to the request in May? It had already been approached, and had refused. This can perhaps be explained in terms of the difference in support for a Commission among the Scottish members on these two separate occasions.

Unfortunately the sources are weak on this strength of feeling. *The Museum*, reporting the February approach, quotes neither names nor numbers, saying only 'the Scotch members'.[59] This may suggest that all of the Scottish MPs made the request, but, had this been the case, it seems likely that this would have been reported. On the other hand, of the deputation that waited on Granville in May, *The Museum* stated that, 'almost every Scotch M.P. attended'.[60] Another piece of evidence lends weight to the implication of near unanimity. A letter to *The Museum* in January 1865, referring to the May meeting, stated that, 'all of our Scotch members, except one . . .' attended.[61] This shows considerable strength of feeling and, perhaps, a threat to the Government. In the same circumstances, it seems most unlikely that Lowe would have rejected the Scottish demands.

On Friday, 10 June, in reply to a question from Mr. Dunlop in the House of Commons, Mr. H. Bruce stated that a Commission, to inquire into education in Scotland, and, in particular, to consider if it was not possible to erect a national system on the foundation of the old parochial system, was to be appointed. Also, the Revised Code was to be suspended, until the inquiry had been completed, provided that this was achieved within twelve months. However, although the Revised Code was suspended as far as payments were concerned, and grants would continue under the 1860 Code, the individual examination of children in the 3 R's would continue.[62]

Conclusion

The evidence, on balance, tends to suggest that the Revised Code, which had been designed to apply to Scotland in 1861, was not implemented in the first instance because of a combination of political and economic reasons. A national system for Scotland would have achieved as much as the Code, in reducing Privy Council expenditure, and possibly more. Consequently, when this measure foundered on the rock of denominational strife, Lowe implemented the Revised Code to achieve the necessary economy. Its suspension in 1864 was brought about, mainly for political reasons, by a Government anxious for survival. The strength of feeling among Scottish MPs, that the country should have a Royal Commission before the Revised Code was introduced, was quite considerable by May 1864. The Government clearly acknowledged this, and responded. The suspension for one year was continued annually until 1872. This was because of delay on the part of the Argyll Commission reporting, and the increasing likelihood of a separate measure for Scotland coming about. When the Education (Scotland) Act, 1872, was passed, the Scotch Code introduced payment by results.

NOTES

1. J. Kerr, *Memories Grave and Gay* (Glasgow, 1902), p. 55.

2. The most recent account is J. F. Dunford, *Her Majesty's Inspectorate of Schools in England and Wales, 1860-1870* (Leeds, 1980).

3. J. Strong, *A History of Secondary Education in Scotland* (London, 1909).

4. A. Morgan, *Rise and Progress of Scottish Education* (Edinburgh and London, 1927).

5. H. M. Knox, *Two Hundred and Fifty Years of Scottish Education, 1696-1946* (Edinburgh and London, 1953).

6. S. J. Curtis, *History of Education in Great Britain,* 3rd edition (London, 1953).

7. *Ibid.,* p. 517.

8. *Ibid.,* p. 258.

9. Knox, *op. cit.,* p. 35.

10. *Ibid.,* p. 34.

11. J. Scotland, *The History of Scottish Education,* Vol. I (London, 1969), p. 236.

12. *Ibid.,* p. 236.

13. *Ibid.,* p. 236.

14. The National Society was founded in 1811 for 'promoting the education of the poor in the principles of the established church'. The British and Foreign School Society was founded in 1814 by the Nonconformists in opposition to the established church body.

15. Sir James Kay-Shuttleworth was the first Secretary to the Lords of the Committee of Council on Education until his retiral in 1849.

16. After the Disruption of 1843, of course, the situation changed. See A. L. Drummond and J. Bulloch, *The Church in Victorian Scotland, 1843-1874* (Edinburgh, 1975), especially chapters 1-4.

17. *Report of the Committee of Council on Education,* 1839-40.

18. *Report of the Committee of Council on Education,* 1846-47.

19. *Report of the Committee of Council on Education,* 1853-54.

20. D. W. Sylvester, *Robert Lowe and Education* (London, 1974), pp. 41-43.

21. *Hansard,* 11 February, 1858, cxlviii, col. 1248.

22. Lingen's evidence to the Newcastle Commission, *Newcastle Report,* VI, p. 552.

23. Letter from Lowe to Granville, 16 February, 1862. *Granville Papers,* P.R.O. 30/29, Box 18, Bundle 12, piece 7.

24. Letter to Earl Granville on the Revised Code of Regulations. Contained in the Minute of the Committee of Council on Education, 29 July, 1861.

25. *Ibid.*

26. D. W. Sylvester, *op. cit.,* pp. 49-56.

27. *Daily News,* 20 January, 1862.

28. *Hansard,* 13 February, 1862, clxv, p. 219.

29. T. R. Bone, *School Inspection in Scotland, 1840-1966* (London, 1968).

30. *Ibid.,* p. 55.

31. *Ibid.,* p. 56.

32. *Ibid.,* pp. 56-57.

33. 'The Revised Code', being the resolutions agreed to at the meeting of the Free Church Teachers' Association, 1861, p. 3.

34. *Report of the Committee of Council on Education,* 1861-62.

35. W. F. Connell, *The Educational Thought and Influence of Matthew Arnold* (London, 1950).

36. L. Woodward, *The Age of Reform, 1815-1870,* 2nd edition (Oxford, 1962), p. 171.

37. *Ibid.,* p. 181.

38. *Ibid.,* p. 179.

39. See note 21 above.

40. *Granville Papers,* P.R.O. 30/29, Box 18, Bundle 12, piece 3.

41. *Report of the Committee of Council on Education,* 1861-62.

42. *Newcastle Report,* I, p. 67.

43. *Ibid.,* p. 327.

44. Quoted in S. J. Curtis, *op. cit.*, p. 257.

45. *The Museum*, January 1862, p. 534.

46. D. G. Wright, *Democracy and Reform, 1815-85* (London, 1970), p. 63.

47. D. W. Sylvester, *op. cit.*, p. 46.

48. *Hansard*, 13 February, 1862, clxv, pp. 218-219.

49. *The Glasgow Herald*, 15 February, 1862.

50. W. H. Bain, '"Attacking the Citadel": James Moncrieff's Proposal's to Reform Scottish Education, 1851-1869', *Scottish Educational Review*, 10, 2 (1978), pp. 5-14.

51. *The Museum*, July 1862, p. 240.

52. *Ibid.*, p. 241.

53. *The Museum*, January 1863, p. 492.

54. *Report of the Committee of Council on Education*, 1863-64.

55. *The Museum*, April 1864, p. 119.

56. *Ibid.*, p. 39.

57. *The Museum*, June 1864, p. 114.

58. *Blackwood's Magazine*, February 1862, p. 250.

59. *The Museum*, April 1864, p. 38.

60. *The Museum*, June 1864, p. 114.

61. *The Museum*, February 1865, p. 38.

62. Individual examinations had begun at the start of May 1864, when the Revised Code had come into force in Scotland.

6

Science, Religion and Education: A Study in Cultural Interaction

Walter M. Humes

1

RAYMOND Williams has defined the theory of culture as 'the study of relationships between elements in a whole way of life'.[1] Elsewhere, he has commented on the immense complexity of the concept of culture and on the need to be aware of the variety of modes of analysis open to the investigator.[2] With regard to the study of Scottish culture, two related tendencies can be detected in conventional approaches to the subject.[3] The first is a heavy reliance on formal institutions as sources of cultural information: the institutions of the law, the church and education, in particular, are regarded as significant and distinctive embodiments of national customs, values and beliefs. And secondly, the culture of Scotland in general (including its institutions) is seen to be constantly under threat from England, which, by virtue of its economic and political dominance, tends to penetrate all aspects of Scottish life.

Behind both of these tendencies can be detected an understandable desire to defend the principle of Scottish autonomy. However, it can be argued that approaches which focus on institutions and which make constant reference to English cultural imperialism provide, at best, an incomplete account of Scottish cultural life. In the case of education, there are some grounds for thinking that the wish to defend the distinctiveness of the Scottish system has led to limited and, in certain respects, questionable interpretations of historical developments: this applies particularly to the modern period — that is, the period of mass compulsory schooling. The separate institutional apparatus for Scotland (the Scottish Education Department, the Scottish Certificate of Education Examination Board, the Consultative Committee on the Curriculum, etc.) tends to disguise the extent to which educational *thinking* has been shaped by a climate of ideas which is by no means peculiarly Scottish. In this essay one aspect of that wider climate of ideas — the influence of 'scientific' forms of enquiry and their extension to social fields such as education — will be examined in some detail, with particular reference to the second half of the nineteenth century. It will be necessary, as part of the exercise, to look at some of the cultural *interactions* (between science, religion and social reform) which Williams sees as crucial and which both amplify and qualify the institutional approach.

The question of the importance attributed to England's influence on Scotland's educational system requires slightly fuller preliminary comment. Those historians who do acknowledge some loss of Scottish cultural identity in education during the modern period explain it in terms of the spread of English (or British) models. James Kellas, for example, has remarked on the degree to which Scottish education has been 'subject to the assimilation process in British society' and has stated that 'the grounds for maintaining it as a distinct form seem less clear'.[4] Certain developments and pressures in the last three decades of the nineteenth century appear to illustrate the tendencies to which Kellas refers. Despite successive calls for a separate national system of state-supported education for Scotland by Sir James Moncrieff and others, full legislation was delayed until after the 1870 Act dealing with provisions in England and Wales.[5] Furthermore, the main deficiency of the Scottish Act of 1872 — its failure to provide properly for secondary education — could be seen as assuming an essentially English pattern of extensive private involvement in post-elementary education. The creation of a separate Scotch Education Department in 1885 did little to mollify nationalist fears. The Department was housed in London, not Edinburgh, and the Duke of Richmond described it disparagingly as 'simply a room in Whitehall with the word "Scotland" painted on the door'.[6] Moreover, the first Permanent Secretary was Henry Craik, himself a product of the Whitehall bureaucracy and later a Unionist M.P. who gave voice to imperialist sentiments.[7]

Developments at University level also seem to lend support to the view that there was a steady erosion of a distinctively Scottish tradition in the face of English pressures. The series of Royal Commissions on Scottish Universities (of 1826, 1858, 1876 and 1889) identified a number of problems regarding the quality and marketability of the traditional general degree — the age of entry to University, the initial qualifications of students, the range of subjects studied, the need for greater specialisation. G. E. Davie has written bitterly and eloquently on both the composition and the recommendations of the 1889 Commission, which, he suggests, found 'solutions' to these problems in Anglicising reforms:

> . . . the members were Scotch neither in feeling nor education, being aristocrats with Anglican sympathies and being connected with Oxford and Cambridge rather than the Scottish Universities.[8]

> . . . unrestricted entry was abolished, and matriculation examinations — of an excessive difficulty at that — were suddenly instituted so as to force up the school leaving age by two years and to favour the pupil of the good fee-paying school in which English values were influential. At the same time, English-style Honours, that other great object of University 'Reform', were at last introduced, and thus provision was made that students with high qualifications should be allowed to specialise from the start.[9]

Explanations along these lines are attractive, in that they appeal to Scottish sentiment, but they are also dangerous. It cannot be denied that they contain a measure of truth, especially when it is realised that there has always been a significant body of Anglicisers within Scotland aspiring to the values of the dominant partner in the Union. Nonetheless, such accounts carry the temptation to ascribe all change to some kind of English conspiracy. The sources of social and intellectual change are many and are not reducible to a single chain of cause and effect. To look only for cases of English 'influence' debases the character of Scottish culture and suggests a very restricted range of appropriate research strategies: comparing Scottish and English legislation; examining the careers of prominent figures in the formulation of policy (for example, Secretaries of State for Scotland and senior civil servants at the Scottish Office who were themselves educated at English public schools and/or Oxbridge); assessing the impact of London-based media on life north of the border. Although such approaches can sometimes yield valuable insights, they clearly have limitations: the conceptual categories they employ are, beyond simple matters of fact, decidedly crude (it is easy to identify a Scottish or English Act of Parliament, but what of a Scottish or English 'idea'?). In addition, they tend by their very nature to exaggerate differences (and the significance of the loss of such differences) and ignore similarities. And, most seriously, as a direct result of their very immediate concern with questions of nationalism, these approaches fail to take proper account of over-arching concepts and ideas which go beyond nationality and help to shape the perceptions and values of men and women in many different cultures. To make this point is not to argue for some kind of 'culture-free' analysis of the history of ideas — the practical expression of human perceptions and values will vary in different cultures, even though they may have some sources in common — but it is to suggest that conventional accounts of Scottish identity, centred on institutions, such as education, and relying heavily on the notion of England as predator, need to be supplemented (and counterbalanced) by an awareness of the part played by intellectual 'keywords' which have an international currency. One such keyword is 'science'.[10] A discussion of some of the interactions between science, nationalism and education will form part of the account that follows, but it will be conducted within a conceptual framework which makes reference to European and American developments, not just British ones.

These observations indicate the need to relocate the study of Scottish education within a broad cultural context which encourages an examination of the 'relationships between elements in a whole way of life'. Thus in the remaining sections of this paper a number of issues that are not mentioned (or treated very cursorily) in the standard histories will be introduced — the reception of evolutionary biology in theological and educational circles in Scotland; the idea of a science of education (which offered a philosophical basis for specialised developments in such fields as mental testing and the psychological study of childhood); the way in which science provided a justification for the extension of bureaucracy and professionalism in education. In shifting the focus of attention towards wider questions of intellectual history, there is, of course, loss as well as gain. The picture that will be presented will be less tidy than that conventionally offered and will leave some problems unresolved. An indication of the scope for further work and of alternative methods that might be employed will be given at the end. The present approach also carries a risk that the practical realities of education may be lost sight of amidst abstract (and perhaps speculative) interpretation. Equally, however, a proper understanding of educational practices requires that regard should be paid to their underlying rationale, not just their substance. The 'formal' curriculum of the history of Scottish education has received a fair amount of attention: this paper represents an attempt to look at some aspects of its 'hidden' curriculum.

2

To say that science has a strong claim to be regarded as one of the leading concepts of the nineteenth century — perhaps *the* leading concept — does not seem extravagant. Michael D. Biddiss, in Volume VI of *The Pelican History of European Thought*, cites Emil Du Bois-Reymond (1818-1896), the German physiologist, to support the contention that science was regarded as the basis of nineteenth-century 'intellectual security and material advancement':[11]

> If there is one criterion which for us indicates the progress of humanity, it is the level attained of power over nature . . . Only in scientific research and power over nature is there no stagnation; knowledge grows steadily, the shaping strength develops unceasingly.[12]

This Baconian emphasis on the *power* of science was amply illustrated at a material level. At the level of ideas, the positivist thinking of Auguste Comte (1798-1857), the French philosopher and sociologist, had done much to enhance the status of science (despite later criticisms by practising scientists). Comte offered a theory of human progress which suggested that every branch of human knowledge passed through three stages: a theological stage, which offers explanations of phenomena in terms of divine (or, at least, supernatural) intervention; a metaphysical stage, which relies on abstract, unverifiable accounts of experience; and finally a positive stage, in which attempts to explain final causes are abandoned in favour of a rational, empiricist accumulation of knowledge, based on observation, comparison and experiment. Comte's ideas gained wide currency among intellectual groups throughout Europe and, in Britain, were discussed eagerly by J. S. Mill and his circle, which included the Scot, Alexander Bain (1818-1903). Bain records in his *Autobiography* that positivism provoked considerable interest among the members of Aberdeen Philosophical Society, and his own application of scientific modes of thinking to the field of education will be considered later.[13]

Positivism claimed to offer an account of the whole of human knowledge, and this points to the need for a broad conception of nineteenth-century science. Although it was in the natural sciences that the greatest advances were made, scientific models and forms of enquiry gradually permeated nearly all aspects of human experience. Thus science in the nineteenth-century sense included not only the accumulated knowledge of 'the sciences' but also all systematically formulated knowledge, as well as the principles regulating the pursuit of such knowledge. Futhermore, to think 'scientifically' was, in an important sense, to develop a particular view of the world and of human nature — a view which, for example, valued rationalism above intuition and materialism above spirituality.

This extension of science to encompass nearly all forms of experience can be seen very clearly in the responses to Darwin's *Origin of Species* (1859). Darwin himself always expressed his theory of evolution in relatively cautious terms — though as Raymond Williams has pointed out, a social dimension, in the shape of the influence of Malthus's theory of population, was always inherent in Darwinism[14] — but in the hands of some of his followers, the language of evolution ('survival', 'fitness', 'selection') was used to support a whole range of theories, many of them of dubious 'scientific' character. Herbert Spencer (1820-1903), for example, though not a strict Darwinist (he was committed to his own brand of Lamarckian evolutionary thinking prior to the publication of *The Origin*), attempted to apply evolutionary principles to the whole of human knowledge, in a vast scheme of synthetic philosophy. J. D. Y. Peel observes:

> Darwin's theory is much more modest than Spencer's . . . Darwin's theory accounted for the secular transformation of each species by the mechanism of natural selection, while Spencer's attempted to explain the total configuration of nature, physical, organic and social, as well as its necessary process.[15]

Translated into social terms, Darwinism provided a seemingly authoritative basis for a wide range of (often conflicting) theories on such subjects as the role of the state in modern society, the economic consequences of capitalist enterprise, and the measurability of inherited intelligence.[16] The history of Social Darwinism can be viewed as a testimony to both the power and the false promises of science.

Scotland, no less than other European countries, was strongly influenced by the spreading ideology of science. Indeed, the contribution of many distinguished Scots — Kelvin, Simpson, Lyell, Clerk-Maxwell and others — to the long list of important scientific and medical advances in the nineteenth century was a considerable one. There was, however, one important area of Scottish cultural life which was potentially hostile towards science — that represented by the Presbyterian Churches. Evolutionary biology, in particular, by challenging the doctrine of a 'special creation' for man, seemed to pose a clear threat to Biblical authority and religious orthodoxy. Bearing in mind some of the bitter exchanges between scientists and theologians in

England, the Oxford debate of 1860 involving T. H. Huxley and Samuel Wilberforce (Bishop of Oxford) being the most notorious,[17] what was the Scottish response?

In *The Church in Victorian Scotland* Andrew L. Drummond and James Bulloch suggest that, in fact, the Scottish reception of Darwinism was generally favourable. They offer several reasons for this: the succession of distinguished Scottish geologists (most notably Lyell) who had helped to prepare the ground for Darwin; the impact on the popular mind of Robert Chambers' *Vestiges of the Natural History of Creation*, published anonymously in 1844, an unscientific but widely read work; the general receptivity of the newly literate to contemporary science; the acceptance of evolution by important public figures such as the Duke of Argyll.[18] The ascendancy of science over Biblical literalism was not entirely uniform, as the stance of Hugh Miller[19] and, later in the century, the fate of W. Robertson Smith[20] indicate, but it does represent the general trend. Drummond and Bulloch conclude: 'Scotland produced no violent repudiation of Darwin . . .'[21]

A good measure of the acceptability of evolutionary thinking in religious circles can be formed from the career of Henry Drummond (1851-1897), who was Professor of Natural Science at the Free Church College in Glasgow and author of *Natural Law in the Spiritual World* (1883) and *The Ascent of Man* (1894). Drummond is of particular interest in the context of the present study for three reasons: his direct involvement in education; his philanthropic work, which allied him to the reform rather than the conservative wing of Social Darwinism; and his influence outside Scotland.

The title of Drummond's inaugural address as Professor of Natural Science was 'The Contribution of Science to Christianity' and in it he says that theology 'borrows' the 'instruments' of science to improve man's understanding of divine creation: in particular, 'the scientific method and the doctrine of evolution' are two such instruments.[22] While the former insists on 'the value of facts, and the value of laws',[23] the latter demonstrates the indivisibility of the natural and spiritual worlds by supplying theology with 'a theory which the intellect can accept and which for the devout mind leaves everything more worthy of worship than before'.[24] Furthermore, the task of interpreting the Bible is greatly eased by evolutionary thinking:

> We see now that the mind of man has been slowly developing, that the race has been gradually educated, and that revelation has been adapted from the first to the various and successive stages through which that development passed. Instead, therefore, of reading all our theology into Genesis, we see only the alphabet there.[25]

Just as the version of creation contained in the Bible requires reinterpretation in the light of the theory of evolution, so too do seeming instances of God acting in a wrathful and vengeful way:

> For instance, we are told that the iniquities of the father are to be visited upon the children unto the third and fourth generations . . . We now know, however, that this is simply the

doctrine of heredity. A child inherits its parents' nature not as a special punishment, but by natural law.[26]

These statements indicate some of the ways in which theology assimilated the findings and methods of science. They represent a condensed form of the argument contained in the essays which make up *Natural Law in the Spiritual World*. This was the volume which gained for Drummond an international reputation: James W. Kennedy actually says that it was 'the most widely read religious book in the world in its day'.[27] Interestingly, it had its origins in a series of lectures delivered to a working men's class in Possilpark in Glasgow,[28] a fact which ties in with the philanthropic motives so strongly apparent in the later work, *The Ascent of Man*. As a student in Edinburgh, Drummond had worked for the College Missionary Society in the poorest parts of the city and became involved in the 'Great Mission' of Moody and Sankey to Scotland, which opened in Edinburgh on Sunday, November 23, 1873.[29] Later, he helped to further the work of the predominantly working-class youth organisation, the Boys' Brigade.[30] This altruistic concern for the underprivileged helps to explain Drummond's desire to stress what he regarded as a neglected element inherent in evolutionary theory. *The Ascent of Man* seeks to balance the struggles for the self—expressed in the notorious slogan 'the survival of the fittest' — with the struggle for the life of the others, evident most clearly in the instinct of parents to preserve their offspring. 'The Ascent of Man and of Society is bound up henceforth with . . . the diffusion of the Struggle for the Life of Others.'[31] Naturally, for Drummond, this aim is most likely to be achieved through the spreading of the Christian conception of Love — 'Love is the final result of Evolution. That is what stands out in nature as the supreme creation.'[32]

Drummond's influence extended in a number of directions. Most obviously, there was the effect of his ideas on the prospective teachers who were his students at the Free Church College. It has, in fact, been suggested that the College, which had started as a 'stronghold of conservatism', became, through the work of Drummond and others, 'a centre of liberal thought'.[33] A wider educational influence can be detected in the reception of Drummond's ideas in the United States, which he visited several times. Dorothy Ross has argued that *The Ascent of Man* was received with special enthusiasm by the psychologist G. Stanley Hall, a major figure in American educational reform in the 1890s and the child-study movement in particular.[34] Again, Drummond's connection with progressive Social Darwinism has led one commentator to draw a parallel with Peter Kropotkin's *Mutual Aid*, which, like *The Ascent of Man*, rejected crude 'survival of the fittest' interpretations of evolution and argued that 'nature, ethics and social policy, if properly understood, were governed by a single universal law'.[35] These international links cannot be explored more fully here, but perhaps enough has been said to suggest the limitations of viewing Scotland's intellectual history simply as an appendage to that of England.

J

The example of Drummond demonstrates very clearly the generally favourable response in Scotland to evolutionary biology. The fact that this receptivity related to a potentially problematic field of scientific enquiry, and occurred in the area of Scottish cultural life which might have been expected to show the greatest resistance, is of profound significance and indicates the high esteem in which explanatory models provided by science were held. It also indicates the extent to which science tended to dictate the terms by which accommodations were reached: religion had to adjust to science, rather than *vice versa*. The immense power and appeal of science lay partly in its seemingly universal character, its supposed objectivity, and the apparent access it gave to 'reality'. These attributed qualities (all of which have been seriously questioned by twentieth-century philosophers) were not seen as the property of a single class or nation seeking to impose or extend its control over others; they were the common property of mankind. The irony is that that claimed neutrality was probably a more potent instrument in reducing cultural variation than any overt oppression from other cultures. Customs, values and beliefs had either to accommodate themselves to the seemingly unchallengeable power of science or be cast aside as archaic. Viewed in this light, religious acceptance of the findings of science was an inevitable and necessary strategy, a way of retaining a measure of credibility, however diluted.

But it is important not to overstate the case. Science did not extinguish religion, in its Presbyterian or other varieties. This serves to remind us that cultural change always involves a complex series of adjustments, which generally take place over long periods of time. New knowledge is assimilated: it does not take over completely. In order to try to do justice to the processes at work, it will be necessary to return later to this difficult question of the interaction of science and cultural identity in Scotland.

One further qualification is required before proceeding. It has been noted that the philanthropic dimension in Drummond's thought had its roots in both science and religion — in science by way of a particular interpretation of the social implications of Darwinism, and in religion through the Christian conception of Love. However, the attempt to translate ameliorative impulses of this sort into practice involved contact with a whole range of other social and cultural forces — for example, class interests, political policies and bureaucratic structures. Efforts to pursue 'the struggle for the Life of Others' on any scale — for example, through mass education — had to be mediated through existing or developing social agencies and re-expressed in an acceptable rhetoric. The accommodations, assimilations and compromises that that process entailed will also form part of the argument that follows.

3

In 1864, James Donaldson, Rector of the High School in Edinburgh and later Principal of St. Andrews University, published an essay in which he addressed himself to 'two much-disputed questions: Is there a science of education? and is that science of use to education?'[36] He answered in the affirmative to both questions, though he was careful to qualify his remarks:

> When . . . we speak of a science of education, we do not mean to assert that education is itself a science, but that it is based on a science; that a set of laws which it is the business of a science to discover can be used in the work of education . . .[37]

In particular, 'physical education is an applied physiology and mental education is an applied psychology'.[38] With regard to the latter, Donaldson admits that the phenomena which bear on the 'science of the mind' will be 'infinitely more complicated than those of matter',[39] but he insists that this complication will not alter the basic principle. The specific practical advantages which he envisages ensuing from a scientific approach relate to educational methodology, the selection of curricula and the evaluation of results.

Donaldson's argument is interesting for a number of reasons. His own initial training was in the Classics and he might, therefore, have been expected to resist influences in education of a potentially mechanistic and anti-humanistic kind. In fact, he refers favourably to the insights given by Herbert Spencer, Alexander Bain and others into the process of mental development and calls for the establishment of 'Professors of the Science of Education'[40] in all the Scottish Universities. Furthermore, there are no hints of moral or religious reservations about the introduction of scientific modes of thought into arguments about the nature and purpose of education. Donaldson held strong Christian convictions and wrote extensively on theological as well as classical and educational topics, but science is not viewed as a threat to the religious purpose which Scottish education was expected to serve. In this respect, he can be seen as anticipating some of the later arguments of Henry Drummond.

Donaldson's approving references to Spencer and Bain relate mainly to their psychological writings, but their specifically educational work merits some attention. Spencer's collection of four essays (originally published as separate pieces between 1854 and 1859) appeared in 1861 as *Education: Intellectual, Moral and Physical:*[41] within twenty years it had been translated into more than fifteen languages and, as early as 1868, had formed the subject of a chapter in a history of educational ideas — R. H. Quick's *Essays on Educational Reformers*, which itself became a standard text for trainee teachers.[42] James Leitch's *Practical Educationists and their Systems of Teaching*, published in Glasgow in 1876, also devotes a chapter to Spencer and, although not entirely uncritical, the tone is generally favourable to his approach.[43]

What were the main features of that approach? First, a scientific study of human development is seen as a necessary preliminary to educational recommendations:

> . . . it is a fact not to be disputed, and to which we must reconcile ourselves, that man is subject to the same organic laws as inferior creatures. No anatomist, no physiologist, no chemist, will for a moment hesitate to assert that the general principles which are true of the vital processes in animals are equally true of the vital processes in man.[44]

This biological model applies to mental as well as physical qualities: 'education must conform to the natural process of mental evolution . . . there is a certain sequence in which the faculties spontaneously develop, and a certain kind of knowledge which each requires during its development'.[45] Knowledge is thus viewed in an evolutionary and utilitarian way, and Spencer actually classifies the whole of knowledge in hierarchical terms: 'those activities which directly minister to self-preservation' are placed at the top of the list, while 'those miscellaneous activities which fill up the leisure part of life, devoted to the gratification of the tastes and feelings'[46] are placed at the bottom. This involves a conflation of individual and social needs: Spencer assumes that because certain skills can be shown to be more vital than others in the maintenance of the human species, it necessarily follows that the education of every individual should reflect that differential utility. Nevertheless, despite gaps in the logic, the broadly scientific basis of Spencer's thinking comes across clearly.

Alexander Bain, Professor of Logic at Aberdeen University from 1860 to 1880 and author of *Education as a Science* (1879), was a friend and correspondent of Spencer. In 1877, in an address to the Edinburgh University Philosophical Society, he stated:

> I deem it quite possible to frame a practical science applicable to the training of the intellect that shall be precise and definite in a very considerable measure. The elements that make up our intellectual furniture can be stated with clearness; the laws of intellectual growth or acquisition are almost the best ascertained generalities of the human mind; even the most complicated studies can be analysed into their components, partly by psychology and partly by the higher logic.[47]

Education as a Science, published two years later, is largely concerned with this very task. It is a dull but rigorous work which sets out systematically the pedagogic lessons to be learned from the insights of logic, physiology and, above all, psychology: 'The largest chapter in the Science of Education must be the following out of all the psychological laws that bear directly or indirectly upon the process of mental acquirement.'[48] In modern terms, his main interests are in learning theory and child development. At the heart of the learning process, for Bain, are the three functions of 'Discrimination, Agreement, Retentiveness'[49] which carry pedagogical implications in respect of the sequence, pacing and reinforcement of material to be learned. In relation to child development, Bain asserts that 'Nothing but observation of cases will avail us here'.[50] This emphasis on careful empirical study — exemplified by Darwin's 'Biographical Sketch of An Infant' (1877)[51] — foreshadows the emergence of the child-study movement of the 1890s. Bain is particularly interested in the order in which the various faculties (language, mechanical aptitude, moral awareness) develop, so that the task of selecting appropriate curricular material and teaching methods can proceed on an informed basis. His stress on empirical study also anticipates the high level of specialisation which has been a feature of twentieth-century educational studies, a development Bain would certainly have approved of, for in his 'Preface' he recommends 'the division of labour'[52] as a way of bringing about further improvements in teaching and learning.[53]

The examples of Donaldson and Bain in Scotland and Spencer in England offer clear evidence of a growing conviction that the application of scientific thinking to education would pay substantial dividends. There was, it would seem, a strong measure of agreement on both sides of the border on this issue: the tireless campaigns of T. H. Huxley (1825-1895) on behalf of the cause of science in education were well received in both Scotland and England,[54] and the Education Society, founded in 1875 with the specific aim of advancing the cause of the science of education, drew its membership from throughout Britain.[55] Furthermore, there are no grounds for supposing that English writers led the way and Scots followed: in practical terms, Bain was every bit as influential as Spencer — *Education as a Science,* for example, was widely translated, reprinted many times (especially in the United States) and used as a prescribed text for trainee teachers.[56] The process was one of mutual reinforcement, deriving from a common acceptance of the ideology of science.

There are, however, two complicating factors which raise again the difficult question of the precise nature of the interaction of science and cultural identity in Scotland. The first arises out of the argument advanced by some historians that, certainly in relation to the earlier part of the nineteenth century, it is meaningful to speak of a distinctively Scottish kind of science. Davie, for instance, refers to 'the accepted Scottish approach to . . . the sciences',[57] which managed to combine experimental and technological interests on the one hand with humanistic and democratic values on the other. He goes on to argue that, in science (as in other aspects of Scottish cultural life), the encroachment of English models, of a more narrowly inductive sort, led to a loss of national identity and that by the end of the nineteenth century the battle had effectively been lost. If this argument is accepted, then it clearly represents a serious challenge to the case that is being developed here. Once again, however, it is important to realise the dangers of over-using relatively simple nationalistic categories to explain complex cultural phenomena. Scottish attitudes to science depended on many factors, and to appeal constantly to Anglicising explanations is misleading. There were general philosophical influences, often international in character, as the example of positivism has shown. There were pressures deriving from the expansion of knowledge and the practical advantages of specialisation. And there were internal forces arising out of developments in social structure — by the mid-nineteenth century science was no longer principally associated with landed élites, as it had been in the Enlightenment period: it had become accessible to the bourgeoisie, who wanted to use it to meet the requirements of modern urban economic life. S. Shapin remarks that, in so far as Scottish conceptions of science did undergo changes, 'the answer has to be sought, not in English scientific imperialism, but in changes within Scottish society itself'.[58]

The second complication relates more specifically to Donaldson and Bain,

though it also leads into broader issues. It appears that their credentials as
defenders of a distinctively Scottish tradition of education are strong. Indeed,
several of the items in the massive collection of his papers held in St. Andrews
University Library indicate Donaldson's keenness to resist alien importations
from the south.[59] Similarly, when the membership of the 1889 Scottish Universities Commission was being considered, the claims of Bain were urged by
many, not just on account of his distinction as a philosopher and teacher, but
also because it was felt he could represent the Scottish tradition of education in
the face of Anglicising influences.[60]

There are several ways of interpreting this dual commitment — to Scotland
and to science. First, it might be held that the two are completely separate, that
a scientific world view need carry no implications for beliefs and values of a
nationalistic kind. Certainly Bain and Donaldson did not perceive science as a
threat to their nationalism, and in their writings the two subjects are not juxtaposed. On the other hand, it seems unlikely that a wide-ranging explanatory
model such as that offered by science would not impinge on many aspects of a
nation's cultural life, though a conscious appreciation of the process may
depend on hindsight. Secondly, it might be maintained that there is indeed a
connection and that science will tend to dominate: in so far as science claims to
provide objective explanations, and especially if (as Spencer argued) such
explanations can extend beyond the natural world to include social and ethical
experience, the status of values and beliefs deriving from national culture and
tradition will be diminished. A third possibility reverses the priorities and sees
science as the weaker partner: one thinks, for example, of Soviet science (the
Lysenko affair, the abuse of psychiatry) in which a state ideology, for a time at
least, manages to control the objects and the findings of 'scientific' enquiry.
Finally, and perhaps most probably, it might be argued that science and
nationalism will interact in complex and subtle ways,' often at an unconscious
level and in conjunction with other cultural forces, and that a process of
mutual adjustment will take place over time: in some areas of cultural life one
or other may tend to dominate, but the pattern will not be entirely uniform.
Although this essay is mostly concerned with aspects of Scottish culture in
which the penetration by science has been considerable, that is not the whole
story and, in the final section, reference will be made to some indications
which suggest the need for careful qualification. Before that, however, it is
necessary to take the process of interaction between science and education a
stage further by examining that other unresolved question: what happened
when the ideology of science came into contact with the expansion of institutional provision and the pressure for social reform?

4

One way of characterising the last few decades of the nineteenth century, as far
as Scottish education is concerned, would be to say that it was a period of
growing bureaucracy and professionalisation. The setting up of administrative

structures, in the form of School Boards, to operate an expanded educational system,[61] went hand in hand with a number of related developments: the introduction of professional 'experts' whose voices carried special authority (for example, the first Chairs of Education in Britain were established in Edinburgh and St. Andrews in 1876); a recognition of the importance of data collection to provide 'hard facts' for the bureaucrats and policy-makers (the massive Argyll Commission Report of 1865-68 is an example of this trend[62]); the demand for 'efficiency' in education, evident in 'payment by results' and in the extension and refinement of examining procedures (as W. Kennedy, Clerk to the School Board of Glasgow, remarked in 1884, 'This is the age of Examinations'[63]). All of these developments, not surprisingly, reflect the dominant economic and social ideologies of the time. Bain's occasional use of metaphoric language in *Education as a Science* serves to illustrate the point further. Moral education is viewed in terms of the 'management'[64] of sense pleasures and emotions. The exercise of intellectual skills, such as memory, is assessed in relation to their physiological 'cost' or 'expense'.[65] More generally, knowledge is conceived of as a commodity, the teacher's duty being to pass on 'a definite amount of knowledge'.[66] It is the language of the bureaucrat, the economist, the man of commerce. The values implied in this language are clearly compatible with those of science. Indeed, the two can be seen as mutually supportive and reinforcing: scientific materialism is both an expression of and a justification for successful capitalist enterprise.

Education was, however, also developing in response to pressures for increased state intervention in a whole range of social welfare matters. The work of Thomas Ferguson and, more recently, Olive Checkland, has demonstrated the growing political and public awareness of social problems deriving from poverty, bad housing and poor or non-existent health care.[67] The philanthropic impulses of Henry Drummond, which found intellectual support in progressive Social Darwinism and spiritual support in the Christian doctrine of Love, were focused on the living realities of urban deprivation. How did education fit into this picture and what kind of mutual adjustments involving science, philanthropy, bureaucracy and professionalisation took place? It will be instructive to look at some contemporary statements which point forward to the social role education was to assume.

First, there is the uncompromising opinion of the Reverend William Leggatt, Governor and Headmaster of the Buchanan Institution of Glasgow, founded in 1859 for the relief of destitute boys. In a pamphlet published in 1871, reviewing the work of the Institute, he asserts:

> Some theorists talk as if they believed that all minds are by nature alike, maintaining that education and training cause all the differences in mind and character which we perceive in after life. The theory is as inapplicable to the individuals of our Society as it is to the races of which mankind are composed. The intellect of a race which never knew cultivation is not more evidently inferior to that of cultivated Europeans, than are the natural powers of children of the unenterprising, thriftless, dependent poor inferior to the inherent capacity of the educated, enterprising classes, who have established and maintained themselves in a

position of comfort and opulence. In a social condition such as ours, where free scope is
given, and a fair field is open to all, it is not chiefly the want of opportunity which keeps
individuals from rising in the social scale, or improving their material condition . . . The
inherent differences of their natural capacity — the want of nervous power, — of mental
vigour in one class which another possesses and freely exercises, must be taken into consideration before the phenomenon can be explained.[68]

Lying behind these assertions, a number of strands can be detected.
Acceptance of a Christian duty to make institutional provision for the
destitute coexists with a belief in the inevitability of a highly stratified society
(despite a 'fair field' being 'open to all'), and, most interestingly, with an
appeal to the hereditary emphasis in the theory of evolution as an explanation
for poor academic achievement. Leggatt would certainly have concurred with
Charles Darwin's own observation: 'I am inclined to agree with Francis Galton
in believing that education and environment produce only a small effect on the
mind of any one, and that most of our qualities are innate.'[69]

Interpreted in the light of these sentiments, the 'science of education'
becomes a matter of measuring innate individual differences and making
differential provision for various 'kinds' of children. A considerable amount of
energy was devoted to just such an interpretation both in England and in
Scotland: the pioneering work of Francis Galton and the now-discredited Cyril
Burt provided a basis for the later efforts of Godfrey Thomson at Edinburgh
and William McClelland at St. Andrews.[70] It has been convincingly argued
that this 'scientific' work offered a useful rationale for policy decisions which
were, in fact, determined by class interests and bureaucratic needs.[71] This is
perhaps an example of a cultural interaction in which science did not
dominate: its power was not directly undermined but it was seriously compromised by being used for disreputable ends.

The crudity of the Reverend Leggatt's statement was, as might be expected,
not a feature of the 'professional' research papers produced a generation later.
The penetration of science into the realms of social policy-making brought
with it a characteristic mode of discourse: cool, rational, detached. This transformation took time, but its roots can be detected in the same decade in which
Leggatt was writing. Paradoxically, a necessary preliminary was the deliberate
exclusion of awkward questions of a political kind about the social context of
educational provision. S. S. Laurie, in his inaugural address as Professor of
Education at Edinburgh University in 1876, is disarmingly explicit:

The education of every human being is determined by potent influences which do not
properly fall within the range of our consideration here. The breed of men to which the child
belongs, the character of his parents, the human society into which he is born, the physical
circumstances by which he is surrounded, are silently and irresistibly forming him . . . With
these things we have to do only by way of a passing reference; we have not to deal with
them.[72]

This evasion of the very questions into which the Reverend Leggatt plunges so
boldly involves cutting out fundamental issues to do with the structure of

society — its economic basis, its class divisions, its differential distribution of power. These, it would seem, lie outside the scope of proper 'scientific' investigation and would take the educationalist beyond his area of expertise. There is, in this, an ironic reversal of the process whereby science had been extended to social matters such as education in the first place: now the field to be examined is restricted, ostensibly in the interests of systematic enquiry.

A subject which offered a manageable area for study was child development, approached in a psychological rather than a sociological manner. And so we find J. M. D. Meiklejohn (the first Professor of Education at St. Andrews University), in the temperate, enquiring language of the academic, listing a series of questions worthy of scientific examination:

> What powers unfold themselves at what times? What special food is best for the nurture of these powers? What powers are in danger of over-stimulus, and what in danger of atrophy? What are the trustworthy indications, and how can we apply tests, of character? How can we diagnose the kind of power in this or that mind? At what point does interference with what seems to be the natural growth of the mind become advisable? And at what point hurtful? How can we best keep alive and nourish the inborn feelings of wonder, curiosity and the power of imagination? [73]

'Observation and experiment' rather than 'the manufacture of hypotheses' are to provide the means of looking into these questions. [74] This is to be the province of professional researchers who will provide 'a body of knowledge which may be useful to the thoughtful parent or to the young teacher, which may give him the true beginning of his work . . .' [75] In an expanding educational system, the 'body of knowledge' will not only be transmitted to prospective teachers by 'experts' in colleges and universities, but also made available to political and bureaucratic decision-makers.

Social reform through education was thus translated into a new rhetoric, defined in limited terms, and mediated through a rising professional class. The ready acceptance of a circumscribed role had at least three related consequences. First, it gave the educational 'experts' a clearly defined set of tasks that were not in any sense socially subversive; secondly, it placed them in a mutually supporting relationship with policy-makers — the experts, carefully avoiding basic issues to do with class, money and power, provided the policy-makers with the restricted answers they wanted to hear and the policy-makers, in turn, confirmed the authoritative status of the experts by consulting and listening to them; and thirdly, this comfortable dyadic relationship served to exclude counter-voices, or at least devalue anything they might say. The powerful ideology of science supported all three elements — detailed, painstaking enquiry necessitated the division of labour (as recommended by Bain); systematic data collection had to be carried out by those trained in specific fields (such as mental testing and child development) and the results made available as 'facts' for use by policy-makers; those who were sceptical either about the ideology itself or about its deployment in this way were, almost by definition, unworthy of serious consideration.

An interesting example of a dissenter, whose criticisms were largely ignored, is Patrick Geddes (1854-1932), Professor of Botany at University College, Dundee from 1883 to 1920.[76] Geddes's own education was unconventional, and no doubt this partly explains the stance he took. He refused to submit himself to competitive examinations on the grounds that they stifled rather than encouraged real learning, and he obtained his professorial appointment, despite the lack of recognised academic qualifications, on the strength of research and publications. What formal education he did receive was gained principally under the tutelage of T. H. Huxley at the School of Mines in London (later the Imperial College of Science), an influence which caused Geddes to become committed to the evolutionary view of life and use it as a basis for his work in an astonishingly wide range of fields — town planning, Celtic publishing, cultural exhibitions, as well as academic and social reform. His interest in environmental improvement took him to Cyprus, India and Jerusalem, in all of which he drew up ambitious schemes for development and regeneration. This strongly internationalist outlook was combined with a deep concern for the future of Scotland, and he wrote scornfully of those Scots who compromised their nationality in the pursuit of 'political honours from the other side of the Tweed'.[77] In these respects, Geddes stands at the centre of the cultural forces which have been juxtaposed in this paper — science, nationalism, social reform.

On educational matters, Philip Boardman has commented on the extent to which Geddes was out of sympathy with the dominant trends of his time:

> He failed to produce even one objective test in his seventy-eight years of life; he was lacking in respect for educational statistics, and — crowning blasphemy — he denied the divine nature of administrators.[78]

Elementary and secondary schools were, for Geddes, 'prisons for body and mind',[79] whose main function was to serve the needs, not of children, but of 'text-book-perpetrators' and 'examination-machine-bureaucrats'.[80] Furthermore, 'Much of our so-called "education" . .'. is literally definable as the *production of artificial defectives*'.[81] The 'routine education of the three R's, despite all machinery of standards, addition of special subjects and what not'[82] does not give access to anything worthwhile: the real world of culture requires first-hand observation, exploration and discovery by the individual learner.

Geddes was not, however, a soft-centred Rousseauesque romantic, as the demanding education of his own children shows.[83] Nor was he a vague, impractical theorist with no experience of educational realities. His quite amazing energy had very concrete results in university extension work, in international summer schools, and in the student hostel movement (University Hall, Edinburgh, was founded by him in 1887). Even at school level, where the forces that Geddes deplored had gained most ground, his ideas contributed towards the introduction of nature study in the curriculum. On a wider front, he met and corresponded with a number of American educators who were directly involved in the promotion of progressive educational theory and practice, including William James, G. Stanley Hall and John Dewey.[84]

But in all of this Geddes operated on his own initiative, outside official channels. It is not hard to see why he was unpopular with the 'establishment' of Scottish education. His scathing references to the 'decaying educational mandarinate'[85] were not calculated to disarm or persuade by sweet reason. A culture, however, reveals as much about itself through those it rejects or dismisses as through those it respects or advances. Geddes's irreverence had its origins in a realisation that the professional and bureaucratic trappings that accompanied mass provision and that drew on science (or pseudo-science) for ideological support were, in relation to the development of individuals, potentially destructive rather than liberating. This was not a message that a rising and expanding class of 'experts' wanted to hear since it effectively challenged the power and authority with which they were rapidly investing themselves.

5

This essay represents an attempt to show, in relation to the development of Scottish culture, that subterranean movements at the level of ideas are just as significant as surface configurations in the form of institutional structures. It has been argued that Scotland, no less than England, was profoundly affected by the ascendancy of scientific forms of thinking and that the church, the institution which might have been expected to resist this cultural shift most strenuously, did not, in fact, do so. Furthermore, the application of 'scientism' to social fields, like education, was equally evident north and south of the border. A concomitant development, the growth of professional experts and bureaucratic machines, drawing on science for their rationale and justification, but stopping well short of a radical analysis of the class basis of society, was similarly not a peculiarly Scottish phenomenon: it can be seen not only in England but also in the United States.[86] Indeed, the immense power and attraction of the scientific world view is evident in the ease with which it crossed national boundaries and in the variety of uses which it served. Inevitably, in this process, there were misinterpretations, wrong directions and abuses. The 'science' of eugenics (promoted by Francis Galton, the founder of the mental-testing movement) is one example.[87]

The account that has been offered is obviously incomplete: three examples will suggest the scope for further work. First, much more detailed information is required about the way in which science was exploited and manipulated by those who exercised power. This will not be easy to come by as, by their very nature, exploiters and manipulators are ungenerous when it comes to leaving written records of their activities, and, in any case, much of the process almost certainly took place at a subconscious level in the shape of instinctual responses to protect vested interests. Nevertheless, the task is an extremely important one since, if evidence is forthcoming, it will serve to qualify the impression that has been given of the power of science: in the realm of political life, other forms of power, operating as economic and social forces, come into play.

Secondly, there is a need to amplify what has been said about the role of religion in the cultural transformations that have been charted. Its relations with science have been discussed, but comparatively little has been said about its relations with education. Despite the challenge of science, the role of the Church in Scottish education remained important, and agnostics like Bain encountered strong opposition when they sought academic advancement.[88] There is clearly scope for further examination, and again the findings may qualify the picture presented here.

And thirdly, the precise nature of Scottish cultural identity needs to be subjected to much closer scrutiny, not only in relation to the effects of science, but also in relation to many other intellectual 'keywords'. Yet again, the need for qualification is apparent. Despite the international character of many forms of scientific thinking, we stop short of saying that all cultures are essentially the same, the products of uncontrollable scientific materialism: we assume, for example, that it is still meaningful to speak of Scottish identity and to distinguish it from English or American varieties. And although we are now familiar with the notion of cross-cultural studies of educational systems (using 'scientific' statistical instruments), and even of proposals for cross-cultural curricula (such as Bruner's MACOS[89]), substantial variation in respect of aims, methods and structures is still apparent. Advances in science and technology may reduce differences between cultures, but they do not eliminate them entirely.

These points act as further reminders of the immense complexity of the concept of culture and the need to approach it from many directions.[90] The concepts of 'language', 'class', 'community', 'democracy', 'industry', 'labour', 'realism', 'romanticism', and many others, could all usefully be applied to the development of Scottish culture in ways that would fill out and modify what has been said above. In addition, there are many strategies which, though hardly new, are poorly represented in Scottish writing. Where, for example, is the Scottish equivalent of Richard Hoggart's *The Uses of Literacy*?[91] Popular culture — the world of the media, sport, entertainment, etc. — offers a rich field for investigation. Again, the study of literature and biography as significant cultural documents (rather than aesthetic objects) would be likely to yield valuable results.

One beneficial consequence of pursuing these alternative approaches would be that they would promote greater awareness of the difference between education and schooling. Understanding of Scottish education (and, by extension, Scottish culture as a whole) has suffered from too ready an acceptance of traditional institutional categories. Schooling is only one cultural agency and, increasingly perhaps, not a particularly successful one. To attribute too much of Scottish identity to it is to oversimplify the complex fabric of cultural life, its structure of customs, values and beliefs, expressed through an immense variety of forms of individual and social action. Within that structure there are inevitably tensions, conflicts and contradictions, and Scotland certainly has her share of these: the paradoxes of forthright speech and subservient conduct, aggressive masculinity and maudlin sentimentality, contempt for and envy of most things English, moral righteousness and eschatological guilt, the democratic myth and the corruption of power, are plain to see but difficult to explain. Of course, these are issues which, like the study of the ideology of science, lead the enquirer far beyond the subject of schooling as conventionally treated in histories of Scottish education. Such a development has one final attraction, quite apart from the worthwhile re-orientation of academic study which it would entail: it would undoubtedly be disconcerting to those who have risen to prominence under the scientific, bureaucratic and professional pattern that has been described, for, in re-defining the terms of the debate, one is also questioning the nature of education itself and the pretensions of those who control the present structure of schooling.

NOTES

1. Raymond Williams, *The Long Revolution* (Harmondsworth, 1965), p. 63.
2. Raymond Williams, *Keywords: A Vocabulary of Culture and Society* (London, 1976), pp. 76-82. See also *The Long Revolution*, pp. 57-88 and *Culture* (London, 1981), *passim*.
3. See, for example, James G. Kellas, *Modern Scotland*, revised edition (London, 1980).
4. *Ibid.*, p. 72.
5. See Wilson H. Bain, '"Attacking the Citadel": James Moncrieff's Proposals to Reform Scottish Education, 1851-69', *Scottish Educational Review*, X, 2 (1978), pp. 5-14.
6. Quoted in James Scotland, *The History of Scottish Education*, Vol. 2 (London, 1969), p. 5.
7. Craik was a strong supporter of the idea of military training in schools. On the relation of this view to the Boer War, see Ian Thomson, 'The Origins of Physical Education in State Schools', *Scottish Educational Review*, X, 2 (1978), pp. 15-24.
8. George E. Davie, *The Democratic Intellect: Scotland and Her Universities in the Nineteenth Century*, second edition (Edinburgh, 1964), p. 97.
9. *Ibid.*, p. 99.
10. See Raymond Williams, *Keywords*, pp. 232-235.
11. Michael D. Biddiss, *The Age of the Masses* (Harmondsworth, 1977), p. 49.
12. *Ibid.*, p. 49.
13. Alexander Bain, *Autobiography* (London, 1904), pp. 153, 156-159.
14. Raymond Williams, 'Social Darwinism', in: *Problems in Materialism and Culture* (London, 1980), pp. 86-87.
15. J. D. Y. Peel, *Herbert Spencer: The Evolution of a Sociologist* (London, 1971), pp. 141-142.
16. See Robert C. Bannister, *Social Darwinism: Science and Myth in Anglo-American Social Thought* (Philadelphia, 1979), *passim*.
17. See D. R. Oldroyd, *Darwinian Impacts* (Milton Keynes, 1980), pp. 193-195.
18. Andrew L. Drummond and James Bulloch, *The Church in Victorian Scotland, 1843-1874* (Edinburgh, 1975), pp. 215-239.
19. Hugh Miller (1802-1856). His *Testimony of the Rocks* (1857) was an attempt to render compatible the 'days' of Genesis and modern notions of geological time, but in *Footprints of the Creator* (1850) he insisted that each new biological species was the sign of a special act of creation.

William Ferguson suggests that 'the tensions produced by the attempt to reconcile science and religion may have had some bearing on Miller's mysterious suicide in 1856': *Scotland: 1689 to the Present* (Edinburgh, 1968), p. 338. See also George Rosie, *Hugh Miller: Outrage and Order* (Edinburgh, 1981).

20. W. Robertson Smith (1846-1894), theologian and orientalist, Professor of Hebrew and Old Testament Exegesis at the Free Church College, Aberdeen; later Professor of Arabic at Cambridge. Robertson Smith's linguistic studies led him to the conclusion that the Bible was an accretion, not a unified divine revelation, a view which seemed to lend support to the evolutionary version of creation. His ideas provoked considerable controversy and, although acquitted of heresy in 1880, he was suspended from teaching the following year. See Drummond and Bulloch, *The Church in Late Victorian Scotland, 1874-1900* (Edinburgh, 1978), pp. 40-78.

21. Drummond and Bulloch, *The Church in Victorian Scotland, 1843-1874*, p. 234.

22. *Henry Drummond: An Anthology* (New York, 1953), ed. James W. Kennedy, p. 68.

23. *Ibid.*, p. 68.

24. *Ibid.*, p. 75.

25. *Ibid.*, p. 78.

26. *Ibid.*, p. 78.

27. *Ibid.*, p. 14. See also Drummond and Bulloch, *The Church in Late Victorian Scotland, 1874-1900*, p. 28.

28. Drummond and Bulloch, *The Church in Late Victorian Scotland, 1874-1900*, p. 28.

29. *Henry Drummond: An Anthology*, pp. 23-31.

30. *Ibid.*, pp. 56-57.

31. *Ibid.*, p. 220.

32. *Ibid.*, p. 218.

33. Drummond and Bulloch, *The Church in Late Victorian Scotland, 1874-1900*, p. 28.

34. Dorothy Ross, *G. Stanley Hall: The Psychologist as Prophet* (Chicago and London, 1972), pp. 261-262.

35. Bannister, *op. cit.*, p. 158.

36. James Donaldson, 'On the Science of Education' in: *Lectures on the History of Education in Prussia and England and on Kindred Topics* (Edinburgh, 1874), p. 167. The essay originally appeared in *The Museum* in 1864.

37. *Ibid.*, p. 168.

38. *Ibid.*, p. 168.

39. *Ibid.*, p. 171.

40. *Ibid.*, p. 184.

41. Herbert Spencer, *Education: Intellectual, Moral and Physical* (London, 1949, 1st edition, 1861).

42. R. H. Quick, *Essays on Educational Reformers* (London, 1868). On the use of Quick's volume in the training of teachers, see J. W. Tibble, 'The Development of the Study of Education' in: *The Study of Education*, ed. J. W. Tibble (London, 1966), pp. 6, 19.

43. James Leitch, *Practical Educationists and Their Systems of Teaching* (Glasgow, 1876), pp. 239-298.

44. Spencer, *op. cit.*, p. 138.

45. *Ibid.*, p. 61.

46. *Ibid.*, p. 8.

47. Alexander Bain, 'Metaphysics and Debating Societies' in: *Practical Essays* (London, 1884), p. 147.

48. Alexander Bain, *Education as a Science* (London, 1879), p. 15.

49. *Ibid.*, p. 15.

50. *Ibid.*, p. 185.

51. Charles Darwin, 'A Biographical Sketch of an Infant', *Mind*, II (1877), pp. 285-294.

52. *Education as a Science*, p. vii.

53. For a fuller discussion of Bain, see Walter M. Humes, 'Alexander Bain and the Development of Educational Theory' in: *The Meritocratic Intellect: Studies in the History of Educational*

Research, eds. James V. Smith and David Hamilton (Aberdeen, 1980), pp. 15-29.

54. See, for example, Huxley's Rectorial address at Aberdeen University delivered during Bain's term of office as a Professor. 'Universities: Actual and Ideal' in: *Collected Essays,* Vol. III (London, 1893), pp. 189-234.

55. A useful entry on the Education Society is to be found in Foster Watson (ed.), *The Encyclopaedia and Dictionary of Education,* Vol. II (London, 1921), p. 529.

56. See Bain, *Autobiography,* p. 431 and Tibble, *op. cit.,* p. 6.

57. *The Democratic Intellect,* p. 105.

58. S. Shapin, 'Science' in: *A Companion to Scottish Culture,* ed. David Daiches (London, 1981), p. 321.

59. For example, Box 11, Item 21 (typescript) on the role of the Scotch Education Department; Box 13, Item 11 (manuscript) on the differences between the Scottish and English educational systems. Donaldson's range of contacts in educational, religious and political circles was extensive, and it is highly likely that a detailed study of his papers would yield valuable evidence about the development of ideas in the period under consideration.

60. See Davie, *op. cit.,* pp. 98-99, 101.

61. See, for example, James M. Roxburgh, *The School Board of Glasgow, 1873-1919* (London, 1971).

62. *Schools in Scotland: Report of Royal Commission.* First Report, PP, 1865, XVII [3483]; Second Report, PP, 1867, XXV [3845]; Third Report, PP, 1867-68, XXIX [4011].

63. W. Kennedy, *Examinations,* a paper read at the Galashiels Congress of the Educational Institute of Scotland (London and Glasgow, 1884), p. 3.

64. *Education as a Science,* p. 178.

65. *Ibid.,* p. 13.

66. *Ibid.,* p. 103.

67. Thomas Ferguson, *Scottish Social Welfare, 1864-1914* (Edinburgh and London, 1958). Olive Checkland, *Philanthropy in Victorian Scotland* (Edinburgh, 1980).

68. William Leggatt, *An Account of the Ten Years' Educational Experiment Among Destitute Boys Conducted in the Buchanan Institution, Glasgow* (Glasgow, 1871), pp. 18-19.

69. *Charles Darwin and T. H. Huxley, Autobiographies,* ed. Gavin de Beer (London, 1974), p. 22.

70. The connections between Galton, Burt and Thomson are explored in L. S. Hearnshaw, *Cyril Burt: Psychologist* (London, 1979). On Thomson and McClelland, see Marjorie Cruickshank, *A History of the Training of Teachers in Scotland* (London, 1970), pp. 181-182.

71. See H. M. Paterson, 'Godfrey Thomson and the Development of Psychometrics in Scotland', a paper presented at the British Educational Research Association Conference in 1975. An abbreviated version can be found in *Research Intelligence,* B.E.R.A. Bulletin 2 (1975), pp. 63-65.

72. S. S. Laurie, *Inaugural Address* as Professor of the Theory, History and Practice of Education in the University of Edinburgh (Edinburgh, 1876), p. 23. Reprinted in *The Training of Teachers and Other Educational Papers* (London, 1882). In fairness to Laurie, it should be pointed out that he did have reservations about the application of scientific and bureaucratic thinking to education, deriving principally from his strong moral and religious convictions — he was, for example, fairly critical of Spencer. Ideas can, however, have consequences which go beyond (or even run counter to) the conscious intentions of those who express them, and the passage quoted in the text certainly limits the study of education in ways that served the interests of the rising class of 'professionals' in education.

73. J. M. D. Meiklejohn, *Inaugural Address* in: *The Study of Education: A Collection of Inaugural Lectures,* Vol. I, ed. Peter Gordon (London, 1980), p. 5.

74. *Ibid.,* p. 4.

75. *Ibid.,* p. 5.

76. There are a number of useful general studies of Geddes, but a detailed examination of his educational ideas is lacking. See Philip Boardman, *Patrick Geddes: Maker of the Future* (Chapel Hill, North Carolina, 1944) and *The Worlds of Patrick Geddes* (London, Henley and Boston,

1978); Paddy Kitchen, *A Most Unsettling Person: An Introduction to the Ideas and Life of Patrick Geddes* (London, 1975); Philip Mairet, *Pioneer of Sociology: The Life and Letters of Patrick Geddes* (London, 1957).

77. Patrick Geddes, *Scottish University Needs and Aims* (Dundee, 1890), p. 3.
79. Quoted in Boardman, *Patrick Geddes: Maker of the Future*, p. 269.
80. *Ibid.*, p. 266.
80. *Ibid.*, p. 266.
81. *Ibid.*, p. 270. Geddes's italics.
82. *Ibid.*, p. 272.
83. See, for example, Kitchen, *op. cit.*, pp. 194-204.
84. See Boardman, *The Worlds of Patrick Geddes*, pp. 175-176, 443.
85. Quoted in Boardman, *Patrick Geddes: Maker of the Future*, p. 278.
86. See, for example, L. J. Kamin, *The Science and Politics of I.Q.* (New York and London, 1974).
87. See Roy Lowe, 'Eugenics and Education: A Note on the Origins of the Intelligence Testing Movement in England', *Educational Studies*, VI (1980), pp. 1-8.
88. Bain was rejected for a number of academic posts prior to his Aberdeen appointment. He gives a frank account of these rebuffs in his *Autobiography*.
89. Jerome Bruner, *Toward a Theory of Instruction* (New York, 1968), pp. 73-101.
90. The recently published *A Companion to Scottish Culture*, ed. David Daiches (London, 1981) is a welcome addition to the literature on Scotland, but it does not attempt to tackle theoretical and methodological problems.
91. Richard Hoggart, *The Uses of Literacy* (Harmondsworth, 1958). The whole field of cultural studies is relatively undeveloped in Scotland: there is certainly no body of work comparable to that produced by the Centre for Contemporary Cultural Studies at the University of Birmingham.

7

The Sexual Division of Labour in the Scottish Teaching Profession, 1872-1914

Helen Corr

NO serious attempt has yet been made to compare and contrast the recruitment and job opportunities for the sexes in the Scottish teaching profession during the late nineteenth century.[1] Consequently, scholars in Scottish universities have become more familiar with existing studies on the position of the sexes in the English teaching profession and remain relatively ignorant about the Scottish dimension.[2] The lack of research on women teachers is particularly serious as they constituted 70 per cent of all existing teachers in Scotland by 1914.

Admittedly, some educational historians like Douglas Myers are aware of the recruitment pattern of the sexes into the teaching profession in eighteenth-century Scotland.[3] He rightly stresses the predominance of the parish schoolmaster within the Scottish educational tradition and the lack of the notion of employing schoolmistresses before the nineteenth century. Yet the process in which the teaching profession became overwhelmingly composed of women teachers has never been the subject of serious research. This is quite surprising, given that one of the most notable developments in the history of the profession was that, while in the 1850s it was numerically dominated by men, by the 1890s it was largely comprised of women. The changing composition in the sex ratio of teachers during the nineteenth century represented a unique and distinctive feature of the Scottish educational system. Elsewhere in Britain women teachers already outnumbered their male counterparts and men continued to remain in a minority. A more precise indication of the dramatic shift in the employment pattern of the sexes in Scotland is shown in Table One.

TABLE ONE
% Number of Teachers in Scotland

	1851	1911
Male teachers	65.0	30.0
Female teachers	35.0	70.0

Sources: *Scottish Occupational Census* decennial series (Parl. Papers, 1851, Vol. CCXXVIII); *Scottish Occupational Census* (Parl. Papers, 1911, Vol. CXIX).

The purpose of this essay, therefore, is to describe this feminisation of the Scottish teaching profession and its implications for the development of occupational divisions between the sexes within the educational ladder. The term 'feminisation' is used here to document the sharp acceleration in the numbers of women entering teaching and the process whereby the teaching profession became largely composed of women.

It is within this context that the 1872 Education (Scotland) Act can be seen as an important landmark in altering the balance of recruitment of the sexes into teaching. Within the first decade of the Act there was a sharp rise in the number of female teachers without a corresponding increase of men. The 1881 census recorded that, for the first time, female teachers outnumbered their male counterparts by 8,000 to the latter's 5,515. The implications of the 1872 Act for the development of occupational divisions between the sexes are best considered by referring to some of the relevant clauses. This in turn should lead to some understanding of the structural and ideological forces involved in shaping policy-making decisions which affected the supply and demand for teachers. One of the major provisions of the Act was

> . . . to amend and extend the provisions of the law of Scotland on the subject of education in such manner that the means of procuring efficient education for their children may be furnished and made available to the whole people of Scotland.[4]

This goal was to be obtained by securing the following list of provisions: firstly, a number of suitable schools sufficient to meet the requirements of the population, and secondly, regular attendance at these schools. The fundamental objective of the Act, therefore, was to introduce a national educational system and compulsory education for all children over the age of five. This in turn meant that an increase in the supply of teachers was urgently needed to meet the proposed increase of scholars attending school. Another relevant clause which was to have a striking impact on the teaching profession in Scotland was the ruling that

> . . . no person shall be appointed to the position of principal teacher who is not the holder of a certificate of competency.[5]

Together these stipulations created an extensive range of problems for the Scotch Education Department (SED), who were given the responsibility for putting the 1872 Act into practice. The foremost difficulty they faced was that, on the one hand, they wished to raise educational standards by demanding qualified and certificated teachers, which meant attending a teacher training college for two years. On the other hand, to train teachers was a costly and time-consuming operation, particularly in a period when the demand for teachers was far greater than the supply following the introduction of the 1872

Act. For example, in the year of 1874-5 alone, there was a 23.3 per cent increase in the number of children attending school.

A related problem was that although the SED had overall control of Scottish education, the teacher training colleges were administered by the Presbyterian churches. This feature of the educational system caused a longstanding source of tension between the two bodies over the inadequate provision of training college accommodation. The churches were unable to undertake large schemes of reconstruction to accommodate the sharp rise of students attending college (after 1872) without the aid of extensive funds. The SED felt itself unable to give enormous grants which would increase the value of church property and the power of the church in educational affairs. In effect, the SED desperately wished to reduce the control and powers of the church rather than to extend them. A major step towards reducing the church's stronghold in the educational sphere was taken in 1872. Clause 65 of the Act contained the radical insertion that state schools were to be non-denominational:

> Every public school and every school subject to inspection shall be open to children of all denominations and any child may be withdrawn by his parents from any instruction in religious subjects and from any religious observance in any such school.[6]

This was to mark the end of an era in which the Kirk had retained legal control over public education for over 300 years. Not unexpectedly, the response of the Presbyterian church authority to this clause was a positive one. They were well aware that they could continue to exercise a considerable degree of influence in religious and educational matters with the aid of voluntary schools, but more particularly through the medium of the teacher training college. The nature and use of this strategic weapon (and how it could be employed) was made very explicit in the church reports shortly after the introduction of the 1872 Act. The Education Committee of the Church of Scotland wrote:

> Now the Act is an accomplished fact it is the duty of the church to lend its aid in carrying it out and its influence in directing the administration of it . . . In prosecuting this object they will best serve the interests of a religious education for they will thus furnish successive bands of teachers trained under the auspices of the church.[7]

The control of the church in educational affairs was upheld when the Church of Scotland succeeded in its efforts to establish another teacher training college in Aberdeen in 1873. The SED agreed to this demand, but only on condition that it was limited to female entrants of whom the majority would be self-supporting. In 1874 the Free Church followed suit by establishing another training college in Aberdeen exclusively for women. This meant that, by 1875, the Church of Scotland and the Free Church had set up six training colleges in Scotland whilst the Episcopal Church retained its control over a small residential college (numbers averaged about 50 students) for self-supporting female students in Edinburgh.

However, with the Act's recommendation that all principal teachers should be certificated, the churches were even less able to accommodate the overwhelming influx of prospective students into their training colleges. This resulted in a large percentage of potential teachers being forced to seek alternative occupations whilst others were willingly accepted into smaller board schools without any formal qualifications. Moreover, since the training colleges provided the major training vehicle for entry into the teaching profession, the Act had far-reaching implications for the standard of qualifications attained by the sexes.

Rejection from training college had a particularly severe effect on female aspirations and skills. A larger number of women were applying for training college entry during the 1870s. As a result, the sex ratio of entrants to the training colleges was decisively altered from the pattern which had been established in the 1860's.[8] This was particularly true of the attendance figues at the Free Church training colleges. The Education Committee reports recorded that 129 males compared to 217 females were attending colleges in Glasgow and Edinburgh in 1873. By 1878 these figures had increased to 153 and 281 respectively, whilst the Church of Scotland reported in 1876 that out of a total of 477 students attending Scottish training colleges there were 192 males compared with 285 females.

The higher attendance rate amongst female students tended to obscure the fact that a larger number of females were also rejected by the training colleges, even though they had successfully gained 2nd class honours in the Admission examination. For example, in 1877, the number of candidates sitting the entrance examination at the Church of Scotland training college in Glasgow was 75 males and 112 females; the results of the examination showed that 17 males and 10 females had failed to meet the required standard laid down by the Scotch code. However, the actual number of candidates who were successful in securing a place at the college was 50 males and only 52 females. This meant that nearly all of the male candidates were accepted into the training college, but there remained a sizeable number of successful female candidates who were refused entry — principally due to a lack of accommodation. Hence the structural defects of the training college system and the strained relations between the SED and the church authorities created a situation in which many females were not given the opportunity to equip themselves with a training college certificate. This resulted in a pool of unskilled female labour being thrown back onto the teaching labour market in greater quantities than their male counterparts.

Given, therefore, the inadequacy of training college accommodation, the foremost question the SED faced was how to increase the existing supply of teachers without extending the power and control of the church.

The SED responded to this problem by devising a number of new schemes, in addition to those already in operation, which would increase the supply of certificated teachers without their attending a course at a teacher training college. The SED decided to pursue a dual policy in which there was an army of untrained and unskilled teachers alongside an increasing percentage of trained certificated teachers. The policy was ambivalent; on the one hand the overall aim was to improve Scottish educational standards by demanding a body of 'competent' and skilled teachers, but on the other hand an army of teachers was urgently required to meet the rise in the number of children attending school. The decision to implement this policy was reported by Sandon, Gordon and Richmond — Commissioners from the Scotch Education Department in London. In 1875 they wrote:

> . . . the supply of certificated teachers is at present much below the demand . . . A sufficient supply of teachers is not forthcoming and we have therefore slightly modified the article 59 in the code, introduced by our predecessors by which the SED are empowered to grant certificates without examination to persons who having been for some years in charge of elementary schools are reported by the inspectors to be efficient teachers.[9]

The duplicity of this policy led to the development of a well-defined occupational hierarchy within the teaching profession. It comprised various categories of teachers, and each of these teachers could be identified as having varying degrees of status depending on sex and to a lesser extent on qualifications, age and previous teaching experience. A synopsis of the various categories of teachers is necessary in order to locate more precisely the position that each group held within this hierarchical educational structure. During the course of the 1870s the Scotch code recognised five categories of teachers consisting of:

(a) Certificated Teachers
(b) Provisionally Certificated Teachers
(c) Assistant Uncertificated Teachers and Acting Teachers
(d) Female Assistant Uncertificated Teachers
(e) Pupil Teachers

(a) *Certificated Teachers*

This category referred to those teachers who had undertaken a two-year training college course but who only gained a certificate after completing a probationary period of actual service in a school. In practice this category incorporated two distinct groups of teachers: (1) Principal Certificated teachers, which referred to headmasters and headmistresses, and (2) Assistant Certificated teachers, which normally referred to the teaching staff in schools who had undergone a training college course. The distinction is an important one because inevitably Principal teachers had a higher income and greater standing than Assistants.

(b) *Provisionally Certificated Teachers*

This category provides an excellent example of a scheme created by the SED in 1874 in which they presented teachers with a temporary certificate without their going through the formal channels of a training college. It was aptly referred to as 'Provisional' because when the teacher reached the age of twenty-five the certificate was cancelled. Within their short working life, provisionally certificated teachers served a most important function for the smaller school boards in rural districts. They were given the authority to teach up to sixty pupils in a classroom without calling on the services of another teacher.

(c) *Assistant Uncertificated Teachers and Acting Teachers*

These groups were entirely composed of untrained and uncertificated teachers. They were usually employed to teach in a school under the authority and guidance of a certificated teacher. The only factor which distinguished them from pupil teachers was that they were regarded as part of the school staff and they were not required to be annually examined.

(d) *Assistant Uncertificated Female Teachers*

This category was specifically created by the SED to meet the increase in the number of children doing needlework in the junior and senior departments in elementary schools. The majority of needlework mistresses were described as untrained Assistants and their status was comparable to that of pupil teachers in spite of the fact that they had to be eighteen or over.

(e) *Pupil Teachers*

This group was defined as those who served a five-year apprenticeship in a school between the ages of thirteen and eighteen. They were placed under the control of a certificated teacher and their progress was monitored by an inspector.

A closer examination of the internal organisation of the educational hierarchy shows that occupational divisions based on sex were adapted in accordance with educational policy and attitudes. After the 1872 Act the church authorities and the SED actively began to encourage the entry of women into teaching, partly because of an abundant supply of female labour. More importantly, however, there was a particular need for teachers in the infant sector of the elementary school where there was an intense concentration of pupils after universal education had been introduced in 1872. Together these factors resulted in a greater degree of interest in the role of women teachers and the instruction of infants. It was rationalised on the grounds that women had an innate and maternal sympathy with child nature and they were therefore 'naturally' more suited to teaching young children. This view was gaining increasing acceptance in official educational circles. Gordon, Richmond and Hamilton, senior officials in the SED, expressed such a viewpoint in 1878:

> The education of children should be so conducted as to develop grace and gentleness in their manners and deportment. If they are brought up under the gentler, more natural qualities of female teachers, a better result may be expected to be attained, than if trained entirely by men.[10]

This view was accompanied by a growing conviction in some intellectual circles that women teachers should have exclusive responsibility and control of the infant department. James Currie, rector of the Church of Scotland training college in Edinburgh, gave expression to it in the early 1870s:

> I have often expressed my conviction that the education of children up until the age of nine is women's work. They are better fitted for that kind of work than men; and in point of fact they do it infinitely better when they are suitably trained for it. The gradual though slow increase in the number of female schools seems to show that prejudice against women as teachers is dying out.[11]

As Currie's comment suggests, the notion of the infant department being conceived as a 'woman's sphere' represented a notable departure from pedagogic practice in the early nineteenth century. An infant school was generally associated with an infant schoolmaster who was usually assisted by his wife or a young female assistant. The major point of significance was that it was the male who was the dominant figure in this sector of the educational system, and the female mistress played a secondary role. Thus such titles as 'Qualifications of an Infant Schoolmaster' were to be found in the Glasgow training schools under the control of David Stow in the 1830s. Overall the 1870s marked a transitional period when occupational divisions between the sexes were becoming increasingly definite. The shift in the employment and recruitment of women into teaching was closely associated with changes taking place in the internal organisation of elementary schools. The transitional nature of this shift was analysed in a report by James Currie in 1875. He was commenting on the numbers of male and female students who had left training colleges and had subsequently obtained teaching posts:

> Especially noticeable was the rapidity with which female students were appointed. So different from what it was in former years. This is accounted for by the fact that the public school of the country is almost universally conforming to one type of organisation, that in which there is a master responsible for the whole, and the mistress under him for the instruction of the younger children.[12]

Currie's model could be more appropriately applied to small schools in rural localities, but in urban areas with high population density the organisation of the teaching staff in an elementary school was more complex. Even within each geographical boundary of a city the size of the teaching staff could display considerable variations. Generally speaking, however, the occupational hierarchy was organised along the lines shown in Table Two:

TABLE TWO

Educational Ladder in an Elementary School

Headmaster
Deputy Headmaster
Assistant Certificated Master
Assistant Certificated Mistress
Infant Mistress (head of Infant Department)
Assistant female teachers
Pupil teachers

Occupational divisions between the sexes were most marked at the very top and bottom sections of the educational hierarchy; it was in the senior department of the *elementary* school that there was no clearly defined sexual division of labour and, therefore, the relationship between the sexes in this sector of the teaching profession was more complex. By the 1880s women were not only predominant in the infant sector but also in the category of Assistant Certificated teachers.

As a result of greater numbers of girls attending training college during the 1870s, the percentage of females defined as 'skilled' and certificated teachers rose quite dramatically compared to the relatively stable position of male certificated assistants. In percentage terms, the numbers of male certificated assistants constituted 8.7 per cent in 1883 and in 1900 stood at 10.7 per cent. This provided a sharp contrast with the dramatic increase of women in the profession. In 1883 they represented 15.6 per cent of the certificated teaching staff, and by 1900 this figure had risen to 29.2 per cent.

In short, it can be seen that one of the long-term effects of the 1872 Act was a sharp acceleration in the displacement of male entrants into teaching by women. Concern over the question of male shortage was particularly acute among church authorities since they realised that a trend was becoming firmly established in which large numbers of girls were attending training college without a similar response from males. In a determined effort to encourage male entry into training college, the Free Church and the Church of Scotland opened their doors to male students at the Aberdeen training colleges in 1887. This proved to be an unsuccessful venture, principally because of the exceptionally high rate of entry among males into Aberdeen University as a result of the Dick Bequest scheme operating in the three north-eastern counties of Nairn, Banff and Aberdeen.

The high rate of male entry into Aberdeen University was accompanied by an exceptionally low rate of admission into the Aberdeen training colleges. In 1894 it was reported that 100 girls compared with 12 boys applied for a place at an Aberdeen training college. It is clear from the reports of the respective church authorities and the HMIs that the shortage of male candidates in training colleges had reached a crisis point by the early 1890s. John Kerr, senior inspector of training colleges in Scotland, pointed out in his general report in 1893 that only 270 males applied for admission to training colleges as compared with 1,123 females; out of that number only 137 males and 553 females were actually admitted. The heightened pitch of anxiety among church officials prompted a joint meeting of the educational committee of the Church of Scotland and the Free Church to discuss the issue of male shortage in 1895. They addressed a letter to the SED which contained the following heading: 'to direct attention to the Lords of Privy on the small number of male candidates and male teachers'. They pointed out that the percentage of boys offering themselves for admission to teacher training colleges had fallen from 80 per cent in 1890 to 48 per cent in 1894.[13] The letter concluded by emphasising that the supply of male teachers was hopelessly inadequate to meet the demand. In another letter, Dr. Ross, Rector of the Glasgow Church of Scotland college, described 'two evils' resulting from this situation: firstly, that the 'Education committee was forced to admit additional young women to fill the vacancies in the training colleges' and, secondly, 'women would now have to be employed in the advanced classes with a consequent decline in the numbers taught latin and maths'.[14]

This viewpoint contained an implicit criticism of the large participation of women in the workforce and a concern that educational standards would drop as a result of the replacement of male teachers by women. It served as a blunt reminder that a career in teaching was no longer a male preserve and that women's numerical presence in the profession was a staunch one; by 1901, women teachers numbered 17,374 compared to only 8,040 men.

Broadly speaking, the scarcity of male teachers and their reluctance to take up teaching as a career can be linked to three major factors; firstly, the development of other and possibly more lucrative opportunities in occupations like banking, the civil service or clerical administration dating from the 1870s onwards. For example, in the clerical profession alone there was a total of 51,175 male clerks recorded in the 1901 census in Scotland; secondly, the replacement of male teachers by women, which may have diminished male bargaining power in terms of wages, since females could be employed at a cheaper rate; lastly, the existing social and economic grievances that prevailed within the teaching profession which made a teaching career for males appear a less attractive proposition.

It is important therefore to discuss some of the injustices which faced all teachers, to assess if they had a disproportionate effect on women and to consider some of the general social and economic effects of the 1872 Act on the role and position of the sexes in the Scottish teaching profession.

Undoubtedly, two of the most bitterly contested issues in the teaching profession concerned the lack of promotional opportunities and wage differentials, and they received prominent attention from the largest teachers' union — the Educational Institute of Scotland (EIS). Animosity over the question of promotion was particularly pronounced among male certificated Assistants, since promotion to the top sections within the educational hierarchy was severely restricted. The percentage of principals in state schools remained remarkably stable between 1872 and 1914, which effectively blocked the advance of any other groups who aspired to these tightly held positions. This situation caused acute disillusionment among Assistants and it was undoubtedly a contributing factor in accounting for the temporary decrease of male entrants into teaching at the beginning of the 1890s. As one male teacher commented in 1896:

> It is nay, almost impossible to get a lad of promise to enter the profession. The prospect nay almost certainty, of lifelong assistantship with all that that means has a deterrent effect on possible recruits and school boards have sometimes to wait for months before they can secure male teachers.[15]

The scarcity of male candidates was also tied up with the broader question of wage differentials. The most vicious attacks were launched against individual school boards since they had the power to devise their own salary scales in a particular locality. Subsequently salary scales showed the most bewildering variety not only in urban and rural areas, or between the Highlands and lowlands, as one would expect, but also in different geographical areas within a city. The lack of uniformity in school board policy was described by a member of the EIS:

> Because for instance there exists an imaginary and arbitrary line, separating Leith from Edinburgh therefore an assistant of eight years standing whose fate has placed him to the south of that line receives £120 per annum whilst his less fortunate brother simply because he is located two yards north of it receives £95 for precisely similar services. Both do exactly the same work, both produce equally good results yet one only receives three-quarters of the remuneration of the other.[16]

Similarly in the rural districts of Scotland, ranging from Orkney down to Galloway, there were persistent complaints to the EIS regarding the discrepancy in salaries. According to one EIS observer, the low salary scales prompted many men to view the civil service as a 'haven of peace and security'.

Meanwhile, other male teachers directly blamed the huge importation of cheap female labour into the market as the chief reason for the lowering of men's salaries. By the 1890s the feminisation of the profession (corresponding with the male shortage) produced a sharp and bitter reaction from male teachers, particularly from male certificated assistants since it was that sector of the hierarchy into which women were flooding. Consequently not only were women accused of undercutting male teachers' wages but also of lowering educational standards and the respectable tone of the teaching profession. Some of these sentiments were encapsulated in 1894 by a male certificated Assistant teacher:

> We . . . have had to struggle against the downward tendency in wages caused by the continual importation of unskilled [female] labour into the market in practically unlimited quantities. Under the stress of these conditions a reaction has begun. The profession as a means of earning a livelihood is falling into comparative disrepute and men of ability are turning their talents to other and more profitable work.[17]

This evidence suggests that many male teachers strongly believed that existing grievances within the teaching profession could be largely attributed to women's refusal to obtain adequate qualifications and their willingness to accept low wages. Yet it could be argued that the educational structure and the dominant ideologies articulated within that structure actively contributed to women's subordinate position within teaching. In this respect, one of the most powerful ideological forces which determined divisions and internal segregation of tasks in the workplace derived from biological differences between men and women which then served as a justification for sexual differentiation and inequality.

If we take, for example, the question of wage differentials, it is clear that the widespread criticism levelled against women teachers for providing cheap labour was perfectly correct. Parliamentary statistics on the distribution of salaries show quite clearly that female salaries were generally half of male salaries. For instance, in the period 1872-1900 the mean annual salaries of females varied between £62-£72 and the corresponding figures for men ranged between £121 and £143 per annum. An overall view of the percentage distribution shows that by 1914 the majority of male teachers earned above £100, whereas 79 per cent of the total number of female certificated Assistants did not have a salary exceeding £100, and 60 per cent out of the total number of female principals were also receiving below £100.

On the other hand one could argue that the wage differentials in Scotland were justified on the grounds that women teachers were less highly qualified than their male counterparts. This widespread view was certainly valid in the late nineteenth century when there was a large percentage of untrained female teachers, but certain decisive changes took place in educational policy which render this argument less convincing.

The most significant change occurred in 1905 when the Presbyterian churches finally relinquished their control over training colleges and they were placed under the control of the SED. In addition the SED introduced several 'New Regulations' in 1906 which aimed at eliminating all untrained categories of teachers within the educational hierarchy.[18] This was in keeping with the long-term goal, laid down in 1872, of achieving a body of competent and certificated teachers. Between 1906 and 1914 there was a sharp decline in the numbers of pupil teachers and untrained Assistants, while other groups like provisionally certificated teachers and female uncertificated Assistants had been completely abolished by 1914.[19]

These categories of untrained teachers had fulfilled certain necessary functions for the educational authorities in the years following the introduction of the 1872 Act but, one generation later, they were no longer seen as necessary divisions within the hierarchy. The decline in the untrained categories of teachers was accompanied by a further increase in the number of certificated teachers. The practical outcome of the 'New Regulations' was that by 1914 women constituted 65 per cent of the entire certificated teaching staff in Scotland. Therefore, the commonly held assumption that women provided a cheap source of labour on the grounds that they were unskilled and unqualified could no longer be said to be justified. Yet an increase in the standard of female qualifications and the strength of numbers was not synonymous with increased promotional opportunities or a greater measure of status. Indeed the most prestigious post to which women could aspire was usually that of infant mistress in an elementary school.

It is also apparent that male teachers received greater encouragement and assistance in their efforts to attain promotion and formal qualifications. A good example of this discriminatory policy based on sex was reflected in the allocation of bursary allowances to training college entrants. All males received bursary allowances worth £18-£25 per annum, whereas the majority of female students was self-supporting. Moreover, even when a girl was fortunate enough to be awarded one of these coveted allowances, it rarely exceeded £18 per annum. Oral evidence would support this thesis. For example, a former schoolteacher was asked if she ever resented the apparent ease with which male teachers gained promotions:

> Answer: Oh yes! We used to wonder how they did it.
>
> Question: Was it because men were more highly qualified than women?
>
> Answer: Not a bit of it — it was supposed to be a man's privilege. Men were supposed to be better at discipline but a woman could often have done better.[20]

What is interesting about this comment is that although this female teacher was implicitly questioning the extent of male teachers' so-called superior teaching abilities, neither she nor the majority of women teachers were prepared to launch a sustained campaign to remove the inequalities based on sexual differentiation. An examination of the literature on the EIS reveals that there was no separate female organisation (except for a Ladies' Committee) nor was there a national campaign headed by women to obtain equal wage rates before 1914, although on a local level the Glasgow branch of the Scottish Class Teachers' Association did challenge the set of assumptions determining wage differentials between the sexes. For example, in 1914 they called for 'the equalisation of salaries between men and women teachers' and petitioned the Glasgow School Board for a 15 per cent wage increase for females and a 10 per cent increase for men.[21]

They met considerable opposition to this claim largely because the dominant view held by contemporaries was that female earnings merely supplemented the man's wage and the family income. The concept of the family (with the man as chief breadwinner and woman as wife and mother) was of crucial importance in defining the segregation of tasks and wage differentials between the sexes in a range of occupations. The reasons for women's subordinate position in teaching, therefore, ought to be located within a broader social and economic perspective. This perspective should take account not only of an occupational structure but also of male and female attitudes and roles within the family unit. Indeed the relationship between the home and the school (as workplace) provides a vital link in understanding how the enormous influx of women into the Scottish teaching profession after the 1872 Act was viewed by female contemporaries.

With the use of literary journals like the *Educational News*, it can be gleaned that many women viewed their entry into teaching as a 'revolutionary movement' since it provided a vehicle to prove themselves efficient in the workplace and in the home. It gave them a legitimate excuse to pursue an independent career and a chance to prove to their male counterparts that they were not intellectually inferior. As one female teacher wrote in an article in 1900:

There was a time in Scotland certainly within the nineteenth century when public opinion granted that the average woman had a soul but was doubtful about her brain . . . we are called here today to settle this doubt.[22]

The practical outcome of these sorts of arguments was reflected in the linking of women's higher education with infant and primary teaching, which was merely institutionalising an already prevalent feeling that women were naturally more suited to teaching young children. Equally important in this respect was the growing concern with the instruction of domestic economy in the late nineteenth century which corresponded with the influx of women into the teaching sector. It created an area where a minority of female intellectuals could apply their skills in campaigning for the provision of domestic economy for girls in elementary schools. Alongside teaching infants, this provided a distinct and specific area within the curriculum where women could exercise power and influence on policy-making decisions. In practice, however, one primary reason why the campaign to introduce domestic science into schools was ultimately successful was precisely that women did not challenge their traditional role as wife and mother. The sexual division of labour within the educational hierarchy was largely accepted as a natural phenomenon by many women. This point was implicitly made by one female teacher who wrote:

We have sympathy with every movement that makes fresh points of contact between the school and the home . . . There are things inside and outside the household that a woman can do better than a man and things a man can do better than a woman and our system of education should take cognisance of that fundamental fact.[23]

Equally important was the fact that women did not as a rule impinge on or undermine male teachers' authoritative positions in the top categories of the educational hierarchy — either as principals in elementary and secondary schools or the training colleges. This largely resulted in the development and reinforcement of occupational divisions between the sexes in the course of the late nineteenth century. While it cannot be disputed, therefore, that the feminisation of the Scottish teaching profession brought expanding employment opportunities for women after the 1872 Act, it was within a limited social and economic context.

NOTES

1. There are, however, a number of studies focusing on aspects of the Scottish teaching profession. See D. Myers, Scottish Teachers and Educational Policy 1802-1872: Attitudes and Influence (unpublished Ph.D. thesis, University of Edinburgh, 1970); M. Cruickshank, *A History of the Training of Teachers in Scotland* (1970); T. R. Bone (ed.), *Studies in the History of Scottish Education* (1967); R. Rusk, *The Training of Teachers in Scotland* (Edinburgh 1928); J. Scotland, *The History of Scottish Education* (1969).

2. *See A. Tropp, The School Teachers: The Growth of the Teaching Profession in England and Wales* (1957), and F. Widdowson, *Going Up Into the Next Class: Women and Elementary Teacher Training 1840-1914* (1980).

3. Myers, *op. cit.*

4. Reports of Commissioners, *Committee of the Privy Council Reports on Education in Scotland* (Parl. Papers, 1873, Vol. xx).

5. *Op. cit.*, Art. 56.

6. *Op. cit.*, Art. 68.

7. General Assembly Library, Edinburgh; Report of the Church of Scotland Education Committee to the General Assembly, May 1873, pp. 6-9.

8. In the 1860s, the attendance figures between the sexes at the Church of Scotland and Free Church Training Colleges were fairly evenly distributed. For example, in 1860, 111 males and 104 females attended Glasgow Church of Scotland training college.

9. Parl. Papers, *op. cit.*, 1875-6, Vol. xxv, pp. 1-30.

10. Parl. Papers, *op. cit.*, 1878-79, Vol. xxv, pp. 1-30.

11. J. Currie, Reports of the Edinburgh Church of Scotland Education Committee to the General Assembly 1871-73, Vol. VII, 1871 report, pp. 12-13.

12. J. Currie, *op. cit.*, reports 1874-76, Report, May 1875, p. 47.

13. *Op. cit.*, December 1894, p. 15.

14. *Ibid.*

15. *Educational News*, 1896, The Scottish Assistant Teachers' Association, p. 427.

16. *Op. cit.*, 27 January 1894; Paper read at EIS Conference, Edinburgh, *The Position of Assistant Teachers: The Professional Outlook*, pp. 56-60.

17. *Ibid.*, pp. 59-60.

18. Scotland, *op. cit.*, vol. 2, pp. 97-118.

19. There was a total of 4,323 pupil teachers in 1905-6, but by 1913-14 this figure had been drastically reduced to 24, CCES reports 1914-16, Vol. xx, p. 32.

20. Oral testimony, Mrs. Dickson (Glasgow).

21. Glasgow branch of the Scottish Class Teachers' Association, Minute Book, 27 February 1914, p. 254.

22. *Educational News*, October 1900: I. Hamilton, 'Women's Work in Public Schools', pp. 732-733.

23. *Educational News*, 30 August 1907, p. 719.

I would like to thank Roger Davidson and Bob Morris for their invaluable assistance.

8

The Education Departments in the Scottish Universities

R. E. Bell

1

IN 1979 the University of Exeter with 5,957 full-time students supported four chairs of education. In the same year the four ancient universities of Scotland with 28,131[1] full-time students supported only three, and two of those were of comparatively recent foundation. Yet Scotland had been the first country in the British Isles to establish such chairs and had moreover acquired a world-wide reputation both as a centre of educational enthusiasm and of devotion to scientific educational research. Hearnshaw, for example, in his history of British psychology, takes his reader's awareness of such a reputation for granted. He speaks of 'Scotland where the Scottish tradition of education provided favourable ground for psychological developments',[2] describes how strong centres were developed in Edinburgh and Glasgow, how in the former city Professors Thomson and Drever in particular established a centre influential far beyond Scotland and how, in most of the educational developments of which he speaks, 'Scotland . . . has been a jump ahead of England'.[3]

Whatever happened then to the initiative of 1876 that gave Edinburgh and St. Andrews the first British University chairs in what appears to have been a subject of perennial Scottish interest? Why were no further Scottish chairs founded in the next three quarters of a century? Why did St. Andrews eventually abandon its chair and its commitment to the subject? And, given the apparent national enthusiasm, why was there no sudden multiplication of Scottish chairs in the expansive '50s and '60s when Exeter and many other English universities were spawning education chairs with such eagerness?

It may be, of course, that Scotland (unlike England) had gradually discovered that university chairs and large university departments were not necessarily the best guarantee of the country's educational vigour or the best guardians of an efficient system of educational research. Shocking though such a sentiment must seem to English and American enthusiasts for university expansion, there is at least some Scottish evidence to support such scepticism. The very influential Scottish Council for Research in Education, for example, was the first national research centre to appear in the United Kingdom, yet it

had its roots not in university or even college activity but in the research committee of the main teachers' union and in the enterprise of pioneer local
education officers, few of whom had studied education or psychology at
university level.[4] Naturally, university teachers were later involved in the
work of that Council but they were never dominant in its early days. Moreover, the General Teaching Council for Scotland, set up not merely to control
admission to the teaching profession but also to determine its forms of
training, has never considered it necessary to include in its membership
representatives of university departments of education as such, even though
college staffs and universities in general are directly represented.[5] In some very
real senses, therefore, university departments of education have been seen in
Scotland as of no more than peripheral importance.

Of course, it may also be that Scotland's general enthusiasm for educational
studies and educational research has itself been greatly exaggerated. Yet the
evidence for such an enthusiasm is very strong and, indeed, convincingly
demonstrates also a Scottish desire to establish strong links between the
teaching profession and the universities. There are at least seven major pieces
of such evidence:

1. The actual establishment of the two 1876 chairs — twenty years before any similar move
    by an English university and fully backed by the main teachers' organisation.

2. The history of that organisation, the Educational Institute of Scotland, which from the
    beginning has not only acted as the main trades union for Scottish teachers but has also
    claimed to be a learned society, initiating research, receiving theses and awarding fellow-
    ships traditionally referred to as 'degrees'. Moreover, in its early days the EIS attracted to
    its membership not merely the elementary teachers who established the English National
    Union of Teachers but also teachers in the prestigious grammar schools of Edinburgh and
    Glasgow and even university professors outside the field of education itself.[6]

3. The creation in 1928 of the Scottish Council for Research in Education, the first such body
    in the British Isles.

4. The early requirement (in 1906) that all teachers in both secondary and elementary
    schools should be fully trained[7] (some sixty years before any similar move in England),
    followed in 1924 by the official establishment of an all-graduate male profession,[8] both of
    these developments creating *prima facie* a wider potential audience for the findings of
    educational researchers.

5. The establishment in 1966, for the first time within the British Isles, of a Registration
    Council for teachers (on the lines of the General Medical Council), laying down academic
    standards for admission to the profession.

6. The establishment following the first world war of a highly prestigious second degree in
    education in all four existing universities, a degree widely accepted also as an honours
    degree in psychology and forming what Hamilton terms 'an important preparatory
    school for what might be called the superintendent class in education',[9] a training ground
    for an educational clerisy extending significantly into England and the remainder of the
    Commonwealth.

7. A whole array of famous Scottish names ranging from Godfrey Thomson to A. S. Neill,
    which feature regularly in the studies of educationalists throughout the English-speaking
    world and beyond.

At first sight, evidences 1, 4, 6 and 7 appear to demonstrate major commitments by the Scottish universities to the field of education, though evidence 7 in particular must be treated with caution. Holders of famous names do not necessarily share the characteristics of a majority of their colleagues, and too much concentration on them and their activities can disguise a more general reality. Many a university department has earned a reputation as a centre of excellence on the basis of one staff member's bestseller or the work of one research team. Equally, when regarding evidence 5, we must beware of extrapolating too readily to education the effects of such a Council's work on university activities in other professional fields. The ostensible purpose and standing of the Scottish General Teaching Council as outlined in the foundation legislation have been much eroded by the attitude of successive Secretaries of State who have enforced registration only in state primary and secondary schools and have exempted the private sector in a way that would have been fatal to the prestige and effectiveness of the General Medical or Dental Councils had similar exemptions been made in their case.[10] Indeed, so much has the GTC fallen under the control of government and the teachers' unions that the universities as such have played an unexpectedly insignificant role both in its deliberations and its preoccupations.

On the other hand the early enforcement both of graduation on a male teaching profession already given to attending university, and of formal training on all graduates, did lead to a far closer relationship between the teaching profession and the universities and between the training colleges and universities than has until recently been the case in England. As we have seen (evidence 6), the Scottish universities began over sixty years ago to cater for the postgraduate education of leaders in the educational world. The comparative underdevelopment of the Scottish university departments of education does therefore remain an apparent anomaly in a post-war world in which even the English universities, too often neglectful of educational studies, began to expand their departments on a major scale.

When in 1876 Scotland led the field with its two chairs, the Educational Institute could obviously see it as a major advance for their policies of professional development,[11] while the College of Preceptors had supported it as a major event for teachers throughout the British Isles.[12] Yet in 1976 the only celebration of a centenary that might well have been a national event turned out to be a tiny private meeting of the Scottish History of Education Society. Both Edinburgh and St. Andrews universities totally ignored it, and since then the number of Scottish chairs, far from increasing, has actually decreased. Indeed the young, idiosyncratic and small university of Stirling alone has ventured to found more than one; St. Andrews transferred its chair to Dundee, which appears now to be abandoning it; Strathclyde and Heriot-Watt have never even attempted to establish one. What, then, happened to the great hopes of 1876?

L

2

In fact, the two chairs then established had grave weaknesses from the beginning. The first two incumbents, Laurie at Edinburgh and Meiklejohn at St. Andrews, were significant and influential figures in themselves, but the significance and influence of both were created by their general life work rather than through or even perhaps in spite of their being Professors of Education. Indeed, it may well be that the difficulties of those first incumbents still haunt the university departments today.

The chairs were originally endowed by the trustees of Andrew Bell, the advocate of the so-called Madras system of monitorial pedagogy under whose will funds had been allocated for the development of education in Scotland. These funds were administered by a number of separate bodies, and the Education Act of 1872 presented a dilemma to the trustees who had hitherto largely seen their task as one of developing actual schooling in those needy areas that now seemed likely to be adequately served by Local School Boards. An Act of the Court of Session compelled the Town Council of Glasgow to continue to aid the Sessional schools in their area,[13] but in the East it was felt that the money should now be put to different use. A codicil in Bell's will had suggested the financing of lectures on teaching for audiences in Edinburgh, and this idea was now developed into a full-blown proposal for the establishment of a regular university chair.[14]

Such an idea was not new to Scotland. For fifty years or more the idea of the academic study of pedagogy had been discussed. In an article of 1862 in *The Museum*, for example, 'an Edinburgh graduate' had emphasised the far greater need in Scotland than in England to link teacher training to the universities at which so many budding teachers studied,[15] and it was not unknown for university professors with earlier secondary school experience to write of their experience in ordered and academic terms. In particular, Pillans, Professor of Humanity at Edinburgh, had done so[16] and had drawn attention to the now advanced study of pedagogy in Germany and elsewhere. The Educational Institute itself had canvassed the possibility of university chairs and classes,[17] and a similar suggestion by the Headmasters' Conference in England as recently as December 1872 had already helped to produce lectures, if no chair, in Cambridge and elsewhere. There was therefore nothing inherently surprising in the Edinburgh proposal, especially as, since the eighteenth century, the Scottish universities had been far readier to embrace new subjects (especially potentially profitable new subjects) for chairs than had their English counterparts.

While it is difficult now to determine how far there had been preliminary discussions with the university before the Bell trustees' offer was formally made, by the time it was first discussed by the Edinburgh Senatus, the Arts Faculty had already been exploring how the university could serve the needs of the post-1872 teaching profession.[18] The Scottish Act, unlike the English one of 1870, dealt not merely with elementary but also with secondary schools, and it was clear that any expansion of that sector would have repercussions on the work of a professoriate the size of whose salaries was still affected by the number of students they could attract. If the existence of a department of pedagogy might act as an extra inducement to potential teachers to study their other subjects in Edinburgh, then it would have a virtue quite apart from any other public service that it might perform within a expanding education system. In any case, there were sufficient professors in all faculties genuinely concerned with educational issues to give the idea an intrinsic attraction.

Within Senatus there appears therefore to have been no opposition to the idea in itself. All the anxieties, initally at any rate, seem to have centred on the issue of finance. At first the endowment spoken of was £10,000,[19] but when the prospect arose of a government willingness to provide a supplement, as they had done in recent years in connection with the new chairs of Engineering and Geology,[20] it was felt appropriate to lower the Edinburgh offer to £6,000 and to offer the balance of £4,000 to the University of St. Andrews. This was appropriate on a number of grounds. Bell himself had been a native of St. Andrews and a student of the University, an institution now with much reduced numbers and facing bankruptcy. Moreover, the St. Andrews region contained the large city of Dundee and the highly populated county of Fife, but it had as yet no teacher training centre of any kind. The existence of the chair might well not merely offer a needed service but could also draw a new and substantial income to a needy university.

However, in so confidently expecting a state subsidy the Bell Trustees miscalculated. Indeed Edinburgh University had been more nervous. Some members of the Arts Faculty felt that with only £6,000 as endowment for a salary, a lectureship might have been more appropriate than a chair.[21] However, both the trustees and the Senatus had felt that an approach to government was justified. When this, using the Engineering and Geology analogies, failed to produce a satisfactory result, Senatus cautiously postponed a final acceptance of the money.[22] The trustees became incensed at what they felt was the looking of a gift horse in the mouth and pressed the university for a final decision.[23] The reasons for the government's delay and the final refusal to provide the extra endowment, despite the respectable precedents, are now obscure. Certainly Robert Lowe was known to be sceptical about the idea of education as a science,[24] and Ross speaks bitterly of an effective parliamentary pressure group successfully opposing such a grant.[25] But, significantly, the government appears to have proposed reserving to itself the right of initial nominations to the chairs, a right usually accorded to those providing the endowment and certainly accorded in the case of Geology and Engineering.[26] Whether the imposing of such a condition was simply designed to terminate the negotiations by annoying the endowers (which it certainly did) or whether it implied a new desire on the part of government to exercise control over any extension of teacher training into the university sector is not entirely clear. What is certain, however, is that the Bell trustees made their entitlement to nominate the first occupants of the chairs a definite condition of the offer,[27] and both universities finally accepted the albeit inadequate gift horse without further ado and without any government endowment.[28]

The immediate and evident effect was to fix the new professors' basic salaries at a point way below that of their colleagues. How far this in itself gave the chairs themselves a different and lower status is now difficult to judge, but certainly Laurie for one seems hardly to have been accepted as a normal colleague by his fellow professors in the Edinburgh Faculty of Arts, whose deliberations he only once attended during his first two years in office, and that for a meeting at which his own financial disadvantages were being discussed prior to a submission to the University Commissioners.[29] His next major emergence in the Senatus was five years later when he complained of his colleagues' behaviour in arranging classes that clashed with his without prior consultation,[30] a complaint not accepted by the Faculty of Arts when the matter was referred to them.

In St. Andrews the financial situation was even worse than in Edinburgh. Not only was the endowment itself much smaller, but the actual number of potential students in session at any one time was considerably less.[31] Meiklejohn could not even count on a room in which to conduct his classes and, as Maitland Anderson reported, he had sometimes to conduct them in his own drawing room.[32]

But any alienation was not entirely due to financial causes. There were also academic problems. For while many professors supported the new chairs, there were undoubtedly other colleagues who mistrusted the whole idea of pedagogical studies on ideological grounds. Theological, philosophical and physiological objectors to new pedagogical and psychological theory were always present, as they were to be for the following hundred years. But even when colleagues were not inimical, even when they were moderately friendly or well disposed towards them, the problem shared by Laurie and Meiklejohn was that their subject, unlike the others, did not form part of the regular degree programme. Any students who attended their lectures did so as volunteers, and while this produced a willing and co-operative audience, it did not encourage their colleagues to see the Education classes as an integral or serious part of the university's activities or its Professor as a Faculty member equal in status to the rest of them. No doubt the personal status of the two Professors as individuals (Laurie, for example, had been a key figure in the councils of the Church of Scotland) and their high standing with those students whom they did attract did something to mitigate the effects of the exclusion, but they were Professors of theory rather than practical trainers of teachers, and so long as their fellow theoreticians refused to accept them fully into their fellowship, the function and future of their chairs remained continually in doubt.

The doubt was increased by the fact that the world of Scottish teacher training outside the universities was a far more influential and socially prestigious one than was the case in England. The major training centres of the Church of Scotland and the Free Church of Scotland, as they existed following the Disruption of 1843, had a great influence both inside and outside Scotland. Their interests were more than well defended, not only by church leaders but by a laity in both Lords and Commons whose concern with church and educational affairs was far greater than it is today. Laurie, who had himself been one of those responsible for framing the Church of Scotland's educational policy before his university appointment, was only too aware of the need to pacify those who saw the establishment of his chair as a threat or a snub to the college sector. Indeed he so insisted that the colleges had an essential and unique role to perform,[33] that it was sometimes difficult to discern exactly what he saw his own new role to be. Certainly he spoke of the college teachers' right to a share in university teaching for which their intellectual abilities amply equipped them,[34] in a way that was rarely heard again before the 1960s. In fact his gestures of goodwill and the vagueness of his definition of his own role, may well have helped to create the demarcation disputes that were to bedevil the relationship of Edinburgh University and Moray House College eighty years later.

Laurie spoke of 'Faculties of Education'[35] but never made it clear whether he envisaged two in Edinburgh, one inside and one outside the university, or some future amalgam. Under the Scotch Code of 1873 students in the Training Colleges were already allowed to attend two university courses prescribed for graduation. It was clear, both in the Senatus discussion of the founding of Laurie's chair[36] and in his own statements, that his new education course was seen as relating to those students in some way, but it was never clear in what precise way, for they were also College students and the colleges were hardly likely to surrender to Laurie their teacher training function, just as none but the more affluent students were likely to spend scarce resources on a course that did not count either towards a degree or as a training qualification.

As Knox puts it:

> If in England the academic study of education rose out of practical needs, the converse was largely the case in Scotland. These chairs of education were founded first and their practical connection with teacher training was left to be worked out afterwards. In some ways this was an advantage in that it gave greater prestige to education as a university study; in other respects it was to prove a disadvantage in that the marriage between the two parties was never really consummated and ended in divorce.[37]

Unlike England, the colleges were not attended exclusively by elementary teachers. Where Laurie did attract secondary teachers he was accused of poaching, the whole situation seemed fraught with difficulties and things were made even worse by the fact that Glasgow and Aberdeen Universities did not follow suit by founding chairs of their own. Undoubtedly Aberdeen was willing to found such a chair had funds been forthcoming,[38] but Glasgow appears to have had other grounds for rejecting the notion,[39] and as a result no new national structure of teacher training emerged in which the university sector as a whole could be assigned a role. Moreover, initially at any rate, this failure on the part of Aberdeen and Glasgow affected also the admission of Education to the Arts degree curriculum for, far more than nowadays, the degree structure of the four universities was definitely intended by the legislation to keep in step. For all these reasons, during the next forty years, the role of the chairs remained ill-defined and their usefulness and influence remained considerably restricted. In 1902 John Adams accepted the new London chair in preference to the one at St. Andrews, where he had been shortlisted on the death of Meiklejohn, and in doing so was said by his wife to have avoided *'enterrement de première classe'*.[40]

However, it would be misleading to suggest that the Edinburgh chair in particular remained totally moribund for the remainder of the century. Laurie was a man of much enterprise and vision. He was indeed (according to Darroch[41]) almost tempted away during this period to the new Teachers College at Columbia in New York and, whatever the limitations of his Scottish role, he greatly influenced events in both London and Cambridge.[42] But even in Scotland he gradually carved out a recognised, if unofficial, work space for himself. In 1880 he persuaded Edinburgh to award the title of 'Literate in Arts' to those who had successfully completed four compulsory courses of the Arts degree programme plus a fifth optional course which might be Education, and in 1886 he persuaded them to found their first postgraduate Diploma — The Schoolmaster's Diploma, taken either at a general level by passmen or as a specifically secondary diploma by honours graduates.

The very title of Schoolmaster's Diploma conveys its non-elementary school orientation. It is true that the honoured parish school tradition in Scotland had given the term 'schoolmaster' a wider use in the profession perhaps than had recently become the case in England. Even so, it is probable that Laurie saw in the ever-developing private, secondary school system of Edinburgh a fruitful field of operation. There was a type of schoolmaster in such schools as Fettes or the Academy who might accept a period of training at the university when he would turn his back on a college for both social and academic reasons. As the Edinburgh Merchant Company and other bodies reorganised their endowments, the number of such schools grew, and Laurie had been a major advocate of their development, being himself responsible for the reorganisation of the Heriot Trust in such a way that a handsome seventeenth-century orphans' residence became quite suddenly a 'traditional' secondary school whose academic status and involvement grew increasingly during the following half-century.

A further breakthrough for both Laurie and Meiklejohn came in 1892 when the Universities Commission (set up by the Act of 1889) included Education as a full qualifying subject for the M.A. at all four universities and Glasgow and Aberdeen, though still avoiding chairs, were actually forced to found lectureships. Initially these were cautiously made part-time appointments linked to the colleges, thus providing Adams (the Glasgow lecturer), Rusk suggests, with an admirable opportunity to develop that combination of university and college work characteristic of his later work in London, which set the pattern for English graduate training.[43] Such caution was justified. Far from becoming the basis for new Faculties of Education and bringing a strong teacher training function at long last to the Scottish universities, the 1892 arrangement simply succeeded in isolating the academic study of the 'theory and history' of education (two of the three elements in the Bell Chairs' title) from the vital third of 'practice', and in 1906 a major change in the pattern of Scottish teacher training suddenly precipitated what Knox called the 'divorce'.[44] Henceforth all teachers in the state sector had to undergo training; the universities, who were providing general education for a far higher proportion of elementary and not just secondary teachers than their colleagues in England, renounced that task as too formidable. The colleges could train all the graduates. If education remained in the university curriculum, it should remain so purely as an academic discipline. Ironically the success of Laurie's own preaching of the need for universal teacher training had thus destroyed much of what he had tried to develop within the university itself. There is no doubt that he considered the college courses too narrow for graduate needs especially the needs of honours graduates. He, like Meiklejohn, had never (so far as we know) fulfilled the Bell Trustees' demand that from time to time they should preach the virtues of the Madras monitorial system. Now their successors were effectively to be prevented from giving practical training of any kind.

3

As a result, this next generation of Scottish university teachers of education developed new and more appropriate enthusiasms. Darroch at Edinburgh and Edgar at St. Andrews were joined by a new figure in Glasgow, William Boyd, who, though never a Professor, made probably the greatest and most varied mark on Scottish education of any departmental head of education in any University.[45] He considerably developed the study of educational history, and with Darroch he established strong links between Scotland, the New Education Fellowship and the world of Dewey. He was also involved in the child guidance movement and was instrumental in setting up the first Scottish guidance clinic, while his enthusiasm for diagnostic testing first awoke the interest of the Educational Institute in modern educational research.[46] Each Saturday he lectured to scores of Glasgow teachers voluntarily attending a long-running course on current issues, a course which had to be financially self-supporting.[47] Boyd more than anyone else therefore embodied that wide range of interests and enthusiasms that were to keep the Scottish university departments alive despite their eschewing of actual teacher training. Yet all he achieved was achieved without the political power and influence of a chair and often in the face of opposition from a university hierarchy which viewed him with much ideological suspicion.

To praise Boyd is not to disparage Darroch, also a man of broad views, whose influence might well have equalled that of his Glasgow colleague had he not disappeared much earlier. Indeed it was in Edinburgh under Darroch that certain moves were first made which were eventually to stabilise the position of the departments for the next half-century by leading to the establishment of a proper education degree.

Given the decision to shed training and to concentrate on the academic study of education, it was always likely that there would be an attempt to establish such a degree. Indeed the EIS had for long demanded it. However, three decades of editorials in their journal make clear that the Institute could be very confused about what exactly they wanted. Certainly they wanted a place for education in the university. Certainly they wanted chairs, but what exactly the holders of those chairs should do was not always clear. Some EIS leaders saw them as teacher-trainers, others as what they eventually became. Some wanted Faculties that included the colleges, some wanted purely university faculties, doing only academic teaching and research. It was natural therefore that when they spoke of education degrees, some should envisage a degree like the modern B.Ed., awarded after a course of practical training interspersed with undergraduate studies, while others envisaged a postgraduate degree purely concerned with research as in the American and German Ph.D. (as yet unknown in British universities). A third group envisaged a postgraduate degree, however, that was not a research degree but a first Honours Degree in education to be done after graduating in another academic subject (a professional qualification rather like the LL.B.), and that, in fact, is what the Scottish education degree eventually became. There was extensive national support for the idea of such a professional degree and, in seeking to establish it, Darroch and the rest were seeking what was probably the best way of ending the confusion over their own departments' function in the post-1906 years.

Moreover, there were other influences operating, just as telling as the EIS or Scottish teacher opinion. Academic influences, especially from America, were stirring the whole world of educational and psychological studies, and it was natural that the development of thinking about an Edinburgh degree should involve the psychologists. This was doubly natural in that Drever, the head of the Psychology Department, had earlier had an educational orientation. He had been a student of Laurie's attracted to his course after some years in teaching[48] and had actually made his debut as a university teacher lecturing, not in psychology, but in comparative education. According to Rusk,[49] Edinburgh's initiatives were enough to stir Glasgow into action.[50] No doubt Boyd was hardly averse to the development of a degree which he later took up with enthusiasm, but the prime mover appears to have been not him but MacAlister, the university's Principal, who, again according to Rusk, heard of the Edinburgh proposals on an evening visit to the capital and, not to be outdone, sketched out his own proposals in the train on his way home. This story may or may not be apocryphal but what is remarkable is the proposal's subsequent history, for, in a way perhaps unparalleled, the Principal persuaded the University Court to accept his suggestion in the teeth of opposition from the Senatus but with the support of the General Council (i.e. the graduates), of whom of course teachers formed a high proportion.[51] That the Principal's own sudden enthusiasm rather than any move by Boyd and his colleagues was the crucial factor is suggested by the fact that some years were to elapse before any candidates for the degree were to present themselves in Glasgow.[52]

In the end, as was still the Scottish custom, all four universities adopted broadly similar regulations for this Bachelor of Education degree (to be referred to later as B.Ed. in Edinburgh and Ed.B. elsewhere), and it was clear that, far from being a miniature Ph.D. as some of the new research-minded might have hoped, it was to be a first degree (albeit taken at the post-graduate stage) in the parallel subjects of education and psychology. Moreover it was to be regarded as an Honours degree in both and was to incorporate a great deal of undergraduate material. Indeed earlier attendance at relevant undergraduate courses could give exemption from parts of this degree's courses and examinations.

The degree course was divided into two stages: the Diploma and the Degree proper, and it was clearly envisaged that many more students would successfully complete the first stage than would eventually attempt the second. Indeed, a broadly similar diploma course had been running in Edinburgh for some years before the procedures for adopting the Degree Ordinance had been finally completed.

Those attempting the diploma course had either to have been trained as teachers, to have taught successfully for three years or to be undergoing concurrently a form of teacher training. In the end a system developed whereby a sizeable number of graduates in training at the colleges chose to do the local university's diploma course concurrently. A minority did this to qualify themselves for later entry to the Degree course, but the vast majority did so because attendance at the diploma classes in the university not only excused them from what were, rightly or wrongly, supposed to be the far duller equivalent classes in education theory and psychology within the college but also prolonged their stay within a university atmosphere and qualified them for membership of teams, unions and clubs from which they would have otherwise been excluded. The popularity of this diploma had a major effect on the life of the Aberdeen, Edinburgh and Glasgow departments and indefinitely postponed any further questioning of those departments' viability in their respective universities although, for reasons we shall return to, it did little for the St. Andrews chair which could not implement the diploma part of the Ordinance until 1928[53] and postponed the operation of the degree course for thirty years — until 1949. At Aberdeen the courses developed as at Edinburgh and Glasgow but on a much smaller scale.

Yet even in the largest universities one must not exaggerate the size of the degree's scale in the years between the wars. Glasgow's Ordinance was accepted in 1916 but the first person to graduate did not do so until 1922 while, between then and 1939, the average number of graduates per year was only 3 or 4. In Edinburgh also, though graduations began in 1918, the average graduation was little higher than at Glasgow with 5 or 6 per annum. The heyday of the degree was undoubtdly the period after 1945 when the greater incidence of post-graduate grants, especially for ex-servicemen, boosted the numbers. Even so the degree's influence began to be considerable before the end of the 1920s. Graduates became administrators, lecturers and professors in all parts of the British Isles. Many of them had never intended to be so. They had simply intended to widen their horizons as teachers or at best to improve their chances of promotion to headships or other more lucrative positions in schools. But their university teachers saw new career structures emerging hitherto undreamt of, and these teachers (especially Boyd at Glasgow and Thomson at Edinburgh), because of their status as pioneers, were able to exercise a quite unexpected degree of patronage. Nowhere was this more true than in the field of psychology for, at a time when British departments of psychology were few and Honours graduates still extremely rare, these Scottish B.Eds and Ed.Bs were ranked as honours psychology graduates by the British Psychological Society and were able to fill many of the new psychological posts not just in universities but under those local authorities opening clinics or operating psychometrically based selection procedures for secondary education. Scottish graduates were especially valuable in such positions, given that they had also earned, concurrently, an Honours degree in the actual direct concerns of education.[54]

4

After the second world war, while the numbers holding the degree expanded, doubts were raised about the status as a full degree in psychology. This was a natural result both of the expansion of the subject and of the number of regular psychology departments now producing graduates. Even so, the value of the B.Ed/Ed.B. as a broadly based qualification for lecturers and administrators continued to be recognised, while at least a third of graduates in any case remained in the school sector, hopefully enriching the general system in the way that Darroch, Boyd and other pioneers had envisaged.

At the same time, while there is no doubt that the degree was a crucial innovation, giving a real function and sense of purpose to the departments concerned, its own functions have to be treated with some caution. First of all, we must not exaggerate its dominance in Scotland. True, there is much to be said for Hamilton's claim that it was the training ground for the 'superintendent class' in Scottish education. Many Scottish lecturers, administrators and psychologists were and are its holders. At the same time, holding the degree or its equivalent has never been a necessary condition of appointment to any post, whether by regulation or by custom. It is held to have been of great value to administrators, but in 1960, more than 40 years after its institution, only 11 of the 35 directors of education in Scotland held the degree, even if some of those 11 were among the most influential.

Second, in the world where postgraduate degrees are usually assumed to be primarily research-based in their orientation, we must remind ourselves that this was merely a post-graduate honours degree, even if the dissertation element in the final examination grew in importance after the second world war on a scale never envisaged by the degree's founders. Moreover, while there are many graduates prepared to pay tribute to the degree course and the training it provided as the basis for their eventual success as researchers, there are some very distinguished doubters. One Glasgow graduate, for example, who later became a well-known professor in England, is less than enthusiastic about the Ed.B. course:

> The contents were valueless; the only value of the course was formal. They gave me an entrée into university teaching which I wanted and which would have been impossible for me without it. With it I sneaked into a decent PhD University and from there a move to university teaching was relatively easy. It was an entirely formal degree. Its content was negligible at the time and I burnt the lectures many years ago.[55]

On the whole, Thomson's students at Edinburgh are the most wholehearted in praising the B.Ed. course as a preparation for a research career, but even some of them are doubtful about its value as a training ground for psychologists. Edinburgh graduates of that period have particularly emphasised the lack of coordination between the work done by students in Thomson's department at Moray House and that done in Drever's Psychology Department within the university proper. One 1948 graduate asserts that they were quite unrelated and, he says, 'I'm glad I had followed a B.A. Honours Psychology course under Sir C. Burt in London.'[56]

Third, as we said earlier, the degree's importance as a psychology qualification was only temporary. Later, those seeking British Psychological Society recognition as Honours graduates had to specialise in psychological topics in a way not only never envisaged by the degree's founders but also likely so to upset the balance between the two 'sides' that its essential all-round nature was damaged. Even some of those who taught psychology for the Scottish degree have retrospectively expressed doubts about its validity as an Honours qualification, notably Thouless who felt it was 'jolly lucky'[57] to get the recognition it received.

Fourth, the balance between educational theory (history, philosophy, administration) on the one hand and psychology on the other, though probably suited to the educational world of the first half of the twentieth century, was much less suited to the educational world of the second half. Sociology in particular was for far too long excluded from the degree programme while the Edinburgh Education Department's espousal of experimental education and test construction meant that, while they still valued history and philosophy, they inevitably used up some of their space for propounding a form of psychometrics that by rights should probably have fallen on the psychology side of the fence. The blossoming forth of other education disciplines in the 1960s and '70s resulted in an inevitable system of options that finally killed off the original all-round degree.

The degree's major lack of success, however, lay in its failure to impress a sufficiently large number of academics in other parts of the university. Despite all the efforts and successes of the Edinburgh B.Ed. graduates and all the high-level, often world-famous, teaching that had gone into producing them in the fifty years between 1918 and 1968, it was still possible in that latter year for at least a large minority of Edinburgh's professors to question whether a university department of education could justify or could ever have justified its existence.

The truth is, of course, that there had always been in the universities a group with such doubts. Some had been sceptical at the time of Laurie's appointment, just as a Senatus majority could be mustered against MacAlister's degree proposal in Glasgow.[58] There was and is nothing peculiarly Scottish about this. There was doubt in both the United States and in England about the acceptance of education as a true discipline and as a legitimate part of the academic canon. But in those countries the education department at least had a clear function. Formal acceptance there came with the clearly financially profitable introduction of graduate training, and more enthusiastic acceptance came later with the greater research patronage of such departments by government during the 1950s and '60s. But, money apart, there was and is scepticism.

Such scepticism certainly existed in Scotland but it tended to sink from view for some thirty years, between the 1920s and 1950s, as a result of an unexpected series of events. Usually opposition to the university departments manifested itself after 1906 in the wish that 'all this business', by which was meant both teacher training and educational research, should be 'left to the colleges'. No doubt certain élitist professors, especially Englishmen just arrived in a new situation, saw these colleges (the home of what they took to be elementary school teachers and those who failed to make university entrance) as a suitable dumping ground for a not very respectable and embarrassing academic discipline. At the same time, they underestimated both the social and political strength of the Scottish colleges compared with English ones (witness the resilience the Scottish colleges showed in postponing government action on closures during the 1970s) and also the extent to which, as a result of the gestures of Laurie and others, the colleges' own teaching extended into and overlapped with that of the universities. Indeed, many less élitist professors wished education to go into the colleges not because they saw them as a dumping ground but because they admired them and felt a better academic job could be done there. Others (all too often a majority, perhaps) were concerned with the financial issues and saw in any disappearance of the under-populated education departments into the colleges a wonderful opportunity to save university money.

In the end, the government, or at least its committee on the training of teachers, suggested just such a merger, and both Edinburgh and St. Andrews concurred. The Chairs were to remain in existence but they were to be combined with the headship of the largest local college and (presumably) both university and government would save money in the process.[59]

The Edinburgh chair was now filled by Godfrey Thomson, who also became head of Moray House College and thus established an amalgam of activities, some university-sponsored, some college-sponsored, that the world outside simply knew as 'Moray House', so much so that even now, thirty years after the university department and college were re-divided, many people still remain confused and find it difficult to believe that the Moray House tests, for example, are produced not by that college but by Edinburgh University Education Department which, under Thomson, was temporarily housed in the same building. This confusion was doubled by the fact that Thomson, though meticulous in his scientific work was no great respecter of bureaucratic niceties. He admitted part-timers to the degree course, for example, when it was clearly forbidden in the regulations, and he was not one to make clear distinctions between his college class and his University Diploma class, between college research and degree work. The result is that education largely disappeared from the field of university controversy for almost thirty years, much as it did at St. Andrews, though it is of interest that the merger there did not prevent Professor McClelland's activating the Diploma regulation for the first time in 1928, presumably to provide a seedbed for an as yet non-existent degree class.

Academically, of course, the fame of the Edinburgh department during this merger under Thomson was at its height — even if the world thought of it as 'Moray House' — while Boyd, without a chair, produced a large number of highly satisfactory graduates and extended both his clinical and historical work. Both figures were increasingly accepted by prestigious American colleagues and, in the new educational atmosphere of the post-1945 period, Scottish academic attitudes to education as an academic discipline began to undergo a striking (though possibly temporary) change.

Indeed Glasgow, after three-quarters of a century of positive refusal, was so impressed that it finally decided to establish a chair. This might seem a pleasant tribute to Boyd's work in building up a department that had never joined with a college, but it was nevertheless a public slight to him as an individual; he had retired in 1945 without a chair, yet with a prestige and international fame enjoyed by few British professors of the subject.

Suspicion of his personal politics (his social work among the unemployed of Clydebank and his outspoken views on their plight had given him a quite undeserved reputation as a Marxist) appears to have been a major reason why he was never elevated. However, lack of conviction about education as an academic subject appears also to have continued beyond the days of the initial Senatus opposition to the Ed.B. Even Boyd's wish to provide the basic endowment for a chair from the profits of his diagnostic test series appears to have cut no ice.[60] Yet by 1948 the University, encouraged perhaps by the disappearance of the embarrassment of Boyd and by the new North Atlantic vogue in the subject, was not only willing to support such a chair but to finance it *in toto*, a decision perhaps influenced also by massive enrolments for both the Diploma and the Ed.B. An appointment was made in 1951, and twelve years later a professor appeared also in Aberdeen.

A parallel new enthusiasm in Edinburgh University, however, had less happy consequences. Far from solving a long-standing grievance (as in Glasgow and Aberdeen) it actually helped to create a new one. The joining of the University Chair to the Headship of Moray House had provided a period of calm in the relations of the two institutions. Both profited from the financial advantages, the college enjoyed heightened prestige, and those in the university who were dubious about education as an academic subject had it painlessly removed from their midst without their having, embarrassingly, to fight for its abolition. However, to the surprise of many, the retirement of Thomson in 1951 put the whole arrangement in jeopardy, for an influential body of university opinion arose (especially in the Arts Faculty) which now, far from disapproving of education as part of the academic canon, actually felt it was too important an academic subject to be absent from the direct concerns of a major university and too complex and fundamental a topic to be left in the care of a mere Training College. In a sense, these had been Laurie's opinions in defending his original tenure of the chair, though he presented them with a little more delicacy than some of the chair's uncompromising defenders in the 1950s.[61]

Their reasons were not held in common. Some professors like John MacMurray, perhaps the leader of the movement, felt strongly that education was a key issue both in philosophy and in the national future and that it had not been adequately served by Thomson who, however sympathetic to philosophy, remained an amateur and devoted most of his energies to forms of psychometrics seen by MacMurray and others as dehumanising.[62] Others, like many supporters of the new Glasgow chair, hoped that a more independent chair in a less overcrowded department could foster a wider development of American-style research in educational fields other than the purely psychometric. A third group were plainly snobbish, both socially and academically, in their attitudes to what they saw as a state-sector college. Their children, like most middle-class children in Edinburgh, were attending fee-paying non-state-sector schools. To them the really respectable authorities on education were the headmasters of the independent sector brought to birth so enthusiastically by Laurie and his contemporaries. An independent chair could far more easily fall in with the needs of a group which had traditionally mistrusted educational 'theory', especially psychological theory, and despised the preoccupations of the colleges. A typical sentiment of this group was that good teachers were born not made. They might even have seen the major function of a professor of education not as a trainer of teachers, not as a research worker, but as an adorner of secondary school speech days, adding the prestige of university patronage to the work of secondary schoolmasters without interfering too much in the running of the whole business.

It seems likely that a similar array of sentiments was operating in St. Andrews where McLelland, in his joint tenure of the St. Andrews chair and the

Dundee college principalship, had also established a strong reputation in the psychometric field, and there too, chair and college principalship were again divided. Certainly the two eventual, independent professors, Pilley in Edinburgh and Adams in St. Andrews, could not have had preoccupations more different from those of their distinguished predecessors. Adams was a fervent classicist seeking his major inspiration not in North Atlantic psychology but in the work of Comenius and his predecessors. Pilley, though a practical researcher in the physical sciences, based his gospel on actual opposition to the social sciences, their philosophy and methodology and, though having to work with psychologists in both the Diploma and Degree programmes, he always made it clear, with Leavis-like clarity, that he despised their work if not them personally. Yet, ironically, the re-division of university and college functions had actually brought into Pilley's immediate responsibility the very test-construction industry that he had in one sense been appointed to wipe out. Indeed, such was its financial success in that heyday of secondary school selection that neither he nor the university had the will to do anything about it, and the profits of the Moray House Tests underpinned many of the activities and even the full manning of the new, more 'humane' department.

5

As for relations with the college, they went from bad to worse. It may be that Inglis, Thomson's successor as head of the college, had expected also to have the chair. He had had a distinguished career not merely in the college world but also as Boyd's assistant in Glasgow University. But whatever his personal feelings, there was certainly enough patronising of the college by university authorities to justify retaliation. The fact that the University Diploma class, in many ways the cream of the graduate course, opted out of college theory classes and went 'up the hill' to be taught in a different atmosphere was becoming as distasteful to many college lecturers as the creaming of comprehensives by fee-paying grammar schools was becoming to state school headmasters. The college, as a result, could on occasions prove unco-operative over timetabling,[63] while the personal relations between the heads of the two institutions became distinctly soured.

Even so, the college and the university department had managed to pursue separate paths without damaging each other in the half-century preceding Thomson, and those lamenting the strained relations of the '50s and early '60s did not usually envisage the consequences they were to have for the chair when Pilley retired in 1965. By that time a major change was taking place in the general relationship of the colleges to the Scottish universities following the Robbins Report on the future of higher education, published in 1963. Robbins had envisaged a new kind of college undergraduate course combining teacher training with academic study, and leading to a new kind of B.Ed. degree. One minor consequence of this arrangement was that the existing Scottish postgraduate degree (B.Ed. or Ed.B.) had to be swiftly renamed Master of Education, thus leading to final confusion with the many and varied English degrees of that name, most of them based mainly on highly specialised research work and totally unlike the broad-based first-degree-like Scottish formula. But a far more important consequence for the university departments was that the colleges now entered into new negotiations with the universities that were to lead to their undertaking actual degree work (under university supervision, it is true), using their own staff and classrooms.

So, said Moray House College in particular, it they could now directly teach students for the university's own degrees, why could they not teach students for a mere diploma in education, the subject in which they were supposed to be particularly expert? The resentments of many years came to the surface, and in Edinburgh a straight bid was made to take over the major teaching commitment of the university's department and thus to destroy its claim to reasonable staffing and finance, even its major claim to separate existence.

Moreover, this bid received a welcome from within the university hierarchy itself. As we have seen, there had always been two quite distinct élitist attitudes to education as an academic subject in Edinburgh University: one (represented by MacMurray) insisted that education was too important a subject to be entrusted entirely to a mere training college, the other (strong also in Oxford and Cambridge, as we shall see in a moment) insisted that the university was too pure an institution to tolerate a spurious subject like education in its curriculum — far better to leave it to lesser institutions like training colleges. Both these élitisms, of course, could also find support among other élitists of a purely social kind (as we have already suggested), while they could also draw allies from various schools of thought in medicine and theology, depending on prevailing fashions and tendencies.

In the early '50s the MacMurray school was supreme, but by the end of the '60s the 'no education in universities' lobby was once more showing its strength. It drew much (though not all) of its strength from a group of professors originating in Oxford and Cambridge, where the lot of the education departments has always been a hard one. Even now, Oxford has no chair of education and, until recently, Cambridge also, though sporting a chair, was singularly inhospitable both to the local Institute and to an education degree. Indeed, this Oxford and Cambridge attitude had probably always underlain at least some of the prejudice against university departments of education displayed by the Scottish professoriate and by private sector schools both in Edinburgh and Glasgow. Symptomatically, in the 1960s, at a time when Edinburgh was happy to establish a chair of nursing studies and later even a chair of fire insurance, there was inadequate support for a chair of adult education, even though the director of that department already enjoyed high prestige in the world outside and was actually drawing a professor's salary.

A golden opportunity for the holders of such views to attack the Bell Chair itself arose quite naturally in the late '60s when many possibilities hitherto considered unthinkable were suddenly being suggested very widely and prejudices, not merely inhibitions, could be brought into the open in a way that convention had hitherto forbidden. Pleading the perennial financial constraints facing universities in the post-Robbins period, Edinburgh University established a procedure whereby, whenever a chair became vacant, its very existence and future should be questioned, and, following Pilley's departure, this procedure was followed in the case of Education.[64]

To be fair, it has to be emphasised that this was not an *ad hoc* procedure adopted especially by the enemies of educational studies. Indeed, even the Chair of Hebrew, a subject whose claim to serious academic regard was beyond question, was also investigated and actually abolished.[65] But the occasion did present an opportunity for all the department's enemies to gather round its potential corpse. The Oxford- and Cambridge-educated sceptics, the enemies that Pilley had made through his scorn for the social sciences, the older medical and theological professors still pursuing their feud with Thomsonian psychometrics, all of them and others seized the opportunity. Another group, principally lawyers and Scottish historians, on the other hand, seized the opportunity to defend the chair as a bastion of the Scottish heritage under attack from anglicisers (a novel view in the light of the very English Pilley's not very reverent attitudes to his adopted country), while a scattering of Senatus members in all faculties took the commonsense view that, given the national importance of education and given its secure position nowadays in most English-speaking universities, it would be perverse of the Scottish universities, where such chairs originated, to neglect any such opportunity for doing social and possibly academic good.

However, the most telling factor against maintenance of the post-Thomson settlement was the growing belligerence of Moray House College and its demand for the diploma. For this particular crisis in a most dramatic way brought back to public attention the question that had always existed for the Scottish chairs: what was their precise function in the national scheme of teacher education? Even if Edinburgh University decided to keep its chair, the question for Pilley's successor would be the same one that faced Laurie and Meiklejohn on their appointment nearly a century earlier: what is there for me to do? True, the position would be somewhat different in that, even if the diploma disappeared to Moray House, the now celebrated degree would still remain, but even that did not necessarily provide an adequate answer. In Pilley's last years, through his insistence on a two year full-time course, the number of candidates per annum had finally dwindled to two — hardly the basis for a thriving department — and though his colleagues were now planning a part-time course with wider appeal even the department's friends were worried about how it might function without the diploma.

In the end, a compromise was reached. The diploma did go to Moray House but the university department shared in its adminstration and teaching. In the circumstances, the university decided that the chair could be filled. However, the chosen candidate, Hudson, was clearly chosen for his reputation in the

M

world outside rather than for any gifts especially suitable for a professor in Scotland, and while it is true that the same could have been said of Pilley or even of Thomson (for Edinburgh had for half a century appointed Englishmen to a chair reserved elsewhere in Scotland entirely for Scotsmen), both Pilley and Thomson had genuinely attempted to develop a function in relation to the specifically Scottish system in which they found themselves. Neither served that system as directly as Boyd or Laurie, but at least their diploma and degree candidates did spread their ideas in the Scottish world outside the university. Hudson, on the other hand, appeared positively to welcome the lack of any clear duties for his chair within the Scottish world. Quite happy to pass the diploma to the College, he maintained the degree but devoted most of his energies to a band of Ph.D. students, some of whom originated in Scotland, but who could just have easily have carried on their work in England, Ontario or Wisconsin. To the horror of Scottish traditionalists, Hudson even contemplated the possibility of dropping 'education' altogether from the title of his chair.[66] He had found what to him was a paradise but to Laurie and Meiklejohn had been a nightmare — a chair without clear functions.

The two pioneers and their successors had painfully carved out a function for themselves, and it is a tribute to the heads of the Scottish departments that until the 1960s the actual right of their departments to exist had rarely been challenged. There had been a period of doubt in the early '20s at St. Andrews, but the union of chair and college there had overcome that problem. Even the long delay in establishing actual chairs in Glasgow and Aberdeen had never prevented the development of their departments' work and influence. The Hudson episode was, however, a clear turning point. Those who had served in the Pilley department actually decamped and joined the adult education people in a new department of educational studies, quite distinct from the research centre presided over by the professor himself. Although the chair and the department joined up once more upon the arrival of Entwistle in 1979, this was never an inevitable development.

In order to manufacture a respectable function for itself, a Scottish chair must now respond more idiosyncratically and in relation to its own particular local circumstances. Gone are the post-1918 days when all four departments then existing tried to move in unison when framing their degree course and administering their diploma.

In the mid-1960s they realised that they were drifting apart and possibly facing some common threat. It might well have been this feeling that led them to huddle together once a year round the fire of the Burn Conference Centre in Kincardineshire. These Burn Conferences, which were meant to unify, simply highlighted the growing differences. Increasing academic pressures led to differing schemes of specialisation within the previously generalist M.Ed., whose study periods and thesis demands also began to vary more and more. The growing interest in education outside the disciplines of education and psychology led to the presence at the Burn of sociologists and other research agents from SCRE, from government, and from other subject departments never involved in the dilemma inherited from Laurie and Meiklejohn. In any case, a good professor of education now ran a good department on his own lines, probably using many foreign models. Any distinctive Scottish tradition counted for less and less.

Furthermore, by the mid-1970s, two other universities, unheard of even when Pilley retired, were being more and more influential in the education field. Stirling University, exercising a manifest teacher training function to the horror of EIS and College traditionalists alike, clearly stood outside the mainstream of Scottish university departments, not only in the shape of its Anglo-American style M.Ed. but also in its large-scale involvement with undergraduate courses. The Open University now provided Honours degree education courses for far more Scottish teachers in any one year than had ever tackled the old B.Ed./Ed.B. in the whole of its pre-war history. In such circumstances any talk of a distinctive Scottish education degree became more and more meaningless.

Ironically, the 1980s saw the emergence in the Open University itself of a very Scottish dilemma. Its own Faculty of Educational Studies, like most Scottish departments, has no teacher training functions. In its case, this is caused not by the rivalry of colleges but by the mere difficulty of training teachers at a distance, with no supervision of practice and little personal contact. But this divorce of educational theory from actual training has posed for the OU very similar problems to those faced by Laurie and his successors, and these problems were underlined by one of Lord Perry's farewell suggestions on relinquishing the Vice-Chancellorship in 1980. Perry had been Vice-Principal of Edinburgh at the time of the Hudson affair, and he made clear on this occasion his own doubts about the suitability of including education in a university's mainstream honours degree.[67] However, the Faculty's subsequent efforts to vindicate its inclusion in mainstream university activities and its defence of education as an academic concern seem to have strengthened not only its position but also its powers of self-examination.

For similar reasons the uncertain position of the Scottish university departments has had positive as well as negative results. Indeed the phenomenon of doubt about their function seems on most occasions to have been a stimulus rather than a depressant. The degree in its heyday was clearly an achievement that arose directly from the search for a distinctive task and function. Had the departments been encumbered by the chores of teacher training their small staffs in the 1920s might never have attempted such an ambitious project. More recently many of the research programmes undertaken by the Scottish university departments seem to have arisen directly from that recognised independence of both government and teaching profession that is a by-product of their ambiguous position. The work on School Councils at Glasgow, for example, or on school management structures at Dundee immediately spring to mind as projects that might well have been too politically charged to be handled satisfactorily by any other agency. Scottish chairs of education may still be few in number and their future, as always, fraught with uncertainty, but at least that uncertainty has kept them innovative and determined to preserve their independence. They have been spared the dangers of that total acceptance which has spelt the decline of many a more respectable university department.

NOTES

1. *Commonwealth Universities Year Book*, 1980.
2. L. S. Hearnshaw, *A Short History of British Psychology 1840-1940* (London, 1964), p. 256.
3. *Ibid.*, p. 255.
4. R.E. Bell, Godfrey Thomson and Scottish Education, unpublished paper delivered at British Educational Research Association Conference, Stirling 1975.
5. Scottish Education Department, *Review of the Constitution and Functions of the General Teaching Council* (Edinburgh, 1969).
6. A. J. Belford, *Centenary Handbook of the Educational Institute of Scotland* (Edinburgh, 1946), *passim*.
7. M. Cruickshank, *A History of the Training of Teachers in Scotland* (London, 1970), p. 139.
8. *Ibid.*, p. 169. Strictly speaking, university graduation was not enforced outside the academic area. Teachers of art and physical education, for example, were merely expected to qualify within their own specialist institutions.
9. D. Hamilton in an unpublished paper, The Normal Curve and Some of its Abnormalities, read to the annual conference of the British Educational Research Association, Alsager 1981.
10. R. E. Bell, 'Lessons of the Scottish GTC', *The Times Educational Supplement*, 22 January 1971.
11. D. Ross, *Education as a University Subject: Its History, Present Position and Prospects* (Glasgow, 1883), p. 16.
12. In a message to the Senate of Edinburgh University, Edinburgh Senatus Minutes, 28 March 1874.
13. D. Ross, *op. cit.*, p. 34. The Town Council were responsible for administering the Bell fund in their area.
14. H. M. Knox, 'The Chair of Education in the University of St. Andrews', *St. Andrews Alumnus Chronicle*, 33, Jan. 1950.
15. *The Museum*, July 1862. The anonymous author was believed to be Laurie, subsequently the first holder of the Edinburgh Chair.
16. J. Pillans, *The Rationale of Discipline as Exemplified in the High School of Edinburgh* (Edinburgh, 1852).
17. D. Ross, *op. cit.*, pp. 8-9, 16-19.
18. Edinburgh Senatus Minutes, 29 March 1873.
19. H. M. Knox, 'Simon Somerville Laurie 1829-1909', *British Journal of Educational Studies*, X (1961-62), p. 140.
20. Letter from Bell Trustees dated 18 February 1874, quoted in Edinburgh Senatus Minutes, 21 February 1874.
21. Edinburgh University Faculty of Arts Minutes, 24 February 1874.
22. Edinburgh Senatus Minutes, 26 October 1874.
23. In letter of 5 October quoted in Edinburgh Senatus Minutes, 25 October 1875.
24. Quoted by Ross, *op. cit.*, p. 12.
25. Ross, *op. cit.*, p. 18.
26. Edinburgh Senatus Minutes, 25 June 1875.
27. Edinburgh Senatus Minutes, 25 June 1875.
28. Edinburgh Senatus Minutes, 6 November 1875.

29. Edinburgh Faculty of Arts Minutes, 24 February 1877; a further endowment of £4,500 from the Bell fund was forthcoming in 1888.

30. Edinburgh Senatus Minutes, 28 January 1882.

31. Ross, *op. cit.*, p. 27.

32. Quoted by H. M. Knox, 'The Chair of Education in the University of St. Andrews', *St. Andrews Alumnus Chronicle*, 33, January 1950, p. 34.

33. S. S. Laurie, 'The Teaching Profession and Chairs of Education', in *The Training of Teachers and Methods of Instruction* (Cambridge, 1901), p. 6.

34. *Ibid.*, p. 8.

35. *Ibid.*, pp. 11-12.

36. Edinburgh Senatus Minutes, 29 March 1873.

37. H. M. Knox, 'Simon Somerville Laurie 1829-1909', *British Journal of Educational Studies*, X (1961-62), p. 138.

38. Ross, *op. cit.*, p. 17.

39. *Ibid.*, p.17.

40. R. R. Rusk, 'Sir John Adams 1857-1934', *British Journal of Educational Studies*, X, (1961-62) p. 51.

41. A. Darroch, in P. Monroe (ed.), *A Cyclopedia of Education* (New York, 1912), 3, p. 653.

42. Knox, *op. cit.*, p. 141.

43. Rusk, *op. cit.*, p. 51.

44. Knox, *op. cit.*, p. 138.

45. R. E. Bell, Godfrey Thomson and Scottish Education. See note 4 above.

46. *Ibid.*

47. Glasgow University Court Minutes, 12 June 1924.

48. C. Murchison, *A History of Psychology in Autobiography*, II (Worcester, Massachusetts, 1932), p. 22.

49. In conversation with the author.

50. Glasgow University Court Minutes, 14 December 1916.

51. *Ibid.* At this meeting an attempt to delay consideration of the Ordinance was rejected on the motion of the Principal. As recently as 7 November (Senatus Minutes), the Senate had transmitted its opinion to the Court that a separate Degree in Education was not necessary.

52. It was in 1922 that the first graduate took the degree, George Jeffrey Aitken, who had originally graduated as long before as 1896. This was four years after the first Edinburgh graduation.

53. This is discussed by H. M. Knox, 'The Chair of Education in the University of St. Andrews', p. 34. See note 14 above.

54. The extent of the work done by Aberdeen graduates, for example, is noted in an article by Rex Knight, Head of Psychology Department, in the *Bulletin of the British Psychological Society*, 47 (April 1962), p. 9.

55. These comments are derived from responses to a questionnaire survey, by the author, of all traceable holders of the degree.

56 *Ibid.*

57. In conversation with the author.

58. Glasgow Senatus Minutes, 7 November 1916.

59. Cruickshank, *op. cit.*, p. 167.

60. Educational Institute of Scotland, Executive Committee Minutes, 25 August 1928.

61. Amid a flurry of rhetoric promising future cooperation, the university's firm intentions emerge clearly in the minutes of the Edinburgh Provincial Committee, 26 February 1951. Although they still support the idea of a joint appointment, they clearly wish the form of association between the two institutions to change.

62. This view is attacked as unfair by Sir James Robertson in his lecture, *Godfrey Thomson* (Edinburgh, 1964), p. 6.

63. See, for example, letter from the Secretary of the University (dated 22 July 1957) addressed to Inglis and reproduced in the Minutes of the Edinburgh Provincial Committee, 20 November

1957.

    64. Edinburgh University Bulletin, Nov. 1965.

    65. Edinburgh Senatus Minutes, October 1967. It was in fact merged with the Chair of Old Testament Literature and Theology.

    66. An intention declared at a meeting with members of the department, 21-22 February, 1968.

    67. Lord Perry, Open University Senate Minutes, 15 April 1980.

9

Social Efficiency Progressivism and Secondary Education in Scotland, 1885-1905

Mary E. Finn

OPINIONS differ regarding the nature of the changes Sir Henry Craik imposed on the educational system of Scotland during his tenure as first Secretary of the Scotch Education Department from 1885 to 1905. To many of his contemporaries (and some educational historians) his reforms were both 'sound and healthily progressive'.[1] Today, however, Craik exemplifies the high Tory bureaucrat to reformers who are trying to create a more comprehensive and less selective meritocratic school system.

This presents an interesting dilemma for the historian of Scottish education. In many ways the change in opinion corresponds to a changed attitude toward 'progressive education' in the United States. 'Revisionist' historians there have argued that, since the improvements promised have not materialised, it is necessary to consider the possibility that progressive educators did not mean what they said about creating a new society, one both more just and egalitarian. Since the rhetoric and the reality of progressivism seem to have little in common, according to these historians, a new view may be needed of progressives, one in which education for social control and social efficiency is given adequate attention.

While it may be difficult to conceive of any 'progressive educator' who was not a member of the New Education Fellowship, or at least sympathetic to its ideals, some explanation is required for the opinion of Craik's contemporaries that the reforms and changes he promoted were forward-looking and progressive. One way to explain this is to see that more than one variety of progressive was extant in Scotland as well as in the United States. This essay attempts (1) to view Craik's reforms from the perspective of those who approved his policies and saw the changes he introduced as promising progress and improvement of the Scottish educational system; (2) to offer a critique showing how such changes could be both 'progressive' and be designed to keep the underlying structure of social and economic relations the same; and (3) to suggest that these conservative 'social efficiency' progressive reforms were possible, in part, because of the bureaucratic, hierarchical structure of the

Scotch Education Department and that they, in turn, expanded and reinforced that bureaucracy's domain and dominance.

The terms 'progressive' and 'new' education generally conjure up images of non-traditional schools and open classrooms. Historians of Scottish education seem agreed that this type of 'child-centred' education has only recently been found in Scotland's publicly supported schools. James Scotland says, for instance, that the reforms of the American progressive educator John Dewey were not endorsed by the Education Department in Scotland until the 1930s, and were not practised in the classrooms until the 1950s and 1960s.[2] However, it is possible that both this traditional version of progressivism, and the social efficiency variety to be described here, grew out of intellectual and social trends that can be associated with post-Darwinian thought.

Modernising and updating institutions, to take account of the organic nature of society and the effects of ongoing change, was an imperative for all progressives. To the social control and social efficiency progressive, this took the form of providing educational institutions to develop each individual's talents, so each could play his or her specialised part or social role. By looking at the development of secondary education in Scotland during Craik's administration, using Glasgow as a particular example, it is possible to examine these social efficiency progressive reforms and to estimate their significance for today's school.

Redress of Grievances

Craik is usually given credit, or blamed (depending on your view of selective, differentiated or streamed secondary schools) for the development of publicly supported secondary education. His reforms, and those of John Struthers who succeeded him in 1905, were not always popular with the schools or the parents.[3] They did succeed, however, according to Scotland, in transforming what is often referred to as a parallel system of separate schools (primary and secondary for middle classes and elementary for working classes) into an 'organic' whole.[4] The result was a ladder or educational highway provided within the state system to allow children with ability to move from publicly supported elementary school to publicly supported secondary school and on to university and the 'business of life'.[5] The system was arranged, according to Craik, so that 'children above average ability [regardless of social class] could climb to the higher position for which nature intended them'.[6]

A long series of reforms was necessary to accomplish this, but the effect was to redress one of two major grievances many Scots had with the Education (Scotland) Act of 1872. While the Act had established a state system of 'elementary' education, 'secondary' education had been virtually ignored by the Government. The 1872 Act did 'recognise' two types of secondary schools, the higher class *public* (former Burgh) schools and higher class *private* (endowed and subscription) schools, but only the state-aided public (elementary) school[7] was eligible to receive government grants. The latter was to offer both primary and post-primary education as the Education Act specified that 'the standard of education then existing in the public [parish] schools should not be lowered'.[8]

Popularly elected School Boards were responsible for the administration of both the public elementary and the public higher class school, though the latter 'were not permitted to derive support from the local rates'.[9] John Kerr, former Senior Inspector for Craik, identified the problem of the higher class public school as 'the anomalous position of secondary schools in the education field, as compared on the one hand with the primary school well supplied with grants and on the other the university and its large resources of various kinds'. Secondary schools, the 'natural connecting link' between the primary school and the university, had to depend largely on fees and scanty endowments.[10] Parliamentary reforms of various endowments helped some private schools become efficient secondaries. The number of students attending the Merchant Company schools in Edinburgh, for example, rose dramatically after the 1869 Endowed Schools Reform Act. Enrolment went from 428 to 4,100 in two years. Heriot's School, reformed a few years later, went from 180 students to more than 1,000 in only one year.[11] Public higher class or secondary schools, however, declined for lack of funds and attention under the new School Boards. There were only 17 public higher class schools in 1879 compared to 260 private secondaries.[12] Permissive legislation in 1878 did not help the public secondary school because School Boards were reluctant to rate for a type of education that would only be available to a select few. State secondary schools had to rely on fees, Council gifts and occasional endowments.

In 1892 Parliamentary aid was finally offered to the public secondary school. Meanwhile, Craik had taken two important steps which are discussed in detail below. One was to gain control for the Education Department over the entire secondary school sector. The other was to draw a line between elementary and secondary education. The first was accomplished with the Leaving Certificate, instituted in 1888 for higher class schools and extended to the public (elementary) school in 1892.[13] The second was accomplished with the Merit Certificate, begun in 1891 to mark the upper limit of the public (elementary) school course. The result, eventually, was the desired organically connected national system of education, from primary school through to university. By 1920, according to Scotland, there were 196 secondary schools receiving grants according to the secondary school Code for Scotland, and only 13 strictly private secondary schools. Scotland credits reforms instigated by Craik for these results.

In addition to demand for state support of secondary schools, educationists criticised the 1872 Act for introducing 'payment by results' to Scotland, which many felt had narrowed the Scottish schools' curriculum. Established by the Code of 1873, payment by results meant each student was individually tested on his or her ability to read, write and count. Since Parliamentary grants were given on the basis of these test results, too often these basic subjects, commonly called the 'Three R's', were the only subjects which received serious attention from teachers and headmasters whose livelihood depended on their students' performance. Drill and rote memorisation were the major pedagogical tools used to prepare students for the HMI's inspection.

In his first Code, 1886, Craik used grants for 'class' subjects to broaden and enrich the elementary curriculum and thus redress this second grievance. Literature, for instance, was now taught to all students in the elementary standards, along with geography, history and science,[14] in addition to the Three R's. Craik gradually moved to the idea of class exams to satisfy the HMI's that both the class subjects and the basic subjects were being adequately taught. He modified individual exams in the lower standards in 1886 and introduced a relaxation in the higher standards of both standard and class subjects.[15] In 1889 he abolished all fees in the compulsory standards, and in 1890 the individual examination system was abolished. In 1894 fees were eliminated for all elementary standard students between the ages of five and fourteen, and in 1898 the whole system of grants for individual subjects was replaced by a system of block grants based on attendance in the elementary standards.

These reforms resulted in a change of attitude, according to Kerr. Because test performance and grant earning required less attention, ordinary elementary subjects could be taught so that attention was paid to 'permanence, intelligence and development of the whole child's nature'. The object was to make children morally and physically good citizens, 'fit to earn a living and to enjoy their leisure'. These goals were said to be both 'sound and healthily progressive'.[16] According to John Clarke, Craik's 'new educational ideals were reminiscent alike of the fine spirit of the Renaissance and the opulent mind of the Greek'. School work, Clarke said, should

> aim to produce useful citizens embued with a sense of responsibility and of obligation toward the society in which he lives. It should render him, so far as the school can do, fit in body and alert in mind and should prepare him for rational enjoyment of his leisure.

'Auxiliary' subjects, such as nature study, drawing and music, in addition to the class subjects, were introduced by Craik to 'reinforce the Three R's and to establish an organically connected curriculum which would promote intelligence, observation and self expression'. Time was also to be found for 'training in manual and recreative exercises and in morals and manners'.[17]

A. J. Belford, historian of the Educational Institute of Scotland, claimed that as a result of Craik's reforms, and those of his successor Struthers, by 1908 the clear aim of Scottish education was 'education of the whole being, mental, moral and physical, by means of a complete and well articulated system of national schools'.[18] Both aspects of this conclusion, the broadening and enrichment of the elementary curriculum to educate the whole child, and the development of a national system of schools from primary through secondary to university, were related to the 'organic' progressive view. However, instead of fostering development of the social co-operation that interdependence made essential, and of the intelligence each individual needs to thrive in a modern, complex and changing world, the social efficiency minded progressive emphasised the need to find and develop differences among individuals, and to adjust and systematise the various parts to ensure the efficient organisation of the social whole. Eliminating the existing system of specific subjects, which concentrated the higher education subjects in the academic or university preparation areas, became a primary goal of such reformers.

Specific Subjects

When Craik came into office there were no government grants for the higher class (secondary) schools. However, money had been available since 1873 for the teaching of specific subjects in the public (elementary) schools. Specific subjects were extended to Scotland, along with the Revised Code or payment by results, to expand the horizons of the older students and to allow more challenging work for the parish schoolmasters who by tradition taught both the elementary subjects and those required for university entrance. The specific subjects included the university subjects — Latin, Greek and mathematics 'inductively taught'; a group of language subjects — English literature and language, French and German; and a group of science subjects — mechanics, chemistry, animal physiology, light and heat, magnetism and electricity, physical geography, and botany. Each subject consisted of three stages; each stage involved one year of study.

In 1886 Craik's introduction of class subjects had removed certain specific subjects from the schedule. Class subjects were taught to all students, not just those individuals who prepared for specific subject exams. In addition, after 1886, students had to be in Standard V before they could begin to study any specific subject. This meant staying in school one year beyond the six elementary standards in order to do all three stages of a specific subject. In 1890 the Department's schedule of specific subjects was reduced to seven (mathematics, Latin, Greek, French, German, agriculture and domestic economy) and school managers were allowed to select other subjects suitable to their locale, provided the Department approved.[19]

The specific subjects were very popular with students and parents; demand was high and headmasters and School Boards were all too willing, from the Education Department's point of view, to offer advanced work to pupils willing and able to stay in school beyond the Three R's. The 16 subjects in 1886 had increased to between 20 and 24 by 1898. The number of pupils presented for examination grew from approximately 19,000 in 1876 to nearly 69,000 in 1886, after which it ranged around 50,000 to 1899.[20] Glasgow experienced a similar growth (as seen in the chart overleaf), especially in mathematics and French.[21]

The Scottish tradition of preparing for university in the parish school was promoted with this system. University fees were low and admission comparatively easy. If a student lacked adequate preparation for university, he could join a junior or preparatory class. One result was that a large proportion of the Scottish population attended university. In 1884-1885 the

Number of Passes in Academic Specific Subjects in Glasgow Schools

Year Ending	Mathematics	Latin	Greek	French	German
1881	67	270	2	111	1
1885	246	459	22	504	58
1889	569	301	42	1120	167
1892	1606	563	4	2082	259
1895	1392	455	14	2211	220
1899	1376	233	20	2117	269

ratio of university students to population (including junior classes presumably) was 1:5,000 in England and 1:617 in Scotland. As late as 1889 the greater number of University entrants still came directly from the public (elementary) schools.[22] Many reformers complained that this situation hindered the development of secondary schools. University fees were often lower than those of the secondary schools, so the latter suffered from the competition with the university for post-primary students. And the standards of the university were said to suffer, to be lower as a result of the admission of poorly qualified candidates. Raising the standard of university entrance would require developing stronger and more substantial secondary schools. Both the specific subjects available in the elementary school and the junior classes at the university, however, stood in the way.

The process of establishing a national, organically connected education system (with secondary schools the 'natural connecting link') involved, first, a centralisation of the specific subjects into fewer and fewer schools in urban areas. In 1887 Govan,[23] for instance, had five central schools at which the university subjects and certain specialised post-primary courses could be taken.[24] Glasgow had named 13 schools in 1886 where bursary winners were to take higher courses.[25]

In 1892, when the Leaving Certificate and the Merit Certificate were introduced to the public (elementary) schools, five such schools were chosen in Glasgow to offer the Leaving Certificate work in what were called 'secondary departments' which were not on the elementary code or financed with specific subject grants. These secondary departments (sometimes referred to as 'central schools') were in addition to the higher class public schools of Glasgow, the Boys' High and Garnethill; the latter, though still a public (elementary) school officially, was being groomed as the Girls' High. Sixteen other schools (out of a total of 60+ Glasgow Board schools) were cited as having 'higher departments' which offered Merit Certificate work extending one year beyond the standards on the specific subject or elementary code. The majority of other Board schools offered some specific subject work, at least in the early stages.

The Leaving Certificates were awarded for passing individual subject exams which were, at first, confined to the university subjects. The Merit Certificate was to mark the uppermost end of the Board's public (elementary) school course, which included all three years of at least one specific subject and which thus required staying to age 13. While 13 was the official leaving age, an exemption could be obtained if a student was at least 11 years old and had reached Standard V. Only a minority stayed to Merit Certificate level.

Fees were charged for all the certificate or ex-VIth. courses, though various bursaries continued to be available for what was now Merit Certificate work. In addition, a scholarship system was established for the Leaving Certificate work with funds now available from the 'equivalent grant'.[26] This provided an indirect government subsidy for secondary work in the form of 60 scholarships each to the Boys' High and Garnethill and 150 to the five central schools, each lasting three years. One-third were renewable yearly for a total of 90 scholarships which were awarded on the basis of examinations given each year.[27]

The first direct government grants for secondary work were also provided from the equivalent grant. In Glasgow the Burgh Secondary Committee (consisting of representatives of the School Board, Town Council and Educational Trusts[28]) which administered the equivalent grant, awarded £1,800 to the Boys' High School, £1,000 to Garnethill and £2,500 to the five central schools (City, John Street Bridgeton, Kent Road, Whitehill and Woodside) as well as £500 for evening classes which offered higher instruction.[29]

In Govan a total of 370 free places were set aside in 1893 for students at the Merit Certificate level — one year beyond Standard VI. Few of these were at Hillhead which had to maintain high numbers of fee-paying students to make up for grants lost when it became a fully fledged secondary school. The Govan Board received £4 for each free scholar and £1 for each fee-payer from the Burgh Secondary Committee for Govan. In 1895 the students were distributed as follows: [30]

Govan	109 free scholars	0 fee-paying
Fairfield	62	0
Albert Road	46	71
Bellahouston	68	62
Hamilton Crescent	83	98
Hillhead	28	230

In 1896 a qualifying exam was instituted as more students sought free places than were available, though the number of free places had again been increased, to 430. A total of 490 fee-paying places was available. In 1887 fees for various schools in the Glasgow area were: [31]

Glasgow Academy	£12 to £14
Kelvinside Academy	£12 to £14
High School (Boys')	£8
Hillhead Public School	£5 to £6
Garnethill Public School	£3 to £4

In 1894 the Glasgow Board began to urge that students who intended to stay in school, to either the Merit or Leaving Certificate stage, be transferred to the schools which offered certificate courses by the beginning of Standard V (age

11) in order to receive the necessary preparation. As only the five central schools and the two higher class schools offered work to the Leaving Certificate level, it would have been advantageous, if not necessary, to enrol in one of these schools by age 11 if one expected to continue advanced work to university entrance level, or in one of the 16 schools with higher departments if one wished to continue to the Merit Certificate level. Fees were still charged for all ex-standard courses. Several important changes were introduced into all Scottish schools in 1897 as a result of directives in Craik's code for that year. Fees were eliminated up to age 13 for all students, even those who had completed the elementary standards. That is, free schooling had to be made available in some School Board schools for all students who stayed until their thirteenth birthday. This did not result in the abolition of all fee paying in the public schools as Glasgow continued to charge fees, at a differential rate, depending on desirability, in some schools.[32] However, if students finished the six elementary standards in six years, they now had one free year in which they could work on specific subjects in those schools which offered them and which charged no fees. Formerly this ex-VIth. year would have culminated in the Merit Certificate exam, but the Code of 1898 reduced the qualifications for the Merit Certificate so that the exam could be taken at age 12, or the end of the VIth. standard. In addition, the specific requirement for the Merit Certificate was dropped so that the new exam only tested the Three R's and the class subjects. The change in meaning or value of the Merit Certificate was reflected in the statement that the new certificate was a 'certificate of conduct and character as well as attainments'.[33] But perhaps the most significant aspect of these changes was that the Merit Certificate exam had become a *qualifying* exam — that is, it was now necessary to have passed the Merit Certificate exam before being admitted to *any* type of advanced or post-primary course.

The elimination of fees and the institution of block grants for attendance and the teaching of class subjects in all elementary standards also meant special application was now necessary for parents of children who were at least 11 years old and who sought exemption by labour certificate exam after Standard V and before age 13. This, it was hoped, would increase longer school attendance, and in 1898 the Department's policy was to establish a leaving age of 14 by eliminating fees for students in elementary schools up to their fourteenth birthday.[34]

In 1898, then, there were, theoretically at least, two years beyond the Merit Certificate exam (ages 12-13 and 13-14), in which specific subject work could be taken, and in some schools this was wholly free of fees. The Code of 1899, however, eliminated all grants for specific subjects. As a temporary measure six schools were designated by the Glasgow Board as having Advanced Departments where two years of post-standard work based on the old specific subject curriculum was available. A review of the Inspectors' reports for 1899, however, indicates that other non-designated Glasgow Board Schools continued to offer specific subject work, even beyond those 18 still officially listed as having 'higher departments' in 1898.

The availability of advanced work in the neighbourhood school was popular with parents, students and teachers. Though the policy of the Education Department had long been to centralise advanced work into proper secondary-type schools and departments, as late as 1899 there were still 37 Glasgow Board schools offering French to 3,584 students, 47 offering mathematics to 2,404 students and 14 offering Latin to 492 students. Of these, the five central schools and the two higher class schools contained 311 Latin scholars, 1,135 mathematics students and 1,648 French scholars, leaving in the public (elementary) schools, 181 Latin scholars in eight schools, 1,269 mathematics students in 41 schools and 1,936 French students in 31 schools. Elimination of the specific subject grants, however, would bring a swift end to the long tradition of offering advanced work in the public (elementary) school. The result of the Education Department's policy, in Glasgow at least, would be that only those students who passed scholarship exams to go to one of the five central schools to age 15 (now officially called higher grade schools) or a higher class school to age 17, or who were willing to pay fees, were given the traditional academic course. And, unless these students had transferred by age 11 to one of these schools, they might not receive the proper preparation for this advanced work.

Supplementary Courses

For that growing number of students in Board schools who were beyond the elementary standards but did not attend a higher school, the Glasgow School Board began to develop 'alternative courses'. According to the Board's report for 1899, 'rudiments of mathematics and science in connection with arithmetic and nature knowledge' were among the limited options available. According to the 1901-1902 report of the Glasgow Board's Committee on Teachers and Teaching:

> As was anticipated last year the Committee were faced at the beginning of the current session with the need for some provision being made for scholars who had obtained the Merit Certificate and were not likely to remain beyond age 14. For the great majority of such pupils the ordinary curriculum of an Advanced or Higher Grade Department would have neither interest nor value. . . the Board agreed that in eight schools a special curriculum should be provided embracing, beyond revision of the ordinary subjects, for boys, such as Arithmetic, including mensuration, as will be of practical application and where possible manual instruction; for girls, cookery, laundry-work, needlework, dressmaking and where possible housewifery.[35]

Special attention was also to be paid to composition, reading good literature, physical exercise and nature study.

The 1902-03 General Summary of Work (Glasgow Board) reported that the Scottish Education Department Code for 1903 had embodied, in 'supplementary courses', a programme similar to that developed by the Glasgow Board. Preliminary HMI reports indicated that the new system allowed greater emphasis on English, home reading, moral education, less formal work and smaller classes. According to the Board, the new arrangements would allow 'the great mass of their scholars to receive in moral training as well as in ordinary instruction the full benefit of the longer school life and the freer conditions now possible'.[36]

The Board concluded that, while still in transition, 'the broader and less mechanical lines of the new system cannot but make for progress'. The Education Department's call for commercial and industrial courses for boys and domestic courses for girls (the supplementary courses) was seen as easily merged with the Board's present 'special curriculum' for scholars beyond the qualification stage but under 14 years of age. Consequently the Advanced Departments were abolished and, along with them, all remnants of specific subject work in the public (elementary) schools. All post-primary work of an academic nature in Glasgow was now confined to the five higher grade schools and the two higher class schools.

Another provision of the 1903 Code was that at least one year's attendance in a supplementary course was required before the Merit Certificate could be obtained. The Merit Certificate, which for a decade had indicated the ability of a scholar to do traditional or academic post-primary work (that is, it was a certificate of attainment) now marked completion of one year of non-academic post-primary work. The Merit Certificate exam continued to be a qualifying exam but it no longer resulted in the issuance of a certificate. The 'quallie' was now a hurdle to be overcome before work leading to any certificate could be begun. This prompted the EIS to renew its opposition to the qualifying exam:

> Both school managers and teachers have always affirmed that, instead of being a passport to the entrance into Higher Grade Schools and Advanced Departments, it was really a barrier of varying difficulty, which vexatiously and needlessly excluded pupils from higher work in the school.[37]

The effect of these changes, instituted by Craik in the period 1898 to 1903, was to lower the opportunity for traditional secondary work for many students in the Scottish Board Schools. In addition to passing the qualifying exam it was also necessary, in Glasgow at least, to pay fees or win a scholarship to do a course leading to any academic certificate. While the percentage of students who qualified doubled from 1903 to 1919, in 1920 only about 25 per cent of all school children in Scotland were able to qualify at or before age 12, and another 25 per cent were unable to reach this level even at 14 years of age. 'Unsuccessful pupils usually prepared anew and made another attempt to pass the examination. Many of them continued this monotonous process until they reached the age of 14 when they left to escape the "grind" and the school.'[38] Since many students who left at age 14 had not had one year in the supplementary course, only a minority of all supplementary students ever attained the Merit Certificate. The percentage ranged between 34 and 41 between 1903 and 1914.[39]

Since the qualifying exam was an indication of ability to do advanced work,

In the opinion of Rev. Smith, the children who could not or would not attend the higher grade school had to be satisfied to become "hewers of wood and drawers of water" to their more favoured contemporaries, even though they had demonstrated that they were among the élite by passing the qualifying examination at 11 or 11½ years of age.[40]

Most who could, however, did choose the higher grade school. Between 1900 and 1903 the number of higher grade schools in Scotland increased from 27 to 36 and rose to 191 in 1910.[41] By 1920 there were approximately 30,000 higher grade pupils compared to 15,000 higher class pupils and 60,000 pupils in supplementary courses.[42]

According to Wade, 'Many pupils who expected to devote a short time to a post-primary course attended the higher grade schools because they had greater educational and social prestige. Consequently, the growth of the supplementary courses was retarded by the development of the higher grade school.' One result was that few stayed long enough to complete the higher grade course, to age 15.[43] Eventually parents were required to sign a pledge saying their children enrolled in a higher grade school would remain three full years, but this was unenforceable.[44] Wade concluded that, 'The traditional view that the education of adolescents to be of any value had to include "a touch of the classics" died slowly',[45] hence the unpopularity of Craik and Struthers, who promoted the non-academic supplementary course for the majority of post-primary students.

Even given the popularity of the higher grade schools, and their consequent growth, it is questionable just how much progress Craik's secondary education reforms represented. Many contemporaries and some historians seem to believe the development of the selective secondary system was an improvement over the old ways. Roxburgh, in his history of the Glasgow School Board, maintains that there were more than enough opportunities in Glasgow for secondary education, more even than parents were prepared to take up. As evidence he cites the fact that nearly one in every two students in the fee-paying schools was on scholarship.[46] However, in 1897 for example, there were 325 applicants for the 90 scholarships available, leaving one to wonder if elimination of fees would not have led to increased attendance in secondary courses.[47] In addition, there is still the question of the effect of centralisation of secondary courses into seven schools in Glasgow, and the elimination of the specific subjects from the public (elementary) schools. In a speech to the EIS in 1897, Dr Mackay of Edinburgh warned of 'very powerful influences' which he said were planning to prohibit teaching primary and secondary work in the same school. Educators, he said, were being told that after the Three R's were acquired, 'the children should all be drafted out to a secondary or higher centre — that was, all children who were destined to be passed on to higher subjects'. However he continued, 'there could be no drafting from lower to higher schools unless in the first place the pupils received a certain measure of higher education in the lower school'.[48]

These policies establishing a national, organically connected system of schools from elementary through secondary did not necessarily increase the opportunities available for traditional or academic secondary work. More pupils were staying at school longer, but the majority of post-primary students were enrolled in the non-academic supplementary courses, the numbers of which rose in Glasgow from 687 in three schools in 1903-04 (compared to 1,212 higher grade pupils) to 1,744 in 1907-08 in 36 schools (compared to 1,548 higher grade pupils).[49] More pupils may have received more 'schooling' which was based on an expansion and enrichment of courses to educate the whole child, but this did not necessarily mean they received more 'education'.[50]

For that minority of students who reached the higher grade or higher class public school, elimination of specific subjects resulted in a strengthening of the academic programme. Craik progressively raised the standard of the Leaving Certificate, and introduced a second level, the Intermediate Certificate. The higher grade (three year) course led to the new certificate; the higher class (five year) course became mandatory for the full certificate. From a series of individual certificates for individual exams the Leaving Certificate eventually came to represent (in 1908) a set curriculum covering a block of four exams, each of which covered a four-year subject.[51]

The 'progressive' reforms designed to broaden and enrich the elementary curriculum and organically educate the 'whole' child provided the vehicle by which a new curriculum in the form of supplementary courses could be developed. Selective tests were introduced to assist in determining which students would follow this course and which would receive the strengthened pedagogy represented by the Leaving Certificate. Reform of the Scottish universities made this stronger secondary curriculum mandatory. The special-isations thus begun with the division of post-primary students into academic or non-academic streams could be further developed in the reformed university.

University Reform

Scottish universities had been under pressure to change their curriculum for several decades. Opposition was especially strong, according to George Davie, to the traditional three-year Arts degree which, until 1899, was required before specialisation or Honours work on the English university model was allowed.[52] Reforms in 1858 had added an optional fourth or Honours year in which the student could specialise in classical literature; mental philosophy including logic, metaphysics and moral philosophy; mathematics, including pure mathematics and natural philosophy; and natural science, including geography, zoology and chemistry.[53]

The reforms instituted by the University Commissioners, beginning in 1899, were to allow well-prepared students to specialise from the beginning, without doing the M.A. degree, though the M.A. was allowed to stand as an alternative to the Honours course. This permanently weakened the ordinary

M.A., according to Davie, as the M.A. was effectively fossilised in a form which was old-fashioned. Offering a more modern alternative to it meant the M.A. would be side stepped and not revised and updated.[54]

The other significant reform of the University Commissioners was to require that the preliminary or entrance exams to the university be passed before any degree qualifying exams could be taken. Previously the preliminary exam had been optional; a pass had meant a three-year Arts course could be taken rather than the four-year course, which included the junior classes. After 1892 the Leaving Certificates were accepted in lieu of the preliminary exam. A separate exam was required for the open competition bursaries, and those who arrived at the university with presentation bursaries had to pass the preliminary exam. As the bursary exam consisted of the same set of papers as the preliminary exam virtually everyone who began the university with a bursary had to have passed the preliminary exam or its equivalent, the Leaving Certificate exams. Junior classes continued to be offered but the preliminary exam, especially for bursaries, forced up the entrance age and acted as an incentive for the schools 'to send up their pupils in an advanced state of preparation',[55] as was desired by the reformers.

These university reforms contributed to the demand for proper secondary schools. The all-through parish school, using grants for specific subjects, could not offer an adequate preparation for the higher entrance standards. One consequence, then, of the university reforms was the need to develop secondary schools on the model of the English grammar school in which the general or liberal arts education was completed so that the student could specialise at university from the outset.

Another consequence of the trend towards specialisation in the university was the elimination of what has been called the 'class' system, and with it a decline in the traditional Scottish university's emphasis on the humanities. Davie gives an interesting and appealing account of the significance of the elimination of the class system. While most historians see the move towards earlier specialisation and an expansion of the subjects in which specialisation was possible (including the consequent decline in required classics) as a victory for the progressive, forward-looking liberals over the tradition-bound back-ward-looking conservatives, Davie claims that only if

> one regards English values and principles as the only proper values and principles then of course a debate between an anglicising party and its opponents about the future of Scottish education is bound to appear as an opposition between Sweetness and Light (or Progress) on the one hand and narrow provincial obscurancy on the other.

Instead of seeing Scottish educational reform as 'an uninteresting episode in which the bringers of modern civilisation were resisted by devotees of a moth-eaten regional routine', Davie argues it should be viewed as a 'profoundly important argument between those who regard the traditional English point of view as normal and natural and those who regard it as being, in some very important ways, out of line with the western norms'.[56]

The class system, it seems, was an integral part of the ordinary M.A. degree and was, in part, what made the humanities in the university a democractic and liberalising experience. For three years, students who might pursue various postgraduate studies and professions followed a common classical course. As Professor Grierson of Edinburgh University described it, the effects of students of various bents and backgrounds in the same class encouraged even further the Scottish professor's traditional inclination 'in teaching mathematics and science, language and literature, to give an unusually large amount of attention to the first principles and metaphysical ground of the disciplines'.[57] The result was a classical course with a 'characteristically humanist flavour', and the title of Professor of Humanity in place of Professor of Classics, or Latin and Greek.

According to Davie, there may have been a connection between the modernisation of the universities and the social efficiency progressive reforms of the schools. While he does not mention Craik by name, Davie associates him with his predecessor Sir Francis Sandford whose name one Scots MP described as 'synonymous in Scotland with everything that is detestable, obscurantist, reactionary, anti-liberal and anti-Scotch'.[58] The 1885 establishment of a separate Education Department for Scotland, Davie argues, failed to appease patriotic Scots because the appointee Craik, was part of the same hated bureaucracy of the arch-angliciser Sandford. Davie thus implies that school reforms in Scotland resulted from the same anglicising influences as those responsible for university reforms. Davie traces the long history of the anglicisers' campaign to bring the Scottish Universities into line with the English, beginning with the efforts of Sandford's father in the 1820s. However, he does not show satisfactorily why the reformers were so successful in 1889 when they had been unsuccessful for so long. Davie argues that by 1889 the patriotic Scots were too 'demoralised' to resist. 'National prejudice did not achieve articulate constructive expression in the speeches at Westminster', he claimed. The patriots' opinions contained 'more heat than light'. While Davie acknowledges that the demand for English-style Honours degrees (specialist courses) in 1889, as represented by the utilitarian views of Edward Caird of Glasgow University, introduced a 'novel and radical' note to an old controversy, he fails to analyse the nature of these views. He says, instead, the 'Scots were losing their creative touch in education and were content to leave the initiative to the Anglo-Scots'.[59]

Davie also insinuates that fear of losing their peculiar Scottish traditions led the Scots MPs to refrain from launching a vigorous defence of the Universities in Parliament. 'If Scottish education was ever brought before Parliament by itself and independent of English education', Davie quotes the Anglophile Playfair as saying, 'the difference between the two will raise up many enemies in the house to the peculiarities of Scottish education in relation to the higher subjects taught under the Government grant.' But Davie concludes that this refers to the fact that institutions like compulsory philosophy in the university would strike the English members as very odd and foreign. Thus, the behaviour of Scottish MPs in these educational debates was probably due to the fear that a discussion in public about the distinctive Scottish heritage would introduce into Parliament topics of a sort likely to fatigue the majority of its members and so bring Scotland into discredit.[60]

This seems to be a misreading on Davie's part of Playfair's concern which probably pertained to the schools and not to the universities. But while concern over using government grants to teach higher subjects in elementary schools was legitimate in England,[61] such was not the case in Scotland where the Education (Scotland) Act of 1872 had specified that the public schools were to continue to offer education to the standard previously attained, that is, that of the all-through parish school — or at least the Scottish Education Department succeeded in so interpreting the Act for several decades.[62]

The urge towards specialisation which Davie attributes to anglicisers and assimilationists in Scottish university reform was also occurring in American universities and colleges at this time, though the élitism of the English system was specifically rejected by the leading university reformer, Professor Eliot of Harvard.[63] It may not have been because the model was English that it appealed to the social efficiency progressives, therefore, but because it better suited modern times. That is, the need for specialisation for social efficiency may have prompted educational reform in both countries. Selecting and preparing the right individuals for the different social and economic roles that needed to be performed was a function for which schools could be adapted. The process thus begun in the schools could lead to greater efficiency of work in the university where better-prepared students could pursue their specialisation to a higher standard. Craik's desire to develop a secondary school system in Scotland that was more similar to the typical English grammar school than to the Scottish all-through school may have resulted as much from his social efficiency progressivism as from his anglicising propensities. Adoption of the high level of general education, and even the beginnings of specialisation which are associated with the grammar-type school, would allow the admission standards of Scottish universities to be raised so that the specialised Honours courses, relevant to the needs of modern industrial society, could become the standard university course. The old hierarchy of social and economic relations could thus be maintained in the new and changing conditions created by modern industrial and commercial developments.

New Utilitarianism in Education

All education, it seems, was assumed by progressives such as Craik to have a new social role. In the broadened and enriched elementary curriculum, explicit attention was to be paid to the whole child — morals, leisure, citizenship and job prospects. This represented something of a change in the purpose of education; education for life became education for a life of social rather than individual usefulness. According to Professor Darroch of Edinburgh University, who was said to represent the 'new utilitarianism' in education, 'the life of active social usefulness is the only life worth living and that really happy man is he who is efficient to perform his duties in the station of life for which by nature and education he is fitted'.[64]

The school reforms introduced in conformity with this new view were designed to provide each Scottish child with an 'education that will enable him to discharge his duty as a citizen and rise to the level for which he is qualified by natural gifts'.[65] While all education was to be socially useful, the post-primary course was of particular importance as at this point decisions were made about what specific useful contribution each individual could make to society based on these 'natural' gifts.

Before Craik's reforms, any and all who stayed in school beyond the elementary standards expected to pursue academic subjects, including a 'touch of the classics'. After Craik's reforms, more students were in school longer, but there were distinctly different types of post-primary education offered to different students, to prepare for different stations in life, and different social roles. 'Selection by exclusion' was thus replaced by 'selection by differentiation' in the Scottish schools.[66] Post-primary education was no longer a matter of offering university preparation to those who would eventually enter professions, with those who 'chose' to leave school free to select their own work and leisure activities. While the school leavers had never been wholly free from the constraints of physical need and economic deprivation under the traditional conditions, their decisions had been made, for the most part, outside the purview of the school establisment.

It was increasingly recognised, however, that the outcomes of such selection should not be left wholly to chance. Waste of human resources was no longer individual waste, but social waste. The old impulse for social control of the many by the few was thus complemented by the need to efficiently organise society; the welfare of all was at stake. An organic interdependent society, therefore, required a national system of schools which were themselves organic, that is, which provided a *whole* education in the state sector, from primary to university, and which educated the *whole* child.

This education for 'social' or 'national efficiency', as it has been called, required rationalisation and planning to see that all the proper functions of the system were fulfilled. According to the Rev. Smith, it was necessary to approach the planning of educational schemes

as a business problem, demanding a business-like solution. Our system of education should be organised as if it were a business concern, in which all the parts are to be so ordered that each is considered only as it directly serves the definite end in view.[67]

That end, often, was development of upright citizens who were also good workers.[68]

As a result of progressive education reforms, the classical notion of one type of education appropriate for everyone who sought higher education was replaced by a more utilitarian version in which education for social usefulness became education for work as well, the work for which one was best suited as determined by the testing and selection process. The progressive broadening and enrichment of the elementary course gradually softened the pedagogy for the majority student and prepared the way for the supplementary course as one post-primary course. The upgrading of the university entrance requirements made necessary the strengthening of the pedagogy for the selected minority who would attend. The differentiated (streamed) secondary school found in Scotland and the U.S. today was the eventual result of the convergence of these dual trends.

Democratic Reform Progressivism

While social control and social efficiency progressives, such as Craik and the university reformers, were the most successful progressives, they were not the only progressives, it must be remembered.[69] As Davie suggests, the opponents of university reform were perhaps more 'democratic' than the reformers. It may well be that the old ways, the all-through school, the easy access and junior classes at university, the 'class' system, the humanist approach to classics and mathematics and the teaching from first principles, offered *wider* opportunity for intellectual enlightenment than the newly reformed 'national' system.

Had the Scottish universities been allowed to modernise their curriculum in their own way, Davie argues, they might have innovated something more in keeping with the democratic tradition which he claims they sought to defend. This might have involved teaching the newer scientific subjects humanistically and philosophically. Professor Burnet, a classicist from St. Andrews, for example, proposed teaching science as 'thinking about the world in the Greek way'. Professor Thompson, a scientist from Aberdeen, thought that 'Man should seek after science primarily in hope of a clearer vision of the world', and of that wisdom which is necessary, in addition to knowledge, to rule the world. The sciences, he argued, should be taught in correlation with each other, and he emphasised the need, in a democratic society, to teach the scientific method of thinking, of arriving at knowledge through observation, experiment and reflection. Such knowledge is both verifiable and communicable, which makes it more readily accessible and 'public'.[70] This version of the use of 'scientific method' contrasts with the more specialist view of such knowledge promoted by the utilitarians. There is also some indication that the schools were interested in similar 'democratic' modernisation innovations. Minutes of the Glasgow branch of the EIS indicate concern with a variety of new curricula and pedagogies.

The teaching of chemistry to all students in elementary schools, for instance, was the subject of one EIS lecture. The value of such a course was said to be that it could train the intellectual discipline by awakening natural curiosity, cultivating powers of observation, training logical faculties and powers of accurate description and by ascertainment of facts and drawing of correct inferences.[71]

It is possible that such reforms were desired to secure a better education of the traditional type for a larger number of individuals, though to establish such a thesis would require more space than is available here. Had more democratic innovations been implemented, however, it is possible that the result would have been a modernisation and updating of the content of the specific subjects so as to strengthen them. Reform of the pedagogy, more 'learning by doing', might also have made such academic subjects more suitable for more students. Arguments for centralising these subjects might thus have been weakened and the democratic nature of Scottish education strengthened.

Why the reforms of the more democratic progressives in school and university were less successful than those of the social control and social efficiency progressives is an intriguing puzzle. Part of the answer may lie in the possibility that the distinction between these two types of progressive reformers, apparent with the advantage of hindsight, was much less obvious to their contemporaries. Both democratic reformers and social efficiency reformers *were* 'progressive'; both kinds were attempting to cope with urbanisation and industrialisation. Both looked to the schools and universities to bring desired social change, the one by differentiating the curriculum of the schools to allow early selection and specialisation, the other by democratising the intellectual process to promote more widely the 'scientific method of thinking'. Both took account of the new thinking regarding the organic nature of society, and the need to consider the individual in his or her social role. Relevant and useful education, especially in the newer scientific subjects, could be seen as desirable by all progressive, forward-looking educators.

What seemed to be difficult to keep in mind was that not all 'change' brings 'improvement' and not all those who defended the old ways were reactionary conservatives, though the professors who defended the classics and the schoolmen and women who sought to retain specific subjects were easily characterised as such. It is also necessary to keep in mind that recognition of the need to change and adapt to new circumstances does not necessarily ensure that the old status quo will be altered in the process. Sometimes changes and reforms are necessary just to keep the underlying hierarchical structure of society intact, especially in the state of continual flux and change which seems to characterise modern society.

Distinctions seem not to have been made between those progressives whose reforms would reinforce the status quo (social efficiency and utilitarian progressives) and those whose proposals offered possibilities for reforming the structure of society (democratic reform progressives). Changes implemented by the former seemed, on the surface at least, 'progressive'; this may have weakened the guard of the latter against Craik's educational reforms which were in fact élitist and undemocratic. Progressive forces may have even joined together on occasion, given a superficial commonality and the failure to examine underlying assumptions about the nature of the society which the reforms were to promote.

In addition, the centralised, bureaucratic structure of the Scotch Education Department made it difficult for those most affected by Craik's reforms (teachers, students and parents) to influence the changes that were imposed. In the process of administering the Department, Craik was able to institute, piecemeal, over a period of years, changes which, taken together, were of wide-ranging significance. The common post-primary curriculum which had been widely available in neighbourhood schools and which allowed easy access to the universities was replaced by a more systematic method designed to ensure that the right students went to university and that the others were adequately prepared to do something useful for society. While a more tough-minded curriculum was developed in state-supported secondary schools, which allowed students to complete the general education required to pursue a specialised course at university, for the remaining students, who were compelled to stay in elementary school longer, the academic subjects were replaced by practical, occupation-oriented, morally uplifting courses.

Had Craik presented these reforms, in total, as a package to be debated and discussed, his assumptions about the results he intended may have been more readily available for review. It seems unlikely, however, from the halting and groping manner in which he implemented his reforms, over the two decades of his tenure, that he had such a clear-cut programme in mind from the beginning. But the fact that he could, through the process of administering the bureaucracy, make the changes which he did to bring the schools into line with his views, indicates the policy-making possibilities that are available to bureaucrats, and the hazards that are involved in such policy-making.

It is also probably not wholly accidental that these policies expanded the functions of that bureaucracy. The more the curriculum is differentiated, the more need there is for selective machinery and personnel to administer it in order to make decisions about who will take what course, and where and when the different courses will be made available. Such administrative chores gradually consumed headmasters' time, reducing their teaching and classroom responsibilities. Curriculum supervisors, psychological and achievement testing specialists, and vocational and guidance counsellors are additional non-teaching personnel required by the new system. These in turn require supervision and new bureaucratic arrangements to ensure the efficient articulation of the whole system.

In conclusion, while the changes Craik implemented moved the schools closer to the progressive, forward-looking view of their proper role, given the new understanding of the nature of society, these reforms did not change the status quo; they reinforced it. The changes were justified at the time as improvements that would benefit each individual and society as well. Broadening and enriching the curriculum to eliminate rote and mechanical teaching and learning was promised, but differentiated education resulted, in which fewer academic subjects were taught to most students, while more academic subjects were taken to a higher level by a few. The bureaucratic structure made it difficult to examine, debate or discuss the implications of these changes, while new functions were created which required further bureaucratic procedures. The system that resulted emphasised education for one's place in society over education for self-realisation and enlightenment.

NOTES

1. John Kerr, *Scottish Education — School and University, from early times to 1908* (Cambridge, 1910), p. 331.

2. James Scotland, *The History of Scottish Education*, volume II, (London, 1969), p. 50, p. 181.

3. *Ibid.*, p. 27.

4. *Ibid.*, p. 71.

5. Kerr, *op cit.*, p. 277.

6. *Ibid.*, p. 277.

7. The publicly financed and controlled elementary schools were designated 'public' schools. Though they were primarily elementary schools, the term 'elementary' was avoided.

8. N. A. Wade, *Post-primary Education in the Primary Schools of Scotland 1872-1930*, (London, 1939), p. 42.

9. *Ibid*.

10. Kerr, *op. cit.*, pp. 303-304.

11. Scotland, *op. cit.*, p. 63.

12. *Ibid.*

13. T. B. Dobie, 'The Scottish Leaving Certificate, 1888-1908', in T. R. Bone (ed.), *Studies in the History of Scottish Education, 1872-1939*, (Edinburgh, 1967), p. 168.

14. Wade, *op. cit.*, p. 47.

15. John Kerr, *Memories Grave and Gay*, (Edinburgh, 1902), p. 25.

16. Kerr, 1910, *op. cit.*, p. 331.

17. John Clarke (ed.), *Problems of National Education*, (London, 1919), pp. 17-18.

18. A. J. Belford, *Centenary Handbook of the Educational Institute of Scotland*, (Edinburgh, 1946) p. 149.

19. Wade, *op. cit.*, pp. 47-49.

20. *Ibid.*, pp. 58-59.

21. James Roxburgh, *The School Board of Glasgow, 1873-1919*, (London, 1971), p. 114.

22. John Strong, *A History of Secondary Education in Scotland*, (Oxford, 1909), pp. 227-229.

23. Govan Parish schools were under a separate School Board until they were joined with the Glasgow School Board about 1911.

24. Marjorie Cruickshank, *A History of the Training of Teachers in Scotland*, (London, 1970), p. 112.

25. Roxburgh, *op. cit.*, p. 125.

26. In 1891 the so-called 'free school Act' had reduced (but not eliminated) fees for elementary education in England and Wales by providing fee grants. In 1892 Scotland was given an 'equivalent' grant. Since Scotland had already used the 1889 'whisky' money to reduce fees, whereas England used it primarily to reduce rates, Scotland could use the equivalent grant to finance secondary education (see Strong, *op. cit.*, p. 245).

27. Glasgow School Board, *Report of Committee on Teachers and Teaching*, 1896.

28. Roxburgh, *op. cit.*, p. 127.

29. Glasgow School Board, *General Summary of Work*, 1894.

30. Govan School Board, *Minutes of Committee on Secondary Education*, 18 February 1895.

31. Roxburgh, *op. cit.*, p. 137.

32. *Ibid.*, p. 151.

33. Glasgow School Board, *Annual Statistics*, 1897-98.

34. S. Leslie Hunter, *The Scottish Educational System*, (London, 1971), p. 20.

35. Glasgow School Board, *Committee on Teachers and Teaching*, 1901-1902.

36. Glasgow School Board, *General Summary of Work*, 1902-1903.

37. *Educational News*, 21 February 1903.

38. Wade, *op. cit.*, p. 77.

39. *Ibid.*, p. 98.

40. *Ibid.*, p. 85.

41. *Ibid.*, p. 109.

42. *Ibid.*, p. 97.

43. *Ibid.*, pp. 113-116.

44. *Ibid.*, p. 116.

45. *Ibid.*, p. 114.

46. Roxburgh, *op. cit.*, p. 168.

47. Glasgow High School and Secondary Committee, *Letterbook*, 1897.

48. *Educational News*, 2 January 1897.

49. Glasgow School Board, *Annual Statistics*, 1903-1904 to 1907-1908.

50. In Scotland, the supplementary courses were supposed to consolidate previous learning. According to the Rev. John Smith, *Broken Links in Scottish Education* (London, 1914), the 'guiding principle' of the Scotch Education Department in regard to the supplementary courses was that 'no new subject should be taken up save some manual occupation'. To Smith, this overlooked 'the very important consolidation in our intellectual equipment that arises from the advancement to new and related subjects' (pp. 72-73).

51. Scotland, *op. cit.*, p. 69.

52. George Davie, *The Democratic Intellect* (Edinburgh, 1961). For a critical review of Davie's book, see Donald J. Withrington, *Universities Quarterly*, 1961-62, vol. 16, pp. 94-98.

53. Kerr, 1910, *op. cit.*, p. 337.

54. Davie, *op. cit.*, p. 79.

55. Strong, *op. cit.*, p. 237.

56. Davie, *op. cit.*, p. 9.

57. *Ibid.*, p. 13.

58. *Ibid.*, p. 96.

59. *Ibid.*, p. 93.

60. *Ibid.*, p. 70.

61. Eric Eaglesham, *The Foundations of Twentieth-century Education in England* (London, 1967), pp. 17-18.

62. While the Education (England) Act of 1902 severely reduced the higher education of the elementary school in England (Eaglesham, *op. cit.*, p. 33), post-primary education continued to be widely financed under the government grant in Scotland, with the result that at the time of the Hadow enquiry only 98,459 children over age 11 in England were in advanced courses in

elementary school, whereas 71,816 were 'enrolled in the advanced divisions of the primary schools in Scotland [which] . . . served a school population of about one tenth the size of England's (G. S. Osborne, *Change in Scottish Education*, London, 1968, p. 52).

63. For a biography of Eliot, see Henry James, *Charles W. Eliot*, (Boston, 1930) and Edward A. Krug (ed.) *Charles W. Eliot and Popular Education*, (New York, 1961).

64. Alexander Morgan, *Makers of Scottish Education* (London, 1929), p. 218.

65. Kerr, 1902, *op. cit.*, p. 28.

66. Brian Simon, *Education and the Labour Movement 1870-1920* (London, 1965) and 'Classification and Streaming: a study of grouping in English schools, 1860-1960', in Paul Nash (ed.), *Education and History: The Educational Uses of the Past* (New York, 1970) has described the process by which English education was similarly reformed.

67. Smith, *op. cit.*, p. 42.

68. 'Rationalisation' and 'efficiency' were key concepts to progressives in business and in education. The one field often influenced the other. For instance, J. J. Findlay, the well-known 'new' educationist, recommended time and motion type studies in his book on class teaching. It is a wholesome custom,' he said, 'in some Training Colleges for the critics of a lesson to employ a watch fitted with a seconds-hand, and to note down roughly . . . the distribution of time between teacher and taught' (J. J. Findlay, *Principles of Class Teaching*, London, 1902, p. 398). I owe this reference to David Hamilton.

69. Most historians who detail the education reforms of social control and social efficiency progressives in the U.S. acknowledge that more than one type of progressive existed. Different labels are used to make this distinction. Arthur Wirth, *Education and the Technological Society* (Scranton, Pennsylvania, 1972) contrasts 'social efficiency' with 'democratic reform' progressives; Lawrence Cremin, *The Transformation of the School* (New York, 1964) refers to 'scientific', 'romantic' and 'radical' progressives; David Tyack, *The One Best System* (Cambridge, Massachusetts, 1974) devotes his book to the 'administrative' progressives but acknowledges the existence of 'pedagogical' progressives; Robert Church and Michael Sedlak, *Education in the U.S. — an interpretative history* (New York, 1976) distinguish between 'conservative' and 'liberal' progressives.

70. See Clarke, 1919, *op. cit.*

71. Educational Institute of Scotland, Glasgow Branch, *Minutes*, 21 March 1891.

10

Incubus and Ideology: The Development of Secondary Schooling in Scotland, 1900-1939

H. M. Paterson

1

The Scots are not industrious, and the people are poor. They spend all their time in wars, and when there is no war they fight with one another.

(Don Pedro de Ayala, Spanish ambassador to the Scottish court, 1498)

But throughout the whole of Scottish society one basic feature still shows her Celtic element, the structure of kinship. Kinship, cousinship, the ties of a common surname held men together by a band that was so taken for granted that it is difficult to get a clear impression of its importance.

(Rosalind Mitchison, *Life in Scotland*, 1978)

SCOTTISH culture has been dominated for many centuries by poverty, fear and strife, and the greatest of these is poverty. Whether we consider the country's geographical resources, or its financial organisations and achievements, the sustained note is one of relative lack of material wealth. Compared to its southern neighbour, or to many other countries in Europe, Scotland has almost always been underdeveloped, a member of the so-called 'Third World', a nation of the undercapitalised and exploited South rather than a member of the rich North. This material poverty has occasionally lessened, of course, most notably in the golden midsummer of Victorian industrialisation when the character of Scotland's people and the presence of its few natural resources combined in a heady expansion which brought undreamed of wealth to a few. Such moments of relief were always passing, never lasting for more than a few decades at most: invariably, they were succeeded by a return to the former indigence of the bulk of the Scottish people, an indigence made all the more stark by contrast.

The massive determination of this material fact has permanently marked the culture, the social structure and the psyche of Scotland. The presence of penury, or its memory, or its prospect, has made the Scot particularly anxious for security of a straightforwardly tangible sort. Fear of starvation, fear of the poorhouse, fear of the dole — these have been driving forces in constructing the characteristically Scottish urge to 'get ahead' and 'do well', so often remarked upon by others; Tom Nairn's 'peculiarly gritty and grinding middle-class materialism'[1] is not restricted to the Scottish bourgeoisie. Materialism is a structural aspect of the Scottish outlook, and for a very good reason — it is driven by a justifiable fear of material want. That pervasive anxiety, derived from material conditions, leads directly to another consequence of importance for understanding Scottish society — the co-existence of solidarity and division within that society.

In conditions of severe scarcity, winning a share of the few rewards available produces *both* competition *and* co-operation. Many commentators have remarked on the democratic and egalitarian nature of society in Scotland — the non-feudal clan structure, the lack of snobbishness, populist presbyterianism, the parish school.[2] At the same time, division and strife, between groups and individuals, have also been marked: clan fighting with clan, the power of the laird over tenants, sectarian division, and an academic élitist orientation in schools. The structure of Scottish society is, in this sense, quite paradoxical since it embodies powerful forces for fusion which also result in division. Now, such a paradoxical combination is obviously evident in many societies — but, in Scottish social structure, it seems to be marked, and powerfully effective. The *degree* of relative poverty is an obvious explanatory factor here. The more remote the prospect of any kind of fair share in the few material goods available, the stronger the forces driving people towards both solidarity and division and the more definite the polarisation of the society between ideals of both co-operation and competition. This would then explain more fully the twin Scottish drives towards both egalitarianism and élitism — it makes more sense of that common Scottish phenomenon known as 'meritocracy'. The coin, of which solidarity and division are the two faces, is the anxious struggle for survival in a bleak material environment. At times the competition is open, aggressive and bloody; elsewhere, it is submerged, only to surface inexorably in the more socially acceptable (and therefore solidarised) form of competition-under-rules. Both the rules and the competitive drive are crucial; the first is reflected most obviously in the ferocious stress on social conformity so characteristic of Scottish civil society; the second is manifested in the easy acceptance of a ruthless search for advancement to some position of reward, power and status within the undeniable social hierarchy — in the Kirk, in business, in politics, in sport, or in the professions.

All aspects of Scottish civil society show this strong tension, this paradoxical fusion of opposites; but one of the civil institutions where it is most clear is the school system — and here the main paradox can be stated clearly. Scottish schools have often been described as 'democratic', and the system they formed has frequently been characterised as demonstrating the 'democratic' nature of Scottish society. But a closer examination of the facts shows that, far from embodying an abiding concern for the education of 'the whole people',[3] the Scottish school system was designed to neglect the education of the bulk of the population in favour of a few children with a narrowly defined range of talents.

Let us take one example of this — the Scottish system of parish schools, propounded initially in the *First Book of Discipline* (1560), more or less systematically established throughout the country by successive Acts of the Scottish parliament, which reached its zenith in lowland Scotland during the eighteenth century, only to be finally swept away by the legislation of 1872. The schools were not free (usually a small fee was charged); attendance at them was not universal; the curriculum was, for most of the children, restricted to very basic instruction in literacy, numeracy and religion. The apex of the parish school was the 'lad o' pairts', the boy (never a girl) of academic talent who was lucky enough to possess the physical stamina, moral qualities and parental support (as well as one of the minority of gifted teachers available) necessary to carry him to some mastery of subjects such as mathematics, Latin, Greek, French and history at school level, and directly, at an early age, into one of Scotland's universities. There, if he did not succumb to illness or diversion, he could expect the same talents to pay off handsomely in one of the professions — medicine, law, the church — or perhaps in business. There were many like this throughout the long history of the parish school, and they came from the humblest and poorest sections of Scottish society.

But they always constituted a tiny minority. The Secretary for Scotland wrote in 1922, that' . . . the lad o' pairts was always an exception and too often his talents were cultivated at the expense of his less fortunate companions . . .'[4] The Scottish dominie could usually count himself lucky to find one or two lads, with that narrow and specific set of academic talents, during the course of his teaching career. Smout claims that, in a survey of North-East parochial schools carried out in 1832, only five per cent of the pupils learned Latin, and only two out of 7,700 pupils were learning French — and this, it seems, was probably typical rather than exceptional.[5] For the bulk of children, a rudimentary education was the best that was available and sometimes not even that — for example, parish school education in Highland areas before the advent of industrialisation (and many urban parishes afterwards) was sparse or non-existent. Even the supplementation of charity, adventure and other privately funded schools could not make literacy universal in Scotland.

Thus, although the parish school system was nominally open to all who could pay its small fees, its most glorified product was the boy who managed to fight his way through an academic curriculum of crushing illiberality. To do this, he required the exclusive help of a devoted teacher (who had himself managed to complete a similar course) and the concomitant neglect of his fellow pupils. The system is therefore best described as competitive-élitist rather than egalitarian or democratic. Access to the institution was formally open; success within it was closely defined and therefore, of necessity, restricted to a few. The system's close definition of both 'success' and 'talent' ensured that its formal openness was contradicted by its substantive selectivity. The fusion of solidarity and division within the parish school system is clear. It represents a particularly Scottish solution of the problems involved in sieving a nation, by the device of mass schooling, so as to recruit talent to the leader class whilst, at the same time, placating and controlling the many who would never reach such heights. Of course, the definition of 'talent' was handed down to the populace by that very leader class, who thus ensured the continuance of their own hegemony (a strategy we will come across later). Such a system was also not expensive, supported as it was by a mild taxation of land-owners, tenants or municipal councils coupled with the levying of fees and supplemented, where necessary, by local charity. This degree of rationalisation (it *is* possible to speak of a Scottish 'single national system' of schools before 1872) contrasts markedly with the characteristic English model of a number of *separate* systems designed to cater for the school needs of supposedly clear social classes — a public school system for the aristocratic and landowning élite, a grammar school system (linked tenuously with the first at university level) for the aspiring bourgeoisie and, for those in the lowest classes, little or nothing until the advent of the elements of basic instruction provided by the state. It takes money to set up and sustain such a structure and it was precisely the lack of it which encouraged the near approximation to a 'single national system' in Scotland; as Osborne points out, the relative povery is clear from the fact that, in 1864, '. . . the endowments of Eton alone were greater than those enjoyed by all the burgh schools [about 54] and all the universities [five] in Scotland put together'.[6] It was in response to such poverty that the Scottish system of parochial schools concentrated on fostering the career of the 'lad o' pairts' and neglecting the education of all other poor children.

Naturally, the poor children, and their parents, had to agree to be placated and controlled. With some, there was no problem since straightforward hardship dictated the early employment of children (at least seasonally) as a means of supplementing the family income; with others, a modicum of literacy and numeracy sufficed to satisfy demand. For the ambitious, who could yet not manage to do well, the school's narrow definitions of 'talent' and 'success' corresponded to a Calvinistic view of an élite with god-given ability and, together, these two ideologies were sufficiently powerful to convince the unfortunate lad without 'pairts' that it was all his own fault and that he had no option but to rest content with second or third place. The prevalence of such attitudes ensured that, despite clear differences and divisions between social groups, the fusion of division and solidarity in Scottish society was remarkably successful — for a time. It was the arrival of industrialisation, and the development of Scotland's economy as a cutting edge of British capitalism, which was to increase the tension between competition and co-operation and, ultimately, to create a civil society which was sharply divided. In such a situation, the power of the parish school to act as an instrument for social control was finally broken. It could not respond sufficiently to the huge array of social problems which the Industrial Revolution in Scotland was to generate.

The effects of the industrialisation of Scotland's economy are well enough known: an absolute increase in population, a relative increase in the size of urban centres and a concomitant de-population of rural areas, the generation of wealth for the few, the rise of the Scottish industrial and professional bourgeoisie, the construction of a proletariat class, the creation of poverty, ignorance, slums and disease. By the end of the nineteenth century Scottish society was markedly divided along class lines, and yet most members of that society held many attitudes in common: the Scottish bourgeoisie of urban gentry and industrial capitalists had finally risen to power by means of wealth accumulation and collaboration with (or replacement of) the older aristocratic and landowning ruling class; the labouring proletariat — whether of peasant, artisan or craftsman stock — was finally confirmed in its subordinate position. But both espoused their own versions of the dominant free enterprise ideology which was born in Adam Smith's homeland and which flourished there after his death. For the bourgeoisie, revitalised by a renascent Calvinism at the Disruption of 1843, free enterprise ideology brought obvious material and political rewards; for the proletariat, especially the labour aristocracy of Edinburgh and Glasgow, the traditional Scottish virtues of 'respectability' and 'self-help' served to accommodate them to this ideology,[7] and it was not until the financial rewards of living by these virtues became clearly deficient that we see the slow movement of the Scottish working class towards a limited reformist radicalism. The increasing tension between solidarity and division was manifest in all the institutions of Scotland's social structure. It was clearly to be seen in the schools with the rise of a largely separate system designed to cater for the bourgeoisie — the increasing numbers of academies, high schools, proprietary boarding or 'public' schools and other institutions for the children of an affluent middle class bear witness to this. They arose in response to the demands of an anglicised and expanding bourgeoisie who wished to save the expense of sending their children to such schools south of the border.

The gradual absorption of most of this separate system into the state organisation of schools, which took place between 1872 and 1918, resulted in the reaffirmation of a strong élitist tendency in the organisation of secondary schooling. For the bourgeois Scot — whether lawyer, doctor, businessman, minister or teacher — social and material advancement was a defining characteristic of the bourgeois lifestyle, and one main route of such advancement was through education to one of the professions (most notably in Scotland, the legal profession). Such educational advancement

P

required a system of schooling which met two main criteria — first, continuity of stage from 'primary' through 'secondary' to university level; and, second, a tight selection process which would guarantee the emergence and success only of those who were fit to join the existing membership of the dominant class. We have already seen how the old parish school system fulfilled both criteria fairly well in its day. But, with the great social disruption consequent upon industrialisation, and with the resulting greater polarisation of Scottish society, the ladder of advancement embodied in that older tradition was gradually eroded and a new one had to be found. The response of the aspiring bourgeoisie, in setting up a largely separate, privately funded sector of schools for themselves, was a development that policy-makers in the state sector could not ignore; the eventual new amalgamation of state sector and private sector resulted in the ideals and strategies of the latter coming to dominate the former, so that the dual criterion of continuity and selection became paramount, supported by a social analysis in terms of class.

The return of the bourgeois school to the state fold in Scotland was not without its problems. Financially, the difficulties were soon overcome by degrees; administratively, the transference of power from school boards, close to the people, to local authorities based on the county (and dominated there by bourgeois and aristocratic elements) was inexorable. It was simply a question of waiting until the 'rationality' and 'cost effectiveness' of such moves became obvious to legislators. But the problems of access (who would be allowed to enter secondary education?) and content (what would be taught in secondary schools?) were much more intractable. By 1900, the state-funded elementary schooling of the bulk of the Scottish population was accepted as the norm — the imperative need to 'moralise' and control a potentially restive labouring class had ensured this and, although the development of elementary or 'primary' schooling was not unproblematic even then, its relative success served to move the focus of debate and pressure from the schooling of younger children to the schooling of the adolescent. There were (and still are) good reasons for this: the construction of adolescence by Western European civilisation as a problematic period in the life of the individual makes schooling for control a central and intractable issue; the demands of an approaching life of labour, and full adult participation in the economic life of the society add their own difficulties; secondary schooling thus raises major issues of psychic and social adjustment. If we add to this the requirements of an industrialised capitalist economic structure for a differentially trained workforce, it can be seen that the superficially *educational* issues of access and content in fact are generated by strong forces within the *socio-political realm* and raise profound problems in that realm. It is with an analysis of these forces and problems, between the turn of the century and the outbreak of the second world war in 1939, that the remainder of this essay is concerned.

2

> The pride and glory of a schoolmaster's profession will be destroyed; that considerable class
> of scholars, who now go on to the Scotch Universities from the parochial schools . . .
>
> Mr. A. C. Sellar, *Argyll Commission*, 1867

The story of the growth of a state-financed system of secondary schools in Scotland is dominated by confusion. The confusion seems to extend from uncertainty as to the nature and aims of secondary education to the nomenclature to be used in describing the schools in which this education was supposed to occur. There is a perennial swithering (evident in published sources) about what precisely such schools were for, what they ought to be doing, and to whom; there is also a bewildering variety of terminology used throughout the period from about 1900 onwards to describe and label the schools, the children and their courses of study — specific subjects, higher class publics, higher grades, intermediates, supplementary courses, advanced divisions. The list seems endless.

Nevertheless, there are two factors which help in the struggle to arrive at a coherent picture of what happened, and why. The first is the realisation that those who had the power and influence to construct the system of secondary schooling which grew up in Scotland between 1900 and 1939 appear to have held to a dominant *ideology* throughout, which governed their view of the purposes and functions of such a system. This was an ideology rooted in the notion that types of children, for whom types of schooling were more or less appropriate, could be easily identified. The typology was based on assumptions of job-orientation and class origin — these children were assumed to be heading for specific job categories in the economy and they were assumed to come from particular social classes. Thus, it appeared natural and efficient to organise types of secondary school to correspond with these types of children. The second factor which helps to clarify a confusing picture is the realisation that the *rhetoric* chosen to present the fruits of this ideology to the Scottish public alters over the years in response to pressures of a mainly political sort. The character of the language chosen to present the system (based on such an ideology) shifts from descriptions and justifications in terms of social class to descriptions and justifications in terms of 'natural ability'. There is evidence to suggest that such shifts were purely cosmetic semantics reflecting a forced development of the language used but in no way symptomatic of a shift in the basic ideology.

The main effect of the Scottish legislation of 1872 was to threaten the traditional Scottish ladder of meritocratic educational advancement via the parish school and the universities. Sellar may be correct in describing the 'lad o' parts' as the schoolmaster's 'pride and glory'; it is fairly clear that their number was never considerable (as has been previously argued), even in areas such as North-East Scotland where scholarships eased the purely financial problems of protracted study. Nevertheless, the sheer existence of such a route was very important; it provided a necessary avenue, out of poverty and into some wealth and standing, which a significant minority of Scots saw as necessary and just. The arrival of state legislation which delineated a publicly funded elementary schooling but which largely omitted to give the same degree of financial encouragement to schooling beyond the elementary must be seen as the first move in the dismantling of the traditional route. The omission was compounded by a gradual shift of the Scottish universities away from their past role as providers of some elements of such post-elementary schooling (in the form of junior classes) for a relatively youthful student body. What the universities moved towards was a position where a much more high-powered and specialised curriculum, incorporating such developments as Honours degrees, necessitated a raised age of entry consequent upon a raised level of qualification for entry.[8] As Kerr pointed out in 1910:

> Such an education as may fit every working-man's child to face the necessities of life is, in all ordinary circumstances, within his reach, and yet it is scarcely doubtful that, in certain circumstances, the poor man's son has not so good a chance of getting a university education as he had forty years ago . . . Many fathers cannot or will not bear the expense of the three additional years which are now required to bring a son to the door of the university. The age of schoolboys entering the university has gone up from sixteen to nearly nineteen years.[9]

Thus the sealing off of an elementary or primary stage of schooling for the populace, in the same period as the university was increasingly distancing itself from such schooling, resulted in the breaking down of that important ladder for meritocratic advancement which the tradition of the Scottish parish school had represented. However, there was one social group for whom this erosion was not problematic, as indicated earlier — those who could afford to buy the kind of schooling required. Private schooling has always existed in Scotland, but the eighteenth and nineteenth centuries saw a burgeoning of the field as the wealth of the middle classes increased and as their acceptance of curricula based on the classics diminished. Perth Academy was characteristic in many ways. Founded in 1760, it offered an alternative to study at distant universities and to the city's traditional grammar school by teaching the 'modern' scientific and commercial subjects to the children of middle and upper classes of the locality.[10] The academy in Inverness was similarly for the 'upper classes in the Highlands'.[11] Whether academies or other forms of private secondary schools, the whole non-state sector flourished; by 1879, there were two hundred and sixty higher class non-public schools (that is, secondary schools funded largely by private means);[12] by 1905, such private schools were educating almost as many pupils as the state schools,[13] and this was not to alter fundamentally until after the Act of 1918 which made state secondary schooling free and compulsory.

These developments help to explain Sir Henry Craik's rush to institute a Leaving Certificate in 1888, three years after his appointment as Secretary of the Scotch Education Department. Craik was plainly aware of the growing hiatus between state schooling and university education; he may well have seen the popularity and success of the private schools as threatening.[14] In any event, his success in setting up the Leaving Certificate, and in persuading universities and other bodies to accept it as equivalent to their own entrance qualifications, ensured that *academic types of secondary schooling* were strengthened. In this way, the *academic type of child* was reinstated as the dominant consideration in the thinking of Scottish educational policy-makers; it was this child's secondary education which had to be secured, as a matter of priority. If, in effect, this entailed a categorisation of children and schools along class lines, this was simply a reflection of a supposed natural social order in which the accumulating power of the Scottish middle classes had to be recognised.

3

It is evident that the governing class is being increasingly recruited from the middle class, and that it is politically desirable that the latter should, by being well educated, be fitted to contribute to the supply of wise legislation.

John Kerr, *Scottish Education — School and University*, p. 312

The class-orientated nature of Scottish schooling is seldom noted. Instead a large part of Scottish educational mythology rests heavily on the contention that the country's school system was classless or democratic. But there is a considerable amount of evidence to show that, if Scottish schools were ever democratic, they were democratic in a particular way which emphasised social division, competitive liberalism and individual achievement at the expense of others.[15] Nowhere is this more marked than in the system of secondary schooling which was built between 1900 and 1939 on the foundations laid by the Scotch Education Department under Craik. This system is characterised by a twofold division of children and schools — first, the academic child who is to receive an academic secondary schooling either for its inherent value or for its usefulness in qualifying for entry to university and the professions; second, the non-academic child who is to receive an elementary or primary schooling with, at its conclusion, a variety of bits and pieces added on, very few of which will suffice to lead anywhere except to the ordained social rank. These two types of children are recognisable, it is claimed, by the social class to which they belong and by the occupations towards which they are supposed to be heading. Later, as we enter the 1920s and 1930s, it will increasingly be argued that such children can be spotted by obvious differences in their 'natural ability' or 'intelligence'.

Kerr's straightforward assumptions of a class-orientated basis for two types of secondary schooling are not unique. Kerr was, towards the end of his career in 1896, the Senior Chief Inspector for Scotland and, hence, close to the senior civil servants who effectively ran the school system with seemingly little direct political control apart from their own predilections and convictions.[16] Such convictions had produced the view that Scottish working-class children would be sufficiently catered for, in terms of secondary schooling, by a variety of bits added to their elementary schooling. The first such 'bits' had been the system of 'specific subjects' which had lasted from 1872 to 1898 followed by the arrival of so-called 'Advanced Departments' in the latter year. The specific subjects were continued in these Departments but the curriculum was also broadened and deepened in such a way as to incorporate '. . . a practical bias in terms of the probable future occupations of the pupils'.[17] By 1902, however, the raising of the school leaving age had made available two full years in which a different secondary 'bit' could be developed for children of working-class parents who were supposed to be heading for working-class jobs. These new 'bits' were the 'supplementary courses' instituted in 1903.

The origins of the supplementary courses are not totally clear but there is evidence to show that their main purpose was to continue, and foster, the growth of a second-rate secondary schooling for a specific type of pupil. Two examples must suffice here. Shortly before the courses were legislated into existence a certain Mr Smith (probably J. C. Smith, a Departmental Inspector from 1899 and Senior Chief Inspector from 1927 to 1932) wrote an extensive memorandum to John Struthers, Craik's deputy and then his successor in 1904. Smith's memorandum urges the setting up of a new type of secondary curriculum for a particular type of pupil:

> These pupils are not going into professions, nor even as a rule into offices. The boys will become ploughmen, crofters, farmers, artizans: the girls will go into shops or factories, or into domestic service. At the same time it is proper to note that, as these pupils *ex hypothesi* get the merit certificate some time before they are 14, they are by no means duffers and will not generally become mere drudges. We have to consider the future mason, not the mason's labourer.[18]

The memorandum appears likely to have formulated the basic thinking behind the introduction of supplementary courses in 1903, and its implications are startling. First, it shows a simple and dogmatic analysis of career structure in the Scotland of the time; second, it blandly assumes a particular level of motivation and job-orientation in particular types of pupils; and, third, it directly links the new courses with future occupations and, by implication, with social class. Presumably the 'duffers' and 'mere drudges' will have to rest content with an elementary schooling; at secondary level, the incipient professional and commercial class are sharply ·separated from potential masons, crofters, domestic servants and shop assistants, and it is for the latter group that supplementary courses are intended. That Smith's superiors welcomed such analyses is clear from another piece of evidence. An anonymous inspector, who was due to meet members of the Perth School Board just before the introduction of supplementary courses, submitted a list of the members' questions and his proposed answers to John Struthers before the meeting took place. To the question, 'Would free places at the Academy [Perth Academy] not serve the purpose of Supplementary Courses?', the inspector proposed the answer, 'The two forms of education were intended for totally different classes of pupils', at which point the unmistakable hand of Struthers, above the initials 'J. S.', makes the marginal comment, 'certainly'.[19]

Given such views, it is not at all surprising that official policy forged ahead along the lines of making permanent the division of secondary schools into two types. There had been a third type, at one time, in the shape of higher grade secondary schools. Set up in 1899 to provide a form of intermediate secondary schooling and concentrating on providing for the needs of pupils who were willing to devote three years to courses aligned towards industry and commerce, they also reflected the class-occupation categorisations of the educational establishment. But their initial effect was to liberalise to some extent the dour academic tradition of Scottish secondary schooling, and they were thus extremely popular with parents and children.[20] However, they fitted unhappily into the simple twofold division to which the policy-makers were addicted, and their popularity seriously undermined the supplementary courses. They had to go, and, by 1920, most of them were subsumed under the regulations for secondary schools for the able minority. Meanwhile, Circular 374, issued in 1903, had explicitly indicated the need for division:

> My Lords are of the opionion, from a careful consideration of the facts, that the tendency . . . to make one and the same school with one and the same staff serve many different functions is the weak point of educational organisation in Scotland . . and they are satisfied that increasing division of function as between different types of schools is an essential condition of further educational progress.[21]

The classification of pupils into two types also becomes more explicit at this time. We now know that this was based on straightforward class and occupation categories, but its public presentation was simply in terms of 'secondary' and 'non-secondary' pupils.[22] Even this was sufficient to raise storms of protest at the time, and the 'incubus of non-secondary pupils'[23] was to haunt Scottish educational policy-makers from then on.

4

Received Mr. Wheatley. He is an extreme socialist and comes from Glasgow.

Diary of George V, February, 1924

The Education (Scotland) Act of 1918 is usually given detailed attention by historians of education, as it should. But much important educational decision-making was done more quietly and in less public places than in Acts of Parliament. This applies particularly to the period between 1918 and 1939, a period during which government and rulers had to learn to move more circumspectly in the face of various formal and informal threats to their hegemony; perhaps the greatest such threat was the mobilisation of ordinary people as represented by the rise of the Labour Party and the growing electoral power of the working class. Part of that mobilisation, in Scotland as well as England, was a demand for increased access to secondary education for all children, as of right. The strength of this demand necessitated conciliation (however grudging) by those who wished to retain power and control, so that enough was given away to satisfy the demand but not so much as would threaten the power-base. Part of this strategy involved a change in the kind of language used to describe the existing educational scheme, in the hope that an altered rhetoric would convince the people of Scotland of an altered substance. In fact, the substantive changes in Scottish secondary schooling which were intended to bring about a genuine change in access to the schools never materialised; instead, the divided system laid down in the early years of the twentieth century simply continued in more refined form, although the terms in which it was presented and justified were to change from those involving ideas of class and occupation to (it was thought) a more defensible set of notions centred on the idea of 'natural ability'.

Not that the older — and by now politically dangerous — language of class vanished immediately. In 1917, the Permanent Secretary to the Scotch Education Department (Struthers) could still insist that '. . . there is a class of pupils who, after reaching a certain age, will derive more educational benefit from part-time instruction with some direct reference to the occupation in which they are engaged than by a compulsory continuation of whole-time instruction . . .'[24] Similarly, his comment in 1918 that Scottish Roman Catholics constituted '. . . a pariah class and a growing national danger',[25] unless their schools were absorbed into the state system and some of their demands were met, was not a remark that a politically aware civil servant could have made easily a few years later, even in a confidential letter to his political master.

The problem, then, was to safeguard the meritocratic academic ladder by doing as little as possible to meet the demand for secondary education for all, and to dress up the whole exercise in words which would disguise the lack of fundamental change. Safeguarding the ladder involved pouring cold water on any scheme which would alter its fundamental principle of providing a route solely for the academically gifted. Thus, when the Scottish Education Department's own Advisory Council suggested a re-organisation of secondary schooling which could have threatened this principle, reaction was swift.[26] In October, 1920, George Macdonald (Struthers' deputy and then successor) sent a long minute to his superior in which he analyses the Advisory Council's draft scheme in illuminating terms:

They have ignored the fundamental fact that the school population falls into two parts — the majority of distinctly limited intelligence, and an extremely important minority drawn from all ranks and classes who are capable of responding to a much more severe call. It is vital for the body politic that each of these should have the very best education which it is possible to devise, but the education must be adapted to their capacities and matters will not be helped by ignoring the difference between them. The type that is best for one is not necessarily the best for the other, and attempts to establish equivalence may result in harm to both. I am sure it would be far more profitable to admit the difference, to attempt to discover what was the most suitable course of training for each, and then to spare no pains to make these courses as good as they possibly could be. What the Committee seems to me to have done is to draw up a scheme which proceeds on the supposition that all save a few backward children are capable of profiting by the same sort of education.[27]

The old twofold division is still here, but now what is emphasised is that its basis is dependent on recognising the 'distinctly limited intelligence' of the majority. Such recognition is plainly not a problem for Macdonald. By 1920, also, supplementary courses were admitted, by Struthers and his inspectorate, to have failed,[28] and the intractable 'incubus of non-secondary pupils' thus continued to trouble the sleep of tidy-minded bureaucrats.

Surprisingly enough, the simple rhetorical solution of re-labelling *all* post-primary work as 'secondary', while retaining the desired sharp divisions *within* the category, does not seem to have been raised at this stage. There may have been financial reasons for this, in the sense that schooling conducted under a code of regulations for primary schools (as was the case with most of the new Advanced Divisions which replaced supplementary courses) was much cheaper than schooling under secondary regulations which allowed more generous provision for teachers, classes, facilities and grants — and during the era of the Geddes Axe, cheapness was all. Nevertheless, the direct result was that a way was now open for a major political attack on the relatively low level of funding of schools for the poorer classes, and such an attack was not long in coming (the details are discussed below).

In the meantime, the government circulars and school codes of the early 1920s are marked by a reiteration of the twofold division of secondary schooling, by a renaming of the 'bits added on' as Advanced Divisions and by increasing recourse to a rhetoric of 'natural ability' as the ground for such a division. The initial blast occurs in the notorious Circular 44, issued in December, 1921, which proposed, for a small minority 'endowed by nature with the mental equipment',[29] a full five-year secondary course leading to the Leaving Certificate, whereas the majority of children not so endowed would be relegated to Advanced Divisions or other 'bits'. The Circular points out also that such strict division '. . . implies, wherever practicable, an entirely separate organization even in subjects which are common to the secondary and the non-secondary group',[30] and even if such combination was convenient it would be 'educationally unsound'.[31] The ostensible reason for such a division is couched in terms of the need to give 'non-secondary' pupils courses which would be more in line with their supposed lack of ability and greater general attention to their supposed peculiar needs — a line of reasoning quite under-mined by the differential funding of Advanced Divisions which favoured the full secondary schools. The Circular raised a storm of protest, but the Scottish Education Department ignored it all and marched on to issue codes and other circulars in 1923 and 1924 which made the divided system mandatory.

Part, at least, of the reason why they felt able to ignore the protest was that the opposition in Scotland seemed incapable of mounting a coherent case. Many voices rightly stressed the social undesirability of the division[32] but, when scrutinised for detailed analyses of deficiencies or constructive alternative proposals, their perorations show a distinct lack of substance. To take one important example, the Educational Institute of Scotland (the main union of Scottish teachers) had this to say on the draft school codes issued in May 1923:

> The unity of the educational system is entirely lost by any such division as that of non-secondary and secondary, inasmuch as the very terms imply the one group is in the minds of the author or authors of Circular 44 exclusive of the other. This exclusiveness will be strenuously opposed . . . What the country requires and demands is a national system, which involves the complete co-ordination and articulation of the various parts, and offers to the pupils the fullest advance according to their talents . . . it is for us teachers to preach on all occasions the gospel of educational unity. We desire to have a system linked up into one homogeneous whole, and embracing all stages of education, from primary school to the University. No other system can be considered satisfactory . . . [33]

Strenuous opposition must surely require a firmer base than this. When the codes were published five months later, the comment was equally ambiguous and vague:

> The policy of the Institute has for many years been a full secondary education for all pupils. The Advanced Divisions, whatever may be said to the contrary, are palpably intended to furnish certain pupils with an inferior type of education. Unless and until the curriculum for all post-qualifying pupils is the same and carries with it the same privileges and is not separated even in name, the opposition to the Codes will be continued. All post-qualifying education must be the same for all pupils.[34]

Precisely how all post-qualifying (secondary) education could be 'the same' for all pupils remains unanalysed, and the suggested non-separation of names provided too easy a way out for the writers of the codes. It is also as well to remember that the Institute appeared to take a very different line a few years earlier when it agreed that '. . . while school education cannot and should not be vocational in the narrow sense of the term, it is both possible and desirable at this secondary stage to differentiate curricula to suit the varying capacities and probable future needs of different classes of pupils'.[35] The Institute ideal in 1917 thus seems to have been in some accord with that of the Scottish Education Department. The vagueness of their opposing stance six or seven years later would seem to indicate a certain lack of conviction. There were good reasons for this. A proper secondary education for all children would have involved a fundamental re-appraisal of the nature of such education and, in particular, an attack on the grossly restrictive academic tradition of the Scottish secondary school which emphasised a narrow curriculum of examinable subjects pursued grimly and methodically to the Leaving Certificate. Teachers of such subjects had a strong vested interest in maintaining their dominant position in the school curriculum, as did the parents of those pupils who could pass examinations in them. Finally, and perhaps most decisively, the universities would never have countenanced such an undermining of their *raison d'être* and thus their dominance of the system from the top down. In general, then, there was no real heart in the opposition since a coherent counter-argument would have necessarily led to an attack on the foundations of the whole system. Nonetheless, opposition continued sporadically up to the outbreak of war in 1939. When the Education (Scotland) Bill reached the committee stage in March, 1936, its provision for 'non-secondary pupils' was attacked by James Maxton M.P. on the grounds of differential financing to the disadvantage of children in Advanced Division schools. Maxton maintained '. . . that the school buildings for advanced division schools were much inferior to those of secondary schools . . .' and '. . . that the staffing, the equipment, the buildings, and the teachers of secondary schools were better than those of advanced division schools'.[36] The Scottish Education Department were then landed with the unenviable task of disproving Maxton's claims by reference to their own data. Unfortunately, the figures they came up with *supported* Maxton's claims — the lowest building cost per pupil for secondary schools was almost double that for Advanced Divisions (£30 as against £16), and the average size of class in Advanced Divisions was appreciably greater than the average for secondary schools (30.3 pupils as against 23.75 pupils nationally; 36.6 pupils as against 26.5 in Glasgow).[37] This inability to defend the separation, even on such limited financial and numerical grounds, helps to explain what happened next. On 15th May, 1936, J. W. Peck, the newly arrived Scottish Education Department Secretary, wrote to the Lord Advocate about the Bill:

> The underlying idea in the criticism of the Opposition is that the three year pupils do not get as fair a deal as the five year people — in other words, putting it crudely, that the children of the poor go to inferior Advanced Divisions, and the children of the middle classes and well-off people go to the superior secondary schools and 'academies' . . . The intention of the Department is that there should be no distinction except such as is justifiable on purely educational grounds. Different subjects, differently qualified teachers, different make-up of the curriculum, may be appropriate according as the course is three years leading to commerce and industry, or five years leading to higher positions in these or to the Universities. The Department believes that such differentiation is called for, but it has been and will be made on educational, not social grounds.[38]

When the Bill became law at the end of July, all post-primary schools were re-named 'secondary' and Advanced Divisions vanished; the secondary schools were divided into those providing five-year courses leading to the Leaving Certificate ('senior secondaries' as they were to be labelled) and those providing three-year courses to age fifteen and leading to nothing at all ('junior secondaries'). The old division remains, but its locus is shifted from a division of schools to a division into *types of course*, and this separation is thinly papered over by a change of name (the same manoeuvre was to be repeated thirty years later with the advent of comprehensive schools). The advantage of this new basis for division lay in the fact that allocation of pupils to courses could be more persuasively made on the grounds of so-called 'natural ability', and that it was ability which would now determine the type of secondary schooling to be delivered; the schooling, in turn, would determine the occupational slot which the child would occupy, as Peck's letter makes clear. Class is thus no longer explicitly mentioned although it is implicit in the occupation categories used; hence the basic ideology remains unchanged.

But who was to identify the child's 'natural ability' and how could it best be done? To rely on teachers' estimates would have meant laying the authorities open to charges of bias or subjectivity; to rely solely on what was achieved in primary school tests might simply reflect the amount of time devoted to preparing for such tests. Something much more objective and, if possible, scientific, was required, and the growing availability of mass tests of intelligence seemed to provide a ready-made solution. Scotland had its own master of the esoteric art of intelligence test construction in the shape of Godfrey Thomson, Professor of Education at Edinburgh University and Director of Edinburgh's Moray House Training College for Teachers.[39] When the Scottish demand for objective (and cheap) means of assessing 'natural ability' began, Thomson's Moray House Tests of Intelligence seemed to offer the instant solution to administrative problems of allocating children to courses. His view of a national system of schools was that it:

> acts as a sieve, or a succession of sieves, sorting out pupils into different kinds. In its crude form this idea presents the picture of a ladder of education, up which a competing crowd start, the weaklings to be elbowed off as they endeavour to climb . . . This picture is somewhat repellent . . . Since, however, people clearly differ in their qualities and abilities, it is certain that a period of education will always be a period of sorting.[40]

Thomson was an Englishman, but the congruence between these views and those of the Scottish Department are marked — and expressed with more honest brutality. Intelligence testing in Scotland, therefore, seems to have fitted in neatly with a need to find 'scientific' justification for dividing children up into groups according to their ability. In this sense, Thomson's work acted as a legitimator of a pre-existent ideology which had shifted in rhetoric to what was imagined to be safer ground. In addition, a new and relatively enlightened policy of 'promoting' all children at age twelve into one or other form of secondary education screwed the administrative problems of allocation to a higher pitch. It was no longer possible to hold children back until their attainment was satisfactory; under the 'clean cut' policy, the child's age was the main determining factor in the move to secondary courses.[41]

5

Scotland's schools are at the centre of Scotland's perplexity, one of its main causes.

R. F. Mackenzie, *The Unbowed Head*, 1977

. . . expansion of schooling for the masses was usually viewed as a progressive step forward, one generated by humanitarian motives. The possibility that the school was in fact a vehicle of control and repression escaped analysis.

C. Karier, P. Violas, J. Spring, *Roots of Crisis*, 1973

The ability of the Scots to sustain the tension between solidarity and competitive division broke down once and for all as industrialisation gathered pace. That ability had itself been an outcome of structural factors — a largely agrarian and peasant economy, with elements of the clan system and feudalism intermingled, had produced a materially poor but relatively stable Scottish civil society. But the growth of mercantilism and then of capitalist industrialisation destroyed that stability and led to the overthrow or incorporation of nobles and landowners who had ruled the country for their own ends. A new class rose to dominance — the Scottish bourgeoisie. Never very numerous, their political power increased relentlessly with successive extensions of the franchise; their educational needs began to dominate the world of the Scottish school and, when the state entered that world, those needs, backed by that power, had to take priority. But someone had to pay for this order of priorities, and Craik's policy of re-establishing the eroded ladder of meritocratic schooling (previously embodied in the parish school system) indicated that the payment would be made at the expense of the ordinary people of Scotland. His construction of a secondary schooling devoted to certification above all was, in fact, a resurrection of a very old Scottish meritocratic tradition in a new guise. As men of their time, it seemed to Craik and his successors only natural that this divided system should be described in class terms; in doing so, they were only making explicit an accepted Scottish system of social grading which had very deep roots. A system of secondary schooling which separated middle class sheep from the remaining goats, and sent them off to different schools, aroused only pious opposition couched in the vaguest phraseology. But when the goats found some kind of voice and began to threaten the dominance of the Scottish middle class, appeasement became the order of the day. The cry of 'secondary education for all' had to be met somehow but without destroying the meritocratic route. Consequently, an exercise in public relations was called for first of all; a change in the language used to describe the divided system was necessary and the *socially* graded secondary system thus became the *ability* graded secondary system. But, in addition, these restive goats had to be controlled and confined so that, with any luck, their threatening assertion of rights might never arise if they were properly schooled; hence the persistent emphasis on schooling for conformity in Scotland which is so evident in the importance granted to '. . .

understanding the need for co-operation with authority'.[42] The legislation on secondary schools since 1872 and particularly since 1903 has thus been dominated by a gross ideology of social division; it has given Scotland a secondary school system which directly meets the needs of only a small minority and has forced Scottish schooling into a mould which now seems incapable of reasoned transformation.

NOTES

1. Tom Nairn, 'Old and New Scottish Nationalism', in *The Break-up of Britain: Crisis and Neo-nationalism* (London, 1977) p. 170. Nairn's analysis of Scottish culture and of its strengths and weaknesses has not so far been superseded, in my view.

2. The most extensive recent panegyric on Scottish democracy is L. J. Saunders, *Scottish Democracy 1815-1840* (Edinburgh, 1950).

3. The phrase comes from the Education (Scotland) Act of 1872.

4. Quoted in I. R. Findlay, Sir John Struthers KCB, Secretary of the Scotch/Scottish Education Department, unpub. Ph.D. thesis, University of Dundee, 1979, p. 349.

5. T. C. Smout, *A History of the Scottish People 1560-1830* (Glasgow, 1969), p. 428.

6. G. S. Osborne, *Scottish and English Schools — a comparative survey of the past fifty years* (London, 1966), p. 18.

7. See, for example, R. Q. Gray, *The Labour Aristocracy in Victorian Edinburgh* (Oxford, 1976).

8. See G. E. Davie, *The Democratic Intellect* (Edinburgh & Chicago, 1961) and James Scotland, *The History of Scottish Education* (London, 1969), vol. I, chapter 22 and Vol. II, chapter 10.

9. John Kerr, *Scottish Education — School and University* (Cambridge, 1913), pp. 276-277.

10. D. J. Withrington, 'Education and Society in the eighteenth century', in N. T. Phillipson and R. Mitchison (eds.), *Scotland in the Age of Improvement* (Edinburgh, 1970); see also James Scotland, *op. cit.*, vol. I, pp. 104-105.

11. Quoted in James Scotland, *op. cit.*, vol. I, p. 105.

12. James Scotland, *op. cit.*, vol. II, p. 63.

13. *Ibid.*, p. 71.

14. See Thomas Dobie, 'The Scottish Leaving Certificate 1888-1908', in T. R. Bone (ed.), *Studies in the History of Scottish Education 1872-1939* (London, 1967).

15. A. A. MacLaren (ed.) *Social Class in Scotland: Past and Present* (Edinburgh, 1972). In his introduction, MacLaren argues that '. . . the egalitarianism so often portrayed is not that emerging from an economic, social, or even political equality; it is equality of opportunity which is exemplified. All men are not equal. What is implied is that all men are given an opportunity to be equal. Whatever the values attached to such a belief, if expressed today it would be called elitist not egalitarian' (p. 2). This neatly describes in more general terms what I have described as an educational 'meritocracy'.

16. See T. R. Bone, *School Inspection in Scotland* (London, 1966).

17. Newman A. Wade, *Post-primary Education in the Primary Schools of Scotland 1872-1936* (London, 1939), p. 78. Wade's book is a major (and somewhat neglected) source of information and data on the development of the 'bits added on', although his commentary on events has to be treated cautiously.

18. Scottish Record Office, *File ED/7/1/21*, West Register House, Edinburgh. In the remainder of this essay, such files from the Scotch/Scottish Education Department are identified by the prefix S.R.O.

19. *Ibid*.

20. Wade, *op. cit.*, pp. 105-118 gives details of the successful appeal of higher grade schools.

From 27 schools in 1899, the number rose to 196 schools in 1914; pupil numbers increased from 2,561 in 1900 to over 31,000 in 1918, and this was 68 per cent of all secondary pupils in the latter year. In the light of this, it is difficult to understand Wade's comment that higher grade schools were a 'failure' (p. 118); granted, many of its pupils did not complete the course and gain the Intermediate Certificate introduced in 1902, but it is worth noting that the percentage gaining this certificate increased from 11 per cent to 15 per cent between 1908 and 1918. In general, it appears that Wade is following the Departmental line — that the higher grade schools competed unfairly with supplementary courses, to the detriment of the latter. But this is simply a comment on the unattractiveness and poverty-stricken nature of the supplementary courses by their progenitors.

21. Scotch Education Department, *Circular No. 374*, 16 February 1903.

22. *Ibid.*

23. This astonishing phrase occurs during a discussion between the Secretary of the Scottish Education Department and his Chief Inspectors on 21 February 1922 (such meetings were held regularly). See S.R.O. ED/7/4/72.

24. S.R.O. ED/14/159.

25. In a letter to Lord Balfour of Burleigh (Struthers' boss as Secretary for Scotland from 1895 to 1903) dated 24 October, 1918 and quoted in I. R. Findlay, *op. cit.*, p. 302.

26. The Advisory Council on Education in Scotland had been set up by the 1918 Act and duly appeared in July 1920. Its first report to the Scottish Education Department dealt with the general organisation of schools and it recommended a system of three levels of schools for all to correspond with three age-groups of children — primary from 5 to 12 years of age, intermediate from 12 to 15 and secondary from 15 to 18. Plainly, this scheme would have cut across the Department's preferred twofold division of post-elementary schooling.

27. S.R.O. ED/8/3. Macdonald is commenting on the Council's draft scheme which was not published until January 1923.

28. See T. R. Bone, *op.cit.*, p. 183.

29. Scottish Education Department, *Circular No. 44*, 13 December 1921, p. 1.

30. *Ibid.*, p. 4.

31. *Ibid.*, p. 4.

32. Wade, *op. cit.*, pp. 121-123 gives details of the outcry.

33. Editorial, *Scottish Educational Journal*, VI, 25 May 1923. The Journal was the organ of the Educational Institute of Scotland.

34. Editorial, *Scottish Educational Journal*, VII, 11 January 1924.

35. Scottish Education Reform Committee, *Reform in Scottish Education* (Edinburgh, 1917), p. 39. The Committee comprised representatives from the three teachers' unions with EIS members predominating. Its Report makes sorry reading (by comparison with the English equivalent published five years later), since it is mainly a defensive diatribe on teachers' salaries, career prospects and conditions of service — so much for post-war 'national reconstruction'.

36. S.R.O. ED/14/299.

37. *Ibid.*

38. *Ibid.*

39. For an account of Thomson's career and an initial attempt to suggest correspondences between his views and those of the Scottish educational establishment, see H. M. Paterson, Godfrey Thomson and the development of psychometrics in Scotland 1925-1950, unpublished B.E.R.A. Conference paper, Stirling, 1975.

40. Godfrey H. Thomson, *A Modern Philosophy of Education* (London, 1929), pp. 60-61.

41. Scottish Education Department, *Memorandum Explanatory of the Day Schools (Scotland) Code 1939*, p. 6: '. . . the Department will expect that where schemes of promotion do not provide for promotion entirely on an age basis they will at least ensure that the period of retention in the primary division beyond the age of 12 is kept as short as is reasonably consistent with a broad and generous view of the appropriate educational needs of the pupils'.

42. *Ibid.*, p. 10; the phrase occurs in a discussion of the general aims of the three-year non-academic secondary courses and its emphasis should be compared with the stress on self-expression, initiative and leadership in courses for the academically able (p.12).

11

An Angle on the Geist:
Persistence and Change in the Scottish
Educational Tradition [1]

Andrew McPherson

1. Introduction

THE ebb and flow of nationalist fortunes in the past fifteen years has been accompanied by renewed public and academic interest in the nature of Scottish identity and its place in the political process. A variety of commentators has tried to resolve the central and enduring Scottish paradox, symbolised by the political Union and most recently restated in the inconclusive devolution referendum of 1979: how could a national sentiment of such continuity and consequence persistently prove so inconsequential? Was the very idea of a Scottish identity merely a misplaced metaphor, a deluded personification of altogether more complex events? Or was there indeed such an identity, but one so labile, divided or insecure as to be incapable of sustained and coherent political expression? Or was the resolution of the paradox to be found, not in the pathology of Scottish social personality, but in the pathology of a governance that was unresponsive to stable and distinctive features of Scottish civil society? Had Scotland been sold out? Were the rules of the political game manipulated against it? Alternatively, was the government and administration of the United Kingdom altogether *too* responsive to Scottish national sentiment, periodically purchasing Scottish political quiescence through acts of administrative devolution whose long-term effect could only be to extend centralised political control and ultimately to absorb Scottish institutions into alien metropolitan forms?

The mood of the current reappraisal is self-critical, iconoclastic and demythologising. Harvie's twentieth-century Scotland, for example, is a country of 'no gods and precious few heroes',[2] and Nairn describes Scotland as 'the land where ideal has never, even for an instant, coincided with fact'. In its popular culture he finds 'the pathetic symbols of an inarticulate people unable to forge valid correlates of their different experience . . . ' and he talks of 'the universality of (Scotland's) false consciousness and the multiplicity of its forms': 'Scotland's myths of identity are articulated sufficiently to suit everyone . . . [M]inisters of the Kirk, lawyers, lairds, tycoons and educationalists all have their own contrasting angles on the Geist.'[3]

This essay is mainly concerned with one central aspect of the educationist's 'angle', with the nature of Scottish community, its social differentiation and solidarity, and the relationship of its school system to these. In exploring the symbolic and material basis of this world I want, in particular, to suggest how élite educationists' and others' experience of Scottish education, broadly in the first half of this century, was selectively structured so as to confirm for them the validity of an inherited, traditional and egalitarian, view of Scottish culture and institutions. I shall also suggest — there will be little space for elaboration — some consequences of this for educational advice and policy-making in the 1950s and 1960s. My discussion is offered partly in an attempt to relate the substance of Scottish education to social and political process, and partly as a corrective to analyses that dismiss tradition and myth solely as 'false facts' and that fail to cope with the resultant problem of how one explains the persistence of traditional beliefs which facts appear to contradict. The demythologiser is as likely to dehistoricise, to discount the significance of the interplay over time of changing forms and ideas, as is the prisoner of myth who interprets present institutions as the unchanged expression of a timeless ideal. And therein lies a danger in the summary description of tradition, and my reason for not offering one here. Either one describes the forms — for example, the parochial school, the omnibus school, the five-subject Highers curriculum, the open-doors university, and the general degree — and risks assembling merely a catalogue of 'pathetic symbols', of 'invalid correlates of experience', some of which have demonstrably changed, in form or significance, in recent history; or else one tries to describe that experience more directly in terms, say, of the essential egalitarianism of the Scots. One then, however, risks a somewhat mystical metaphysic of the type that recently attracted the reaction:'It is as if Scots are judged to be egalitarian by dint of racial characteristics, of deep social values which apply at the level of the individual in an undifferentiated manner. Man (or a least Scots-man) is judged to be primordially equal . . .'[4]

The authors of this gentle lampoon observe that '(n)o myth is more prevalent and persistent than that asserting Scotland is a 'more equal' society than England (or Britain) and that Scots are somehow 'more egalitarian' than others in these islands'. They trace the myth to various sources, among them seventeenth and eighteenth-century Presbyterianism, the late eighteenth-century romantic discovery of the 'sturdy clan communalism' of Scottish Gaelic culture, and the late nineteenth-century flowering of Scottish Kailyard literature, which 'celebrated egalitarianism at its most clannish and communal'. 'The myth', they conclude, 'describes putative conditions in the typical pre-capitalist and pre-industrial community, rural or urban. Social identity is one of community, not of class . . . The locus of egalitarianism is the parish, religious and secular, whether in the country village or the small town.'

But did literature imitate life? Did life imitate literature? My exploration of these questions will reinforce the view that the locus of social identity has indeed been that of the village and small town and not that of the city; and especially not that, I would add, of the Clydeside conurbation with Glasgow at its centre. Yet, in 1951, this conurbation accounted for one-third of the Scottish population; over half the population lived in the four cities and the large burghs, and over 80 per cent was urbanised. In 1901 this last proportion had already been about three-quarters.[5] I shall point also to a close and puzzling parallel between the persisting locus of social identity and the locus of influence in the formation of Scottish educational policy and advice, a parallel that is all the more intriguing in the light of Hanham's characterisation of Scottish nationalism as a 'small man, small town' movement.[6] However, I must warn that my essay is intended to extend, and not be a substitute for, the account of the changing Scottish tradition that my colleagues and I have offered elsewhere; it is essentially programmatic in that I have preferred here to strike the balance between suggestiveness and conclusiveness in favour of the former; further evidence and elaboration is required on a number of points; and I do not deal directly with epistemological problems concerning the explanation of actions and beliefs and the representation of beliefs as true or false.[7]

2. Aspects of the form and content of the Scottish tradition.

Since Durkheim sociologists have often wanted to reserve the term 'myth' not for beliefs that could simply be dismissed as false but for folk stories that had two simultaneous functions: to celebrate identity and values and to describe and explain the world in which these are experienced or sought. Logically, myths may be expressive *and* true, or expressive *and* false; though the explanations that they offer and the 'facts' that may confirm or refute them are never closed to dispute.

Public statements about Scottish education often have the logically dual character of myth. For example the nineteenth-century Scottish concern to maintain a socially accessible national education system was often made explicit in the form of a story about the burgh and parochial school since Knox.[8] This story was simultaneously celebratory, descriptive and explanatory. The descriptions contained a measure (sometimes large, sometimes changing) of truth. By the mid-nineteenth century, for example, the parochial school could not sustain a weight of empirical interpretation commensurate with its symbolic importance to contemporaries.[9]

Examples of the continuity of public statements about equality and tradition in Scotland between the 1860s and 1960s have been given elsewhere[10] and one alone must suffice here. McClelland wrote in 1935 that the 'key' to the Scottish education system was that 'the Scottish people value education and that the central and unbroken strand in our long educational tradition is the recognition of the right of the clever child, from whatever social class he may come, to the highest and best education the country has to offer'.[11] Here the present is explained as the realisation of an inheritance that is made potent for the future through the public consent it commands. McClelland's later, and highly influential, work on selection for secondary education derived from this view.[12] Thus the secondary account may mesh with the primary action. Can one pull the stories away without some of the facts sticking?

Several other introductory, but somewhat compressed, comments are necessary. I have talked elsewhere of the nineteenth-century Scottish emphasis on a 'collectivist' principle that, through public and not private provision, university education should be made equally accessible to all social classes and areas of the country, and also to a proportion of the population that was high relative to the then prevailing standard in England. This nationwide emphasis continued well into this century and heavily influenced the form of Scottish secondary education at least until the 1960s, a contest-mobility form with a didactic pedagogy ('the distinctive feature of a contest-mobility system is that . . . more [pupils] are given a chance (in a formal sense) for longer . . .').[13] Since 1888 the influence of the 'accessible university' on the schools has been communicated principally by the Leaving Certificate, controlled by the Scottish Education Department (SED). A continuing element in the Scottish tradition is, then, that of national standards, leading to central national control ('centralism'), often explicitly legitimated in terms of collectivism (in the special sense I give it here).[14]

Working against the collectivist principle, however, was the advised neglect of the pupil or student to whom public provision had given a chance: pupils and students should be helped by the public, but not too much; 'the half-starved Scottish hound' would 'win the race before the overfed spaniel', cosseted within the walls of its English college.[15] From the 1860s, if not earlier, it was regularly argued that Scottish character emerged from the struggle, in the trying circumstances of a non-residential university, for eminence in the rank of merit ('individualism').[16] Also contributing to Scottish character was a disputatious university pedagogy to which the written, terminal examination was seen as hostile, especially when it was external to the lecture class and linked to certification (nineteenth-century Scottish 'examination' was understood simultaneously as teaching *and* learning *and* assessment; to detach one of these elements (assessment) was to distort all of them).[17] This 'liberal' pedagogy was thought to be integral to general ('liberal') education, because it brought diverse ideas and diverse students into a living relationship that formed the basis of 'profession', of individuals' future character, motivation, thought and action. It thereby promoted social reproduction and adaptation and a lifelong involvement in the democracy of knowledge.[18]

The liberal element has been increasingly dominated by the centralist. The former achieved its fullest, though possibly its final, expression in the Scottish Advisory Council on Education's (SACE) report, *Secondary Education* (1947).

There it was treated as the appropriate pedagogy, not only for the university, but also now for the omnibus school that the SACE recommended as the 'natural way for a democracy to order the post-primary education of a given area'. Centralism was antipathetic to this form not only because it diminished teachers' professionalism but also, tellingly, because 'the surest way to distort a School Certificate . . . is to peg it to university matriculation requirements'.[19] We may take the SED's negative riposte of 1951/2 as marking the demise of 'liberal' pedagogy and curriculum, at least for the next generation.[20]

This is not the place to review the truth value of the descriptive and explanatory claims that are made by statements like McClelland's about equality of educational opportunity between the social classes in Scotland. Much depends upon definition. Colleagues and I have discussed the conceptual and epistemological problems and much more of the evidence elsewhere.[21] In general, however, I would argue that, *relative to England and Wales*, such claims have had a considerable validity during the last one hundred years, a validity which, though diminishing over time, and possibly disappearing altogether, was nevertheless still apparent in the two decades following the second world war.[22]

There are, moreover, several reasons why the egalitarian claim should have appeared valid to the educationists who made and influenced policy for the post-war period. First, teachers who became involved in advice and policy-making at a national level after the second war had received their education during a period when, relative to England, the Scottish myth had real substance. Second, there is evidence from as late as the 1960s and 1970s that the bipartite areas of the Scottish secondary system had a higher level of class inequality of educational attainment than the rest of the system where the omnibus schools, mainly serving the small towns and other non-city areas, were common. This 'may in large part have been a result of the much older tradition of the omnibus school' whose long history in certain areas 'might be both a consequence and a cause of a more egalitarian class structure, which in turn influenced the educational attainment of children'.[23] The omnibus school was, of course, only a part of the Scottish tradition, but it had been a larger part before the second world war, and especially before Circular 44 of 1921 denied it to the cities (*see* note 14).

Then, third, there are considerations relating to the way in which educational selection structured the experiences and perceptions of this generation of educationists, both as pupils and later as secondary school teachers. 'Academic' secondary education was, of course, selective, but generously so.[24] The individualist ethic could explain away the relatively high 'wastage' of able working-class pupils through 'early' leaving.[25] Among those who lasted the five-year course for Highers, social class differences in attainment were smaller than in the general school population. Indeed, by the early 1960s, within the population attempting Highers, mean social class differences in Highers attainment were very small indeed (they would of course have been larger if all pupils in the age-group who did not take Highers were 'scored zero').[26] At this time class differences in Highers attainment within the Highers population were non-existent in the omnibus sector,[27] and non-existent also in the six-year schools for areas of scattered population wherein local communities were served by 'truncated' secondary schools.[28] Until the 1960s the Scottish universities maintained an 'open doors' policy for virtually all applicants with minimum Highers qualifications, or better.[29] A relatively high proportion of graduate entrants to school teaching had working-class origins,[30] and anecdotal evidence indicates that such teachers were well represented among those who rose from teaching to the Inspectorate in the 1950s: 'I remember once entertaining a group of Russian educationists . . . with a group of inspectors . . . [O]f the eight I think seven were of working-class origin, which impressed the Russians so much that [they thought] we had chosen them deliberately, but we frankly hadn't. This kind of thing happens more frequently in Scotland than anywhere I know, that's one of the features of Scottish education that pleases me.'

3. Literature, politics and education

The Senior Chief Inspector (HMSCI) who said this was one of sixteen influential educationists, politicians and administrators of the post-war period whom Charles Raab and I interviewed at length between 1976 and 1980.[31] In section 4 I shall look further at these interviews. But first I want to use some biographical and literary evidence to suggest how the first half of the twentieth century made a version of the nineteenth-century tradition available to Scotland after 1945.

In 1971 Sir Charles Illingworth published a life of Sir Hector Hetherington, Principal of Glasgow University from 1936 to 1961. The task he set himself was to explain how Hetherington, a 'descendant of blacksmiths', who came of 'simple country stock' and was raised among 'douce respectable villagers', 'rose through his own efforts to the acknowledged leadership in University affairs in the country and throughout the British Commonwealth'. The occasion for *explanation* is also taken, however, as one for the *celebration* of the last of the 'acknowledged chieftains of their academic families', a man whose biography 'must therefore epitomise every campus activity as well as University developments in the country as a whole'.

Thus established, the subsequent iconography is predictable. From the Solway village in Dumfriesshire where 'many a Hector Hetherington lies buried' and from a small Dumfriesshire town, Hetherington's family moved eventually to the small town of Tillicoultry, near Stirling. There his father imparted to him 'the traditional Scottish respect for the church, for education and the learned professions . . .' His talent '[began] to emerge in the three years he spent at secondary school in the neighbouring small town of Dollar'. He became dux and entered Glasgow University through the bursary competition in 1905. The story continues, 'In Scotland traditionally University students have been drawn from every social class' and 'Glasgow educated them with due regard for their moral rectitude and the paternal purse'. Hetherington joined that 'grey homespun multitude' 'to work and learn and his whole energy was bent on success'. When this was achieved, '[t]owards the later part of his career there was . . . never a hint of bombast. To a friend who suggested he ought to aquire armorial bearings he replied that in view of his ancestry of blacksmiths and farmers the only suitable escutcheon would be a hammer and sickle'.[32] One is grateful for the humour; but a pestle and mortar would actually have been more appropriate because, for all that Hetherington's paternal grandfather had indeed been the Lockerbie blacksmith, his father had been apprenticed to a pharmacist cousin who owned his own shop in Moffat, and at Tillicoultry was himself the village chemist and Justice of the Peace. Young Hetherington's family had, in other words, already risen from the peasantry to the petty bourgeoisie.

A comment on humour, ambivalence and the Scottish self-image is appropriate here. The playwright James Bridie, a student contemporary of Hetherington's at Glasgow, captured the essential point in 1949 when he commented in relation to Kailyard sentiment that 'a great deal of what is called Scottish sentiment *is* funny . . . The Scot himself, greeting *(sic)* heartily beneath his bonnie briar bush, has been known to smile through his tears'.[33] Such ambivalence ultimately arises, I suggest, from the implications for Scottish civil society of the political Union. On the one hand there has been the wish to see the integrity of things Scottish either tested or protected in the world of politics; on the other there has been the southerly orientation that this entails with its threat (though to some a promise) of ultimate assimilation to a genteel society of armorial bearing. Role-distance, role-exchange, mimicry and the like help to manage this ambivalence and become a source of humour. We can see these qualities in Bridie's own treatment of class and education in Scottish and English society: 'We have a tradition of sound education in Scotland . . . It is our substitute for the English tradition of gentility. It is not, we feel, a thing to make a song and dance about. Perhaps I should not have mentioned it.'[34] Ten years earlier he had written in his autobiography, 'In Scotland we do not regard a person as belonging to the sweeper or untouchable caste because he has been educated by an Education Authority. On the other hand we do not rate highly the Scotsman who has succeeded in becoming an Englishman . . . We are too apt to search him too closely for signs of affectation; and in Scotland alien affectations are treated very harshly indeed.'[35] Nevertheless, Bridie can reassure the parent who is concerned with how 'the little Glasgow bourgeois may be fitted to take a distinguished part in the Drift South' that his review of the origins of archbishops, baronets, knights, right honourables and 'many acknowledged leaders of the Church, Big Business, the Bar, the Stage, Literature, Politics, Medicine, Sport, Aviation, Engineering, War, Art and Homeopathy' indicates that '(t)here appears to be plenty of room at the top for a Scotsman who has *not* been to an English public school'.[36]

Sir Walter Scott, it is claimed, 'taught Scotsmen to see themselves as men whose reason is on the side of the Union and whose emotions are not, and in whose confusion lies their national character',[37] and Bridie also conveys something of this. Though not, of course, as influential as Scott or Barrie (of whom more below), Bridie is nevertheless interesting as the product, and the chronicler, of a pre-1914 university culture whose influence on Scottish thought and politics in the 1930s and 1940s was to be considerable. He and Walter Elliot, a future Conservative Secretary of State for Scotland and, like his friend Bridie, a former pupil of the independent school, Glasgow Academy, dominated the clubbish literary life of the Glasgow University Union. Bridie, though not at that time Elliot, was active in its politics.[38] Also active at Glasgow in the same years was another future Secretary of State for Scotland, Tom Johnston, sponsor of Keir Hardie in a Rectorial Election.[39] Hetherington and Johnston both sat in Henry Jones' Moral Philosophy class. Hetherington's 1924 biography of Jones relates that it was conducted on broad and disputatious lines, and also that its members were 'for the most part of very modest means and had to make their way in the world by hard work and in a country where university honours are prized'. Its members would supply 'the leaders of national life in the succeeding generation'.[40] Johnston recalls how he engaged the Welsh Professor in prolonged political debate, though mainly in writing.[41] As a student the industrious Hetherington moved in circles that overlapped but little with the 'high indifference' of the Academy-dominated Union of Bridie and Elliot, but he was later to become close friends with them.[42] In the 1930s and 1940s this generation of students, diverse though it was in social origin and political allegiance, was to make common cause in pressing a Scottish case in British politics. One element in this case was their shared understanding of Scotland's past, a past that they felt they had experienced in the forms of their own education, and a past that they made available to a wider public through biography, essays, lectures, fiction, journalism, and politics itself.

Hetherington's lectures on the philosophy of civil society published in 1918 are suggestive of the beliefs that might unite the homespun country student with the urbane, Academy-educated Glasgow bourgeois in an identity 'of community, not of class'. Using classical analogies (common in such writing at this time) Hetherington traces the origins of civic virtue and leadership to the individual's solidary commitment to his local neighbourhood, a commitment more characteristic of the small community than of the sociologically problematic forms of the city; and he comments that

> it is a notable and instructive fact that Scotland and Ireland with their distinctively national traditions and institutions have furnished political and intellectual leaders to the Empire in numbers out of all proportion to their populations . . . And it is quite possible that, if the analysis of origin were pursued further, certain areas within Scotland . . . might be found to be more productive of leaders than others and these areas are precisely those in which the breath of local life blows most strongly.[43]

Thirty years later he was reported as returning to this theme in an address to the centenary meeting of the Glasgow local association of the Educational Institute of Scotland, at which he was made an Honorary Fellow of the Institute:

> Rural depopulation, the concentration of the vast mass of their people in Glasgow and in the narrow lands between Clyde and Forth . . . these were matters . . . which gave them pause. But . . . under the leadership which they saw moving in Scotland . . . they were in better heart . . . to attack the situation and . . . he [Hetherington] believed that one of the best grounds for confidence was that the Scottish tradition had never been allowed to die. In country school houses, in country mansions such as he knew when he was a boy, and in the recruitment from there to the schools and churches of their expanding cities there had been a noble assurance that the best part of life lay in spiritual values . . . [A]s these things were defended so was served the cause of democracy . . .[44]

Hetherington himself had a considerable record of public service to the United Kingdom, especially in labour relations. (But why did a more vigorous sociology, and a more eclectic study of education, not develop out of the potentially fertile conjunction of Scottish moral philosophy with the changing and contrasting social forms that were experienced by so many of the students, in particular in Glasgow?)

When the 'romantic' Walter Elliot[45] wrote in 1932 of a Scotsman's heritage of 'democratic intellectualism', it was in the context of a discussion of the springs of just such leadership, and of the authority whence it derived. Whilst he talked of the 'fierce egalitarianism . . . respect for intellectual pre-eminence and . . . lust for argument on abstract issues [that] . . . are the traditions of Scotland today', he also commented, revealingly,

> [It] is a heritage where the ordinary man exercises his right of vote . . . but afterwards does not have the right to recall it again. It is a heritage of nomination and not of democracy. It is a heritage wherein discipline is rigidly and ruthlessly enforced, but where criticism and attack are unflinching, continuous, and salt with a bitter and jealous humour. It is a heritage wherein intellect, speech and above all, argument are the passports to the highest eminence in the land.[46]

My contention is that the shared symbolic space of parish, academy, Scotland and Empire, and a shared background in classical studies and in a general university culture wherein, despite a substantial representation of working-class students,[47] 'an Oxonian would have found himself thoroughly at home',[48] all helped to mould a sense of common identity that subsequently played a part in holding a variety of political opinions to the common cause of the nationalistically tinged programme of reform.

John Buchan further illustrates this argument. Yet another student, and later a close friend, of Henry Jones at Glasgow, he had moved to his position as Tory MP for the Scottish Universities (1927-35) through Oxford, the Bar, journalism, imperial service, and a phenomenally successful career as a teller of popular tales about Scotland, leadership and the Empire. In his final years Buchan claimed that his Scottish upbringing 'had made any kind of class feeling impossible'. His friends and close associates at Westminster included liberal Tories like Elliot; Tom Johnston and the Red Clydeside MPs (among them Maxton, another of Hetherington's generation of Glasgow students); and also Ramsay Macdonald who, as the somewhat isolated leader of the national government, depended heavily on his fellow Scotsman for emotional support. Buchan saw the Prime Minister as a romantic Celt whose career 'could only have been possible in a true democracy'. As regards policy, Buchan supported, among other things, progressive measures in education and administrative devolution for Scotland; and Tom Johnston particularly remembered Buchan's 'interest in my effort to get the Labour Party swung away from an anti-colonialist attitude to a pro-Empire one'. The Clydeside MPs and Johnston regarded Buchan as 'a good Scot who had done well by his country's history and song, a decent man who (like Walter Elliot) had got himself into the wrong party'.[49]

Harvie has described reformist 'middle-opinion' of Scotland in the 1930s as made up of writers, architects, planners, industrialists, professionals and politicians, whose 'predominantly academic and professional leadership overlapped with one another and with moderate nationalist politics'. Tom Johnston, for example, helped found the Saltire Society in 1935 and he, Hetherington, Bridie and Elliot all appear in the Society's 1948 list of members. When Johnston became Secretary of State for Scotland in 1941 he invited Walter Elliot, along with the other living former holders of that office, to join the wartime Council of State that he had persuaded Churchill to accept. This Council gave considerable impetus to collectivist reform in wartime Scotland and to proposals for post-war reconstruction.[50] Among these proposals was the report in 1947 of the SACE on *Secondary Education*.

This remarkable document did much to convince educationists in the years after the war that they were heirs to an actively democratic system of national education serving a society characterised by, among other things, 'pride', 'democratic patriotism' and 'freedom from class consciousness'.[51] Many of our interviewees spontaneously referred to it as inspirational and wonderfully written. Its principal author, Sir James Robertson, had also been active in the Saltire Society in its early years (was this how he first came to public attention?).[52] Robertson later attributed the overall emphasis of the report to Johnston's political leadership,[53] and the report itself drew heavily on the work of the Society in representing the traditions of the nation and of its education system.[54] But Johnston left national politics (though not public life) after the war, and the report's proposals for a national system of omnibus schools reconciling social and intellectual diversity through a general curriculum and 'liberal' pedagogy (section 2) were not implemented, partly because of the SED's wish to retain control of the Leaving Certificate and, through the certificate, control of the schools.

When, in 1961, George Davie returned to Elliot's 'felicitous phrase' in naming his widely acclaimed study of the nineteenth-century Scottish Universities *The Democratic Intellect*,[55] this served, in the context of English debates of the time about social class inequalities of access to educational opportunity in England, only to confirm to Scottish opinion the egalitarian pedigree of the national institution that Scotland had substituted for English gentility. But such an inference was some way from what Elliot meant by 'democratic' or 'egalitarian' just as the twentieth-century forms of general education that were popularly supposed to realise these traditional values were far from the nineteenth-century forms that Davie discusses.[56] Nevertheless, the rhetoric, at least, persisted. One may, for example, find the HMSCI telling the (Kilbrandon) Commission on the Constitution (1969) that the distinctive institutional features of Scottish education were 'reflections of our national characteristics: we have an interest in the common man, therefore we have an interest in a broad education'.[57]

The Kailyard qualities in Illingworth's life of the chieftain are, then, symptomatic of a culture in which life and literature had interacted in many ways, and over a long period, to reproduce an image of the national character and of education's part in it. Indeed, one of our interviewees spontaneously invoked the work of the Kailyard's principal author, J. M. Barrie, to express this character. He recounted the episode in Barrie's *Mary Rose* in which a young English couple, wanting to exchange confidences in the presence of their ghillie, decide to converse in French. To their consternation, the young Scotsman is obliged to explain that, as a student at Aberdeen, he unfortunately knows the language. Our informant continued: 'This is what puts it in a nutshell, that the opportunities have been there for the laddie, that he has been encouraged to be a lad o' pairts'; and he added that he and all the other significant educational figures in post-war policy-making, whom we had discussed with him, shared this experience.

Kailyard or not, such sentiments seem to have been pervasive. We found, for example, that the majority of the eleven Scottish-educated educationists whom we interviewed spontaneously identified their own origins with the lad o' pairts and that, with differences of emphasis, virtually all described the post-war Scottish system as socially open. One ex-HMSCI told us that many in the influential Association of Directors of Education shared this view, as did his colleagues in the SED. Both former Secretaries to the Department confirmed this last judgement, one of them saying 'it was something in our blood'. And, in a radio interview in 1973, Bruce Millan, Parliamentary Under-Secretary of State with responsibilities for Scottish education at the time of comprehensive reorganisation, commented, 'I think there is a stronger democratic tradition in Scottish education . . . perhaps we tend to over-emphasise it now and believe that equality of opportunity has gone further in Scotland than it has in England . . . it's perhaps not quite as true nowadays but I still think there is a stronger democratic tradition' (but *see also* note 99 below).[58]

4. The symbolism of the Kirriemuir career

I shall now suggest one other way in which the reception of the egalitarian myth into the world of post-war policy-making may have occurred. Sir James Robertson, a 'classic' and also the author of the 1947 SACE report, *Secondary Education*, subsequently became vice-chairman of the SACE of 1957-1961 and chairman of the Scottish Council for the Training of Teachers. In 1962 he was interviewed on television by Esmond Wright:

Lets look at your own career — It started in Kilmarnock?

(JJR) In Kilmarnock, a co-educational school, then moved to Glasgow, a little while in Hutcheson's Grammar School; and then . . . a sixth year in the High School of Glasgow.

Until you retired three years ago you were Rector of Aberdeen Grammar School . . . Before that you were Rector of the Royal High in Edinburgh; before that you were Rector of Falkirk High School for nine years; before that you were Rector of Fort William Senior Secondary. Why so many moves?

(JJR) Well . . . when I trained after the First World War, I started in Glasgow; and Dr. William Boyd — wise counsellor as well as a great teacher — said to us 'Now get out of Glasgow. Glasgow is so big, the schools are so big, that of necessity promotion will come very late, be very slow — get out of Glasgow.' I got out of Glasgow, I quickly got promotion as a principal teacher, I tried that out in two schools and then I applied for a smaller school, in the Highlands . . . Fort William was a typical small town school, the one which is repeated almost endlessly in the pattern of Scottish life. It had a wide range of ability, it had quite a wide social and economic range, and a school like that was a very good apprenticeship. The same in a measure was true of Falkirk High School, though it was more highly selective. In Aberdeen Grammar School the selection, intellectually, was not too rigorous. There was a certain selection socially — it was a fee-paying school — but we had great variety of types and many levels of ability . . .

This movement is still somewhat unusual, surely, in the experience of Glasgow?

(JJR) It's bound to be. You see, there are no small schools . . .[59]

William Dewar, another 'classic', also served on the SACE of 1957-61 and on other public bodies (section 5). In 1976 he gave us the interview from which the following extracts are taken:

(WD) I myself had been a bursar at Morrison's [Morrison's Academy, Crieff] . . . many a 'lad o' pairts' wanted to go into teaching . . . the tremendous advantage that I had over most teachers in Scotland [was that] I served in four different areas and I knew my own country town of Crieff as well . . . I was unemployed for about two months when I came out in 1929 . . . A post appeared in Aberdeen . . . The Grammar School was fee-paying . . . but there were bursaries . . . After three and a half years there I went as Senior Classics Master to Dumfries Academy, which was quite a contrast; from a city and large port to a relatively small town of about 36,000 inhabitants with one senior-secondary school [in] a sprawling county, but with several well formed, almost independent communities, Annan, Langholm, Lockerbie, Beattock, Moffat . . . Each of these towns had its own identity. In each there was a three-year secondary school, comprehensive in the sense that, in Moffat, for example, all the children from the country schools round about Moffat . . . came to that school. Nobody was sent to Dumfries in the very first year; but at the end of year III those who were judged fit . . . were transferred . . . There was no question of class distinction, none whatever, although

Dumfries Academy had its own primary department, and this was still a common thing in Scotland. We hear, incidentally, if I may go off slightly at a tangent, far too little about this practice in Scotland, of having the whole of the child's education in one school, and it is not confined to the grant-aided schools. You get it . . . in Kirriemuir, if you want a present example. There's any number up and down Scotland . . .

Largely rural schools?

(WD)   Provincial, I prefer to use the expression 'provincial'.

What's the distinction?

(WD)   I think of 'rural' as embracing a very large number of very small schools . . . whereas for me 'provincial schools' are larger without being large absolutely, and they serve a wider area . . .

Provinces with respect to Glasgow and Edinburgh?

(WD)   These are urban areas, big urban areas. Suppose you go out into Angus. Now that's a province . . .

Dewar later remarked, 'I have always been keenly aware of the situation of the fellows and the women who are away out on the periphery of Scotland in the provinces . . .' (see section 5). After Dumfries he moved to Greenock Academy and thence to George Heriot's School, Edinburgh. He emphasised how, at all his schools, poor boys had had bursaries.[60]

Several points may be made from these extracts. Robertson and Dewar between them named eleven six-year secondary schools where they had been pupils or heads. At the time of their association with them, all were either burgh schools (mostly fee-paying) or city schools (all fee-paying); in 1968 seven of the eleven were still fee-paying. All of the eleven but Fort William, a 'good apprenticeship', had either been among the 52 burgh and parish schools classed as 'secondary' by Grant in 1876 (I shall call these 52 'Grant 1876' schools),[61] or else were city foundations of the seventeenth century or earlier (though Heriot's Hospital only became a boys' day school for fee-paying pupils in 1886). There is no mention of an education authority (EA) secondary school in a city that was non-fee-paying by 1946 (there were 24 such schools in 1921 — *see* note 90). Robertson saw the school at Fort William as 'typical', and 'repeated almost endlessly in the pattern of Scottish life'. When Dewar searched for examples, he turned to Angus and to Kirriemuir. The 'provinces' were prominent in his mental map of the country.

There is here, I suggest, a symbolic axis that parallels the axis of careers that were traced through the historical heartland of the pre-industrial education system. One might say that this symbolic world is bounded by Angus, standing for the East and North and with Kirriemuir at its heart, by Dumfries in the South and, in the West by a Glasgow academy, perhaps the Academy. In this world, I suggest, the secular career is also a moral career. We might call it the Kirriemuir career after J. M. Barrie, educated in Angus at Kirriemuir and Forfar High School, at Dumfries Academy and at Glasgow Academy (not entirely fortuitously since he attended the two Academies whilst lodging with his teacher brother who went to a classics post at Glasgow Academy and thence to Dumfries and promotion to the Inspectorate).[62] On the basis of the empirical evidence summarised in section 2, I contend that the Kirriemuir career took one through schools and communities in which social intercourse and educational attainment were less deeply differentiated by social class relationships than they were in the cities. The education authority schools of the city had no place on this career path ('Get out of Glasgow') and no place, either, on the symbolic map. For the ambitious lad o' pairts the career frontier lay, not in the West, but in the East, North or South; not in the city and the future but in the parish and the past.

This, then, may be one reason for the relatively uncritical reception that was given to the egalitarian myth after 1945; namely that it was not subject to the challenge of the city, or of Glasgow, or of the West in the day-to-day experience of the secondary teachers who came to influence advice and policy (I support this claim further in the next section).

A second reason concerns, I think, the symbolic importance of poverty in the Kirriemuir career and a continuing post-Reformation ambivalence concerning the moral implications of secular success. Sir Henry Jones described his betrothal in Glasgow in 1882 as follows: 'I persuaded my sweetheart that if I could not be a professor, I could be a minister; if I could not be a minister, I could be an elementary school teacher . . . and if I could not get a school, I could make shoes.'[63] A career in the commercial world of Glasgow was not one of his options. The highest consummation of the Kirriemuir career was to witness to God's world; the dominie recruited the lad o' pairts from the secular world for that purpose, and he and the minister stood apart from its material concerns. Thus secular success might be a somewhat ambivalent indicator of the divine, and humanly unknowable, judgement of one's moral life; much, I suspect, depended upon the quality of one's leadership, say as a politician, university principal or educationist, or on the quality of one's witness as an author, say, or playwright or journalist (one thinks of the *British Weekly* and, again, of Bridie and Barrie).

The treatment of death in the stories of the myth expresses this ambivalence to the secular world. Georgie Howe, the lad o' pairts in MacLaren's story of that name (published in 1894 in *Beside the Bonnie Brier Bush*), himself died at 21. Fired by religious enthusiasm ('I hae longed a' thro' thae college studies for the day when ma mooth wud be opened wi' this evangel'), Georgie had made a clean sweep of university prizes and medals. A local farmer had financed Georgie's university career after some persuasion by Georgie's dominie that '[i]t wud be a scan'al to the parish if a likely lad cudna win tae college for the want o' siller' (the 'collectivist principle'). Georgie's mother had, of course, hoped 'he wud hae been a minister o' Christ's Gospel here' and took comfort that in death 'he 'ill be judge over many cities yonder'. Another neighbour, however, thought his death 'an aufu' lesson . . . no to mak' idols o' our bairns for that's naethin' else than provokin' the Almichty'. Georgie's lying-in was an 'idyll of Scottish University life' attended by Georgie's college friends, 'characteristic men' who 'could only have met in the commonwealth of letters': a Scottish Catholic aristocrat, a Harrovian Jew, and a crofter's son from Barra (there was no-one from a Scottish city).[64]

When J. M. Barrie received the freedom of Dumfries in 1924, he told the true-life story of just such a Georgie Howe, a boy he himself had known at Dumfries Academy, a 'thin, frightened-looking boy, poorly clad and frail' but possibly 'the greatest boy that ever sat on the forms of the old Dumfries Academy . . . in scholarship he was of another world from the rest of us . . . he went to Glasgow University and afterwards to Oxford, until — someone turned out that light. He was too poor was that brave little adventurer. I think that explains it all.' Barrie added, '[w]e all accepted him as our wonder one. That this could have been so is a good mark for the Academy, and is perhaps a proof . . . that Dumfries is a Scottish town.'[65]

Later that day Barrie was told publicly at a ceremonial dinner in his honour that Scots found in his Scottish works 'our national characteristics portrayed with . . . vital force . . .'[66] And they found them in his life as well. As we have seen, one of Barrie's brothers rose to the Inspectorate in Dumfries. A second had caught the public imagination through his death at university, reputedly from malnutrition; whilst Barrie, rewarded with the Rectorships of St. Andrews and Edinburgh Universities, chose burial in Kirriemuir itself.[67] Barrie enjoyed the fact that his old dominie had also had Ramsay Macdonald as a pupil.[68] Secular success, indeed the occupancy of the highest office in the land, or, alternatively, early death in obscure poverty; either might consummate the moral career of the lad o' pairts. The difference between them was a matter of divine, and therefore to human eyes, arbitrary, will. As long as Scotsmen remained wedded to the moral interpretation of poverty and success, there was little ultimate point in searching for secular descriptions and explanations of the incidence of social inequality; though they could always 'throw lifebelts into the seas we have scrambled out of'.[69]

There is abundant evidence of the persistence and pervasiveness of this 'individualist' ethic (section 2). One of John Buchan's first acts on arriving in Oxford in 1895 was to tell readers of the *Glasgow Herald* that Oxford lacked 'the pinching, the scraping for an education, the battering against want and ill-health, which makes a Scots college such a noble nursery of the heroic'.[70] A quarter of a century later an SED Inspector cautioned in an annual SED report that '[t]he acquisition of knowledge is not the only, perhaps not even the principal, purpose of school life'. Those who were 'agitating for the removal of all things that prevent school from becoming an earthly paradise for the pupil' were reminded that '. . . education is a preparation for life's battle . . . and that the world outside of the schoolroom does not usually go out of its way to smooth the rugged path or to temper the winds of adversity'.[71] And forty years after this, Hetherington can be found telling the graduates of Glasgow University 'that if the basic rate [of student grant] is set too high, the incentive to real excellence of performance may be weakened'.[72] The Scottish student grant arrangements have had a lower parental exemption level than those for

England and, unlike the English grants, have been based on a criterion of individual 'need'.[73] Dewar sat on the Anderson Committee on student grants (1958-60)[74] and his approach to policy for certification, evidenced below, is also, I think, a product of this moral world.

Is it too fanciful to suggest one further point of articulation between the symbolic and material aspects of the Kirriemuir career that made it more deeply persuasive? It is that the forms of the parish were, for many, the forms of childhood and of innocence, whereas the city was for adults and a place of 'bawbees'.[75] One should not perhaps rest too much on Barrie here, but *Peter Pan* was born in a Dumfries garden of Barrie's schooldays;[76] whilst an attempt by Glasgow to offer a 'model for mankind' only persuaded Barrie that 'everything I had done all my life was wrong'. 'Is Glasgow good?', he asked. 'How many tortured souls and bodies must have gone out from Glasgow without knowing it; some of them perhaps are even today flitting from this . . . mighty and squalid city, as all great cities are.'[77] A plausible case could be made, I think, though space does not allow it here, for extending Raymond Williams' analysis of the symbolic and ambivalent significance of the city in western culture to the place of the city and, in particular, the place of Glasgow in the Scottish scheme of things.[78] Moreover, all of the persons mentioned hitherto in this essay had spent a substantial part of their childhood outside the great cities[79] and most (I am not sure about Bridie) show signs in their later thought of a normative orientation towards the supposedly more solidary forms of the smaller community. To get out of Glasgow was not only to pursue ambition, it was to pursue a proper ambition. The Kirriemuir career produced the sort of person that could be invited into the councils of the state.

5. *Postwar policy for certification: the Kirriemuir Council and its aftermath*

Throughout J. S. Brunton's period as Senior Chief Inspector (1955-1966), Dewar was centrally involved in the HMSCI's development of national policy for curriculum and certification, and his national involvement continued after Brunton's retiral. Dewar had gone to Dumfries Academy in 1932,[80] just eight years after Barrie's speech there, and the year Brunton left his own post at Dumfries Academy to join the Inspectorate.[81] Later Dewar sat on Brunton's working group of 1955-59 that developed proposals for the introduction of the O grade,[82] and Brunton used Dewar's school, George Heriot's, to test the feasibility of the group's emerging proposals.[83] Dewar was appointed governor of Moray House College and was elected chairman of the governors. The College nominated him to the newly formed Scottish Council for the Training of Teachers (SCTT) that in 1959 took over from the National Committee for the Training of Teachers (NCTT). Of the eight secondary teachers on the SCTT, only one was from a school in the West (that is, in what is now the Strathclyde Region). This was another 'classic', the Rector of Glasgow High School, previously Rector of Elgin Academy (yet another of the 'Grant 1876' schools (section 4)). A further five secondary teachers were also from schools in the 'historical heartland' (that is, 'Grant 1876' schools or city fee-paying schools of mid-Victorian foundation or earlier): Edinburgh Royal High School, George Heriot's (Dewar), Fettes, Aberdeen Grammar School (Robertson), and Nairn Academy. The remaining two were from Holy Cross Academy, Edinburgh, an EA Catholic fee-paying school, and from Morgan Academy, Dundee. Founded in 1868 as Morgan Hospital, and in 1889 as Morgan Academy, Morgan had supplied four of the five teachers recruited from Dundee secondary schools to the Inspectorate between 1921 and 1960.[84]

Dewar was also nominated as one of several extra members for two of the three 'special committees' that were established by the newly reconstituted SACE of 1957-1961. The three secondary teachers on the Council itself (which had not met since 1952) were Robertson, Bell (Rector of Dollar Academy ('Grant 1876'), formerly at Glasgow Academy and Elgin Academy,[85] and also a member of the Saltire Society [86]), and Craigie (from Musselburgh Grammar School, an east-coast burgh school and, again, 'Grant 1876'); Craigie had been in the east for many years [87] and was deeply versed in Scottish literature and educational history.[88] For the SACE 'special committee' on teacher supply they were joined by secondary teachers from a Glasgow grant-aided school, from another east-coast burgh school (North Berwick High School) and from a junior secondary school in the burgh of Greenock (in the West).[89] For the two SACE 'special committees' on the transfer from primary school, and on the post-fourth-year examination structure, Dewar was added along with the Headmistress of James Gillespie's High School, Edinburgh (an EA fee-paying school) and the Rector of another east-coast small burgh EA school, also fee-paying, Mackie Academy, Stonehaven. There was only one additional secondary teacher from the West, the 'mandatory' Catholic, from a Glasgow EA school.[90]

It was, indeed, a Kirriemuir Council. To summarise: of the thirteen men and three women sitting as secondary school teachers on the SACE of 1957-61 (including the special committees) or on the SCTT of 1959, only four were from the West (two of these were women, one being a junior secondary school head teacher). Nine of the sixteen held posts in independent, grant-aided, or EA fee-paying schools at the time of their appointments to these national committees; a further three were from 'Grant 1876' schools, another was from Morgan Academy (see above), and only three were from EA non-fee-paying schools (as at 1968) founded after 1890. Thus the secondary teachers who became involved in the making of policy and advice in the later 1950s were almost exclusively representative by position, and also, largely, by previous professional experience, of deeply traditional areas of the school system.

It is, perhaps, not surprising that it was these traditions that were *re-presented* to the public in the deliberations of the Council on school organisation and curriculum. The Council, for example, reaffirmed the Scottish emphasis on the generous provision of selective courses at twelve years, invoking the lad o' pairts and arguing that '[l]ack of attention to the intellectually able is quite contrary to the Scottish educational tradition'.[91] To 'stretch' able pupils it recommended a sixth-year examination but, in order to avert hostility to the 'anglicisation' of the system that this implied,[92] it also recommended the retention of the fifth-year Higher. A further argument here was based on the 'small local academy' serving the 'typical' pre-industrial community of 'the small provincial town': to replace a five-year with a six-year course might reduce such a school's numbers and '[t]he problems which would arise would therefore be nationwide in their incidence'.[93] The image of Scotland as a nation of small towns and, implicity therefore, a Protestant nation, was still powerful. Also powerful, I contend, were ideas of leadership of the sort that Hetherington had associated with the traditional areas, areas where 'the breath of local life blows most strongly' (section 3). These underpinned the Council's emphasis, in line with other ideas of the time, on the economic arguments for developing the talents of 'specially gifted pupils'; and they also, I think, interpreted the Council to the members themselves. Dewar, for example, was deeply conscious of the need for leadership: '[I]f the teachers had produced the natural leaders, men with vision, men with the intellectual capacity, men with the academic attainment to impress the Department, we would have got somewhere [in post-1945 provision].'[94]

These people, these arguments, and these symbols were all part of the post-war consensus among Scottish educationists that the country already had a 'comprehensive' education system, even in the cities, and that any development should preserve existing institutions.[95] (It was Tom Johnston himself, after all, who had refused to allow Glasgow Corporation to abolish fee-paying in those of its schools where it occurred.)[96] No doubt the Scottish mental testing movement also contributed ('the lad o' pairts,' said the Glasgow Professor of Zoology in 1932, is 'the boy who started with a big supply of biological capital'[97]), as did Scottish sociology of education.[98] This consensus was ruptured in the mid-1960s when 'new men' in Scottish local and national politics, many of them breaking free from the influence of local Directors of Education, implemented initiatives coming mainly from the English Labour Party.[99] But the form of comprehensive education developed since 1966 still contrasts starkly with that proposed by the SACE in 1947; values and methods are heavily influenced by preponderantly academic certificate courses; and 'centralism', legitimated anew by Circular 600's 'collectivism' (section 2), still predominates.[100]

With impending comprehensive reorganisation, the leading exponent of mental testing in Scotland, Dr Douglas McIntosh (another member of the SACE of 1957-61), left the post of Director of Education for Fife, which he had held for two decades, and accepted the post of Principal of Moray House College (where Dewar was chairman of the governors). McIntosh joined the newly formed Scottish Certificate of Education Examination Board (SCEEB) (1964-1977) and became Deputy Chairman. Dewar became Convener of the Board's Examination Committee. These brief edited extracts from Dewar's account of his convenership (1964-1973) throw light on the continuity of the centralist strand in the Scottish tradition with its attendant moral connotation and its antipathy to internal assessment of the type exemplified in the 'liberal tradition' (section 2) or, more recently, in 'mode 3' of the Certificate of Secondary Education (CSE):

(WD)   We wanted people who were themeselves good teachers and had reliable judgment; basically the test was that they had, in fact, got good Certificate results and were recommended by the Inspectorate. It was left to me as convener of the Examination Committee to make the selection [of the members of the Subject Panels] in order to ensure the involvement of people from all over Scotland . . . I have always been keenly aware of the situation of the fellows and the women who are away out on the periphery of Scotland 'in the provinces' and we felt that it would be a tremendous boost to morale, as well as spreading the work and the interest, if we could try to ensure that over the whole picture people were involved from all over Scotland . . . Let's watch this word 'representation'. What we were endeavouring to ensure was that, in respect of this work of assessing papers and evolving new syllabusses and so on, we should go all round the country. Now this did not prevent any part of the country from making representation. This didn't mean that we said 'All right, there's nobody coming from Glasgow' . . .

Were you not getting pressure from teachers on the Subject Panels for something like CSE?

(WD)   None at all. I cannot recollect a single occasion. We were very careful about the Subject Panels. I chose them from the very beginning . . . [A]s Convener of the Examinations Committee I went down to England with Ian Urquhart, as the Director of the Board and [HMCI] Neville Fullwood from the Department to look at CSE . . . We brought back a very full report a copy of which is in the hands of the Board but formally the report is the property of the Department.

Why was Fullwood on that party going to England and why was the report lodged with the SED? Was this a matter not solely for the Board?

(WD)   No. As a matter of fact we were sent down by the SED. Fullwood was an assessor on the Board. The Board itself was not looking into CSE at that time. It was the Department that wanted us to be brought into this survey at that early stage. The Board at that time, however, was under continuous pressure, it was not severe but it was continuous pressure from, I think the EIS, and certain members of the EIS [Educational Institute of Scotland], to go over willy-nilly to certificates for everybody . . . what failed to impress us [in England] were the safe-guards against misuse . . . Concerning CSE mode 3 (which is essentially internal examinations with external moderation), here we took the view that [in England] there was a certain amount . . . of teaching directly towards the examination paper.

And would that have mattered given that this wasn't formal certification in the sense that O grade and H grade might have been a formal certificate?

(WD)   I think this brings us to the basic question. The real question here is, 'What does the Certificate certify?' If it is certifying that this particular child, given a very restricted area on which to work, and given pleasant circumstances, and pleasant conditions, plus firm direction, did well, if that is what it's going to certify, then let's say so. But let's not pretend that this is something comparable with a highly academic certificate . . . I must confess I had to fight against a certain inborn prejudice of my own . . . but I felt that if you want really and truly to certify anything, your certificate should be something that is understood by those who are going to act on it.

The feeling was then that the possibility of national examinations comprehending the entire age group wasn't on, as far as you're concerned?

(WD)   It's never been on![101]

Interestingly, the argument on the Board in favour of a CSE Mode 3 style of examination for the large majority of sixteen-year-olds was made by the head teacher of a secondary school in Glasgow's East End and presented publicly as virtually the official view of the EIS.[102] (Dewar was a founding member of the Scottish Secondary Teachers' Association (SSTA)). Present proposals for the piecemeal implementation of the Munn[103] and Dunning[104] reports seem likely to result in provision for the 1980s not too dissimilar from that envisaged by Dewar. And one further continuity: following the teacher unrest of the early 1960s, much of it originating in the EIS and in the West, West of Scotland secondary teachers began to appear on the new national bodies that replaced the Advisory Council in proportions approximating the rough 47:53 ratio one would expect (if Strathclyde Region were taken as the West). Nevertheless, in the Subject Panels of the SCEEB, and in the sub-committees and working parties of the CCC, the statistical under-representation of secondary teachers from the West of Scotland has persisted steadily to this day. Since 1965, secondary schools in the Strathclyde Region have provided only between 30 and 37 per cent (according to body and date) of all the secondary teachers involved in this executive and advisory work.[105] What perspectives do teachers from the different regions bring to their work for national bodies and what are the consequences for their subsequent careers of the close contact with the Inspectorate and other influential professionals that such work entails?

Indeed, can similar patternings be found in the careers of Inspectors themselves and of other élite educationists? I think it is possible. Between 1921 and 1966 (and excluding the war years) there were about 100 appointments made from Scottish secondary schools to the Inspectorate. West of Scotland secondary schools (all types, including fee-paying and independent) contributed under a third of these appointments, though they contained, of course, almost half the school population. If Glasgow Academy and Glasgow High School are excluded, along with the Hutcheson's Grammar Schools, the West of Scotland proportion, 1921-1966 (excluding the war years) falls to one fifth. Over half of all secondary school appointees came from schools that were fee-paying (as at 1968) or from 'Grant 1876' schools, this proportion being a little lower after the second war. These two categories of secondary school accounted for half of the schools offering SCE H grade courses in the 1950s, but well under a fifth of all secondary schools. Between 1945 and 1966 only a fifth of the appointments from Scottish secondary schools to the Inspectorate were from schools in the four cities *other than* fee-paying schools (as at 1968) or 'Grant 1876' schools. This proportion falls from a fifth almost to zero (two appointments, one in 1959 and one in 1960) if the contribution of Glasgow schools alone is considered.[106] Virtually all of the post-war entrants to the Inspectorate from Scottish secondary schools had steered clear of Glasgow or had followed 'Boyd's law' and had got out of the city. The Inspectors-to-be who remained within five miles of Glasgow Cross had almost all moved to fee-paying schools that were to survive as such at least until the late 1960s.

Like many of the data in this article, these figures are not conclusive; one would wish, for example, to trace all career stages and not simply the last before elevation to the Inspectorate or, say, to Head Teacher. But they do, again, support a strong presumption in favour of the type of career process and network I have tried to describe. And they help us to understand how a tradition with its origins in pre-industrial Scotland could command assent throughout much of this century.

6. Some concluding comments

The implicit and programmatic argument of this article is that social reproduction (persistence and change) must be understood in terms of the interplay over time of policy and process, idea and form, person and institution. Particularly in the small world of Scottish government and administration it is necessary to find ways of describing how certain ideas and persons become part of 'a convincing body of experience', whereas others are excluded or edged towards the shadows. Dewar, for example, was one of several distinguished educationists of like background and mind with whom the SED and Brunton found they could work from the mid-'50s onwards. This arguably gave the SED confidence in its moves to replace the SACE in the 1960s with executive and advisory structures that extended 'lay' involvement without sacrificing central control.[107] It was, in turn, Dewar's understanding of the Scotland that was there to be *re-presented* that influenced the character of public involvement in one of these new structures and the content of the messages thereafter transmitted between centre and periphery. The form of pedagogy and control used in the classroom thereby derives from, and reinforces, this 'centralist' strand in the Scottish tradition. Why Brunton and the SED chose to operate through this tradition must await a separate discussion, though it is of interest that Brunton said that he himself had at one time worked 'in very close harmony . . . with Sir Hector Hetherington'.[108]

I have discussed elsewhere some ways in which the Scottish myth has functioned to restrict the constructs through which people experienced the education system and has thereby facilitated the reproduction of the dominant categories through which control is exercised.[109] A convincing body of alternative experience cannot be accumulated about ideas or forms that are not practised or whose practice has been forgotten owing to the selective operation of myth on the past. Along with the ideas that are excluded from 'good currency' or incorporated only selectively, we can also begin to think of educationists who have had an analogous experience in public life. All of them had a breadth of vision in relation to the philosophical and sociological context of education that could not be contained within prevailing concepts or practices, and most of them were associated in various ways with older 'liberal' interpretations of the Scottish tradition (section 2). They include Patrick Geddes,[110] Boyd,[111] Thomson[112] and William McClelland.[113]

Robertson himself left the SSTA over its hostile reaction to *Secondary Education;* he was persuaded by a senior administrator in SED not to accept the offer of a Scottish university chair of education on the grounds that he might not cope with the psychometrics [114] and was, arguably, denied the chairmanship of the CCC when it was formed in 1965.[115] We must also be aware that the contribution of the parent disciplines to what now counts as the study of education has been restricted by this process. The varying strength and character of psychology, sociology, philosophy and history in Scottish educational studies is surely also part of the explanation of the uncritical and selective reception that the post-war world has given to the idea of the Scottish educational tradition.

We started with one paradox which we may now state as two; I think this may be claimed as progress. First, how was it that Robertson, an exemplary product of a traditional education, if my Kirriemuir argument is correct, came to propose the radical adaptation and extension of that tradition in 1947? Clearly a materialist explanation of belief is not always possible; in the 'pathetic symbols' of traditional forms he found, it seems to me, both a challenge (to make them 'valid' in a post-war context) and, *pace* Nairn, a source of articulacy. Second, how is it that his resultant *Secondary Education* (1947) was almost unanimously recognised as the finest-ever expression of the Scottish tradition, but was, nevertheless, consistently disregarded as a basis for action? The answer to the first question may lie in Robertson's undoubted insight into the dual function of myth, as celebration and explanation.[116] The answer to the second question, or much of it, may well lie in West Register House in Edinburgh.

NOTES

1. I am grateful to R. Bell, P. Burnhill, P. Cuttance, D. Raffe and P. Weston for comments on an earlier draft; to the Moray Fund of Edinburgh University for financial help with the interview-study of policy-making; to the participants in that study, named and unnamed; to C. Raab, the co-director of that study, for his numerous suggestions and comments; to T. Bone for permission to use his doctoral thesis; to J. Hughes for research assistance; to the staff of the National Library of Scotland; to N. Phillipson and O. Dudley Edwards for advice; to M. MacDougall and C. Holliday for their patient and skilled word-processing; and to A. Arnot. Responsibility for any remaining errors is mine. The pun in the title is pre-emptive.

2. C. Harvie, *No Gods and Precious Few Heroes* (London, 1981).

3. T. Nairn, 'The Three Dreams of Scottish Nationalism', in *Memoirs of a Modern Scotland*, ed. K. Miller (London, 1970), pp. 34-54. See also H. J. Hanham, *Scottish Nationalism* (London, 1969), 'With the myths of Scottish culture this book is largely concerned' (p. 25) and, more recently, articles by C. Harvie, T. Gallagher, J. Hunter and others in *The Bulletin of Scottish Politics*, 2, Spring 1981.

4. D. McCrone, F. Bechhofer and S. Kendrick, 'Egalitarianism and Social Inequality in Scotland', Paper given at the Annual Conference of the British Sociological Association, University College of Wales, Aberystwyth, 6-9 April 1981. They contend that '[s]trictly speaking egalitarianism and social inequality are not directly comparable. Egalitarianism refers essentially

to a set of social values, a social ethos, a celebration of sacred beliefs; social inequality is a characterisation of the social structure referring specifically to the distribution of resources and opportunities'.

5. D. J. Robertson, 'Population and Movement', in *The Scottish Economy*, ed. A. K. Cairncross (Cambridge, 1954), pp. 9-20. 'Urbanised' in this context pertains to communities of over 1,000 persons.

6. Hanham, *op. cit.*, p. 175; my phrase.

7. See A. F. McPherson, 'The Generally-Educated Scot: an Old Ideal in a Changing University Structure', in A. McPherson, D. Swift and B. Bernstein, *Eighteen-plus: The Final Selection* E282 Units 15-17 (Open University, Bletchley, 1972), pp. 5-52; A. F. McPherson, 'Selections and Survivals: a Sociology of the Ancient Scottish Universities', in *Knowledge, Education and Cultural Change: Papers in the Sociology of Education*, ed. R. Brown (London, 1973), pp. 163-201; A. F. McPherson and G. R. Neave, *The Scottish Sixth: A Sociological Evaluation of Sixth Year Studies and the Changing Relationship Between School and University in Scotland* (Slough, 1976), especially chapters 6 and 7; and J. Gray, A. F. McPherson and D. Raffe, *Reconstructions of Secondary Education: Theory, Myth and Practice Since the War* (London, 1982 *in press*). Chapters 16 and 17 in particular discuss epistemological problems in the explanation of myths and other beliefs and take a somewhat different view from that offered in McCrone, Bechhofer and Kendrick, *op. cit.*, and n. 4 above.

8. See McPherson 1973, *op. cit.*, p. 190, nn. 24 and 25.

9. *Ibid.*, p. 171 and p. 192, n. 39.

10. Gray, McPherson and Raffe, *op. cit.*, chapter 3.

11. W. McClelland, 'Distinctive Features of Scottish Education', *The New Era in Home and School*, 16, 17, pp. 172-174. C. Raab drew this to my attention.

12. W. McClelland, *Selection for Secondary Education* (London, 1942), and Gray, McPherson and Raffe, *op. cit.*, Part 2.

13. McPherson 1973, *op.cit.*, p. 165. Evidence and elaboration may be found in *ibid.*, pp. 164-175; Gray, McPherson and Raffe, *op. cit.*, Part 2 and McPherson and Neave, *op cit.*, p. 119.

14. SED, *Circular 44* (no title) (London, 1921), through which the SED introduced the principle of institutionally separate provision for secondary education and argued in effect against the omnibus school in populous areas, is an example of the legitimation of central control in terms of the collectivist principle.

15. J. S. Blackie, *Classical Literature in its Relation to the 19th Century and Scottish University Education: An inaugural Lecture delivered in the University of Edinburgh, November 2 1852* (Edinburgh, 1852).

16. See McPherson 1973, *op. cit.*, pp. 168-171 and section (4) below.

17. McPherson 1972, *op. cit.*, pp. 25-26 and references; A. F. McPherson, 'Nobody Wants an Ordinary Degree', *The Times Educational Supplement (Scotland)*, 12 January 1973 (McPherson 1973a).

18. As note 17. See also J. Burnet, *Higher Education and the War*, (London, 1917); G. Davie, *The Democratic Intellect: Scotland and her Universities in the Nineteenth Century* (Edinburgh & Chicago, 1961) and H. J. C. Grierson, 'The Scottish Universities', in *Problems of National Education*, ed. J. Clarke (London, 1919), pp. 311-362. Henry Jones' account of the voting for prizes in Caird's Moral Philosophy class at Glasgow is a revealing example of the democracy of the class at work; see Sir Henry Jones, *Old Memories*, ed. T. Jones (London, 1923), pp. 135-9. See also an anonymous article in the *North British Review*, XXVIII, (Edinburgh, 1858): 'The characteristic excellence of the Scottish colleges is the existence of an actively wrought lecture-system, combined with constant and searching catechetical exercise, under the highest responsible authorities of the respective classes. This, indeed, is the grand distinguishing feature which, in spite of great shortcomings, has largely contributed to stamp on the national character one of its peculiar marks . . . The professor is ever in communication with his pupil directing his energies, encouraging his exertions, resolving his doubts . . . In a word, bringing into play, in the small community of the class-room, those powers and habits which shall, in after years, be most frequently and most influentially employed in the active business of everyday life' (p.377).

19. SED, *Secondary Education: A Report of the Advisory Council on Education in Scotland* (Edinburgh, 1947), Cmnd. 7005, p. 58 and chapters 6 and 7. A fuller study of the political and intellectual influences on this report is urgently required.

20. SED, *Secondary Education: The Report of the Advisory Council* (Edinburgh, 1951), Circular 206. SED, *Education in Scotland in 1951* (Edinburgh, 1952), Cmnd. 8515, pp. 7-23 can be read as a counter to the SACE's views on curriculum and certification.

21. McPherson 1973, *op. cit., passim*; Gray, McPherson and Raffe, *op. cit.*, chapters 12 and 14. The logical status of 'mythical' beliefs is discussed in chapters 16 and 17.

22. See McPherson 1973, *op. cit., passim*.

23. Gray, McPherson and Raffe, *op. cit.*, chapter 14. Re-analysis of extant data-sets from the 1947 Scottish Mental Survey (*ibid.*, chapter 2) and the Scottish Mobility Study (see note 47) could throw further light on this conclusion.

24. McPherson 1973, *op. cit.*, pp. 164-170, 173.

25. *Ibid.* and Gray, McPherson and Raffe, *op. cit.*, chapter 16.

26. *Ibid.*, chapters 12 and 14.

27. *Ibid.*

28. Unpublished calculations by the author from the Scottish Education Data Archive (for which see Gray, McPherson and Raffe, *op cit.*, chapter 2).

29. McPherson 1973, *op. cit.*, n. 9.

30. A. F. McPherson and G. Atherton, 'Graduate Teachers in Scotland — A Sociological Analysis of Recruitment to Teaching Amongst Recent Graduates of the Four Ancient Scottish Universities', *Scottish Educational Studies*, 2, 1, pp. 35-55. National, Scottish evidence is not systematically available for the first half of the century, but see A. Kelly, 'Family Background, Subject Specialisation and Occupational Recruitment of Scottish University Students: Some Patterns and Trends', *Higher Education*, 5, Table 3, for supporting evidence from the 1930s and 1950s.

31. The fullest published account of this research to date is to be found in C. Raab, 'The Changing Machinery of Scottish Educational Policy-Making', *Scottish Educational Review*, 12, 2, 1980, pp. 88-98. The sixteen include two former Secretaries to the SED, a former Minister, and a number of 'educationists', among them two former HMSCIs and three former Directors of Education. Raab and I plan to publish a further account of this reasearch at a later date.

32. Sir Charles Illingworth, *University Statesman: Sir Hector Hetherington* (Glasgow, 1971), Preface and pp. 1-5, 8-11, 145.

33. J. Bridie and M. McLaren, *A Small Stir: Letters on the English* (London, 1949), p. 50.

34. *Ibid.*, p. 5.

35. J. Bridie, *One Way of Living* (London, 1939), p. 86.

36. *Ibid.*, p. 84.

37. N. T. Phillipson, 'Nationalism and Ideology', in *Government and Nationalism in Scotland*, ed. J. N. Wolfe (Edinburgh and Chicago, 1969), pp. 167-186.

38. Bridie 1939, *op. cit.*, chapters 4 and 5; C. Coote, *A Companion of Honour* (London 1965), chapter 1.

39. T. Johnston, *Memories* (London, 1952), chapter 6.

40. H. J. W. Hetherington, *The Life and Letters of Sir Henry Jones* (London, 1924), p. 72 and chapter 4.

41. Johnston, *op. cit.*, p. 42.

42. Illingworth, *op. cit.*, pp. 9, 10.

43. J. H. Muirhead and H. J. W. Hetherington, *Social Purpose: A Contribution to the Philosophy of Civic Society* (London, 1918), pp. 168-9 *et seq.* The introduction makes it clear that Hetherington wrote this passage. F. Campbell, 'Latin and the Elite Tradition in Education' in *Sociology, History and Education*, ed. P. W. Musgrave (London, 1970), pp. 249-264, discusses an apposite theme on which I can only touch in this essay.

44. *Scottish Educational Journal*, 14 November 1947, p. 640.

45. Hetherington's description, Illingworth, *op. cit.*, p. 9.

46. W. Elliot, 'The Scottish Heritage in Politics', in Atholl *et al.*, *A Scotsman's Heritage*

(London, 1932), pp. 53-65. Bechhofer, McCrone and Kendrick, *op. cit.*, discuss the logic whereby either a radical or a conservative programme may be derived from the one, egalitarian view of society.

47. I. McDonald, Educational Opportunity at University Level in Scotland . . ., unpub. B.Ed. thesis, University of Glasgow 1964, Table R2b, estimates that, in 1910, 35 per cent of students of Glasgow University's Arts Faculty had fathers in manual occupations. Proportions at the other Scottish universities (all faculties) were probably between 20 per cent and 30 per cent; see McPherson 1973, *op. cit.*, nn. 29 and 30 and Scottish Mobility Study (Department of Sociology, Aberdeen University), 'Scottish Education, Fact Sheet no.1: Social Class and Success in Secondary Education', 'Substantial' relates to the standards of the time.

48. Coote, *op. cit.*, p. 35.

49. For this para., see J. Buchan, *Memory Hold-The-Door* (London, 1940), pp. 36 and 40; and J. Adam Smith, *John Buchan* (London, 1965), p. 319 and chapter 11.

50. C. Harvie, 'Labour and Scottish Government: The Age of Tom Johnston', *Bulletin of Scottish Politics*, 2, Spring 1981, pp. 1-20. 'Collectivist' is intended here in a more general sense than that given to the term in section (2).

51. SED 1947, *op. cit.*, Appendix 2.

52. See, for example, J. Robertson's contribution to *Scotland Tomorrow: Report of a Conference of the Saltire Society*, 15 February 1941, pp. 16-18. H. Bell, Rector of Dollar Academy (see section (5) below) spoke at the same conference.

53. Sir James Robertson, 'Climate of Dissatisfaction', *The Times Educational Supplement (Scotland)*, 28 March 1969.

54. SED 1947, *op. cit.*, Appendix 2.

55. Davie, *op. cit.*, p. 75.

56. R. E. Bell, '"Home Rule" and the Scottish Universities', in Wolfe, *op. cit.*, p. 112; McPherson 1972, *op. cit.*, pp. 20-30; 1973, *op. cit.*, pp. 180-186; and 1973a *passim*.

57. Royal Commission on the Constitution 1969-1973, *Minute of Evidence 11, Scotland, 29-30 September 1969* (London, 1973-4) Cmnd. 5460, para. 733.

58. B. Millan, transcript of interview, Open University Education Programme FW004.

59. Sir J. Robertson, transcript of interview with Professor Esmond Wright, 4 April 1962.

60. Transcript of interview of W. McL. Dewar with A. F. McPherson and C. D. Raab, 22 June 1976, with amendments 13 May 1977. All interviewees received an interview transcript to edit and amend with a view to agreeing with the researchers on a version for public use.

61. J. Grant, *History of Burgh and Parish Schools in Scotland* (London and Glasgow, 1876), pp. 507-510. Unless the context says otherwise, the term 'fee-paying' refers to the status of the school in 1968; see J. Highet, *A School of One's Choice* (London and Glasgow, 1969).

62. D. Mackail, *The Story of J. M. B.* (London, 1941), pp. 1-51.

63. Jones, *op. cit.*, p. 152.

64. A. Maclaren, *Beside The Bonnie Brier Bush* (London, 1894), pp. 3-53.

65. J. M. Barrie, *M'Connachie and J. M. B.* (London, 1938), pp. 88-9.

66. *Ibid.*, p. 98.

67. For a 'demythologising' account of all that this funeral was taken to imply, see G. Blake, *Barrie and the Kailyard School* (London, 1951).

68. Barrie, *op. cit.*, p. 205.

69. *Ibid.*, p. 166.

70. J. Adam Smith, *op. cit.*, p. 48. The excellent analysis of the themes of leadership, community, salvation and death in Buchan's last novel *Sick Heart River* is highly apposite; *ibid.*, pp. 462-8.

71. His Majesty's Chief Inspectors of Schools in Scotland, *General Reports for the Year 1921* (London, 1922), p. 48.

72. H. J. W. Hetherington, *Principal's Letter to Graduates* (Glasgow, 1960).

73. McPherson 1973, *op. cit.*, p. 168.

74. Dewar, *op. cit.*, and Committee on Grants to Students, *Report* (London, 1960).

75. Barrie, *op. cit.*, p. 93; not Barrie's word.

76. *Ibid.*, p. 193.

77. *Ibid.*, p. 194. Barrie was speaking about new housing designs at the opening of the Glasgow Health Exhibition of 1929.

78. R. Williams, *Marxism and Literature* (London, 1977). McCrone, Bechhofer and Kendrick, *op. cit.*, drew this to my attention. See, for example, E. Muir's 1935 essay on Glasgow in chapter 4 of his *Scottish Journey* (Edinburgh, 1979). My thesis is not, however, limited to Glasgow. Clearly the place of Edinburgh, in particular, should also be considered.

79. With the possible exception of McClelland, one-time Director of Education for Wigtownshire, though he was educated at the Ewart Institute before moving to Leith Academy; see *Scottish Biographies* (London and Glasgow, 1938).

80. Dewar, *op. cit.*

81. T. Bone, School Inspection in Scotland 1840-1966, unpub. Ph.D. thesis, University of Glasgow, 1967. The published version of this study (same author and title, London 1968) does not contain the detail used in my calculations.

82. SED, *Report of the Working Party on the Curriculum of the Senior Secondary School: Introduction of the Ordinary Grade of the Scottish Leaving Certificate* (Edinburgh, 1959).

83. Dewar, *op.cit.*

84. *The Scottish Educational Journal*, 27 March 1959, pp. 234-5.

85. *Scottish Biographies* (London, 1938).

86. Saltire Society, *List of Members* (Edinburgh, 1948).

87. He had been on the Midlothian executive of the EIS since 1928; *The Scottish Educational Journal*, 13 March 1959.

88. J. Craigie, *A Bibliography of Scottish Education before 1872* (London, 1970) and *A Bibliography of Scottish Education 1872-1972* (London, 1974).

89. *The Scottish Educational Journal*, 22 February 1957, pp. 98-9.

90. *Ibid.* In judging the representativeness of these appointments, one should remember that Scotland had about 900 secondary schools in the early 1950s of which about 200 offered the full, five-year course for Highers. In 1965 there were 668 EA schools of which 204 offered five-year (or six-year) Highers courses; SED, *Education in Scotland in 1965* (Edinburgh, 1966), Cmnd. 2914, p. 33. In 1968 there were 21 EA secondary fee-paying schools, and 29 grant-aided secondary schools (J. Highet, *A School of One's Choice* (London and Glasgow, 1969), chapter 1); and only about five independent schools whose staff had ever figured in those parts of the public system I discuss. In 1921 there were 148 GA and EA secondary schools. Sixteen were GA schools; 18 were EA schools that still charged fees in 1968 (including some 'Grant 1876' schools); a further 26 were 'Grant 1876' EA schools that had never charged fees or had ceased to charge them by 1968. The residual category of 98 schools (EA, non-fee-paying, (as at 1968) and 'non-Grant 1876') already comprised two-thirds of all secondary schools by 1921; see His Majesty's Chief Inspectors of Schools, *Return*, (London, 1923), pp. 5-76.

91. SED, *Transfer from Primary to Secondary Education: A Report of a Special Committee of the Advisory Council on Education in Scotland* (Edinburgh, 1961), Cmnd. 1538, paras. 21, 59, 67, 84-91.

92. See, for example, the leader in the *The Scottish Educational Journal*, 15 December 1961, p. 885.

93. SED, *The Post-Fourth Year Examination Structure in Scotland: A Report of a Special Committee of the Advisory Council on Education in Scotland* (Edinburgh, 1960), Cmnd. 1068, paras. 15, 17 and 19.

94. Dewar, *op. cit.* See also W. McL. Dewar, 'Our Representatives', *The Times Educational Supplement (Scotland)* 25 November 1977, for an article that, *inter alia*, bemoans the quality of Scottish political leadership and looks for solutions to educational problems that 'would adapt without too much difficulty to meet the needs of the more sparsely populated areas of Scotland . . .'

95. Gray, McPherson and Raffe, *op. cit.*, chapter 14.

96. Mentioned in J. Highet, 'Education', in *The Third Statistical Account of Scotland: Glasgow*, ed. J. Cunnison and J. B. S. Gilfillan (Glasgow, 1958), pp. 531-2, n.1. But see also Highet 1969, *op. cit.*, p. 21.

97. G. Kerr, 'Scottish Education', in Atholl *et al.*, *op. cit.*, p. 71.

98. See J. Highet 1969, *op cit.*, Introduction and *passim*. Highet was appointed to the special committee of the SACE on the supply of teachers (see note 84 and text).

99. Gray, McPherson and Raffe, *op.cit.*, chapter 14. Based also on unpublished interview transcripts (see section (3)). Bruce Millan's comment is relevant. He saw Circular 600 '[n]ot at all as the importation of an English issue. I think there is a lot of misunderstanding about this, and a lot of myth as well. People seem to think that before Circular 600 . . . we had a pretty-well-comprehensive system in Scotland anyway. That is just utterly untrue. We had a selective system in Scotland, as they did south of the border . . . I think I would accept that there really were better chances of, as it were, working your way through the system in Scotland than there were in England. But on the principle of selection the argument was exactly the same . . . Of course there were a number of schools in the highlands and elsewhere where there was something very much more approaching what one would call a comprehensive school, and it was perhaps for that reason that we had less hostility towards the idea in Scotland, than they had in certain areas of England . . . But the system was basically selective for the vast majority of pupils . . . ' Transcript of interview of B. Millan with A. F. McPherson and C. D. Raab, 28 March 1980, with amendments 15 October 1980.

100. Gray, McPherson and Raffe, *op. cit.*, Part 2 and chapter 14.

101. Dewar transcript, *op cit.*

102. N. Currie in SCEEB, *Report of Conference on Examinations* (Edinburgh, 1970), pp. 6-24. In SCEEB, *Supplement to the Scottish Certificate of Education Examination Board and its Work* (Edinburgh, 1971), Currie is listed as 'Teachers' Representative(s), Educational Institute of Scotland'. He made it clear he was speaking virtually in that capacity. Dewar's reply (*ibid.* pp. 25-42) is also relevant.

103. SED, *The Structure of the Curriculum in the Third and Fourth Years of the Scottish Secondary School*, (Edinburgh, 1977).

104. SED, *Assessment for All: Report of the Committee to Review Assessment in the Third and Fourth Years of Secondary Education in Scotland* (Edinburgh, 1977).

105. This is the range of six percentages calculated from the reports of the CCC for 1965-68 (Edinburgh 1969), 1968-71 (Edinburgh, 1972), 1971-74 (Edinburgh, 1975) and 1974-1980 (Edinburgh, 1980); and from the annual reports of the SCEEB for 1970, the earliest in which data were published (Edinburgh, 1971) and 1977 (Dalkeith, 1978). The General Secretary of the EIS at the time of the Glasgow teachers' strike of 1961 later commented: 'That single strike in Glasgow had repercussions that went on for a long time. It shook people and the memory of it continued to shake them; the Department was very much shaken, I think.' Transcript of interview of G. Bryden with A. F. McPherson and C. D. Raab, May 1977, with amendments of June 1978.

106. My calculations from the commendably detailed tables in various chapters of Bone, *op. cit.* Information is not available on posts held prior to the post from which appointment was made to the Inspectorate. Thus these proportions conceivably may not reflect the regional balance of overall experience; but I think it likely that they do. Appointments from colleges were not numerically important until after 1960.

107. C. D. Raab, 'The Quasi-Government of Scottish Education', in *Quangos in Britain: Government and the Networks of Public Policy-Making*, ed. A. Barker (London, 1982).

108. Transcript of interview of J. S. Brunton with A. F. McPherson and C. D. Raab, December 1976, with amendments of March 1977.

109. McPherson and Neave, *op. cit.*, chapter 6.

110. See P. Kitchen, *A Most Unsettling Person: An Introduction to the Life and Ideas of Patrick Geddes* (London, 1975). I am thinking of his ideas on extension education, and on the forms of community and schooling.

111. Like Geddes, Boyd also was concerned with the relationship between social solidarity, the forms of the city and the implications of these for education. A study of his life and thought is badly needed.

112. See, for example, the comment of Sir James Robertson in his *Godfrey Thomson* (Edinburgh, 1964) that Thomson 'saw clearly . . . [t]hat once a nation is committed to secondary

education for all even up to fifteen, its educational thinking must swing sharply towards sociology' (p.17). For one of several introductions see S. A. Sharp, 'Godfrey Thomson and the concept of Intelligence', in *The Meritocratic Intellect: Studies in the History of Educational Research*, ed. J. V. Smith and D. Hamilton, (Aberdeen, 1980), pp. 67-78.

113. Relations between the SED and McClelland apparently deteriorated badly during the latter's period as head of the National Committee for the Training of Teachers, partly because McClelland reputedly gave more time than was considered appropriate to the production of general analyses and prescriptions for Scottish education.

114. I hope to be able to publish my evidence for this statement at a later date.

115. *Idem.*

116. Sir James Robertson, The Place of Classical Studies in Education, (unpublished(?), 1970) contains a penetrating analysis of the relationship between myth, history and identity. I am grateful to Lady Robertson for supplying me with a copy of this article and for much other help besides. A full-scale study of 'JJ' is also overdue.

12

Freudianism, Bureaucracy
and Scottish Primary Education

F. J. McEnroe

THIS essay is an analysis of the 1965 *Memorandum on Primary Education in Scotland* which has been hailed as the most liberalising Scottish document on primary education of the twentieth century. The author will contest this view, although conceding that it was a 'revolution' of a sort, and argue that:

  (i) the *Memorandum*, in spite of frequent references to liberal sentiments, envisages education as an instrument for promoting the value-system of a reified society;

 (ii) the acknowledged influence of Piaget on the *Memorandum* is minimal in comparison to the profound influence of Sigmund Freud as expressed through the writings of the analysts of the British Psycho-Analytical Society;

(iii) the *Memorandum* advocates a new bureaucratisation of the primary school with the head teacher in complete control of the schooling process;

(iv) the two elements, Freudianism and bureaucratisation, are mutually reinforcing, and constitute the kernel of the *Memorandum's* strategy to pattern the pupil (intellectually, morally, emotionally, and socially) in order to make him acceptable to society.

1

In the Foreword the Secretary of State for Scotland said that the purpose of the *Memorandum* was to provide 'an up-to-date appraisal of the best practices in primary schools in Scotland and of the principles on which, in the view of those most closely associated with its development over the past decade, primary education should be based'. Although the Secretary of State claimed that the committee which prepared the document was representative of the teaching profession, colleges of education and Her Majesty's Inspectors of Schools, the representation was skewed heavily in favour of Inspectors and head teachers: together they comprised 15 members out of a total of 19, and the Chairman was Her Majesty's Chief Inspector. There was no representative from the ordinary teaching ranks and none from any Scottish university.

Nevertheless, the *Memorandum* was welcomed with delight by most educators as the most liberalising Scottish document on primary education of the twentieth century. That it changed primary education or that it represented a change of heart on the part of the Scottish Education Department was believed by many. G. S. Osborne, Vice-Principal of Aberdeen College of Education, believed that it was a radical change from former documents. He stated:

> That primary education in Scotland has nevertheless not stood still is evidenced by a second *Memorandum*, published in 1965.[1]

> Then, suddenly, in 1965, children as seen through the eyes of the Scottish Education Department became quite different creatures.[2]

> In the Preface to the *1965 Memorandum on Primary Education in Scotland* an attempt is made to suggest that the difference between the practice of the primary schools now and the primary schools of twenty years ago is the result of a steady development . . . In fact the new document represents nothing short of a revolution.[3]

S. L. Hunter, Senior Lecturer in Education at Jordanhill College of Education, was convinced that its advocacy of the 'latest' teaching techniques was of the greatest value for Scottish education:

> The memorandum is heavily biased towards the *children learning* approach, and by giving official Departmental support to more progressive and experimental teaching techniques, it has initiated a general reappraisal of teaching methods in the primary school. No greater service could be performed for Scottish primary education.[4]

Hunter had no doubt that its recommendations were an improvement on past practices:

> This increased freedom for the primary schools means that the way is now clear — at least in theory — for the development of the improved curricula, methods and approaches recommended in the *1965 Memorandum on Primary Education in Scotland.*[5]

A superficial reading of the *1965 Memorandum* might well justify the optimism with which it was welcomed. Many of the statements are echoes of the 'progressive' pronouncements of the most outstanding educators from Rousseau to the present time. We read that:

   (i) the pattern of education must 'above all have regard for the nature of the child';[6]

  (ii) the teacher must realise that 'the child is not an adult in miniature: he does not feel, or act, or think like an adult';[7]

 (iii) education should be 'based on the needs and interests of the child';[8]

 (iv) 'corporal punishment should not be necessary in the modern primary school'.[9]

The most radical sentence of all appears in the paragraph on The Need for Freedom:

> The primary school child has a natural curiosity and a desire to learn which make him capable of seriously and deliberately pursuing his own education on lines of his own choice.[10]

This is an important change from the *1950 Memorandum* which stated merely that the child should be a 'willing collaborator'.[11] The 1965 statement must be one of the most radical in the history of Scottish primary education, and A. S. Neill would have agreed wholeheartedly with its credo. It is not surprising that Osborne should have envisaged the *Memorandum* as a revolution or that he should claim that it represents a complete reversal of most of what the Scottish Education Department had been saying in 1950.

2

But what are the implications of this new freedom for the child? If the Scottish pupil is capable of seriously and deliberately pursuing his own education on lines of his own choice, then what will be the role of the teacher? Will she become a passive observer engaged in documentation of the child's autonomous progress for future reference? And what will be the role of the head teacher? Let us examine these in turn.

The role of the teacher

As the *Memorandum* asserted that the child is capable of seriously and deliberately pursuing his own education on lines of his own choice, we would expect advice to be given to the teacher as to how she could make this possible. Advice is given, of course, and she is told that her pupils 'like the sense of security created by her quiet authority and by an organisation which establishes a consistent routine but allows them to use their own initiative and to exercise responsibility'.[12]

From this it would appear that the pupils will be allowed to use their own initiative within a class organisation whose 'consistent routine' is established by the teacher. It must be admitted that a teacher could establish a routine which permitted the use of initiative on the part of her pupils to the satisfaction of all but the most radical of educators. This admission, however, has to be reviewed in the light of the *Memorandum's* recommendations for schemes of work.

The purpose of a scheme of work 'is to indicate in broad outline the scope of the work at each stage in the school'; it should 'take the form of a policy document, embodying the general aims and objectives of the school . . .'[13]

It should be drawn up by the head teacher in consultation with his teachers, 'each of whom should have a copy, not only of that part of it that most concerns her class, but of the entire scheme, so that she may see her own work in relation to what is being done at other stages, particularly those which immediately precede and follow her own'.[14]

The scheme will predetermine the topics, skills and activities which the adults consider to be important:

> The class teacher's job is to prepare, within the framework of the scheme, and in co-operation with the head teacher, a more detailed programme of work for her class for perhaps a month ahead, setting out the topics that are to be covered, the skills that are to be learned, and the activities that are to be undertaken, and allowing for the differing needs and abilities of the pupils.[15]

The topics, skills and attitudes are not limited to one or two areas of the curriculum but cover the whole spectrum: 'language arts, environmental studies, art and craft activities, music, physical education, projects, outdoor activities and so on'.[16]

The programme will be under 'continual review' to ensure that there are 'no serious omissions'. When this framework has been established for a month ahead, 'the teacher must plan a programme for each week or each day covering all the activities which she wishes to include . . .'[17]

We search in vain for some clue as to how the child will be able to pursue his own education 'on the lines of his own choice' when the topics that are to be covered, the skills that are to be learned, and the activities that are to be undertaken, have already been decided for him.

The role of the head teacher

By reason of the overall view which the head teacher has of the whole establishment the *Memorandum* considers that it is essential 'that his should be the last word on organisation and planning, the content of the curriculum, the utilisation of time, teaching methods and rules of behaviour'.[18]

The area of responsibility designated for the head teacher is greater than that recommended by the *1950 Memorandum*, although this is wide-ranging too:

> He should view the school as a whole, determining the organisation, arranging the time-tables, deciding the teaching methods (individual, group, class), and prescribing the method of instruction to be used in a particular subject when — as in subtraction — the same method ought to be used throughout the school.[19]

The *1965 Memorandum* is careful to point out that education authorities should not encroach on the domain of the head teacher. It admits that their schemes of work 'can be useful guides to head teachers in the framing of their educational policy', but insists that they should be concerned 'only with broad matters of policy and that the detailed application of the principles they contain should be left to individual head teachers'.[20]

If education authorities, however, should give more specific guidance on content and methods, the *Memorandum* stresses that 'there should be no suggestion' that the guidance should be followed rigidly by all schools, and concludes:

> head teachers must be given freedom and encouragement to think out for themselves the type of education that is best suited to the needs of their own pupils, the resources of their own staff, and the nature of the environment in which their own particular school is situated.[21]

Let us summarise the situation: the head teacher will decide on how the various classes are organised, what to include in the curriculum, how much time is spent on the various activities, what teaching methods are utilised to ensure the successful attainment of his objectives, and what behaviour is acceptable; the teacher, in accord with the educational policy of the head teacher, will decide what topics the children will study, the skills to be acquired, and the daily activities to be undertaken, across the entire spectrum of the curriculum; the education authority is advised to leave the day-to-day running of the school to the head teacher.

And what of the pupils of this 'child-centred' education? The pupils receive no mention at all, beyond the bland assertion that they enjoy the 'security' of this 'quiet authority'.

It would be difficult to think of any other educational document from any other country in the world which recommends more power to a head teacher than the *1965 Memorandum*. Indeed, in view of the power conferred on him, we could reasonably claim that its recommendations are 'head teacher centred' and not 'child centred', as Scottish writers have claimed.

In its hierarchy of control the primary school as envisaged by the *1965 Memorandum* is more bureaucratic and less liberal than its predecessor, the *1950 Memorandum*, which is less definite in its advocacy of control and leaves the individual teacher with more scope for personal initiative:

> Although the syllabus of instruction *may* be indicated in outline in a county scheme of work, and *perhaps* at greater length in the headmaster's scheme for the school, many of the decisions about details of content are made by the teacher . . .[22] (emphases added)

3

Reification

But is the *Memorandum* guilty only of an increase in bureaucratisation? Another accusation can be levelled against it, much more serious than this: namely, that its recommendations are formulated for a society which has been objectified to the point of reification. Berger and Luckman (1976) define reification as 'the apprehension of human phenomena as if they were things, that is, in non-human or possibly supra-human terms. Another way of saying this is that reification is the apprehension of the products of human activity as if they were something other than human products — such as facts of nature, results of cosmic laws, or manifestations of divine will'.[23]

As a result of their reification the authors of the *Memorandum* regard the school as a 'thing' which young people must learn to belong to; they regard 'adult standards' as 'things' which young people must learn to accept; and they regard society as a 'thing' which young people must learn to adjust to.

The process of 'belonging to' society is carefully structured by the *Memorandum*. First, the school is advised to begin the process of 'catching' the child *before* he officially begins as a pupil in the first class of infants:

> Generally, it has been found useful to give the new pupil a brief glimpse of the school before he begins his attendance there. If, for example, he can see something of the premises — the classroom which will be his base, the cloakrooms and toilets, the playground — and if he can perhaps sit at one of the little tables or desks, he feels that he already 'belongs'.[24]

The pupil should next learn to 'belong' to his class:

> The child needs to feel that he is accepted and liked, that he 'belongs' to the class community, that the contributions he makes are appreciated by his teacher and his fellows.[25]

He should now learn to 'belong' to his school:

> He should learn to 'belong' to the school, to take pride in its beauty, its equipment, its surroundings and its achievements.[26]

The work of the architect is an important concomitant of this process:

> The design of the building itself and its decor should be such that the pupils find the school an attractive place to be in, providing an environment which not only gives them pleasure but also contributes to the development of their aesthetic awareness.[27]

Eventually, the pupil will learn to 'belong' to society:

> There are many ways of fostering a desirable school spirit. Opportunities of meeting regularly as a unit, and of taking part in school activities such as concerts, religious services, parties, excursions, clubs and inter-school sport enlarge the child's understanding of what a school is and encourage his urge to share in its larger identity. A school badge, or song, or dance can also contribute to this end. A house system may be another useful way of providing the child with a cause towards which he can make his own effort individually and in co-operation with others. Care should be exercised not to encourage exaggerated attitudes of group rivalry, which too easily may become arrogance, and might tend to develop a class or sectarian bias; but school loyalty is a valuable step in the development of wider loyalties.[28]

In tone and substance the preceding quotation could have been an address by Dr Thomas Arnold of Rugby to his staff at the beginning of term!

Adult standards and values are reified too. The *Memorandum* regards the school as a microcosm of society — the ultimate 'thing' — and the teacher as the representative of society's cherished ideals. This is a terrible responsibility to place on the shoulders of teachers, and the *Memorandum* does not shirk giving them advice on how the cherished ideals can be transmitted.

Thus we read that the teacher has the right to insist on her standards being accepted by her pupils, but she is warned that impatience may spoil the process:

> She must realise that the child is not an adult in miniature; he does not feel, or act, or think like an adult. It is her function to supply means of assisting his natural development, and not to distort it by adopting a logical approach or by insisting too early on adult standards for which the child is not yet ready.[29]

As the child matures, however, the school will educate him to accept the values of society and suppress his own:

> During these years the child is also coming to a knowledge of the values held in esteem by society and learning to do what he ought rather than what he would like.[30]

The 'moral development' of the child is charted according to the standards of conduct and taste of the teacher:

> The teacher who is patient and understanding in her treatment of him, and who herself sets an example of the standards of conduct and taste which she expects in her charges, makes a considerable contribution to his moral development.[31]

The *Memorandum* is obviously worried that audio-visual material, carelessly used, may subvert its social philosophy, and warns teachers:

> Every piece of equipment and material brought into use should have a definite purpose.[32]

Every facet of the child's development — intellectual, emotional, moral and social — will be *patterned* to suit society:

> there are things that he has to be taught, not only in the intellectual sphere, but also in order that his emotional, moral and social development may follow a pattern which will make him acceptable to the society in which he will live as an adult.[33]

The whole ethos of the school, from the conduct of school meals to the 'Weltanschauung' of the teachers, will *condition* the characters of the pupils:

> The school routine, the organisation of the classroom, the teachers' methods, the content of the programme of work, the conduct of school meals and other social occasions, and particularly the outlook and example of the head teacher and the teachers, all help to condition the attitudes and behaviour of the pupils.[34]

These recommendations and statements of the *1965 Memorandum* are astonishing and disquieting in their implications. They are also a complete negation of the warning issued by the Advisory Council in 1946:

The danger of imposing an artificial pattern of life applies with equal force to the State. Pupils must not be 'conditioned' to any set and predetermined ways of thinking and acting. They will have to live their own lives in circumstances we can but dimly guess. They should therefore by the encouragement of sturdiness of body and mind be made fit for any emergency.[35]

The Advisory Council, of course, was writing one year after the final defeat of Hitler's Third Reich, and the memory of his evil was still fresh in people's minds. The *1965 Memorandum* was written twenty years after the holocaust had ended, and perhaps the lesson of how Hitler and his 'educators' had manipulated the minds of an entire nation had been forgotten. This is not to suggest, of course, that the Scottish Education Department has any such evil intention for Scottish schoolchildren. But its advocacy of 'conditioning' as an educational strategy to be used by teachers does suggest a view of education which regards children as pieces of plasticine to be patterned to suit the wishes of adults, and is sinister in its implications.

The Scottish Education Department reifies society and the values of adults, that is, regards them in non-human terms as if they are facts of nature. It is not, of course, being argued that an objective world does not exist, but rather that the reification of this social world is not always recognised.

This kind of mystification implies that we are able to forget our own authorship of the human world, and the Marxian dialectic between man, as producer, and his products is reversed in consciousness. Man, the producer of his world, comes to regard himself as the product, and loses the awareness that, however objectivated, his social world was made by him, and can be remade by him.

4

The new freedom for the Scottish pupil has revealed itself as a new bondage to the authority of the teacher and head teacher. How, then, can Osborne claim that the *Memorandum* represents a 'revolution' and that children became 'quite different creatures' as seen through the eyes of the Scottish Education Department? The revolution is not evident in the socio-educational objectives which are more reactionary than ever before; but it *is* manifest in the 'progressive and experimental teaching techniques' advocated to realise these objectives.

Osborne claimed that the *1965 Memorandum* 'was obviously written very much under the influence of the teachings of Piaget'.[36] It is true, of course, that Piaget has influenced the writing of the *Memorandum*, but there is another influence, much more pervasive and important, which appears to have escaped recognition and comment: the influence of Sigmund Freud, who has had a profound influence on twentieth-century thought and practice. Meisel (1981) reminds us that Freud's teaching is so profound and pervasive that we are often unaware of its influence:

The writings of Sigmund Freud have become so decisive a factor in our culture, particularly in America, that it is more difficult than ever to attribute to them the stance of a dispassionate science that simply narrates those unconscious processes of mind discovered by its founder. It is probably more accurate to say that Freud's work has itself become an example of those unconscious determinations that influence us when we least expect it.[37]

Freud, of course, inspired a legion of disciples who have extended and revised to varying degrees his basic theories. At the risk of over-simplification, we can recognise two main movements which have been a response to Freud's biological assumptions. On the right wing, the movement associated in particular with the work of Melanie Klein and her supporters within the British Psycho-Analytical Society penetrated (to a deeper level than Freud himself attempted) the traumas of infantile experience; on the left wing, the movement associated with the heterodox neo-Freudians in America — Adler, Rank, Horney, Sullivan, Thompson, Reich, Fromm, Erikson — rejected or de-emphasised Freud's biological bias, and focused their attention on the importance of social and cultural variables as determining influences on the development of human personality.

The right-wing approach is, of course, implicit in Freud's theories, and it is not surprising that the analysts associated with the movement — Ernest Jones, Melanie Klein, Anna Freud, Joan Rivière, Susan Isaacs, Donald Winnicott, Roger Money-Kyrle, John Bowlby — consider their views to have more in common with Freudian orthodoxy than the theories of the neo-Freudians in America for whose work they tend to have little regard.

It is not being suggested that the former array of British analysts represents a homogeneous collection of individuals. There have been dissensions and bitter controversies within the British group, and shortly after the Second World War there was a major split between the followers of Anna Freud and those of Melanie Klein. The nature of the dispute is not the concern of this essay, but it is interesting to note in passing that the views of Melanie Klein have received the support of several leading psycho-analysts — Rivière, Isaacs, Winnicott, Roheim, Money-Kyrle, and Ernest Jones, the doyen of British analysts, who was the greatest populariser of Freud's theories in Great Britain.

It is proposed now to give some examples from the *Memorandum* to indicate the extent to which Freud and his followers have influenced the 'emotional climate' of Scottish education. It will become apparent that the analysts of the British Psycho-Analytical Society have been particularly successful in altering our approach to the problems of educating the young.

Alfred Adler is the only neo-Freudian who appears to have influenced to any extent the thinking of Scottish educators. In a sense he bridges the gap between the British and American movements: in his early works he was quite as individualistic and biologistic as Freud, but his burgeoning Socialist beliefs led to a study of interpersonal relationships within a wider social setting, and a desire to spread the evangelism of psycho-analysis beyond the sphere of a small coterie of affluent, bourgeois citizens. Adler is especially important, because many of his concepts have become integrated into the systems of other schools, and, with the exception of Freud, it is doubtful whether any other psycho-analytical writer has had a greater influence upon the thought of others.

The examples are presented under four headings:

1. The parent-child relationship;
2. The teacher-pupil relationship;
3. The emotional climate of the school;
4. The role of aggression.

5

1. The parent-child relationship

The *Memorandum* is convinced of the fundamental importance of the parent-child relationship on which, of course, the whole edifice of orthodox psycho-analysis rests. Thus the 'emotional climate' of the pupil's home is a crucial determinant of his subsequent physical, mental, moral, and social development:

> During the pre-school years and after, not only the child's physical and intellectual development, but also his behaviour and attitudes depend largely on the extent to which the conditions and atmosphere in the home are propitious for the successful nurturing of his capabilities.[38]

The *Memorandum* uses the Freudian concept of 'introjection' to explain how the child's view of himself often mirrors the judgement of his parents:

> Even his developing view of himself as 'good' or 'bad', 'clever' or 'stupid', reflects in large part the approval, tacit or expressed, of his parents.[39]

The child's affectional bonds within the family will affect his relationships at school:

> His experience of affection and discipline and his relations with others at home also affect his ability to adjust to other people, whether they be children of his own age, older children, or adults.[40]

Anna Freud (1930) warned teachers that the psycho-analytical concept of 'substitution' is a common occurrence among school children:

> The children whom you call quarrelsome, asocial, envious, and discontent are substituting their schoolmates for their siblings, and there, at school, are fighting out with them conflicts which have remained unsolved at home.[41]

The *Memorandum* adopts the psychic determinism of Freudian theory to explain the behaviour of neglected and pampered children:

> If there is parental indifference or neglect he may never have gained confidence in himself, and if he is over-indulged he may have acquired an undue sense of his own importance.[42]

Alfred Adler (1932) divided children into three groups whose problems, he believed, constituted the greatest danger to 'normal' emotional development: children with imperfect organs; pampered children; neglected children. He said this of the neglected child:

> Such a child has never known what love and co-operation can be: he makes up an interpretation of life which does not include these friendly forces. It will be understood that when he faces the problems of life he will overrate their difficulty and underrate his own capacity to meet them with the aid and good will of others.[43]

Adler thought the pampered child is, potentially, most dangerous:

> The pampered child is trained to expect that his wishes will be treated as laws. He is granted prominence without working to deserve it and he will generally come to feel this prominence as a birthright . . . These grown-up pampered children are perhaps the most dangerous class in our community.[44]

Adler was the first psycho-analyst to pay particular attention to the psychic significance of the place of the child in the family. The *Memorandum* also considers this to be important:

> It may also be useful in some cases to have information about the child's social background, his parents and his place in the family.[45]

Adler believed that this 'phenomenon' is a basic determinant of the child's emotional development:

> Individual Psychology has opened up a very wide field for research work by inquiring into the advantages and disadvantages for children according to the order of their birth. To simplify a consideration of this, we shall suppose that the parents are co-operating well and doing their best in the training of the children. The position of each child in the family still makes a great difference and each child will still grow up in quite a new situation.[46]

2. *The teacher-pupil relationship*

As a corollary to the parent-child relationship, the teacher-pupil relationship is central to the 'emotional world' of the school. If the teacher can arrange the 'emotional atmosphere' of the classroom satisfactorily' 'almost everything he does is favourably affected'.[47]

Thus the teacher is advised to be 'patient and understanding',[48] to 'tactfully suggest',[49] to 'keep a watchful eye',[50] to give a 'gentle hint',[51] to give 'judicious suggestion and guidance',[52] to teach 'without obtrusive attempts to criticise or correct'.[53]

This is a radical change in tone from the *1950 Memorandum*, which said that 'rules should be known to everyone, and conformity to them should be constantly and consistently expected'.[54]

The relaxed, permissive atmosphere advocated by the *1965 Memorandum* is in perfect tune with Freudian analytical techniques. Philip Rieff[55] claims that the required tone for Freudian pedagogy is not a 'deliberate attentiveness' which might induce an unbearably professional strain. Rather, it is the 'calm', 'quiet', 'evenly-hovering' awareness best suited to the pursuit of one unconscious by another. This is the approach which the *1965 Memorandum* advocates to produce the most effective results.

3. The emotional climate of the school

As indicated, a 'healthy' climate in the school is considered fundamental to the success of the *Memorandum's* recommendations. It is perhaps inevitable that the new philosophy should dethrone the exalted position which Knowledge has enjoyed in the Scottish curriculum:

> More than ever before, too, the primary school has to concern itself with the emotional and social development of its pupils . . .[56]

> It cannot be too strongly stressed that education is concerned as much with the personal development of the child as with the teaching of subjects.[57]

The *Memorandum's* assertion is but a belated affirmation of what Ernest Jones said in 1910; indeed, some of the very words are similar:

> it is desirable that education should concern itself more than hitherto with what may be called the human side of the child, and not exclusively with the intellectual.[58]

There can be little doubt that an intellectual curriculum which belittles the emotional aspect of education imposes a strain on many pupils; and any kind of tension is upsetting to the emotional equilibrium which the *Memorandum* seeks to establish. To safeguard this precarious equilibrium, various strategies are recommended, and three concepts in particular emerge as fundamental to the successful implementation of the social philosophy of the *Memorandum*:

(i) Anxiety

The *Memorandum* frequently draws the attention of the teacher to the importance of anxiety: when a child plays, he 'obtains a sense of security and perhaps relief from anxiety';[59] streaming is undesirable because, among other reasons, it results in 'unhappiness and anxiety for the pupils';[60] the teacher should 'guard against the dangers of an over-emphasis on health and hygiene, which may produce feelings of anxiety in sensitive children';[61] in school the pupil 'should be happy and contented and free from fear, frustrations, anxiety and bewilderment . . .'[62]

Calvin S. Hall said that anxiety 'is one of the most important concepts in psychoanalytical theory. It plays an important role in the development of personality as well as in the dynamics of personality functioning.'[63]

Associated with the attempt to reduce anxiety for the pupil is the provision of a secure environment with adults whom he can trust.

(ii) Security

The *Memorandum* emphasises the importance of a sense of security:

> the provision of an environment in which the child feels secure and sure of being understood is one of the teacher's most important responsibilities.[64]

Psycho-analysts have always emphasised the healing power of the sense of security and Donald Winnicott, a former President of the British Psycho-Analytical Society, wrote of its importance for growing children:

> What are we aiming at in bringing up children? We hope that each child will gradually acquire a sense of security. There must build up inside each child a belief in something not only something that is good but also something that is reliable and durable, or that recovers after having been hurt or allowed to perish.[65]

(iii) Suggestion and persuasion

In the relaxed atmosphere recommended, there is no place for the stern didacticism of traditional Scottish education. Instead, the teacher is advised to adopt a more gentle and sympathetic approach to her pupils: she will 'tactfully suggest';[66] pupils 'will listen more readily to an occasional gentle hint';[67] 'judicious suggestion and guidance given informally by the teacher to individual pupils' is beneficial;[68] 'the teacher can do much by a word, a query . . .'[69]

Ernest Jones observed as early as 1910 that 'suggestion' is perhaps the most widely used of all techniques:

> Of all therapeutic agents suggestion, applied consciously or unconsciously, is perhaps the most widely used, and in the case of the psychoneuroses many writers sum up the discussion of treatment in the one word, 'suggestion'.[70]

4. The role of aggression

The Freudian influence is apparent also in the approach adopted by the *Memorandum* to the problem of aggression in school. The traditional Scottish school would not have tolerated any display of aggression by pupils — that privilege was reserved for teachers — and any teacher who permitted acts of violence or rebelliousness would have lost personal esteem in the eyes of her colleagues. But some display of aggression is now considered inevitable, and the suggestions of the *Memorandum* are psycho-analytical in substance.

Before giving examples from the *Memorandum* as verification, it is instructive to read Melanie Klein, whose theory of aggression represents the orthodox psycho-analytical viewpoint. She claimed that efforts to improve humanity have always failed because the reformers have taken a negative view of aggression and attempted to stifle its expression:

> The repeated attempts that have been made to improve humanity — in particular to make it more peaceable — have failed, because nobody has understood the full depth and vigour of the instincts of aggression innate in each individual. Such efforts do not seek to do more than encourage the positive, well-wishing impulses of the person while denying or suppressing his aggressive ones. And so they have been doomed to failure from the beginning.[71]

The approach of the *Memorandum* to the problem of aggression in school follows very closely the psycho-analytical stance. The following examples should make this evident:

(i) Sublimation

The *Memorandum* urges the knowledgeable teacher to divert the pupil's acts of aggression against authority into other channels:

> In an atmosphere of security and affection, however, and in the hands of teachers who understand the developing pattern of his emotions, his increasing desire for independence, which occasionally reveals itself in hostility and rebelliousness against authority, can be diverted into rewarding channels, and used to motivate him in the pursuit of his own education.[72]

Ernest Jones made the same comment in 1911; indeed, the *Memorandum* uses the same hydraulic metaphor as he does:

> The spontaneous activities and interests of children are totally different from those which are the aim of educational strivings, and they have to be replaced by these . . . This replacement is not so much the putting of fresh educational interests in the place of the earlier spontaneous ones as the diverting of fundamental desires and interests into new channels; it is utilising of the same energy in other ways.[73]

(ii) Abreaction

All children love to play, and the *Memorandum* suggests that this could be used as a catharsis of 'unhealthy' feelings:

> Feelings of exasperation, rage and many other emotions may be 'exploded' harmlessly by means of play.[74]

Freud and Breuer (1893) warned that ideas could become pathological if abreaction were denied:

> It may therefore be said that the ideas which have become pathological have persisted with such freshness and affective strength because they have been denied the normal wearing away processes by means of abreaction and reproduction in states of uninhibited association.[75]

(iii) Self-expression

The *Memorandum* advocates opportunities for self-expression as a similar strategy to abreaction:

> By being provided with opportunities for self-expression, the child is given an outlet for his feelings and helped to gain some control over his emotions.[76]

Anna Freud and Dorothy Burlingham (1944) advised educators to take early instincts seriously, because they help the child to conform to the adult world:

> Early instinctive wishes have to be taken seriously, not because their fulfilment or refusal causes momentary happiness or unhappiness; but because they are the moving powers which urge the child's development from primitive self-interest and self-indulgence towards an attachment and consequently towards adaptation to the grown-up world.[77]

It is obvious from these examples that the *Memorandum* has adopted the Freudian view of aggression as innate to human beings and liable to lead to neurosis if a cathartic outlet is denied.

6

The psychology of the group

Freudian techniques are incorporated in the approach of the *Memorandum* to the psychology of the group. It is here also that Freud's theory of group-harmony provides the final, perfect support for the social philosophy advocated by the 1965 document. The group is a key concept in social training, and the *Memorandum* defines it: 'a group is a "team", a number of children working together with a common purpose'.[78] It is not surprising that the *Memorandum* should pay particular attention to the psychology of the group. There are two major reasons for this: first, the group serves as a good introduction to the various group-pressures which will be exerted on the pupil in the future as an adult; second, the group can be used by the teacher to further her programme.

The *Memorandum* envisages the process somewhat as follows: in his early years at school the play of the child is 'self-centred and solitary'. Eventually, however, the child attains a capacity for co-operative play, and the common interests which ensue lead to the formation of groups. At first these are small, and frequently changing, but more formal groupings follow with bureaucratic features: their own identity, their own loyalties, and their own rights of entry. Within these more formal groupings certain children emerge as leaders, revealing an ability to organise the resources of their group 'towards known and desired ends'. (The *Memorandum* does not specify these 'ends' or who determines what they should be, but there can be little doubt that they are determined by the teacher.) This is the critical stage in the evolution of the group, and the description of the process is strongly reminiscent of Anna Freud's advice to teachers:

> It is now that the child is ready to play his part in a team, keeping to the rules, subordinating his personal desires to the wishes of the group, obtaining emotional satisfaction from identification with others. The enlightened teacher can now use the group to foster both emotional and moral development.[79]

We should be quite clear here as to what the *Memorandum* is advocating. Once the children have been emotionally 'caught' in the group, the 'enlightened teacher', that is, the teacher who has a knowledge of the sociopsychological processes of group behaviour, can use the group to guide the emotional and moral development of the children.

The process which the *Memorandum* describes is strikingly similar to the analysis which Freud first formulated in *Group Psychology and the Analysis of the Ego* (1921). He explained later what he had attempted to do:

> In 1921 I endeavoured to make use of the differentiation between the ego and the super-ego in a study of group psychology. I arrived at a formula such as this: a psychological group is a collection of individuals who have introduced the same person into their super-ego and, on the basis of this common element, have identified themselves with one another in their ego. This applies, of course, only to groups that have a leader.[80]

In educational terms Freud's formulation could be paraphrased: a group of pupils is a collection of individuals who have introduced the same person (invariably the teacher) into their super-ego and, on the basis of this introjection, have become a united group.

Freud postulated that the group is held together by emotional relationships:

> We will try our fortune, then, with the supposition that love relationships (or, to use a more neutral expression, emotional ties) also constitute the essence of the group mind. Let us remember that the authorities make no mention of any such relations. What would correspond to them is evidently concealed behind the shelter, the screen, of suggestion.[81]

Freud himself paid little attention to the implications of psycho-analysis for education, and was content to leave psycho-pedagogical research to his daughter and her followers. Anna's *Four Lectures for Teachers and Parents* (1930) — published in Britain in 1931 with the title *Introduction to Psycho-Analysis for Teachers: Four Lectures* — were commissioned by the Board of Education of the City of Vienna, and were followed by a regular seminar for nursery-school teachers conducted by Dorothy Burlingham and herself. Anna informed Austrian teachers that they had the right to expect the submission of their pupils:

> the teacher inherits more than merely the child's Oedipus complex. He assumes for each of the children under his control the role of super-ego, and in this way acquires the right to their submission. If he merely represented a parent for each child, then all the unsolved conflicts of early childhood would be enacted around him; moreover, his group would be torn asunder

by rivalry and jealousies. But if he does succeed in representing their super-ego, the ideal of the group, the compulsory obedience changes into voluntary submission. Moreover, all the children under his guidance will develop ties to each other and become a united group.[82]

What is the nature of this super-ego which the teacher will represent, and which Anna refers to as the 'ideal of the group'? Apparently it is moulded by the influence of the parents who use the love-relationship to establish their wishes:

> The part which is later taken on by the super-ego is played to begin with by an external power, by parental authority. Parental influence governs the child by offering proofs of love and by threatening punishments which are signs to the child of loss of love and are bound to be feared on their own account.[83]

When the domination has been completed, the child introjects the moral demands of the parents; this introjection becomes the super-ego of the child, and it lives an autonomous 'existence' ever after. Freud reminds us, however, that we accept too readily this process as being 'normal':

> It is only subsequently that the secondary situation develops (which we are all too ready to regard as the normal one), where the external restraint is internalised and the super-ego takes the place of the parental agency and observes, directs and threatens the ego in exactly the same way as earlier the parents did with the child.[84]

Thus the super-ego of the child is the introjection of the moral commands of its parents. But parents — and subsequent educators — educate their children according to the dictates of *their* own super-egos which contain the moral interdicts of *their* parents:

> The super-ego is the representative for us of every moral restriction, the advocate of a striving towards perfection — it is, in short, as much as we have been able to grasp psychologically of what is described as the higher side of human life. Since it itself goes back to the influence of parents, educators and so on, we learn still more of its significance if we turn to those who are its sources. As a rule parents and authorities analogous to them follow the precepts of their own super-egos in educating children. Whatever understanding their ego may have come to with their super-ego, they are severe and exacting in educating children. They have forgotten the difficulties of their own childhood and they are glad to be able now to identify themselves fully with their own parents who in the past laid such severe restrictions upon them.[85]

Thus the super-ego is historically determined, and is, in effect, the 'vehicle of tradition'; this analysis, as Freud points out, has practical implications for education:

> Thus a child's super-ego is in fact constructed on the model not of its parents but of its parents' super-ego; the contents which fill it are the same and it becomes the vehicle of tradition and of all the time-resisting judgements of value which have propagated themselves in this manner from generation to generation. You may easily guess what important assistance taking the super-ego into account will give us in our understanding of the social behaviour of mankind — in the problem of delinquency, for instance — and perhaps even what practical hints on education.[86]

Freud criticises Marxism for claiming that human ideologies are merely part of the superstructure of prevailing economic conditions. Freud accepts this as partially true, but Marx's analysis ignores the fact that traditional values and beliefs are transmitted by the educator's super-ego from generation to generation:

> It seems likely that what are known as materialistic views of history sin in under-estimating this factor. They brush it aside with the remark that human 'ideologies' are nothing other than the product and superstructure of their contemporary economic conditions. That is true, but very probably not the whole truth. Mankind never lives entirely in the present. The past, the tradition of the race of the people, lives on in the ideologies of the super-ego, and yields only slowly to the influences of the present and to new changes; and so long as it operates through the super-ego it plays a powerful part in human life, independently of economic conditions.[87]

It is quite clear that Freud's model of group behaviour blends perfectly with the static society portrayed by the *1965 Memorandum*.

It is important to realise that Freud's analysis of group psychology is morally neutral. He does not moralise as to whether the super-ego *ought* to operate in this manner or not. He observes merely that this is what happens in any group which is united with an emotional tie to a leader. Roger Money-Kyrle has pointed out that the super-ego morality is an essentially relative one.[88] Its primary taboos — those on incest and parricide — are, of course, common to all mankind; but since its basic aim is to appease, by obedience, a feared authority, it is as varied in its superstructure as the will of the authority to be obeyed. There is, however, one common element in the super-ego moralities of different societies or sub-groups; they all alike demand the same unquestioning obedience, but to codes of very different kinds.

7

We have come a long way from the statement that the Scottish primary school child is capable of seriously and deliberately pursuing his own education on lines of his own choice to the point where the school is advised to 'condition the attitudes and behaviour of the pupils' with every strategy at its command, in order to make them 'acceptable to the society' in which they will live as adults. That teachers *know* what knowledge, behaviour and attitudes *will* be acceptable to society decades from now is, of course, taken for granted. This kind of assumption is indicative of a quasi-Platonic vision of society which is unchanging and unchangeable, the eternal paradigm for everyone entrusted with the education of the young. Indeed, there is a resemblance between the *1965 Memorandum* and Plato's *Republic:* both consider education to be a fundamental instrument towards the production of the 'good society' and approve of a meticulous censorship and conditioning to achieve their objectives.

The part played by Freudianism in the *Memorandum* is an interesting one.

Psycho-therapeutic techniques are central to its social philosophy, and they are employed to win the 'trust' of the pupil and create a 'secure' environment which the enlightened educator can manipulate to achieve the objectives of the school.

It is ironic that Erich Fromm, a distinguished psycho-analyst, should warn us of the dangers of being fooled by the 'soft' allurement of liberal education:

> Liberal and 'progressive' systems of education have not changed this situation as much as one would like to think. Overt authority has been replaced by liberal and 'progressive' anonymous authority, overt commands by 'scientifically' established formulas; 'don't do this' by 'you will not like to do this'. In fact, in many ways this anonymous authority may be even more oppressive than the overt one. The child is no longer aware of being bossed (nor are the parents of giving orders) and he cannot fight back and thus develop a sense of independence. He is coaxed and persuaded in the name of science, common sense, and co-operation — and who can fight against such objective principles?[89]

According to Rieff,[90] a lack of concreteness on Freud's part has allowed critics to accuse him of supporting a conception of the well-adjusted personality. The Freudian ethic supplies a rationale for the current rage for conformity: man's development is measured by his social adjustment and interpersonal skill rather than by his individualistic accomplishments. According to Whyte,[91] the changes in child-rearing from an entrepreneurial to a bureaucratic society have been incorporated into the school system. The schools to which the 'organisation man' sends his children have a new emphasis: 'the curriculum has borne down very heavily on the pragmatic and the social, and the concept of adjustment has been dominant'.[92]

These trends, bureaucratisation of society and the popularisation of Freudian ideology, provide the backcloth for twentieth-century conceptions of psychological maturity. On the one hand, individuals can be measured against the norms of bureaucratic organisation, and those who fail or refuse to adjust can be considered 'abnormal' or 'immature'. On the other, individuals can be measured against the health-orientated standards of the Freudians and neo-Freudians, and those whose behaviour is unusual or erratic can be considered 'neurotic'.

Although Freud was opposed to unorthodox interpretations of his theories, some of his followers — Reich, Ferenczi, Fromm, Neill, Marcuse, Laing — would hope for psycho-analysis to play a more radical role in challenging the 'false consciousness' of western society; to this end they advocate more freedom for the child in education.

But Freud is not an advocate of this; among other reasons, he was aware that his new brainchild of psycho-analysis would not make any headway in academic circles if it challenged the bourgeois structures of respectable society. Thus, in one of the few pages that he wrote on education, he could say that 'education must inhibit, forbid and suppress, and this it has abundantly seen to in all periods of history . . . It is even my opinion that revolutionary children are not desirable from any point of view'.[93]

This unequivocal position, however, is representative of Freud in old age, and disguises his ambivalence to social authority. In his earlier work Freud spoke against parental exploitation in the name of the integrity and freedom of the child. However, if we consider the intensity of Freud's adherence to the patriarchal authoritarian system of the late nineteenth century, it is not surprising that he later abandoned this radical position. He concluded, in agreement with his libido theory, that the child is a little 'polymorphous pervert' who only in the course of evolution of the libido matures into a 'normal' human being. Thus Freud painted a picture of the 'sinful child' which resembles the Augustinian and Calvinistic painting of the child in essential points. Erich Fromm suspects that 'Freud was motivated in this change of opinion not so much by his clinical finds, but by his faith in the existing social order and its authorities'.[94]

The Scottish Education Department advises the teacher to change the tone of the classroom from the authoritarian approach of Calvinistic-Presbyterian tradition to the relaxed, permissive approach of the Freudian school. In this situation it is almost impossible for the pupil not to be persuaded that he is doing the right thing following the advice of the teacher; conversely, it is almost impossible for the teacher not to be convinced that the new techniques *ought* to be used since they are patently more effective than the old. Philip Rieff had this point in mind when he wrote that the Freudian text expresses our conviction that the old systems of repressive authority are enfeebled; and from this perspective of depth it could be argued that Freud undermines the old systems of authority. Nevertheless, this tampering with our repressions may itself foster a new dependence because the 'new freedom leads to a certain calculated conformity; psycho-analysis finds no more legitimate reasons for being rebellious than for being obedient. It is in this sense that Freudianism carries nihilist implications.'[95]

8

Postscript: the 1965 Memorandum still points the way

In 1980 the Scottish Education Department published a report by Her Majesty's Inspectors of Schools: *Learning and Teaching in Primary 4 and Primary 7* which makes frequent and approving reference to the *1965 Memorandum*. The report is fulsome in its praise and regards the *Memorandum* as a seminal work in primary education: '*Primary Education in Scotland* became an authoritative statement[96] . . . that watershed document[97] . . . has materially influenced the primary school system and much of its approach has become a fact of our educational lives[98] . . . H.M. Inspectors have reported a steady advance and improvement in the state of our primary schools since 1965 . . .[99]

The *1980 Report*, surprisingly, suggests that 'the time has come for some kind of review . . . of the extent to which the recommendations of 1965 still hold good, and whether its expectations have been, or can be, realised in practice'.[100] If they cannot, then the Report declares that major decisions will have to be taken about what direction primary development should take in the future. The Inspectors waste no time in further reflection and decide that the easiest course of action is to proceed in the direction charted in 1965:

> However, it will be difficult to reverse the movement begun in 1965 and two important factors are likely to confirm that the way is forward from the *Memorandum:* Education authorities are still committed to its principles, and the influential teacher training system has furthered the development of these principles.[101]

NOTES

1. G. S. Osborne, *Scottish and English Schools* (London, 1966), p. 105.
2. *Ibid.*, p. 120.
3. *Ibid.*, p. 120.
4. S. L. Hunter, *The Scottish Educational System* (Oxford, 1972, second edition), p. 88.
5. *Ibid.*, p. 94.
6. Scottish Education Department, *Primary Education in Scotland* (Edinburgh, 1965), p. 3.
7. *Ibid.*, p. 3.
8. *Ibid.*, p. vii.
9. *Ibid.*, p. 91.
10. *Ibid.*, p. 12.
11. Scottish Education Department, *The Primary School in Scotland* (Edinburgh, 1950), para. 71.
12. *Memorandum (1965)*, p. 29.
13. *Ibid.*, p. 39.
14. *Ibid.*, p. 39.
15. *Ibid.*, p. 39.
16. *Ibid.*, p. 70.
17. *Ibid.*, p. 70.
18. *Ibid.*, p. 27.
19. *Memorandum (1950)*, para. 563.
20. *Memorandum (1965)*, pp. 39-40.
21. *Ibid.*, p. 40.
22. *Memorandum (1950)*, para. 41.
23. P. L. Berger and T. Luckmann, *The Social Construction of Reality* (Harmondsworth, 1976), p. 106.
24. *Memorandum (1965)*, p. 24.
25. *Ibid.*, p. 11.
26. *Ibid.*, p. 23.
27. *Ibid.*, p. 22.
28. *Ibid.*, p. 23.
29. *Ibid.*, pp. 3-4.
30. *Ibid.*, p. 7.
31. *Ibid.*, p. 7.
32. *Ibid.*, p. 74.
33. *Ibid.*, p. 12.
34. *Ibid.*, p. 90.

35. Advisory Council on Education in Scotland, *Report on Primary Education* (Edinburgh, 1946), para. 25.
36. G. S. Osborne, *op. cit.*, p. 331.
37. P. Meisel (ed.), *Freud* (New Jersey, 1981), p. 1.
38. *Memorandum (1965)*, p. 15.
39. *Ibid.*, p. 15.
40. *Ibid.*, p. 16.
41. A. Freud, *Introduction to Psychoanalysis* (New York, 1974), p. 87.
42. *Memorandum (1965)*, pp. 15-16.
43. A. Adler, *What Life Should Mean To You* (London, 1980), p. 17.
44. *Ibid.*, p. 16.
45. *Memorandum (1965)*, p. 51.
46. Adler, *op. cit.*, p. 144.
47. *Memorandum (1965)*, p. 22.
48. *Ibid.*, p. 7.
49. *Ibid.*, p. 100.
50. *Ibid.*, p. 124.
51. *Ibid.*, p. 116.
52. *Ibid.*, p. 122.
53. *Ibid.*, p. 100.
54. *Memorandum (1950)*, para. 461.
55. P. Rieff, *Freud: The Mind of the Moralist* (London, 1960), p. 87.
56. *Memorandum (1965)*, p. 36.
57. *Ibid.*, p. 37.
58. E. Jones, *Papers on Psycho-Analysis* (London, 1920), p. 591.
59. *Memorandum (1965)*, p. 9.
60. *Ibid.*, p. 42.
61. *Ibid.*, pp. 193-4.
62. *Ibid.*, p. 11.
63. C. S. Hall, *A Primer of Freudian Psychology* (New York, 1954), p. 61.
64. *Memorandum (1965)*, p. 11.
65. D. W. Winnicott, *The Family and Individual Development* (London, 1965), pp. 30-31.
66. *Memorandum (1965)*, p. 100.
67. *Ibid.*, p. 116.
68. *Ibid.*, p. 122.
69. *Ibid.*, p. 161.
70. E. Jones, *op. cit.*, p. 319.
71. M. Klein, *Contributions to Psycho-Analysis* (London, 1950), p. 276.
72. *Memorandum (1965)*, p. 6.
73. E. Jones, *op. cit.*, pp. 608-9.
74. *Memorandum (1965)*, p. 9.
75. S. Freud and J. Breuer, *Studies on Hysteria* (Harmondsworth, 1978), p. 62.
76. *Memorandum (1965)*, p. 101.
77. D. Burlingham and A. Freud, *Infants Without Families* (London, 1947), p. 82.
78. *Memorandum (1965)*, p. 66.
79. *Ibid.*, p. 10.
80. S. Freud, *New Introductory Lectures on Psychoanalysis* (Harmondsworth, 1979), p. 99.
81. S. Freud, *Group Psychology and the Analysis of the Ego* (London, 1955), pp. 91-92.
82. A. Freud, *Introduction to Psychoanalysis*, p. 120.
83. S. Freud, *New Introductory Lectures on Psychoanalysis*, p. 93.
84. *Ibid.*, pp. 93-94.
85. *Ibid.*, pp. 98-99.
86. *Ibid.*, p. 99.
87. *Ibid.*, p. 99.

T

88. R. E. Money-Kyrle, 'Psycho-Analysis and Ethics', in *New Directions in Psycho-Analysis*, eds. M. Klein, P. Heimann, R. Money-Kyrle (London, 1955), p. 430.

89. E. Fromm, *Man For Himself* (London, 1978), p. 156.

90. P. Rieff, *op. cit.*, p. 55.

91. W. Whyte, Jr, *The Organisation Man* (London, 1957), chapters 2, 28.

92. *Ibid.*, p. 383.

93. S. Freud, *New Introductory Lectures on Psychoanalysis*, pp. 181-186.

94. E. Fromm, *The Crisis of Psychoanalysis* (Harmondsworth, 1978), p. 63.

95. P. Rieff, *op. cit.*, p. 328.

96. Scottish Education Department, *Learning and Teaching in Primary 4 and Primary 7* (Edinburgh, 1980), p. 6, para. 2.

97. *Ibid.*, p. 54, para. 30.

98. *Ibid.*, p. 54, para. 31.

99. *Ibid.*, p. 54, para. 32.

100. *Ibid.*, p. 54, para. 30.

101. *Ibid.*, p. 54, para 30.

Index

Aberdeen 17, 61, 68, 74, 144
Aberdeen Philosophical Society 118
Aberdeen University 92, 144, 157, 161, 166, 170, 173
ability 7, 176, 200, 203, 205, 208, 209, 212, 213
    See also intelligence
academies 72, 80, 201
Adams, J. 158, 173
Adams, J. W. L. 167
Adler, A. 252, 253, 254, 265
adolescence 202
adult education 26, 27, 39, 168, 170
Advanced departments/divisions 203, 206, 209, 211
Aitken, G. J. 173
Aitken, W. P. 48
Allen, D. E. 52
Allen, W. 20-21, 24
Althrop, Lord 57, 60, 61
Altick, R. D. 53
Anderson, M. 156
Anderson, W. 48, 50
Anderson Committee 231
Andersonian Institution 40
anglicisation 81, 82, 87, 115, 116, 117, 125-126, 169, 187-188, 189, 233
Annual Register 19
antislavery movement 48
Argyll, Duke of 108, 120
Argyll Commission 75, 103, 111, 112, 127, 135, 203
Ariès, P. 50
Arnold, M. 104, 105
Arnold, Dr. T. 249
Arnot, A. 237
assessment 219, 234
Association of Master Cotton Spinners 24
astronomy 25, 32, 51, 52
Atherton, G. 239
Atkinson, T. 23
attendance 68, 70, 89, 94, 138, 139, 178, 182, 199
autonomy 6, 76

Bain, A. 118, 123-127, 129, 132, 133, 134, 135, 136

Autobiography 118, 133, 136
Education as a Science 124, 125, 127, 134, 135
Bain, W. H. 114, 133
Balfour, Lord 215
Bannerman, R., MP 74
Bannister, R. C. 133, 134
Barker, A. 242
Barnes, B. 48, 50, 52
Barrie, J. M. 223, 226, 228, 229, 230, 231, 240, 241
Bebb, C. S. 49
Bechhofer, F. 237, 238, 240, 241
Belford, A. J. 92, 172, 178, 194
Belhaven, Lord 58
Bell, A. 19, 154, 155, 159, 168, 172, 173
Bell, H. 232, 240
Bell, R. E. 6, 172, 173, 237, 240
benevolence 22, 27-28
Bentham, J. 16
Berger, B. 52
Berger, P. L. 52, 248-249, 264
Bernstein, B. 238
Bible 39, 58, 62, 65, 119, 120
Biddiss, M. D. 118, 133
Blackie, J. S. 238
Blackwood's Magazine 144
Blake, G. 240
Boer War 133
Bone, T. R. 8, 103-107, 113, 149, 194, 214, 215, 237, 241, 242
bourgeoisie 29, 46, 50, 198, 200-202, 213
Bowlby, J. 252
Boyd, W. 159, 160, 161, 162, 165, 167, 170, 227, 235, 236, 242
Boys' Brigade 121
Braverman, H. 23
Breuer, J. 257, 265
Bridie, J. 222, 223, 225, 229, 231, 239
Briggs, A. 49
Bright, J. 111
British and Foreign School Society 59, 60, 96, 113
British Psycho-Analytical Society 244, 252, 256
British Psychological Society 162, 163
British Weekly 229
Brougham, H. 19, 48, 51, 56, 57, 59, 68, 69,